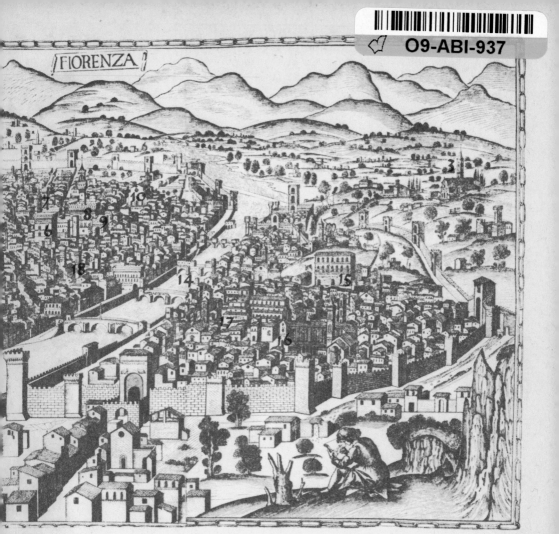

FLORENCE

About 1486 - 90

Giotto's frescoes were already old, but Brunelleschi's Pazzi Chapel was of the most modern design, while his Innocenti, the foundling hospital (11), bore medallions in glazed terra cotta, the recent invention of Luca della Robbia. Nearby is San Marco (12), Fra Angelico's monastery. On this map the Medici live in a *casa* (13), a house, while the Pitti might cross the Arno by the Ponte Vecchio (14) to their *palazzo* (15). On this side of the river are two important churches, the Carmine (16) and Santo Spirito (17). The bridge of Santa Trinità leads to the church of the same name (18). While the youth in the foreground was drawing this view of Florence, the boy Michelangelo was mixing colors for Ghirlandaio in Santa Mario Novella (19), and Botticelli, in Ognissanti (20), was executing commissions for the Vespucci family, whose kinsman Amerigo was to give his name to a continent not yet discovered by Columbus.

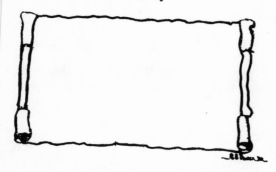

Titian: Venus with a Mirror (canvas, 49⅛ x 41 in.), National Gallery, Washington. (Mellon Collection)

Contents

PART III

Illustrations

ILLUSTRATIONS

PART III

FOLLOWING PAGE 208

Foreword

VASARI

« 1511-1574 »

BORN, *as he tells us in a charming anecdote, into the same family that produced Signorelli, Giorgio Vasari, painter and architect of Arezzo, lived in the High Renaissance. He was a busy and successful artist, an able businessman, a courtier of the Medici, and the devoted friend of Michelangelo. He was in the swim, and the tide he swam in was the rip tide of the Renaissance.*

The Renaissance—il rinascimento—*the very word was coined by Vasari. His* Lives of the Most Eminent Architects, Painters, and Sculptors of Italy *gives, by means of a series of biographies, a picture of the growth of the human spirit during the two hundred and fifty years that witnessed man's greatest artistic flowering since the age of Pericles. In the High Renaissance men stood on a pinnacle of history. Proud, self-sufficient, and discriminating individuals examined their newly-discovered heritage. They took from antiquity the forms of classic art and the humanism of Greece and used their knowledge to produce works of art that were brilliantly new.*

At the very beginning of the Italian Renaissance, Dante wrote The Divine Comedy. *The poem is modeled on* The Aeneid, *which, in turn, was modeled on Homer. Dante went so far as to describe himself as being led by Virgil. He could search through the realms of hell and purgatory for a moral guide to life only with the help of the classic poet. But Dante wrote in Italian. What could have been more revolutionary than that in a time when not only had no serious work been written in the vernacular but men were accustomed on formal occasions to conversing in Latin? We see by the evidence of* The Divine Comedy *that, two hundred years before Vasari, the Renaissance was well begun. But Giotto, the friend of Dante, and familiar doubtless with the classical knowledge that formed the basis of Dante's conceptions, carried the Italian Gothic style to its apogee. The multiple strands of influence and derivation are interwoven, and even in the High Renaissance we shall find Raphael using symbols in his mural*

xi

paintings that carry our thoughts directly back to the elaborate carving above the portals of twelfth-century Gothic cathedrals.

One must remember that the Renaissance was a time of furious building. The old was being torn down. Everywhere there were new churches, and in the old churches there were new pictures on old walls. The cities were full of scaffolding and wet plaster. Men gloried in their new prowess. They strode large, vainglorious, and well known in the narrow streets. "I will take the wall of any man or maid of Montague's," says Capulet's servant in the opening scene of Romeo and Juliet. Even on the streets of Florence, there was hardly room for two coxcombs to pass, and one of them had to muddy his feet in the slime. A stranger within the walls of this city of a hundred thousand people was instantly spotted, for in Florence everyone knew everyone else, at least by sight. A foreigner must be on guard, and the man who belonged was aware of himself and of his own importance to an extent we can hardly imagine today. Now, we must find our way between vast, towering buildings, across wide avenues, among a swarm of strangers. In the Renaissance a man's importance accompanied him on his travels. How extensive those travels were we shall see.

The artist Vasari, part and parcel of this turbulent time, had a devotion to his calling which led him, "not to acquire praise as a writer," as he says, in dedicating his monumental work to Cosimo de' Medici, the reigning descendant of the great Cosimo, "but to revive the memory of those who adorned these professions [painting, sculpture, architecture],* who do not merit that their names and works should remain the prey of death and oblivion." This is an exact description of what he accomplished. He rescued the early painters from oblivion. His work is our prime source of information. In fact, it is the key to our knowledge of Italian art. Vasari examined every available record. He read whatever had been written; he collected anecdotes and recorded traditional stories; he looked at every example of art with the eye of a craftsman, an artist, a historian, and a man of the world. He knew what he was writing about.

In his first edition (1550), Vasari had included only one living painter, Michelangelo. In 1568, he brought out a new edition, which was almost a new work, built on the roughly sketched lives of the first. It was illustrated with a portrait for every biography, a woodcut framed in a fancy design. These portraits were drawn from the traditional likenesses of the artists to be seen in old paintings, medallions, or drawings. Vasari added a great deal of information he had gathered in the eighteen years between the first and

---

* Brackets within the text contain either translations or precise information where Vasari presumes a common background of knowledge.

second editions and included biographies of many more painters, some still living. Between the first and second editions Vasari lost some of his provincialism—or should we say patriotism?—which led him to see excellence only in Florentine art. His point of view broadened with the years, but it retained in general outline his conception of the history of art. We shall read, in the introductions to the sections of his book, that Vasari admired Greece very much but Rome even more, deplored the ruin of all culture after the fall of the Roman Empire, and finally, saw the very summit of accomplishment in the art of his own day.

The present abridged edition is based on the almost word-for-word version of Mrs. Jonathan Foster, published in 1850. This was the first complete translation of Vasari into English. For scholars nothing will take the place of the whole Vasari, in its five volumes. It is a veritable gold mine of information. Students will pore to the end of time over Vasari's interminable descriptions of crowded compositions, hoping to recognize a trait of style, a characteristic gesture, or a personage. Should an unknown Italian picture dating from the thirteenth to the middle sixteenth century appear, what a turning of the leaves of some edition or other of Vasari there would be!

For there are many editions. A distinguished edition appeared in 1759, with annotations by Giovanni Bottari. An edition of 1821, by Padre della Valle, incorporates many original documents in the commentary. The tenth Italian edition (Florence, 1832-38) has notes by Giovanni Masselli. In 1878-82, Gaetano Milanesi brought out his edition in Florence. (This is the edition most frequently consulted.) In 1897, E. H. and E. W. Blashfield and A. A. Hopkins abridged and edited Mrs. Foster's translation, stressing in the commentary matter most interesting to artists. Gaston du C. de Vere translated Vasari anew in 1912-15. His work has more style than Mrs. Foster's translation, but it proves by the similarity of the sense, how faithful both versions are. For laymen who are interested in painting, sculpture, and architecture Vasari uncut is a formidable mountain of information. The material is artlessly presented, for Vasari was no writer, having a living to make, as he says in his dedication, and time only for studies of the pencil, meaning by "pencil" drawing and painting skills.

Vasari was presenting material of the greatest interest to his contemporaries. He obviously believed that his book would be interesting forever, not only to artists but to the public in general. The conviction that this is a fact has inspired the present edition. Until now Vasari has been used by artists and critics. The present edition attempts to extract the facts of interest to the general reader of today. Birth and death dates have been

checked with the most recent scholarship. In cases where the variation was
a result of the confusion between old and new style calendars, the latest
information has been used without comment. Where modern scholarship
has arrived at dates that vary widely from Vasari's, the fact is noted in the
comment at the end of each life.

The editorial notes are intended to shed light on the text. I have con-
densed Vasari's narrative and comments. In some instances I have trans-
posed material. I have omitted references to works which have disappeared
without a trace, believing nothing so depressing as to read an account of
a masterpiece, only to discover in a footnote that "of this work nothing
remains." On the other hand, descriptions of lost works which have influenced the development of art, such as the decorations of the Hall of the
Grand Council in Venice, which burned in 1577, have been retained. Mrs.
Foster's translation, complete and so accurate, except for an occasional
lapse,* has been used as the basis of this work for several reasons. The
quaintness of the phraseology helps to bridge for us a four-hundred-year
lapse of time. The stilted "Then, by the will of God, was born" helps us
to relish the flavor of the Renaissance. A new translation from the Italian,
tempting though the task would be, might gain little and at the same time
lose this valuable though fortuitous asset of Mrs. Foster's admirable work.
For the sake of picturesque flavor, ducats and crowns have been retained,
as these terms are familiar to us, but braccia have been roughly translated
into feet. When Vasari said Michelangelo's Moses was five braccia high,
he meant to convey the impression of something ten feet tall. To translate
this dimension into nine feet six inches would neither give Vasari's meaning nor be strictly accurate.

While Vasari was alive Luther nailed his theses to the door at Witten-
berg, Magellan's men circumnavigated the globe, Cortes conquered Mex-
ico, Francis I, Henry VIII, and Charles V met on the Field of the Cloth
of Gold, the peasants rose in southern Germany, Machiavelli published his
Prince, Pizarro conquered Peru, the Turks invaded Hungary, Loyola organ-
ized the Jesuits, Cartier sailed up the St. Lawrence, Coverdale's English
Bible was published, Calvin introduced the Reformation at Geneva, the
Spaniards operated the mines at Potosí in Bolivia, the Council of Trent
was held, Cervantes was born, Rabelais was born, Hawkins sold the first
Negro slaves in America, and Shakespeare was born.

Is it not remarkable that a man, then living in one of the great cities of
the world, had the patient diligence and devotion to perform Vasari's self-

---

* For example, Mrs. Foster called Mantegna "The Florentine Painter." Vasari wrote,
Pittore Mantuano, "The Mantuan Painter."

imposed task? Artists and critics had at last succeeded in lifting painting and sculpture from the level of mere crafts and had established them among the liberal arts. Vasari was accepted as a peer by the most accomplished artists of his day. Yet he judged the work of the primitives with an appreciation that was lost in the criticism of the centuries between his generation and the time of the pre-Raphaelites in England. In all that time men could not see beyond the glory of Titian, Raphael, Michelangelo, and Leonardo. Ruskin and the pre-Raphaelites were the first to lift the veil. Benozzo Gozzoli, Ghirlandaio, and Filippo Lippi came into view. In our own time interest has gone back, faster and faster. We have admired in the primitives their strong statement of pattern and line and color. But though in this way we have covered Vasari's ground, and passed it, too, taking up early Greek and Egyptian and Mesopotamian art, and even African Negro sculpture, we have hardly seen what Vasari appreciated. In every case he evaluates the work both on its own terms and in terms of the lusty age in which he lived. He points out the action "so true to life." His praise is for lifelike expressions, forms, or gestures. When these are rendered with the quality of "grace," he is most enthusiastic. He tells the story in each picture with never-flagging interest. He examines the material substance of the work of art and admires the way in which technical difficulties have been overcome. Vasari recognizes and admires the artist's knowledge of classic art, anatomy, and perspective.

This edition is dedicated to all in our time who like to look at pictures, to look at the subject matter in pictures, to look through pictures to the times that made them, to read a picture as if it were a book.

PART I

CIMABUE

Painter, of Florence

《 CA. 1240-1302 》

WHEN the barbarian hordes devastated unhappy Italy, they not only destroyed the buildings, but exterminated the artists themselves. Then, by the grace of God, in the year 1240, Giovanni Cimabue was born in the city of Florence to give the first light to the art of painting. The boy was so intelligent that his father sent him to Santa Maria Novella to study letters under a relative who taught in the convent there. But Cimabue, instead of learning to read and write, spent his time drawing men, horses, houses, and other fancies in his books. This natural inclination was favored by fortune, for the boy was often able to escape from school and watch some Byzantine painters at work in the Gondi chapel in Santa Maria Novella. These artists had been invited to Florence by the governors of the city expressly to restore the art of painting, which had not only degenerated but was quite lost. The artists were impressed by the boy's intense interest and, with his father's permission, accepted him as an apprentice student. He soon surpassed them in design and color. For these masters cared little for progress or innovation and worked in the rude Byzantine style. Therefore, though Cimabue imitated his instructors, he improved the art by releasing it from their uncouth manner. Examples of his work in Florence prove this. One is a small panel, a Saint Francis drawn from a living model, on a gold background, with twenty small pictures around it that tell the whole story of the saint.

Cimabue made great efforts to justify the high opinion already formed of him when he undertook to paint the large *Madonna* on a gold ground for the abbey of Santa Trinita in Florence [now in the Uffizi Gallery, Florence]: the Virgin holds the child in her arms and is surrounded by worshiping angels. As he progressed in reputation and power, Cimabue departed still more from the dry, formal manner of his instructors, rendering all more flexible and natural. He painted a colossal Crucifix on wood for the prior of Santa Croce, which gave great satisfaction. The prior caused

3

the artist to accompany him to Pisa, where Cimabue painted a Saint Francis which was considered a work of extraordinary merit, having more beauty of expression in the head and more grace in the draperies than had been seen up to that time, not only in Pisa, but in all Italy.

Cimabue became widely known by these and other labors, and he was invited to Assisi, where, in company with certain Greek masters, he painted a portion of the vaulted roof of the lower church of San Francesco. He so greatly surpassed the Greek masters that he began alone to paint the upper church in fresco. His subject was certain passages from the history of the Virgin: her death, when her soul is borne by Christ to heaven upon a throne of clouds, and the coronation, when, in the midst of a choir of angels, He places a crown upon her head. He also painted the five vaults of the roof. In the first vault, over the choir, he placed the Evangelists, larger than life, so well done that even in our day the freshness of the flesh tints proves that painting in fresco was, thanks to the labors of Cimabue, making important advances. Every alternate vault was painted dark blue, with gold stars upon it. The other vaults were decorated with medallions containing sacred figures: Christ, the Virgin, Saint Francis, and John the Baptist in the third; and the Doctors of the Church in the fifth. When this great labor was finished, Cimabue painted the whole interior of the church in fresco, except a portion of the lower wall, which many years after was done by Giotto. This work, truly great and rich, must have caused the utmost astonishment in the world of that day. I, who saw it for the second time in 1563, thought it most beautiful, especially when I considered the miracle of Cimabue having seen so well in times so dark.

After his return to Florence, Cimabue did many works which show that he was gradually approaching the general method of modern times. He painted a Virgin for the church of Santa Maria Novella [supposed to be the Rucellai Madonna—see this illustration], the figure larger than any done before. This work was an object of so much admiration to the people that it was carried in solemn procession, with the sound of trumpets, from his house to the church. There is a story, which may be read in certain records of old painters, that King Charles the elder of Anjou, brother of Saint Louis, as he passed through Florence, was shown the picture while Cimabue was painting it in a garden near the gate of San Pietro. It had not been seen by anyone. All the men and women of Florence crowded to see it with all possible demonstrations of delight. They ever afterward called the place Borgo Allegri [Joy Town], a name it still retains.

In Pisa there is a small picture in tempera of Christ on the Cross. Angels hold words written around the head of Christ which they direct toward the ear of the Virgin on the one hand and toward John the Evangelist on the other. The words are: *Mulier ecce filius tuus* [Woman, behold thy son] and *Ecce mater tua* [Behold thy mother]. A third screed, supported by another angel somewhat apart, reads: *Ex illa hora accepit eam discipulus in suam* [From that hour that disciple took her unto his own home]. So we see that Cimabue originated the use of words in art for the better expression of the meaning—certainly a new and peculiar expedient.

Cimabue had now acquired a great name and large profits and was appointed, with Arnolfo di Lapo, the architect, to superintend the building of Santa Maria del Fiore in Florence. But when he had lived some sixty years, he departed to another life, having achieved little less than the resurrection of painting from the dead. He left many disciples, among others Giotto, a most eminent painter, who long dwelt in the house of his master in the Via del Cocomero [in Florence].

Giotto obscured the fame of Cimabue, as a great light outshines a lesser. Although Cimabue may well be considered the first to have restored the art of painting, Giotto threw open the gates and showed the path to that perfection which art displays in our age.

The portrait of Cimabue was painted by Simone of Siena [Simone Martini] in his *Church Militant and Triumphant,* in the chapter house of Santa Maria Novella. He is seen in profile, the face meager, the beard short, reddish, and pointed; his head is enveloped in a hood, which is folded gracefully under the chin and closely wraps the throat.

Editorial Notes on Cimabue

VASARI's dramatic beginning of the LIVES is of course, not strictly true; for art in Italy was never "exterminated." Vasari himself, in fact, mentions in his introduction that there was great artistic activity in the eleventh and twelfth centuries. At that time huge cathedrals were built and elaborately decorated with Byzantine and Roman ornament. The men of the Renaissance were bound to inquire into their artistic lineage and fix upon one individual as the very first painter of modern times. The shadowy figure of Giotto's teacher was given more and more importance by popular legend. While Vasari was a boy, the first list of Cimabue's works appeared. Vasari took this list and added to it many more pictures. At present few pictures are attributed to Cimabue. We even think Vasari was mistaken about the Madonna that was carried in triumph from the Borgo Allegri

—that probably received its name from the Allegri family—to Santa Maria Novella. Moreover it is doubtful if any picture seen by Charles of Anjou could have been destined for that church which was not completed until ten years after his passage through Florence. In the year 1285 Duccio signed a contract that is thought to apply to this very picture, the Rucellai Madonna. Vasari, we are bound to notice sooner or later, gives to Florence the laurels in art. And Duccio was a Sienese.

The introduction that Vasari wrote to Part I of the LIVES is specific. In it he describes Italy overrun by the barbarians. Each LIFE is prefaced by a paragraph of general observations, often rhetorical. I have taken the facts from the introduction and with them supplanted such vague phrases as "overwhelming floods of evils." The sense is wholly Vasari's.

Santa Maria Novella, in Florence, is a church of which we shall hear more and more. The Church was a center of the refinement of life. Connected with Santa Maria Novella were a school and a hospital. Rich persons, such as the Gondi, and the guilds built their own chapels, not only to beautify the church, but also for the glory of God and the good of their own souls. The embellishment of the church was a continuous process. The wonder is that any pictures at all remain in the primitive style. The Renaissance believed in itself and had little time to cherish the recent past. It was busy with its own glorious achievements.

The "rude traditional style of the Byzantines" lived on in Russia until very recently, almost as it was in Cimabue's time. The Eastern or Greek Orthodox Church contained none of the yeast of passionate humanity which in the West found expression in the life and sayings of Saint Francis of Assisi. He embraced all nature in his tenderness and pondered so deeply on the sufferings of Christ that he received the stigmata, his hands and feet bearing the marks of wounds such as Christ had received at his crucifixion. Saint Francis died fourteen years before Cimabue was born. The Roman Catholic Church had ceased to hold the people by dry dogmatism, and the Virgin was on the threshold of her long journey from the throne of heaven. That journey we can follow, picture by picture, as Mary changes before our eyes from a celestial Queen, with God on her knees, to a loving mother holding her baby.

The portrait in the chapter house of Santa Maria Novella is not now considered to be either of Cimabue or by Simone Martini. But we are tempted to respect a tradition that even in Vasari's time was already hundreds of years old. So many generations since then have honored that hooded head that we too think of Cimabue when we look at the thin man with the reddish beard.

ARNOLFO DI LAPO
(Di Cambio)
Architect, of Florence

« ? - CA. 1302 »

Abrief account of the state of architecture at this time will not be out of place.

After the fall of Rome, when it was sacked first by the Visigoths under Alaric and then by the Vandals from Africa, all the best artists suffered the same fate as the works of art. They were submerged and buried beneath the slaughter and the ruin of the cities. But infinitely more ruinous than all the other enemies of art was the fervent zeal of the new Christian religion, which had finally annihilated the ancient creeds of the pagan world. To build the churches of the Christian faith, this zeal destroyed the most renowned temples of the heathens. It also destroyed the wondrous statues, paintings, and mosaics of the pagan deities, solely for the purpose of bringing into contempt those ancient gods. Then Totila rose against Rome, razed her walls, and put the whole city to the sword. Some art was preserved by the fall of the buildings. The lower rooms of palaces were buried by the rubble of the upper stories. The immediate successors of those times, believing all to be totally ruined, planted their vineyards on the sites. The rooms thus buried were named grottoes by the moderns who discovered them and recovered many admirable works. The paintings that they discovered they called "grotesque."

No trace, no vestige of excellence in art now remained. Yet, impelled by nature and refined to a certain degree by the air they breathed, men set themselves to work, not according to the rules of art (which they no longer possessed), but each according to his own talent. It is to the masters of these times that we owe buildings vast and rich rather than well constructed, but erected at enormous cost in a rude manner.

In Florence, meanwhile, the practice of architecture began to improve. The church of Sant' Apostolo [the Santi Apostoli], built by Charlemagne, was very beautiful, though small. In fact, Brunelleschi did not disdain to

7

use it as a model. From this beginning the art of design began to make progress in Tuscany. The building of the cathedral at Pisa was a great undertaking. It was designed by Buschetto, a Greek, and had five naves. It was covered with marble within and without. The Pisans were then at the very summit of their greatness and brought an infinite amount of spoils to adorn their cathedral. Columns, capitals, bases, and cornices were arranged with great judgment to make the whole. Other people were fired by the beauty of Pisa to undertake noble enterprises.

Architects began to be known by name. Among the first of these was Buono, who signed only his baptismal name. It was he who built the campanile of San Marco in Venice and constructed the foundations so ably that it has never sunk, even by a hairsbreadth. It is not remarkable for any other quality than this of sound construction. The architect of the campanile at Pisa, a German named Guglielmo [William], did not secure the piles sufficiently, and the tower sank before it had attained half its height. This tower is admired only on account of its eccentricity of form. No one who looks at it can fail to marvel that it should stay up.

By now there were many and important buildings in Italy. The order of Friars Minors of Saint Francis was founded about this time, and there was hardly a city that did not build churches and convents for them. A Maestro Jacopo, a German, was invited to Arezzo to build the mother church, which he did on a much more magnificent scale than the original plan. He acquired so much fame that he was later invited to Florence. The Florentines called him Lapo, according to their custom of abbreviating names. Here he lived the rest of his life, building churches and bridges, planning the drainage of the city and the paving of the streets with stone, and building the Podestà [the Bargello]. These works completed, Maestro Jacopo died, leaving Arnolfo, his son, heir to his talents. [This is Arnolfo di Lapo, or di Cambio, the subject of this history.]

Arnolfo, by whose labors architecture made as much progress as did painting under Cimabue, was born in 1232. When Lapo died, Arnolfo, who was then thirty years old, was considered the best architect in Tuscany. He built the outer walls of Florence in 1284, and many churches and convents in the city. When these undertakings had been completed, the Florentines resolved to construct a cathedral of such extent and magnificence that nothing more could be desired from the power or industry of man. Arnolfo made a model of the temple, directing that the walls should be encrusted with marbles, cornices, pilasters, columns, carved foliage, figures, and other ornaments—which we now see brought almost to completion. But what was most wonderful was the fact that the foundations were able to support the enormous weight of Brunelleschi's dome, which Arnolfo had probably not thought of placing thereon.

The laying of the cornerstone was celebrated on the birthday of the Virgin, in the year 1298, by the papal cardinal legate in the presence of the bishop and all the clergy, as well as all the officials of the city, with the whole assembled population of Florence. The church received the name of Santa Maria del Fiore. As the cost was expected to be very great, a tax was levied on all exports from the city, and a poll tax was imposed. The Pope also granted large indulgences to any who contributed toward the building. Arnolfo has well merited infinite praise and eternal fame for the grandeur of this work. That all may know the extent of this marvelous building, I add the measurements. The length is about one hundred and eighty-five yards, and the height of the cupola, from the pavement to the base of the lantern, is three hundred feet.

Arnolfo was now considered a most excellent architect, and no work of importance was undertaken by the Florentines without his advice. Arnolfo had built the outer walls of the city when he began to work on the Palazzo de' Signori [Palazzo Vecchio, the old palace, or Town Hall], on a plan similar to that of the castle of the Poppi, in the Casentino, built by his father, Lapo. He was forced to accommodate his plan to existing buildings, so that the foundations are awry and out of square. Arnolfo was compelled to bring the tower into the center of the building and to surround it with the walls of the palace. These walls were found to be still in excellent preservation when the painter and architect, Giorgio Vasari, was restoring the palace by the command of Duke Cosimo in 1551. Arnolfo made the tower so secure that it was not difficult for the masters who succeeded him to erect the lofty campanile that we now see there.

After he had accomplished all these things and many others, Arnolfo died, in the seventy-eighth year of his age. We have written the life of Arnolfo as briefly as possible. He showed those who came after him the true path to perfection. Giotto painted his portrait in the figure of one of two men speaking together in the foreground of a picture of monks lamenting the death of Saint Francis [see illustration]. In the chapter house of Santa Maria Novella a painting of the cathedral may be seen. It was the work of Simon of Siena [Simone Martini], painted from Arnolfo's wooden model. It is obvious that Arnolfo intended the dome to rise immediately above the first cornice, at the point where Brunelleschi interposed the drum with the windows. Unhappily, the model itself, as well as Brunelleschi's and others, has been lost through the carelessness of the persons in charge of the church in later years.

Editorial Notes on Arnolfo di Lapo

As in the life of Cimabue, I have made use of the introduction, taking Vasari's account of the state of architecture in Italy and making it a part of the story of Arnolfo di Lapo, or di Cambio, as he is now more generally called.

The statement that the men of Italy were "refined to a certain degree by the air they breathed" carries the imagination on a flight indeed. What is it, we may well ask, in the soil—or the air, if Vasari likes—of Italy that makes art so strong there? Consider how the Etruscans changed the transplanted art of Ionian Greece. Compare a sixth-century Apollo with the Etruscan Warrior in the Metropolitan Museum of Art in New York. Contrast a Greek head and a Roman portrait. The first is ideal, the second real. The air must have some sort of spiritual iron in it.

Actually, Santa Maria del Fiore was first named Santa Reparata, after an obscure saint.

The life of Arnolfo, short as it is, is packed with material for reflection. It is amusing to think of the tower of Pisa still standing, to the amazement of all beholders, while the wonderful campanile at Venice is, in its original state, no more. It collapsed in a heap on July 14, 1902. An exact reproduction has since been built.

NICCOLÒ and GIOVANNI

Sculptors and Architects, of Pisa

« Niccolò, CA. 1220—BETWEEN 1278 and 1284

Giovanni, CA. 1250–CA. 1317 »

WE HAVE treated of painting in the life of Cimabue, and of architecture in the life of Arnolfo di Lapo. We will now consider the art of sculpture in the lives of Niccolò and Giovanni Pisano. It was they who liberated sculpture from the rude manner of the [Byzantine] Greeks.

Niccolò Pisano first worked under Greek sculptors who were executing the figures and ornaments for the cathedral of Pisa. Among the spoils of marble brought to Pisa were several antique sarcophagi, one of which surpassed all others. On it was carved with great truth and beauty the chase of Meleager and the Calydonian boar, the nude and draped figures being perfect in design and executed with great skill. This sarcophagus was placed in the façade of the cathedral because the Pisans so admired it. There it was used as a tomb for the mother of the Countess Matilda.

Niccolò was attracted by the excellence of this work and the many other valuable relics around him and studied them so diligently that soon he was the best sculptor of his time. Besides Arnolfo, the only other eminent sculptor in Tuscany was a Florentine architect and sculptor, Fuccio. This artist did the tomb of the queen of Cyprus, in the church of San Francesco at Assisi. It was a monument in marble adorned with many figures, particularly the portrait of the queen herself, who had left large sums of money for the completion of the building. To typify her force of mind, she is shown seated on a lion. But Niccolò, having proved himself a better artist than Fuccio, was invited to Bologna, where he made the tomb of Saint Dominic, who had but recently died. He also planned the rebuilding of the church and the convent there.

Niccolò certainly had a hand in the building of the abbey of Settimo; he also built the old palace of the Anziani in Pisa. This edifice has been demolished in our own day by Duke Cosimo to provide a site for the erection of a magnificent palace after the plans and models of the Aretine painter and architect, Giorgio Vasari, who has done his best with the old walls, accommodating to them as much as possible the new. Many other palaces and churches were constructed in Pisa by Niccolò, but his most ingenious, most beautiful, and most extraordinary architectural work was the campanile of San Niccolò in Pisa. Externally this building has eight sides, but within it is circular, with a spiral staircase. Within the stairs a free space is left, like a well, while on every fourth stair columns support arches which follow the spiral line. The roof of the staircase is supported on these arches. The ascent is of such sort that the spectator at the foot sees all who go up, and those above see those remaining below. This remarkable invention was afterward applied by Bramante, in Rome, to the Belvedere of Pope Julius II.

Niccolò was no less excellent in sculpture than in architecture. In Lucca, for the church of San Martino, he did a Deposition of Christ in half relief, which is full of admirable figures finished with extreme care. Many artists of Niccolò's day devoted themselves to the study of sculpture, particularly in Milan. Here Lombards and Germans assembled for the construction of the cathedral. They were afterward dispersed all over Italy by the hostilities between the Milanese and the Emperor Frederick [I].

It was in the time of Niccolò that the Florentines, in order that the people might suffer less in the strife between the Guelphs and Ghibellines, began to demolish the old, barbarous towers all over the city. But the tower called Guardamorto [Deathwatch] had walls of such thickness that they would not yield to the pickax. They were also very high. Niccolò cut through one of the sides at the foot of the building and shored it up with wooden props about a yard high. To these supports he then set fire, and when they were consumed the tower fell of itself, a total ruin.

Niccolò then went from place to place, from Siena to Florence, to Naples, to Volterra, and back to Pisa. Here he constructed the marble pulpit of San Giovanni [the Baptistery]. He was most diligent in building the pulpit because he desired to make it a memorial to himself. The people of Siena, impressed by the fame of this admirable work, offered Niccolò the construction of the pulpit in their cathedral. On this Niccolò represented various passages from the life of Christ, with figures well-nigh detached from the marble background. By all these labors the fame of Niccolò was continually extended, and he was invited by Pope Clement IV to Viterbo and by Charles I to Naples. From Naples he returned to Tuscany, stopping at Orvieto. He there worked in company with certain Germans and executed some figures in high relief for the façade of the church of Santa Maria.

Among other children, Niccolò had a son called Giovanni, who was constantly with his father and attained great proficiency under his care. He soon became his father's equal in skill. When Niccolò, in his old age, retired to Pisa, he left the management of their labors to his son. So it was that when Pope Urban [IV] died in Perugia, Giovanni was summoned to construct that pontiff's sepulchral monument. He built a fountain in Perugia with three basins one above the other: the first, of marble, raised on twelve steps; the second, also of marble, on columns; the third, of bronze, supported on three figures, has griffons which pour the water forth on all sides.

When this undertaking was completed, Giovanni resolved to return to Pisa to see his father, now old and indisposed; but passing through Florence, he was compelled to tarry there to assist with the construction of the mills on the river Arno. At length he heard of his father's death and departed for Pisa. He was received with great honor. Everyone rejoiced that, although Niccolò had passed away, Giovanni remained to them, the heir to his virtues as well as to his abilities.

Giovanni's first work in Pisa after his father's death fulfilled the high expectations that were held of his power. He made some changes in the small but richly ornamented church of Santa Maria della Spina. This work must have been considered wonderful in those times, especially as Giovanni here portrayed his father in one of the figures. The people of Pisa, when they beheld the success of this work, and having long thought— nay, even spoken—of making a general burying ground so that too many might not be buried in the cathedral, resolved to confide the construction of the Campo Santo to Giovanni. They spared no expense and roofed the building with lead.

After this Giovanni worked in Naples, Siena, Arezzo, and Orvieto. He then repaired to Florence, partly to view Santa Maria del Fiore, then in process of construction under Arnolfo, the architect, but also to visit Giotto, whose fame met him everywhere on his travels. But he had scarcely arrived when he was given an order to execute the Madonna which stands between two angels over a door of the church, a work that was then greatly commended.

It is no wonder that Giovanni and his father Niccolò should have executed so many works, for they both lived to a ripe old age, and they were the first masters in Europe in their day. There were few undertakings of importance in which they did not take part. Besides those I have already mentioned, Giovanni spent four years in Pistoia on a pulpit for their church of Sant' Andrea, and a font for the church of Saint John the

Baptist. This is in marble. The font is supported on three figures: Temperance, Prudence, and Justice. The work was considered very beautiful and was placed in the center of the church.

Giovanni thought of going to Rome to profit, as his father had done, by the study of the few antiquities to be seen there, but did not because the papal court had just gone to Avignon. He returned, therefore, to Pisa, where he was commissioned to do the principal pulpit for the Duomo. This work was finished in 1311. It was much admired, though it now seems deplorable that so much care, industry, and money were used without any approach to the good style or without any merit in design.

In the old parochial church of Prato, under the altar of the principal chapel, the girdle of the Virgin was preserved. This relic had been brought from the Holy Land by Michele da Prato in 1141. In 1312 a plot for the theft of the holy girdle was uncovered. The criminal was put to death. But the people were alarmed and resolved to build a strong and suitable receptacle for its preservation. They summoned Giovanni, then an old man, and by his counsels built a chapel within the chapel, wherein they deposited the girdle.

At length, having now become very old, Giovanni Pisano died, after producing many more works in sculpture and architecture than are mentioned in this history. Truly, we owe much gratitude to him and to Niccolò, his father, who, from the midst of profound darkness, cast light on all pertaining to art.

Editorial Notes on Niccolò and Giovanni Pisano

NICCOLÒ PISANO, also called Niccolò d'Apulia, was the first great sculptor of the Renaissance. His sculpture is comparable to the antique carvings he so much admired. Niccolò's drawing is as masterly, his composition has as large a plan as that on any Roman sarcophagus. Niccolò was fortunate that many fragments of antique sculpture were to be seen in Pisa. Many of the stones used to build the cathedral were excavated from ancient sites. The erroneously called Chase of the Calydonian Boar was not used, in spite of Vasari, as the tomb of the Countess Matilda's mother.

Perhaps Niccolò's earliest patron was Frederick II, Holy Roman Emperor, the mighty Hohenstaufen, whose court at Palermo was the intellectual center of the age. Frederick was as great an innovator in statecraft as Niccolò was in art. Frederick aimed at the complete destruction of the feudal system. Under his government the individual of extraordinary abilities was liberated from the feudalism whereby son had to follow father in set pattern. Frederick's autocratic methods of government control supplied his treasury with ample funds for patronage of the arts.

The time was not ripe, however, for the full tide of the Renaissance. It is an extraordinary fact that Niccolò had no immediate followers. Giovanni Pisano was equal to his father in technical skill but he created works totally lacking, as Vasari points out, in the classic style. Another hundred years were to pass before sculpture was inspired by Greek and Roman art. The still vigorous heritage from Byzantium was to find expression in Italian Gothic art and architecture. This Italian Gothic, however, was quite different from the Gothic art of France and Flanders. In Italy a man could look about him and see on every hand relics of antique glory, an artistic mold into which to pour his growing strength. Niccolò, as we have seen, used this mold as though he were a true Roman. His work is classic. Giovanni used the forms he saw to convey the sense of stress and strain of the late Middle Ages. Turbulence and passion animate every inch of the surface of Giovanni's work. Giovanni, we say, was a Gothic artist. The classification, inconclusive though it is, is a convenience in ordering our ideas. In our time, we cannot condemn, as Vasari does, everything that is not classic.

GIOTTO

Painter, Sculptor and Architect, of Florence

« CA. 1266 - 1337 »

GIOTTO alone, in a rude and inept age, when all good methods in art had long been lost, dead and buried in the ruins of war, set art upon the path that may be called the true one. The birth of this great man took place at Vespignano, fourteen miles from Florence. His father, Bondone, was a simple farmer and brought up the clever, lively, likable boy as well as he could. When Giotto was about ten years old, Bondone gave him his sheep to watch, and with them the lad wandered, now here now there, near the village. But, impelled by nature herself, he was always drawing. On the stones, the earth, or the sand, he drew pictures of things he saw or of his fancies. It chanced, one day, that Cimabue happened to see the boy drawing the picture of one of his sheep on a flat rock with a sharp piece of stone. Halting in astonishment, Cimabue asked Giotto if he would go with him to his house. The child said he would go gladly if his father would allow it. Bondone readily granted his permission and his son went off to Florence. Under Cimabue's guidance and aided by his natural abilities, Giotto learned to draw accurately from life and thus put an end to the rude Greek [Byzantine] manner. He introduced the custom of drawing portraits, which had not been done for more than two hundred years. Among his portraits was that of Dante Alighieri, his intimate friend. This portrait is in the palace of the Podestà [the Bargello] in Florence.

The first pictures of Giotto were painted for the chapel of the high altar in the abbey [the Badia] of Florence, where he executed many works considered extremely fine [but no longer in existence]. Among these, an Annunciation is particularly admired. The Virgin seems almost ready to take flight, so great is her fear and astonishment as she receives the salutation of Gabriel. Four chapels in Santa Croce were also painted by Giotto. In the Bardi chapel is portrayed the life of Saint Francis; in the Peruzzi chapel are two passages from the life of John the Baptist and two from the life of John the Evangelist; the Giugni chapel is dedicated to the

*Giorgio Vasari: Lorenzo the Magnificent (wood, 35⅜ x 29⅝ in.),
Uffizi, Florence.*

Cimabue: Fresco on west wall, north transept, Upper Church, Assisi.

Arnolfo di Cambio: View of the Seignoria, Florence.

Niccolò Pisano: The pulpit (marble) in the Baptistery, Pisa.

Giovanni Pisano: Detail of the pulpit (marble) in the Cathedral, Pisa.

Giotto: The Meeting at the Golden Gate (fresco), Arena Chapel, Padua.

Giotto: *Death of Saint Francis (fresco), Bardi Chapel, Santa Croce, Florence.*

Andrea Pisano: Weaving (relief, marble), from Giotto's Campanile, Florence.

*Simone Martini: Christ Bearing the Cross (wood, 9⅞ x 6¼ in.),
Louvre, Paris.*

Orcagna: *Christ Conferring Authority upon Saint Peter and Saint Thomas Aquinas (fresco), Strozzi Chapel, Santa Maria Novella, Florence.*

Duccio (follower of): The Rucellai Madonna (tempera on wood, 14 ft. 9⅛ in. x 9 ft. 5¼ in.), Strozzi Chapel, Santa Maria Novella, Florence.

*Spinello Aretino: Episode in the Life of Alexander III (fresco),
Palazzo Publico, Siena.*

Apostles; and that of the Tosinghi and Spinelli families, to the Assumption of Our Lady. Here Giotto depicted the Birth of the Virgin, her Marriage, the Annunciation, the Adoration of the Magi, and the Presentation of Christ in the Temple. This last is a most beautiful thing. The warmest expression of love is to be seen on the face of the old man, Simeon, and the gesture of the child, who is afraid of him and turns toward his mother, is depicted with exquisite tenderness. In the chapel of the Baroncelli family, in the same church, is a picture in tempera of the coronation of the Virgin, with a great number of small figures and a choir of saints and angels, very carefully finished. Artists who reflect on the period in which Giotto did these paintings, so admirable in drawing and in color, will be compelled to grant him their respect and admiration.

After these and other works were finished, Giotto went to Assisi to complete the paintings begun by Cimabue. There he painted, in the upper church and under the corridor which traverses the windows, a series of thirty-two frescoes, sixteen on each side. He earned great fame from this work. The variety in these pictures is remarkable. Every gesture and attitude, every composition, and the different costumes are true to life. Among the figures there is one of a thirsty man bending to drink from a fountain with such eager desire that you almost think him a living man, actually drinking. I will not describe the whole work for fear of being too discursive. Giotto's highly developed facility is obvious in every part of the work: in the beauty of the figures, the just proportion, and the life of the whole. Giotto deserves to be called the disciple of nature rather than of other masters, for nature was to him a never-failing source of inspiration.

Giotto then painted the upper part of the walls of the lower church near the high altar, together with the four angles of the vault, beneath which the remains of Saint Francis repose. The subjects of these paintings are the glorification of Saint Francis in heaven and the virtues of Obedience with Prudence and Humility; Chastity with Purity and Penitence, and Poverty, who is being wedded to Saint Francis, with Hope and Charity in attendance. The paintings on the wall are extremely fine. The portrait of Giotto himself, very well done, may be seen in one of these pictures. Over the door of the sacristy is a fresco representing Saint Francis at the moment when he received the stigmata. His expression is so full of life and devotion that this picture seems to me to be the best of all.

Giotto returned to Florence and immediately painted a picture to be sent to Pisa. This is also a Saint Francis receiving the stigmata. It exhibits a landscape with many trees and precipices, which was a new thing in those times. In the attitude and expression of Saint Francis is expressed his most eager desire to receive the stigmata; Christ in heaven above, where He is seen surrounded by the seraphim, grants the stigmata with a look of lively affection.

It is not surprising that Pope Benedict IX [actually, Boniface VIII], who proposed to have certain pictures painted for St. Peter's, heard of Giotto's fame and sent a courtier to investigate him and his works. On his way to visit Giotto the messenger spoke with many artists in Siena and collected designs from them. He proceeded to Florence and called one morning on Giotto in his workshop. He told his errand and asked for a drawing to take to His Holiness. Giotto, who was very courteous, took a paper and a pencil [brush] dipped in red. Then, resting his elbow on his side, with one turn of his hand he drew a circle so perfect and exact that it was a marvel to behold. He turned to the courtier, smiling, and said, "Here is your drawing." "Am I to have no more than this?" asked the latter, thinking it a joke. "That is enough and to spare," replied Giotto. "Send it with the rest and you will see if its worth is recognized." The messenger went away very dissatisfied. But he sent Giotto's drawing in to the Pope with the others. The Pope instantly perceived that Giotto surpassed all other painters of his time.

So Giotto was invited to Rome, where he was very honorably treated. He was instantly appointed to paint a large picture in the sacristy of Saint Peter's and five others in the church itself. The subject of these latter paintings was the Life of Christ. They were done with so much care that no better work in tempera ever came from the hands of Giotto. He well deserved the reward of six hundred gold ducats that the Pope commanded to be paid to him.

The Pope was infinitely pleased with Giotto's work and commanded that he paint subjects from the Old and New Testaments all around the walls of St. Peter's. Giotto began with an angel in fresco more than thirteen feet high, which is now over the organ. This was followed by many other pictures, some restored in our own day, while others have been either destroyed or removed. In order to move one Madonna, it was cut out of the wall and, supported by beams and bars of iron, was carried away and set under the organ. The mosaic over the doors of the portico of St. Peter's, known as the Navicella, is also a work by Giotto. It is praised not only for the merit of the design but for the grouping of the apostles, who labor to sail the boat through a tempestuous sea, while the winds belly out the sail. It must have been very difficult to produce this effect with mere pieces of glass; it would be hard enough to do it with paint.

After painting a large Crucifixion for the church of Minerva [Santa Maria sopra Minerva], Giotto returned to Florence, after an absence of six years. Soon Clement V was elected pope at Perugia, and Giotto was obliged to go with the papal court to Avignon. He painted with his usual success not only there but in other parts of France, and when all was done he was dismissed with many presents. Among other things he brought back with him to Florence was the portrait of the Pope, which he gave to his disciple, Taddeo Gaddi. He was not allowed to remain long in Florence, for he was invited first to Padua and then to Verona. Here he painted several pictures for Messer Cane [Can Grande della Scala, lord of Verona] and one for the Franciscans. He started to return to Tuscany but was compelled to halt in Ferrara, where he worked for the Signori d'Este both in their palace and in the church of Sant' Agostino. Dante was in exile in Ravenna and persuaded Giotto to visit him, and there Giotto painted some frescoes which are moderately good. Turning homeward, he stopped at Urbino and at Arezzo for a picture or two and at last arrived in Florence.

Dante died in 1321, to the great sorrow of his friend. A year later, Giotto went to Lucca and, at the command of Castruccio [Castracani], then lord of that city, painted a picture of Christ hovering in the air above the four patron saints of Lucca. They appear to be recommending to Him a pope and an emperor, who, as many believe, are the antipope, Nicholas V, and Frederick of Bavaria. Many also maintain that Giotto designed the castle and fortress of Giusta, which is impregnable.

Some time after this, Robert, king of Naples, sent for Giotto to adorn the new church and convent of Santa Clara. Giotto went most willingly to serve so great and renowned a monarch. He painted subjects from the Old and New Testaments. It is said that the passages from the Apocalypse were the inventions of Dante. It is true that Dante was then dead, but Giotto and he may have discussed these subjects.

Giotto painted many pictures in the Castel dell' Uovo which greatly pleased the king, who liked to watch Giotto work and to talk with him, for Giotto was always ready with a jest. One day the king told Giotto that he would make him the first man in Naples. "That I am already, as I live at the Porta Reale." [This was where the first houses of the city stood.] Another time the king said, "Giotto, if I were in your place, now that it is so hot, I would rest a while." "And so I would," replied Giotto, "if I were in your place." Again, the king asked Giotto to draw him a picture of his kingdom. The painter drew an áss, bearing a packsaddle loaded with a crown and scepter and pawing another saddle under foot. Giotto explained that the kingdom was like an ass and its burdens, always wanting to change rulers.

From Naples Giotto went to Rome and then to Rimini, where he painted pictures which have since disappeared. He then went to Ravenna, where he painted frescoes in a chapel in the church of Saint John the Evangelist. He returned to Florence with sufficient worldly wealth and rich in honors. There he painted two Crucifixes, one for San Marco and one for Santa Maria Novella, in which latter work he was assisted by his pupil, Puccio Capanna.

In 1327, Guido Tarlati da Pietramala, bishop and lord of Arezzo, died at Massa di Maremma when he was returning from Lucca after a visit to the emperor. It was decided to raise a monument worthy of the great man, lord spiritual and temporal and chief of the Ghibelline party in Tuscany. So two men of Arezzo wrote to Giotto and asked him to design a splendid tomb, sending him the required measurements. They asked him to engage a sculptor, the best in Italy. Now, when Giotto went to Naples to work for King Robert, he had stopped at Orvieto to study the works in progress there under the Pisani. The work of the two young sculptors, Agostino and Angelo, had pleased him more than that of all others. Giotto praised them and received them as friends, and now, to their great satisfaction, he recommended them for the job of constructing the tomb of the bishop of Arezzo.

A chapel and four pictures were painted by Giotto for the Umiliati d'Ognissanti in Florence. Among these were a Virgin surrounded by angels, and a Crucifix on a panel which was used as a model by Puccio Capanna for the many replicas of this work scattered throughout Italy. When this book of the Lives of the Painters was first published, there was, in the church of the Umiliati, a small picture in tempera, painted by Giotto with infinite care, of the Death of the Virgin, with the Apostles around her and Christ receiving her soul into his arms. This work was prized by all artists, and most especially by Michelangelo Buonarroti, who said that nothing could be more true to life. It rose still higher in public estimation after the publication of this book. It has since been carried off, perhaps for the love of art. The work may have seemed to the robber to be not sufficiently reverenced, and he, out of piety, thus became impious.

On July 9, 1334, Giotto began to build the campanile of Santa Maria del Fiore. The foundations were of concrete and masonry and rested upon massive stone. The height is two hundred and ninety-two feet. The first stone was solemnly laid by the bishop himself. Lorenzo Ghiberti has written that Giotto not only made the model and planned the historical subjects which were the basis of the ornament, but himself did those of the sculptures which show the origin of the arts. Giotto's design called for a spire or pyramid, but modern architects have always approved its omission, the building appearing to them better as it is. Giotto received not only the honor of citizenship of Florence but also a pension of a hundred gold florins for this work. He was also appointed superintendent of the work, which he did not live to see finished.

In the great hall of the Podestà in Florence, Giotto painted a picture, the idea of which has been frequently borrowed. He represented the commune seated in the character of a judge, holding a scepter in her hand, and with equally poised scales over her head. The figure is surrounded by four virtues: Force, Prudence, Justice, and Temperance. This is a very beautiful picture, of appropriate and ingenious invention.

About this time Giotto went once more to Padua, where he painted in the Arena chapel, both to his honor and his profit. In Milan he also produced many paintings, which are scattered about the city. Finally, and soon after his return from Milan, having spent his life in the production of so many admirable works, Giotto resigned his soul to God, to the regret not only of his fellow citizens, but of all who had ever heard his name. He was honorably entombed in Santa Maria del Fiore, as his high deserts merited. He was loved by all, most especially by eminent men of all professions. The memory of Giotto is not only preserved in his own works but is consecrated in the writings of the authors of his time, as the true restorer of the art of painting.

By command of the elder Lorenzo de' Medici, of glorious memory, who greatly admired the talent of this distinguished man, the bust of Giotto, sculptured in marble by that excellent sculptor, Benedetto da Maiano, was placed in Santa Maria del Fiore.

Editorial Notes on Giotto

Ille ego sum per quem pictura extincta revixit.
[I am he by whom the extinct art of painting was revived.]
—ANGELO POLIZIANO*

GIOTTO's great light, as Vasari says in the life of Cimabue, outshone his master's. It has dazzled posterity, too. Art experts still speculate concerning the authorship of pictures of Giotto's time, or soon after it. Vasari, with his passion for Florence and everything Florentine, went astray like the

* First line of the epitaph on Giotto, inscribed on the monument erected by Lorenzo the Magnificent in Santa Maria del Fiore.

rest. I have omitted some paintings he ascribes to Giotto because documents prove that they belong to a later date. Giotto never went to Avignon and never to Pisa, they say. When Vasari tells us that Puccio Capanna made replicas of a Giotto Crucifix, "which are scattered throughout Italy," he gives us one reason for the difficulties of exact attributions of works to Giotto.

Vasari does not make it clear that Giotto developed out of the Roman school of art. This is true, however. Rome never lost the memory of classic art. With Giotto we can trace an unbroken line. But Vasari is right in saying that Giotto was the greatest of innovators. He was as great as Dante. The Renaissance was well begun.

The success of the pictures that filled the interior walls of churches depended on how well they told the episodes of the continued stories, and on how clear they made the doctrine or pointed the moral precept. If we look at them as we look at modern art, as solutions of the problems of form and color, we miss the experience of seeing what the people of the fourteenth century were like.

There were two castles in Naples, the Castel dell' Uovo and the Castel Nuovo. In any case, it was in the latter that King Robert heard the brilliant repartee reported by Vasari. One example of Giotto's wit Vasari does not mention. The painter, tripped by a pig, picked himself up laughing saying it was only right that he be so treated; for although he had used pig bristles every day of his life, he had never done anything for a pig in return.

I introduce the story of Giotto's kindness to the two young sculptors, Agostino and Angelo, from the vita that Vasari devoted to them.

Vasari does not mention some things because he could take for granted a community of knowledge and emotion with his readers. He never says that Giotto was short and conspicuously ugly. These were bywords in Florence. He never tells us that the campanile of the Duomo of Florence is one of the loveliest buildings on earth. A public decree had said: "The Florentine republic desires that an edifice shall be constructed so magnificent in its height and quality that it shall surpass anything of the kind produced in the time of their greatest power by the Greeks and Romans."

ANDREA PISANO

Sculptor and Architect

« 1270-1348 OR 9 »

THE arts of painting and sculpture are sisters, born at the same time, guided and nourished by the same spirit. A proof of this is presented by Andrea Pisano, who devoted himself to sculpture as Giotto did to painting. Andrea was especially celebrated for his castings in bronze and was so honored and largely rewarded by all, but most particularly by the Florentines, that he changed his country, his connections, his property, and his friends. Andrea's work so far surpassed the rude work of the masters in sculpture who had preceded him that it seemed a miracle.

It is true that when the art of sculpture is lost in a barbarous age, it is easier to restore than painting is. Sculpture follows directly the rounded forms of life, while painting must translate shapes into pure outline. Fortune, too, favored Andrea because of the great treasure of antiquities to be seen in Pisa, as well as the work of Niccolò and Giovanni Pisano, which provided a source of study far more valuable than any within Giotto's reach, since ancient painting had not been preserved as the sculpture had. And although statues are often overthrown and broken and burned, yet the fragments allow us to distinguish the long, straight figures of the Egyptian from the Greek, which shows knowledge and study of the nude but has impersonal heads; and the Greek from the bold, rude Tuscan, and also from the Roman, which is so admirable in expression and in movement that it is superior to all—absolutely divine.

In Andrea's day the only art was that being done by the rude Goths and the modern Greeks [Byzantines]. On this Andrea brought his more accurate taste and finer judgment to bear by profiting from Giotto's method of design. His talent was recognized while he was still very young, and he received a pressing invitation to go to Florence and work on the construction of Santa Maria del Fiore. The façade, with its three doors, had been begun, but there was a dearth of sculptors able enough to carry out Giotto's designs. As the Florentines were anxious to please

Pope Boniface VIII, they ordered his portrait to be done first of all. Andrea put his hand to the work and did not rest until he had done the statue of the Pope, with Saint Peter on one side and Saint Paul on the other, and these three figures were placed on the façade of Santa Maria del Fiore. Andrea next did certain small figures of the prophets for niches in the central door.

His work was so far in advance of that of his fellow artists that it was determined to give him, and no other, all the important figures to do. Saint Jerome, Saint Ambrose, Saint Augustine, and Saint Gregory, the Fathers of the Church, were soon completed and were so admired that Andrea was asked to do Saint Stephen and Saint Lawrence.

Andrea had studied architecture in his youth. The commune of Florence employed him when, Arnolfo being dead and Giotto absent, they needed an architect to design the castle of Scarperia, situated in the Mugello, at the foot of the Alps. Some say that Andrea passed a year in Venice doing figures for the façade of St. Mark's. When he returned to Florence, the city was in great fear of the emperor [Henry VII] and employed Andrea in great haste to build the exposed portion of the walls fifteen feet higher. He was also ordered to build stockades and earthworks.

Andrea was commissioned to execute the bronze doors of the Baptistery of Florence, for which Giotto had made the designs. [This he did after the work of casting had been attempted by a bell founder of Venice, who had failed. The subject was the life of John the Baptist in low relief.] Although many think this work lacking in perfection, yet Andrea deserves the highest praise for making a start and paving the way for the work on the other doors. Andrea's door was moved from the central position when Lorenzo Ghiberti's door was placed there.

In this same period of his life the master completed, after the designs of Giotto, the small figures in marble which adorn the door of the campanile [Giotto's Tower] of Santa Maria del Fiore. And around the tower he placed the seven planets, the seven virtues, and the seven works of mercy, in oval compartments, small figures in half relief, which were then much praised. Andrea further executed the three figures, eight feet tall, which were placed in the niches beneath the windows on the southern side of the tower.

Gualtieri [Walter of Brienne], duke of Athens and tyrant of Florence, desiring to make himself more secure in his palace, engaged Andrea as an architect. He had Andrea build the rustic masonry walls thick enough to enclose a secret stair. In this wall he also placed the large door which is now the entrance to the customhouse, and over the door the duke's arms were carved. These arms were later effaced by the Council of Twelve, who wished to destroy all remembrance of the duke. He also desired to construct a fortress, and Andrea prepared the model for it; but it was not used, because the duke was driven from the city in 1343. Before he was expelled by the fury of the people, the duke delayed the building of the Ponte Vecchio, a work of necessity, by taking the hewn stones and woodwork prepared for the bridge and using them for building his palace fortifications.

By long and honorable labors Andrea Pisano not only became rich, but was made a citizen of Florence and a magistrate. His works were honored not only when he was alive but after his death, for there was no one of his ability until the time of Niccolò of Arezzo [Niccolò Lamberti—1350-1417], Jacopo della Quercia, Donatello, Filippo di Ser Brunelleschi, and Lorenzo Ghiberti.

Andrea was buried by his son Nino in Santa Maria del Fiore. His inscription says he worked in bronze, in gold, and in ivory.

Editorial Notes on Andrea Pisano

NOTHING is more subject to the whim of fashion than art criticism. Vasari was stating an obvious truism of his day in his analysis of the Egyptian, Greek, Etruscan, and Roman styles. His views have been out of fashion for so many years that we are startled by his bold characterisation. We are used to thinking of the sculpture of Greece as pre-eminent. The only disagreement has been as to the merits of the different stages of Greek development, early or late. Vasari places before us the very quality of Roman art. The least we can say is that if there were no Greek sculpture, nothing could be more wonderful than the Roman, with its power of expression, its movement, and its force.

It is not probable that Andrea Pisano followed Giotto's designs, either for the door of the Baptistery or for the sculptures on the campanile. Andrea was too important an artist. Even though he may have carried out a plan created by Giotto, Andrea, in his sculpture, is original and vigorous.

In the paragraph about Andrea as architect, the city of Florence is described as having been in great fear of the emperor. This was Henry of Luxemburg, crowned Holy Roman Emperor as Henry VII. The Guelphs of Florence were in power and opposed him and his local allies as dangerous to their own liberties. Henry besieged Florence without success, perhaps unable to pass Andrea's walls and stockades. To read of the politics of that time is to be bewildered by the alliance of the city-state of Florence with distant powers. When Henry VII attacked Florence, the Florentines put themselves under the protection of King Robert of Naples.

SIMONE MARTINI

Painter, of Siena

« 1285-1344 »

Happy *the man who is a born artist!* Not only is it an honorable and profitable life but, what is more important, he earns undying fame. More fortunate still are those who are socially acceptable. Most fortunate of all—I am here alluding to artists—are those who add to these qualities the advantage of living at the same time as any celebrated writer, who, in return for some little favor, a portrait or some such thing, may mention the artist once only in his writings. Here is eternal fame! Painters, whose work lies simply on the surface, cannot hope that their creations will endure forever, or as long as those of the sculptor or the architect, who work in bronze and marble. Great, then, was the good fortune of Simone, who knew Petrarch. For Petrarch wished to have the portrait of Madonna Laura, and having received it from Simone—beautiful as he could imagine or desire—he immortalized the memory of the painter in two sonnets. These sonnets have given more luster to the poor life of Maestro Simone than it has received or ever will receive from all his works, which are rapidly perishing, while the works of Petrarch shall survive to all eternity.

Simone Martini of Siena was nevertheless an excellent painter, distinguished in his day and greatly esteemed at the Pope's court. After the death of his master, Giotto, whom he accompanied to Rome, he won high credit for the Virgin which he did in the portico of St. Peter's. Especial praise has been given to the portrait of a sacristan who is depicted hurriedly lighting lamps before the saints. Simone was summoned to Avignon, where he produced many good pictures in fresco and tempera. He then returned to Siena, where he was appointed to paint one wall of the palace in fresco. The subject was the Virgin with many figures around her. To prove that he could do as well in tempera as in fresco, he painted two pictures for the cathedral, and a third of the Virgin holding the Child in her arms. The attitude of this figure is very beautiful, and the angels supporting a standard and hovering around the Virgin while they turn their eyes toward certain saints who stand below display much grace and infinitely increase the beauty of the work. When all this was completed, Simone was invited to Florence to paint in the chapter house of Santo Spirito. About this time he painted a Virgin and Saint Luke and other saints in tempera for the Gondi chapel in Santa Maria Novella. He signed this picture.

Finally Simone returned to Siena, his native city. Simone commenced a work of vast extent, a Coronation of the Virgin. It contained an extraordinary number of figures, but the master left it unfinished when he fell ill and died. The whole of Siena mourned for him, but more than all the rest, his brother Lippo. Simone was honorably interred in the church of San Francesco.

Editorial Notes on Simone Martini

VASARI'S account of the life of Simone Martini is a long tale of which only this extract is credible in the light of modern research. Even this much is questionable. There exists no evidence that Simone Martini ever went to Rome or ever studied under Giotto. It is now thought that the chapter house of Santo Spirito was decorated with paintings while Simone was out of Italy, at Avignon, where he died in 1344. I have omitted the description of the pictures because Vasari was mistaken about their authorship. In spite of Vasari's unreliability as a historian of Sienese painting, his record is a valuable, even indispensable, source of information on the Sienese school.

ANDREA ORCAGNA

Painter, Sculptor, and Architect, of Florence

« 1308?-1368 »

WE SELDOM find a man, distinguished in one art, who cannot easily excel in other arts. We have a case in point in the Florentine Orcagna [Andrea di Cione], who was at once painter, sculptor, architect, and poet. Born in Florence, Andrea began to study sculpture, while still but a child, under Andrea Pisano. After some years he took up drawing, which led him to painting in color, both in fresco and tempera, with so much success that his brother, Nardo Orcagna, took him as an assistant to work on the Ricci chapel in Santa Maria Novella, where the brothers painted the *Life of Our Lady*. When this was later injured because of the leaky roof, Ghirlandajo repainted it, using Orcagna's composition. In the same church the chapel of the Strozzi was also decorated by the brothers. On the walls of this chapel, to which you ascend by a flight of stone steps, was painted *Paradise*, with all the saints in the robes and headdresses of that day. On the wall opposite was the *Inferno*, with abysmal dungeons, circles of fire, and all, after the description to be read in the works of Dante. In San Piero Maggiore, Orcagna did a rather large Coronation of the Virgin.

Moved by the fame of these works, the men who then governed Pisa summoned Andrea to paint part of one of the walls of the Campo Santo. Andrea set earnestly to work to paint a Last Judgment, with fanciful inventions of his own on the side of the building nearest the cathedral and next to the *Crucifixion* by Buffalmacco. Orcagna painted gentlefolk of every degree seated in a flowery meadow beneath a delicious grove of orange trees. Cupids hover over the young girls of the party shooting their arrows at the maidens. Knights and nobles listen to music or watch dancers who rejoice in the gladness of their youth and love. Orcagna here portrayed Castruccio [Castracani], lord of Lucca, a handsome youth wearing an azure blue cap and holding a falcon on his hand. Here is depicted everything the world has to offer of joy and delight, as far as space would permit, and according to the requirements of art.

On the other side is a high mountain occupied by holy hermits whose days are passed in the service of God. With great animation some pray, while others work. One hermit is seen milking a goat, a most truthful figure. At the base of the hill Saint Macarius is calling the attention of three kings, who ride to the chase with their ladies and attendants, to human misery as exhibited by three monarchs lying dead within a sepulcher. The living kings in varied and beautiful attitudes regard this spectacle with grave attention. Andrea painted the likeness of Uguccione della Faggiuola of Arezzo as one of these sovereigns in the figure holding his nose to avoid the odor of the putrid bodies. In the center of the picture is Death in the form of a black-robed woman flying through the air. Crowds lie dead upon the earth in vast numbers—rich and poor, young and old, men and women, the strong and the faded. Because Andrea knew that the Pisans were pleased with the invention of Buffalmacco, who made words issue from the mouths of his figures, he filled his whole work with such inscriptions. He himself composed the verses, which are now almost indecipherable. Devils move among the bodies, tearing the souls of the departed from their mouths and carrying them off to a fiery gulf. Opposite the devils are angels who approach the good among the dead and bear their souls to paradise. In the ornamental border of the picture are nine angels bearing other inscriptions on scrolls, some in Latin and some in Italian. That they were not admitted to the body of the picture for fear of spoiling the effect displeased the author, by whom they were considered most beautiful, and so perhaps they were, according to the taste of that age.

Orcagna then began the Judgment scene, in which he represented Christ and the twelve Apostles on high amidst the clouds. The misery of the condemned is balanced by the joy and gladness of the good. And deplorable it is that no writer recorded the names of all that crowd of personages, all evidently drawn from life. The pope in this picture is said to be Innocent IV, the friend [actually, the enemy] of Manfredi [Manfred, king of Sicily, the natural son of Emperor Frederick II].

When he returned to Florence, Orcagna repeated this picture in Santa Croce, substituting portraits of his Florentine friends in paradise and his foes in hell. Among the good may be found the portrait of Clement VI with the triple tiara on his head. This pontiff was well disposed toward the Florentines and owned and valued highly many of Orcagna's pictures. Also among the blessed is Messer Dino del Garbo, an eminent physician, who wears a doctor's robe and a hat lined with gray miniver. An angel leads him by the hand. Among the damned Orcagna has placed Guardi, sergeant of the commune of Florence, being dragged along by the devil with a hook. Andrea did this because Guardi had seized his goods for debt. The judge and the notary concerned in the affair were also placed in hell among the sinners. A hypocritical friar furtively tries to mingle with the good, but is discovered by an angel who drives him into the midst of the condemned.

Andrea used to model reliefs in clay to help his brother Jacopo, who was an unsuccessful sculptor. This gave him the inclination to try marble, with the creditable results that will be recounted later. Andrea next applied himself to the study of architecture. When the Florentine commune decided to erect a building where citizens might assemble in bad weather, Andrea's design for the loggia [dei Lanzi] was universally approved. The whole fabric was one of infinite grace and beauty and was completed in a very short time. If only the builders had had the forethought to turn its back to the north and place it beside San Romolo, it would have been as useful as it is beautiful. As it is, no one can endure to remain long in the loggia in winter because of the sharpness of the wind. Andrea sculptured seven marble figures in half relief to place between the arches of the front.

While occupied with any one of his three professions, Orcagna did not neglect the other two. While he was engaged on the loggia, he painted a tempera altarpiece for the Strozzi chapel [in Santa Maria Novella]. This he signed because he believed that it would bear more conclusive testimony to his skill than his works in fresco. Andrea did other pictures, also on panel, which were sent to the Pope at Avignon.

The Brotherhood of Or San Michele [the church of the guilds of Florence] had a full treasury derived both from ordinary almsgiving and from large donations received on account of the high mortality prevailing in the year 1348 [the plague]. The brothers decided to build a tabernacle around their Madonna, rich with sculptures, adorned with precious stones, and decorated with mosaic and bronze. They wished this tabernacle to surpass all others, and so confided the whole to Orcagna, the most excellent artist of that age. He prepared so many designs that at length one was found to please those who ruled in the matter. Orcagna engaged sculptors to do all but the figures, which he and his brother did. When finished, the whole was so carefully joined together—without cement, but with fastenings of lead and copper—that one would think it made of a single block of marble. Although it is in the Teutonic [Gothic] manner, it is so gracefully proportioned that it is the foremost work of that period. The composition consists principally of large and small figures in half relief, of angels and prophets surrounding the Madonna. Wonderful is the casting of the bronze girders and supports, which are all carefully polished. The strength of the work is no less remarkable than its beauty. How earnestly Andrea labored to show his genius in that still uncultivated age is revealed in the large composition on the back of the tabernacle. In it there are the twelve Apostles, figures about a yard high, looking up at the Madonna, who is ascending to heaven in a "gloria" surrounded by angels. In one of these Apostles, Orcagna has left us his own portrait as an old man, which he then was, with shaven beard and round, flat face. It seems that a fortune was spent on this work, and certainly it is not surpassed by any work of the period, and for the part he had in it Orcagna deserves eternal praise.

It was the custom of this master to sign himself Andrea di Cione, *Sculptor* on his paintings, and *Painter* on his sculpture, for he desired that men should be aware of his claims to both these arts. Finally, having attained the age of sixty, he finished the course of his life. In addition to his talents, Andrea was endowed with a cheerful disposition and a kind heart. No man was ever more amiable or had more pleasing manners.

Editorial Notes on Orcagna

THE picture in the Campo Santo at Pisa is now ascribed to Pietro Lorenzetti, of the Sienese school, but the description is too amusing to omit. It seems odd that Vasari did not recognize that the three living kings were looking at their own deaths. Holbein, in Vasari's lifetime, was still expressing this medieval thought. His Dance of Death shows each personage shadowed by his own particular death.

The Loggia dei Lanzi was designed by Benci di Cione. The sculptures, other than those on the tabernacle, are also by other artists.

And the Inferno in Santa Maria Novella is said to have been completely repainted. When I saw it last—as Vasari might say—when, in fact, I was looking at this work with a student's intense interest, some years ago, I was startled and disconcerted by a confidential whisper from the monk-custodian: "Ecco, i Fascisti!" and his finger indicated some particularly evil characters suffering their just deserts. Repainted or not, the picture was real enough to him.

DUCCIO

Sienese Painter

« CA. 1255-1319 »

ISTORIANS pay most attention to the inventors and originators, no matter how great the development and improvement of later men, though by these the original invention be brought to perfection. And this is reasonable, for without the beginning there could be no progress or final flower of beauty. Duccio of Siena, therefore, was a painter much esteemed, who appropriated a large amount of the fame of the artists who followed him. He was the first to decorate the pavement of the Sienese cathedral in chiaroscuro. Duccio worked in the ancient manner but gave his figures a certain grace of outline in spite of the difficulties of mosaic.

Duccio also executed a picture for the cathedral, a Coronation of the Virgin, partly in the Byzantine manner, but partly in modern style. As the high altar stood free of the walls, the picture was painted on both sides. The artist represented all the principal events of the New Testament on the back, very beautifully painted with infinite care in the small figures. Duccio painted many pictures on gold grounds for Siena, Florence, Pisa, Lucca, and Pistoia, which were all highly praised and brought him large profits. When Duccio died, what relatives, disciples, or property he left are unknown, but he must be numbered among those benefactors who have adorned our art and promoted its progress.

Editorial Notes on Duccio

DUCCIO [Duccio di Buoninsegna], as our knowledge increases, is slowly taking Cimabue's place as the forerunner of the great Italians. Vasari was so unaware of Duccio as an important link in the history of art that the fragment I have extracted is all of his life that has any semblance of accuracy. Vasari slights Duccio by ascribing to Cimabue all innovation in painting—to Cimabue and to Florence. We now believe that the flame of art first burned brightest in Siena. If Florentine art developed out of Sienese perfection and the never-extinguished classic art of Rome, which in the late Middle Ages was expressed in mosaic, we do not find that fact mentioned in Vasari. To find out about Duccio we must read other authors.

SPINELLO ARETINO

Painter

« CA. 1346-1410 »

ON ONE of the many occasions when the Ghibellines were driven out of Florence, Luca Spinelli moved to Arezzo, where his son—the boy was named Spinello—was born. This child was so bent on being a painter that at twenty, almost without any instruction, he did as well as many a practiced artist. Spinello attached himself to Jacopo di Casentino when he was painting in Arezzo and soon proved himself to be as good a painter, though Jacopo was then an old man. Thus beginning to be recognized Spinello painted some stories in fresco in Santa Maria Maggiore in Florence. This work he executed so carefully that it appears to be the work of one day rather than of many months, as was the fact. He continued to work in Florence for some time with good success.

The fame that Spinello won caused the council of sixty citizens who governed Arezzo to recall him to paint an Adoration of the Magi in the church of the Duomo Vecchio. This ancient temple, once filled with sepulchral monuments, bones of saints, and other memorable things, is now totally destroyed. The church was dedicated to Saint Donatus and was enriched both inside and outside with the spoils of antiquity which had been previously dedicated to idols. To be brief, this church, at the time of its destruction, was as beautiful as any temple could be.

Spinello painted an Annunciation, with other figures. These are greatly admired for their boldness and facility. He also painted a Pieta for the Brotherhood of Santa Maria della Misericordia, for Spinello was a member of the society and in his turn visited the sick, buried the dead, and performed other pious duties; and he desired to leave a memorial of these things. The subject of this work is a Madonna, whose mantle, opening in front, discloses the people of Arezzo sheltered beneath it. Among them are the portraits of many men of the brotherhood, each bearing the wallet on his shoulder and carrying in his hand the wooden mallet with which he knocks on doors when seeking alms.

Afterward Spinello painted for the hermits of the celebrated abbey of Camaldoli a picture for the high altar. This work was removed in 1539, when the church was entirely rebuilt and a new painting was executed by Giorgio Vasari. Summoned to Florence by Don Jacopo d'Arezzo, abbot of San Miniato-sul[al]-Monte, Spinello painted the stories from the life of Saint Benedict on the ceiling and four walls of the sacristy in fresco and an altarpiece in tempera. The abbot left Florence to become governor of the monastery of San Bernardo in Arezzo. The arrival of the abbot occurred just when the building was completed. He engaged Spinello to paint in fresco the two chapels on each side of the lady chapel and two others. All are works of great beauty.

The people of Arezzo had built a church on many columns of marble and granite to honor the holy martyrs who were put to death by Julian the Apostate on that very spot outside the city walls. This they dedicated to Saint Stephen. Here Spinello painted a great number of pictures with infinite diligence and such care with the coloring that they remained fresh until they were destroyed a few years ago. Besides the stories of Saint Stephen, with figures larger than life, there was another remarkable work in that place—a Saint Joseph in Adoration—watching with delight the kings as they opened their treasures and offered them to the divine child. There was also a Virgin presenting a rose to the infant Jesus. This most beautiful figure was held in such reverence by the Aretines that, when the church was destroyed, they had the wall cut out, regardless of expense, and carried the picture to another church within the city so that it could continue to be an object of devotion. This is not surprising, since there is an air of grace and modesty in whatever Spinello did that lent an expression of sanctity to his saints, especially to his Virgins, who breathe a kind of divinity that invites mankind to veneration.

In a hospital near the gate that opens on the road to Rome was a portico painted entirely by Spinello. Among these pictures was one of Christ lying dead in the arms of the Marys, which showed so much genius, so much knowledge of the art of painting, that it proved that Spinello equaled Giotto in design and surpassed him in coloring. Here Spinello also did a seated Christ—a theological allegory very ingeniously expressed; the three persons of the Trinity were placed within a sun, so that the sun's rays and the same splendor seemed to come from each of the three. The paintings of this portico have suffered the fate of so many other works and have been demolished to make way for the fortifications.

For the Brotherhood of the Holy Trinity, Spinello painted a tabernacle in fresco still to be seen outside the church. While he was engaged on this work, Don Jacopo d'Arezzo was made general of the order of Monte Oliveto. This happened nineteen years after he had commissioned Spinello to do the paintings in Florence and Arezzo of which we have spoken. Don Jacopo, as was customary, lived for the most part at Monte Oliveto di Chiusure, the principal seat of the order. Wishing to have a very beautiful picture made for that place, he summoned Spinello, who had so often served him well before. The master painted a great number of figures half life-size on a ground of gold. The picture was framed in richly ornamented wood-carving and moldings of stucco. For this Spinello received large rewards and great kindness from the general and the monks. He returned to Arezzo where, however, he did not remain long, as the city had been recently sacked and was much disturbed by the quarrels of the Guelphs and Ghibellines. Spinello therefore took his family to Florence, where he had many relatives and friends.

He was then invited to Pisa to paint the spaces on the walls of the Campo Santo left empty by Giotto and the rest. He was engaged on work in the church of San Francesco after the Campo Santo was completed, and would have remained in Pisa, where he was popular and highly paid, had not that city been thrown into an uproar when Messer Pietro Gambacorti was killed by the Lanfranchi [1392]. He returned to Florence, an old man, and tarried there to paint some pictures, though he longed to return to his native Arezzo.

Spinello was seventy-seven years old, or perhaps more, when he did return to Arezzo, and there he lived until his death, at the age of ninety-two. He was old and rich enough to have lived without labor, but he was unable to remain idle, so he undertook to paint some scenes from the life of Saint Michael for the Brotherhood of Sant' Angelo. These he sketched roughly in red color on the plaster of the wall—as the old artists almost always did—and painted one story by way of example. Having agreed on a price, Spinello painted the whole of the wall, besides the high altar where he represented Lucifer fixing his seat in the North and the fall of the angels, who are changed into devils as they descend to earth. In the air appears Saint Michael in combat with the serpent with seven heads and ten horns, while in the center of the picture is Lucifer already changed into a most hideous beast. Spinello was so anxious to make this figure look frightful that, so they say, the figure he had painted appeared to him in his sleep demanding to know where the painter had seen him looking that ugly and how he dared offer him such an affront. The artist awoke so terrified that he could not cry out. His wife hastened to his assistance. But he did not long survive the shock and lay dispirited, his eyes without intelligence. It was thus that Spinello closed his career, leaving his friends in heavy sorrow for his death, although it is true that he had attained a great age. He was buried in Sant' Agostino at Arezzo, where his gravestone bears his fanciful escutcheon, a hedgehog.

Spinello drew even better than he painted.

Editorial Notes on Spinello Aretino

VASARI's account of Spinello's long lifetime is not borne out by the research of modern scholarship. Actually, the artist was about sixty-five when he died.

When artists in the fourteenth century painted fresco, they first drew the design of the picture in red chalk on the dry plaster of the wall. Smooth plaster was laid on this rough wall surface. Just enough of this top plaster to paint in a day was put on at a time. The dry powdered color was moistened in water, and the artist painted on the smooth plaster while it was still damp. The wall and the painting dried together so that no matter how strong the color of the picture, it sank into the plaster to a certain extent. Frescoes have a chalky look. The following day's work must meet and join the part already painted and partly dry without leaving a line. Therefore it is possible to see quite clearly in almost all frescoes just how much was done in a day. Even later on, when the practice prevailed of first making a cartoon and then tracing the design, as it were, on the wet plaster, it was evidently difficult to match the color exactly. It is high praise, indeed, to say that a large fresco looks as if it were all done in one day. It strikes us as remarkable that the artist could ever match the colors, in different stages of wetness, so that they would all dry alike. The artist often planned his day's work with this difficulty in mind, laying on the surface plaster according to his pattern, and ending his daily stint at the edge of a new color.

PART II

VASARI'S
Introduction to Part II

When I first undertook to write these lives, it was not my purpose to make a mere list of the artists or a catalogue of their works. This I could have done by means of a chart or table, without using my own critical judgment. But historians do not content themselves with a simple narrative of events. They must investigate the means by which successful results have been attained, and the points about which errors have been made. Being persuaded that history is the mirror of human life, they set forth the underlying currents, the character of events, for from these details men learn the true government of life. This, then, is the purpose of history. There is, besides, the pleasure of reading about the past as though it were the living present.

When I undertook to write the history of the noblest masters of our arts, I determined to be a true historian so far as I was able, wishing above all to honor the arts and those who labor in them. I have tried not only to tell what has been done, but to distinguish the better from the good, and the best from the better. I have also sought to discriminate among the different methods, processes, and even the various fantasies, inventions, and modes of treatment of the artists.

Now I feel the time has come to set forth the plan of my book, an explanation of my intention, and the reason I have divided the work into three parts.

Distinction in the arts may be attained in many ways. One man may work hard at it; another may study; another may imitate; a fourth may approach his problems with scientific inquiry; others, by several of these methods together, or even by all of them. I divide the time from the revival of the arts down to the present century into three parts, and in each of these there will be found a very obvious difference. In the first, the formative period, as we have seen, a beginning was made, and though obviously imperfect, the work has deserved a larger share of glory than if it were being judged by the strict rules of art. In the second period, richer invention was displayed, with more correct drawing, a better manner, and improved execution. The arts were freed from that rust of old age which still clung to them. Still, who can say that any artist of those times could do what we can do today? The third period has the credit of reaching such perfection that we must fear that art will sink rather than hope that it may still rise to a greater achievement.

Reflecting upon these things, I came to the conclusion that it is the peculiar nature of art always to be crude, stiff, and unreal in the beginning, and to develop by gradual steps to perfection. This was true of the sculpture of the Greeks, and painting must have followed exactly the same progression as sculpture. But for antiquity, we are compelled to trust the opinions of others, who often disagree even concerning the periods when the work was done. Let us therefore consider our own times and what we can see for ourselves. Can we not see at a glance the changes that Arnolfo di Lapo and Giotto brought about in architecture? It is true that their decorations were complicated and confused, and they used columns without distinguishing the orders, whether Doric, Corinthian, Ionic. This may have been partly their invention, but more likely it was the result of using ancient fragments in their new buildings. Their plans were often imperfectly carried out, and the finished work was very different in form from the model.

The same remarks may be applied to sculpture, which still retained some remains of excellence at the first moment of the revival of the arts, though the statues were inflexible and without attitude. When Giotto improved the art of design, figures in marble and stone improved also. The forms became less rigid, the draperies flowed more freely, and expression began to appear in the heads. We must never forget that these artists received no help from those who preceded them. Every beginning, however humble, deserves all the praise and credit that we can give it.

Nor had painting much better fortune in those times, though the devotion of the people called it more frequently into use. There were more painters at work and so progress was more obvious. Thus we have seen the hard, angular lines of Byzantine mosaic and painting first attacked by Cimabue and then entirely extinguished by Giotto. Then began what I would like to call the manner of Giotto, originated by him, imitated by his disciples, and finally honored by all. The hard lines by which every figure was bound, the senseless eyes, the feet planted upright on their extremities, the sharp, formless hands, and the absence of shadow, and every other monstrosity of those Byzantine painters were done away with. The heads began to express vivacity and spirit, the draperies began to have natural folds. Human passions were, in some sort, expressed in the faces. The early manner had been harsh and rugged; that of Giotto became softer and more harmonious. If in Giotto the figures did not have the limpidity and beauty of life, if his hands had not the articulation of nature, or his beards the flow of hair, remember that Giotto had never seen a better painter than himself. Giotto's followers improved manner, outline, expression, and color without originating a new direction.

Sculpture, painting, and architecture had up to the times here alluded to been but roughly sketched out and had they not made further progress, the improvement they had made would have earned them slight praise. But, considered as the beginning of the great things that were to come, we must admit that they are not only beautiful but wonderful. The examination of these beginnings is a source of infinite pleasure. This is why I have felt bound, not only to describe the lives of the older masters most diligently, but to give each one his due praise with all love and confidence, as I have done. I cannot believe this will be wearisome to my brother artists, who may even be assisted by my work. This would be to me the most precious reward of my labor.

Now that we have raised these three arts from the cradle, so to speak, and through their childhood, we come to the second period. Here they seem improved at all points, drawing, manner, coloring—so that little more is required to approach the truth of nature. Even where there is little facility, the works show much thought and care. By the study of the great Brunelleschi, architecture first recovered the proportions of the antique, in the round columns as well as in the square pilasters and the rusticated and plain angles. Only then were the orders distinguished from each other. Care was taken that all should be done according to rule. Buildings were given a better grace, were finely proportioned, magnificently arranged, and richly adorned. The cupola of Santa Maria del Fiore, the graceful, rich, and variously ornamented church of Santo Spirito, San Lorenzo, and the magnificent and lordly beginnings of the Pitti Palace are remarkable erections of that time. This was not the best possible work; we shall see more refinement and delicate finish in the third part of my book, but we are bound to admit that these works are good and beautiful. In fact, certain work then done is so admirable that nothing better has been accomplished, or is likely to be. One of these is the cupola of Santa Maria del Fiore in which Filippo Brunelleschi had the courage to imitate the vast size of the antique and the daring to raise it on higher walls.

. What is said of architecture applies as well to painting and sculpture, in both of which many extraordinary works were executed by the masters of the second period; for instance, the frescoes of the church of the Carmine by Masaccio. Speaking generally, however, the second period did not reach the perfection of the third period, of which we shall speak in due time.

To treat first of the sculptors, their art in the second period made so decided an improvement over that of the first as to leave little for the third to accomplish. Statues began to assume the appearance of living men. Of this we will have proof in the life of Jacopo della Quercia. Still more was accomplished by Lorenzo Ghiberti on the gates of the Baptistery, where fertile invention, correct design, and admirable treatment are combined with figures which seem to move and to possess a living soul. Donato also lived in this period, but for a long time I could not decide whether I was not called upon to place him in the third. His work is the equal of good work of antiquity. It is certain that if we assign him to the second period, we must hail him as the representative of all the other masters of that period, since he summed up all the qualities in himself which were divided among the rest. His work bears comparison with that of later times, and even with that of the ancients themselves.

Similar progress was made at the same time in painting. Masaccio delivered it entirely from the manner of Giotto, restoring the practice of foreshortening. Thus the masters constantly endeavored to reproduce what they saw in nature, and no more. Minute attention to the effects of light and shade succeeded, and efforts were made to improve composition. Landscapes also were attempted.

We will now begin with the life of Jacopo della Quercia, the Sienese, whom I have selected as the honored leader of this second part, and will gradually proceed to discuss and elucidate, in the lives themselves, the difficulties of these beautiful, laborious, and most honorable arts.

JACOPO DELLA QUERCIA

Sienese Sculptor

《 CA. 1376-1438 》

T HE sculptor Jacopo, son of Maestro Piero di Filippo of Quercia, which is a place near Siena, was the first, after Andrea Pisano, Orcagna, and the other masters, who showed that sculpture might make a near approach to nature.

Jacopo did his first big job when he was only nineteen. It happened that the captain of the Sienese army, then in action against the Florentines, died of an illness that he had contracted in camp. The Sienese honored him with a most superb funeral. They built a sort of pyramid of wood and surmounted it with an equestrian statue of their dead leader, Giovanni d'Azzo Ubaldini. This statue, larger than life, was the work of Jacopo della Quercia, who constructed it in the most ingenious way. He built a framework of wooden struts and planks; this he covered with hay, tow, and hemp, carefully secured and bound with ropes. He covered all with a mixture of clay, paste, glue, and rags. It was a great success. It looked enough like marble when it was painted white, and yet was light, and, best of all, it was not likely to crack.

Jacopo executed the figures of some of the prophets, still to be seen on the façade of the church in Siena. He would doubtless have continued to labor in Siena had not pestilence, famine, and discord caused the Sienese to expel his patron, Orlando Malavolti. Jacopo went to Lucca, therefore, where he did a mausoleum for the wife of Paolo Guinigi, then lord of that city. On the base of this tomb are figures of boys holding a garland. They seem rather of flesh than of stone, so finely are they carved. On the sarcophagus is the figure of the lady who is buried within, and at her feet a dog is carved, symbolizing her fidelity to her husband. When Paolo Guinigi was driven out of Lucca in 1429, this sepulcher was removed from its place, and, because of the hatred of the name Guinigi, almost

45

totally destroyed; but on account of the admiration for the beautiful figure, the people of Lucca placed the sarcophagus and the statue near the door leading into the sacristy.

A rumor now reached Jacopo of the proposed second door of the Baptistery in Florence, which was to be constructed at the expense of the guild of clothworkers. He presented himself to make a model for the competition from which was to be chosen the best example of a finished bronze. His effort gave great satisfaction. If he had not had Donatello and Brunelleschi as competitors, that great work would have been entrusted to him. But, as the affair concluded differently, our artist went to Bologna, where he executed the principal door of the church of San Petronio. This door is in marble and, as Jacopo did not want to alter the manner in which the work had been begun, he continued it in the Gothic style, adding the reliefs above the columns [see illustration facing p. 48]. Twelve years were devoted to this work. His compositions are in low relief and represent passages from the Old Testament, from the creation to the deluge. In the tympanum the master made three life-size figures in marble—the Virgin with the Child in her arms, and two saints. The people of Bologna were infinitely pleased with these extremely beautiful figures, and surprised as well, because they had been sure that there could be nothing finer than the work of the sculptors Agostino and Agnolo.

Jacopo was recalled to Lucca to execute an altarpiece for Federigo di Maestro Trenta del Veglia. This work, full of grace and beauty, comprised a Virgin with the infant Christ and four saints. In the predella are stories in half relief representing events from the lives of each saint. This part is greatly and deservedly admired for the way in which the figures are placed on different planes, retiring as they fall into the background. Jacopo's example encouraged other artists to enhance their works by new and original inventions. On the sepulchers of Federigo and his wife, Jacopo executed their portraits in low relief.

Jacopo again went to Florence. His high reputation won him the commission from the wardens of Santa Maria del Fiore to make the decorations over the door which faces the Annunziata. Here, within a mandorla, he represented the Virgin being borne to heaven by a choir of angels who are singing to the accompaniment of various instruments. The movements and attitudes of these figures are exceedingly beautiful. Their flight exhibits a force of motion and an air of triumph such as had never before been seen. The Virgin's garments fall and flow about her with much grace. They clothe the form without concealing it. The whole work was completed in four years with all the perfection that Jacopo could possibly give it. He was incited to do his best by the competition of Donatello, Brunelleschi, and Ghiberti, who were also working in Florence. Even to this day, this work of Jacopo's is considered a most unusual production. On the side of the Madonna opposite that occupied by Saint Thomas is a figure of a bear climbing a pear tree. Much has been said about this caprice of the master's, but I will not repeat any of the speculations it has aroused. I prefer that everyone should be allowed to draw his own conclusions about what Jacopo meant.

Jacopo now wished to return to his native city. He had no sooner arrived in Siena than an opportunity presented itself to make and leave behind him a monument worthy of his talent. The city council of Siena commissioned him to decorate the fountain in the piazza at the cost of twenty-two hundred gold ducats. The master prepared a model, sent for the marble, and began to work. He ultimately completed it so greatly to the satisfaction of his fellow citizens that they called him Jacopo della Fonte [Jacopo of the Fountain] for the rest of his life. In the center, the sculptor placed the glorious Virgin Mary, the special advocate and protector of the city of Siena, a figure of singular grace and beauty. About her he placed the seven theological and cardinal virtues—all delicate and charming figures. About the base in low relief he put the *Creation of Adam and Eve* and the *Expulsion from Paradise*. The fountain took him twelve years to complete. The decorations consist of beautiful children and other ornaments, with the lions and wolves belonging to the arms of Siena—all of the most wonderful workmanship. Here Jacopo departed entirely from the old manner of making figures in one unbending piece without beauty or movement. The master gave to his forms the softness of flesh, bestowing life and grace upon the marble. He finished every part with infinite delicacy and patience.

He also made three lovely half reliefs for the font of the baptistery. For all these works and for the conspicuous uprightness of his life, Jacopo was made a knight and appointed a warden of the Duomo of Siena. Never before or after were the works of that edifice more prudently directed. The master survived his appointment only three years, but effected in that short time many useful and creditable improvements.

Jacopo della Quercia, though but a sculptor, drew extremely well. His drawings seem almost to be the work of a miniature painter. When he died, worn out by his perpetual labors, he was lamented not alone by his friends and relatives but by the whole city. He was fortunate in this, since it rarely happens that distinguished men are universally beloved and honored in their own country.

Editorial Notes on Jacopo della Quercia

IN THE artistic lineage of Michelangelo no single individual was more important than Jacopo della Quercia. In fact, it is impossible to imagine the style of Michelangelo without this heritage. Jacopo's sculpture has a lively twist and fling and all the enchanting flexibility and grace that Vasari talks about so well. Vasari says that Jacopo did not choose to alter the Gothic style of the Bolognese door. But, if we look beyond Jacopo della Quercia to Michelangelo, we might look beside him to the sculptors of Burgundy, who were already carving massive, flowing, dramatic figures. When Vasari speaks of German artists or workmen, he often means Burgundian. Jacopo, of all his wonderful generation, was the one who absorbed the influence of the Gothic North and transmitted it to Michelangelo by means of his own superb and passionate sculpture.

*Jacopo della Quercia: Creation of Eve (relief, marble),
San Petronio, Bologna.*

Luca della Robbia: Singing Gallery (detail, marble),
Cathedral Museum, Florence.

Paolo Uccello: Sir John Hawkwood (fresco, now transferred to canvas; life size), The Duomo, Florence.

Lorenzo Ghiberti: Bronze door of the Baptistery, Florence.

Masaccio: The Tribute Money (fresco), Church of the Carmine, Florence.

Masaccio: The Trinity (fresco), Santa Maria Novella, Florence.

Brunelleschi: View of the Duomo, Florence.

Brunelleschi: Abraham's Sacrifice (bronze), Bargello, Florence.

Ghiberti: Abraham's Sacrifice (bronze), Bargello, Florence.

Donatello: David (bronze, 6 ft.), Bargello, Florence.

Donatello: Crucifixion (bronze), relief on the pulpit in San Lorenzo, Florence.

Piero della Francesca: Portrait of Federigo di Montefeltro, Duke of Urbino (wood, 18½ x 13 in.), Uffizi, Florence.

Piero della Francesca: Portrait of Battista Sforza, Duchess of Urbino (wood, 18½ x 13 in.), Uffizi, Florence.

LUCA DELLA ROBBIA

Florentine Sculptor

« 1400-1482 »

Most Florentines in Luca della Robbia's day learned not only to read and write but also to do accounts. After this sort of schooling, Luca was placed with a goldsmith to acquire his art. When he had learned to draw and model in wax, he abandoned the trade of goldsmith and gave himself entirely to sculpture. He then did nothing but work with his chisel all day and draw late into the night, with such zeal that in winter he often had to keep his feet warm in a basket of shavings. This does not surprise me, since no man distinguishes himself in any art who is not ready to bear heat, cold, hunger, and thirst. And he who imagines that he can become great by taking his ease in pleasant surroundings is much mistaken.

Luca was barely sixteen when he joined a band of young sculptors going to Rimini to work on the tomb of the wife of Sigismondo Malatesta. He did very creditably, and some of his reliefs are still to be seen there. He was recalled to Florence by the wardens of Santa Maria del Fiore to execute five small compositions to carry out the design that Giotto had left for the campanile. Luca filled the empty spaces with figures symbolizing the arts: Plato and Aristotle for philosophy, San Donato as teacher for grammar, a figure playing the lute for music, Ptolemy for astronomy, and Euclid for geometry [the *Liberal Arts*]. These designs are far better than the two completed by Giotto—one of Apelles to signify painting and one of Phidias for sculpture. The success of this work, as well as the patronage of Vieri dei Medici, a great and popular citizen of that day, procured for Luca the commission to do the marble ornaments for the organ then being built in Santa Maria del Fiore. He carved a frieze of singing children [the *Singing Gallery*], dancing and playing musical instruments. Though the figures are thirty feet or more from the ground, one can see the throats swelling with song and the very gesture of the leader as he beats the measure with his hands. On the grand cornice of this work, Luca made two nude angels of gilded metal, finished with great skill. The whole work was considered one of rare beauty, although Donatello, who afterward did the ornaments for the organ opposite to this, used better judgment by leaving his work rough and freely sketched, so that it carried better at a distance.

Artists should remember that sketches carry better if the work is to be seen from a distance. Moreover, a high finish often dulls the poetic fire of the first inspiration. Whoever has a clear idea of what he wants to do, as all ought to have from the first instant, will march with confidence toward the perfection of his work. Nevertheless, some minds work at a slower pace than others; but it is a general rule that slow, careful work is often merely the means of concealing defects in essential qualities. High finish, however, is often praised by the unthinking vulgar more readily than really good work, the product of ability and judgment.

But to return to Luca, who was now commissioned to do the bronze door for the sacristy. This he divided into ten square compartments, five on each side, and, by way of ornament, at every angle he placed the head of a man in the border. No two heads were alike, and each was beautiful in its own way. In the compartments themselves he put subjects from the New Testament. The delicacy of the whole shows how much Luca had profited by his goldsmith's training.

However, when all was done and the master had reckoned up his earnings and the time spent, he saw that his gains were small. He determined to find an easier medium than marble and bronze. Reflecting that clay was easily managed and that all that was lacking was a method of making the clay durable, he made many experiments with terra cotta. He finally perfected a glaze of tin, litharge, antimony, and other minerals and mixtures, and with this he covered his clay and fired it. The result was perfection. He secured an almost endless durability for his works in clay.

Not content with this remarkable, useful, and charming invention, so valuable for places subject to damp, he went on to add color to his white glaze—to the delight of all who beheld his works. Among the first who patronized this new invention was Piero di Cosimo de' Medici, who had Luca decorate a small room in the palace built by his father Cosimo. Technically this was a very difficult job, but Luca completed the whole with perfect success. The fame of this work spread all over Europe. The Florentine merchants kept Luca continually at this work, to his great profit, until at last he was not able to supply the demand alone. He took his brothers, Ottaviano and Agostino, to work for him. [The two were brothers, but were not related to Luca.] They earned much more than they had before, for their terra cottas went not only to patrons in Tuscany but also to France and Spain.

At a later period Luca experimented with painting a flat surface of clay with glazes, besides coloring a garland of fruit and foliage, made of terra cotta, as naturalistically as a painting in oils.

After Luca's death, the work was carried on by Ottaviano and Agostino and Luca's nephew, Andrea della Robbia [1435-1525]. Andrea completed an almost infinite number of works in the course of his life of eighty-four years [actually ninety years]. The medallions of the babies in swaddling clothes on the loggia of the Foundling Hospital in Florence are by Andrea, who died in 1525. I remember talking to Andrea when I was a boy, and I have heard him say that he was one of those that bore Donatello to his burial place. I remember, too, that the good old man seemed to take great pride in this.

To return to Luca. That master was buried in the tomb of his fathers in San Pietro Maggiore. Andrea was buried there too. The latter left two sons, who received the cowl from Fra Girolamo Savonarola, who was ever held in great honor by the Della Robbia family. Andrea had three other sons who were sculptors: Giovanni, Luca, and Girolamo. Luca specialized in glazed terra cotta, while Girolamo worked also in marble and bronze. Employed by King Francis [I] in France, Girolamo became rich and famous. He invited Luca [Andrea's son] to join him to share his success, but Luca died soon after he arrived in France, and Girolamo went back to Florence. There he was disappointed in his hope of commissions from Duke Cosimo, who was wholly occupied with the war with Siena. Therefore he returned to France to die, and not only did his house remain closed and his family become extinct, but art was deprived of the true method of working in glazed terra cotta. It is true that attempts have been made since, but none have ever approached the excellence of Luca the elder, and Andrea and his sons, Luca and Girolamo. If I have expatiated on this subject, let my readers excuse me. I thought it should be treated at some length since Luca invented the process. And if, after closing the life of Luca, I have described his descendants who have lived even to our own days, it was so that I need not recur to them again. Although Luca passed from one occupation to another, it was not because of instability or levity, but because he was searching for a method in harmony with his tastes. He enriched the world with a new and beautiful decoration and for himself won undying glory.

Editorial Notes on the Della Robbia Family

THE Della Robbias are a wonderful example of the place of the artist in
Renaissance society. Art was a thriving industry practiced by skilled craftsmen. Ingenuity and energy, experimentation, and studious application to
the principles of drawing, and an understanding of the science of anatomy
were the tools of the artists. We must put aside our notions of "self-expres-
sion" and "gifted" individuals. Imagine, if you can, a "temperamental"
Della Robbia!

The fifteenth century was an age of individualists. Many of them happened to be artists. When Luca della Robbia was a young man, Florence
was teeming with artists, his fellow craftsmen. Later, when Vasari was writing, things had changed; artists had become the peers of the great noble-
men of the world. They moved from court to court. And yet the Della
Robbias were still turning out charming, completely satisfactory terra-
cotta sculpture of "almost endless durability."

PAOLO UCCELLO

Florentine Painter

« CA. 1397-1475 »

PAOLO UCCELLO might have been the most original and inventive genius in the art of painting, since Giotto's day, if he had but spent half the time on drawing men and animals that he threw away in the study of the fine points of perspective. For although these studies are good enough in their way, they tend to develop a dry angularity of manner in drawing and a highly unsocial attitude of mind. This happened to Paolo Uccello, who knew no greater pleasure in life than solving almost impossible problems of perspective. It is better far to live a balanced life than to give way to too severe studies. It is only when the spirit of inspiration is roused that good work is done; then only do great thoughts come, and only then are great things accomplished.

Paolo Uccello spent his life without any intermission on the study of the difficulties of art. He established the rules of linear perspective. From the ground plan to the cornices and summit of the roof, he reduced all to strict rules by converging the lines toward the center, after having fixed his point of view higher or lower to suit himself. He found means to make his figures really seem to be standing on the floor plane and showed how they must diminish in the distance. This had formerly been done by chance, as best the artist could. Paolo also discovered a way of turning the arches and vaulting of ceilings; of foreshortening floors by converging the beams; of carrying a line of columns around the sharp corners of a building to efface the angle. To pore over these things he remained in seclusion for months at a time. This use of his time kept him poor all his life. When he sometimes showed this labor of love to his intimate friend Donatello, the latter said, "Ah, Paolo, with this perspective of thine, thou art losing the substance for the shadow. This is for men who work at the inlaying of wood—these circles, spirals, squares, and all."

Much of Paolo's work has disappeared. Among others, he painted a series of pictures in fresco of the lives of the Holy Fathers in San Mineato, near Florence. These frescoes were almost all in *terra verde* [a monotone of green], but partly and arbitrarily colored. Fields were blue, cities red, and buildings variously tinted. Herein he committed an error, for stones should look like stone. It is said that while he worked on this series, the abbot gave him scarcely anything to eat but cheese. Being too shy to complain, Paolo decided not to work there any more. The abbot sent to ask why he stayed away, but when the monks came looking for him, he was not to be found. And if he met any of the brothers on the street, he hurried away as fast as he could. One day two of the friars, men much younger than Paolo, ran after and caught up with him and asked him why he had fled. "You have so murdered me," said Paolo, "that I not only run from you but I am afraid to stop near a carpenter's, for fear of being melted down into glue. I have eaten such mountains of cheese that I am turned to cheese." The monks, leaving him amidst peals of laughter, went back to the abbot, who promised no more cheese dishes.

Paolo delighted in painting animals. He had numbers of painted birds, cats, and dogs in his house, and every other animal of which he could get a likeness; but he was too poor to keep the living creatures.

Of pictures by Paolo that do remain, there are those in the cloister of Santa Maria Novella. Here he painted the creation of animals, in infinite variety. There are some lions who are about to fall on each other with open jaws and whose fierce rage is expressed with the utmost truth, as are the swiftness and timidity of the stags and deer in the same picture. Birds and fish are painted with the greatest exactitude in every feather and scale. He also painted the creation of Adam and Eve and their fall. He varied the coloring of the trees, which was unusual at that time. In fact, he carried landscape painting much further than former artists, though, of course, much better work has been done since his day. Paolo was satisfied when he drew things according to the rules of perspective: fields, ditches, furrows— all without selection. Afterward in the same cloister he painted *The Flood*, in which Noah's ark appears. In all the terror and violence of the deluge, dead bodies are admirably foreshortened, one much swollen by the water. There are many expressions of human passion and feeling. Two men quite oblivious of their danger are fighting on horseback. We see the extreme terror of death of a man and woman mounted on a buffalo, which is sinking beneath the water. Beneath this, Paolo represented the drunkenness of Noah, wherein is a cask in perspective with lines curving in different directions, which was considered very fine, though the cask does not follow the diminishing lines of the floor. I am surprised that an artist so careful and exact should have made such an obvious mistake. Paolo also painted the Sacrifice of Noah, showing the open ark in perspective, with ranges of perches, in the upper part, for the birds flying out in flocks. In the air above the ark appears God the Father, presiding over the sacrifice. This is the most difficult figure of any that Paolo did, for the head is foreshortened, flying toward the wall with such force that it seems to press through and divide it. The whole painting is so full of harmony and grace that it is beyond comparison Paolo's best work.

In Santa Maria del Fiore, Paolo Uccello painted a memorial to Sir John Hawkwood, the English commander, who died in 1394. It is a terra verde painting, designed as though it were a sarcophagus with an equestrian figure above, about twenty feet high. It was considered very fine then and still is to this day. If he had made the action of the horse a little more natural in gait, it would be perfect, but he did not know much about horses, as he did not himself ride. He signed it Pauli Uccelli Opus.

Many houses in Florence possess small pictures by this master painted on ends of couches, beds, and other articles of household use. There are also four battle pictures in wood, with the horses and armed men in the splendid vestments of that day; and among the figures are portraits of Paolo Orsini, Ottobuono da Parma, Luca da Canale, and Carlo Malatesta, all great captains of those times. These have been restored in our own day by Giuliano Bugiardini, who harmed rather than helped them.

Paolo Uccello was induced by Donatello to visit him in Padua while he was working there. The gigantic pictures in terra verde that he did for the entrance of the house of the Vitali [Vitaliani] family were held in the highest estimation by Andrea Mantegna. Paolo also painted the arch of the Peruzzi. On it he depicted the four elements, symbolizing the earth by a mole, with a fish for the water, a salamander for fire, and for the air a chameleon. But as he had never seen a chameleon, he made a camel with mouth wide open swallowing air into its distended belly.

Paolo's labor must have been very heavy, because he left whole chestfuls of drawings. Although it is a great thing to produce many sketches, it is still greater to carry out finished pictures, which have much more vitality than mere sketches. In our collection of drawings* we have many studies of birds and animals admirably done. This master was an eccentric character, but he was a true lover of ability in the arts. To perpetuate the memory of five distinguished men, he made and kept in his house a drawing of Giotto, who gave new life to art; Brunelleschi, for architecture, Donatello, for sculpture, and himself, for perspective and animals; the fifth was his friend Giovanni Manetti, the mathematician.

* Vasari refers to his own collection of drawings. It is dispersed.

There is a story that he took great pains with a picture of Saint Thomas seeking the wound in Christ's side. It was above the door of the church dedicated to that saint in the Mercato Vecchio. While he was painting it, he had it enclosed with planking. One day Donatello met him alone and asked him, "What kind of a work is this that you are shutting up so closely?" "All in good time," replied Paolo. Donatello did not press him, thinking that when the time came he would see a miracle. It chanced that Donatello was buying fruit one morning just as Paolo Uccello was uncovering his picture. After Donatello, whose opinion was asked at once by Paolo, had examined the painting very minutely, he turned to Paolo and said, "Why! Paolo, thou art uncovering thy picture just when thou shouldst be shutting it from the sight of all!" These words so grieved the painter and so depressed him that he withdrew into the seclusion of his own house and devoted the rest of his life to the study of perspective. He died in the eighty-third year of his life [actually in his eightieth] and was buried in Santa Maria Novella.

His wife said that he used to stand the whole night through at his table. When she asked him to rest, he would reply, "Oh, what a delightful thing is this perspective!" And doubtless his work, delightful to him, has been invaluable to others of later times.

Editorial Notes on Paolo Uccello

THE fifteenth century seems to have been a pivot point in the history of Europe. Knowledge of the past and a zest for discovery and invention were balanced in the minds of wondrously endowed individuals. These men were but contributing the parts to a whole yet unformed. The High Renaissance was going to fuse with a thousand other factors the craftsmanship of the Della Robbias and the painstaking study of perspective and natural science of Paolo di Dono, called Uccello. Someone had to give his life to the solution of the problems of perspective. It would never have served the purpose of an artist of the High Renaissance to place figures receding on a plane "as best he could." He had to know. Paolo Uccello was the man who worked it all out.

The perspective of the Van Eycks is faultlessly observed. Flemish art in its very beginning reached perfection in exact observation and of impeccable execution. Reality can be rendered in paint no more precisely. The contemporary Italians were not content to use the art of painting to this end alone: their minds were called upon to manipulate the forms they used. Florentine artists often studied mathematics as a hobby. Perspective is a branch of mathematics.

I believe that the reason the laws of sculpture and of bas-relief governed painting as well as sculpture at this time was that the antique served as model. All that men then knew of antique art was learned from sculpture.

LORENZO GHIBERTI

Florentine Sculptor

« 1378-1455 »

A GIFTED man is a guiding light to mankind, not only to his contemporaries, but to those who come after him. The rewards and honors which such gifts bring to their possessors are in themselves a stimulus to rouse the minds of men to effort, and to make endurable the heavy labor of the artist or the man of learning. At any time there are infinite numbers of men striving for the distinction and for the rewards which will be conferred on only a few. Talent can rarely escape the persecution of envy. But it was the high merit of Lorenzo Ghiberti that induced Donatello and Brunelleschi, both distinguished men, to acknowledge that he was a better master in bronze than they. This act redounded to the glory of these two artists, as it should confound the envious and malicious.

Lorenzo was the son [stepson] of Bartoluccio Ghiberti, an excellent goldsmith. Aided by his natural ability, he became a better goldsmith than his father [stepfather]. He delighted in design and sculpture and sometimes worked in colors and at other times employed himself in casting small bronzes. He imitated the dies of ancient medals and coins. He also often made portraits of his friends. Ghiberti's studies were interrupted by an outbreak of the plague in Florence in the year 1400, and he was compelled to fly to Rimini. Here he was employed by Pandolfo Malatesta on the painting of a chamber. However, he continued his studies by modeling reliefs in wax and stucco, for well he knew that such works are to sculptors what drawing exercises are to painters. He did not stay long away from Florence. When the pestilence ceased, the Signoria and the guild of merchants resolved to proceed with the doors of the Baptistery. Florence then possessed many able sculptors, foreigners as well as Florentines, and after long discussion, the time seemed ripe for action. Those in authority thought that the work should be done as well as discussed and gave orders that all masters of eminence throughout Italy should come to Florence and present samples of their ability by trials of skill in the execution of a composition similar to those which Andrea Pisano had done on the first door.

Bartoluccio sent the news to Lorenzo, urging him to return to Florence to show what he could do, saying that this was a rare opportunity, from which they might win such advancement that neither of them need ever again work on mere jewelry. Lorenzo tore himself away from his appreciative patron and his fellow artists. Every minute seemed a thousand years until he was well on his way to Florence. On his arrival he found a great concourse of foreign artists assembled. Of these seven were chosen—three Florentines and the rest Tuscans. Each was given a sum of money and told to bring in a finished composition, the size of one of the compartments of the door, in a year's time. The subject chosen was Abraham's sacrifice. This subject calls for landscape, human figures, both nude and clothed, and animals in three kinds of relief—full, half, and low. The candidates were Brunelleschi, Donatello, Ghiberti—all Florentines; and Jacopo della Quercia, Niccolò d'Arezzo [Niccolò Lamberti], Francesco di Valdambrina [Francesco di Domenico Monciatto], and Simone da Colle. Each promised to produce his trial piece complete in a year. All set to work. They kept their labors entirely secret that they might not copy each other's plans. Lorenzo alone, under the guidance of Bartoluccio, who insisted on many models before they decided on any one, allowed everyone to see his work and listened to all criticisms. He finally produced a model without any defect whatever. He then cast it with entire success. Lastly, he polished it with such love and patience that no work was ever so carefully finished.

When the time arrived, the trial pieces were submitted to the guild of merchants for their judgment. They were carefully examined by the syndics and by many other citizens, and also by the foreigners in Florence —painters, sculptors, goldsmiths. These people were all invited to give their opinion. There were thirty-four judges. There was some disagreement on minor points, but all the judges agreed that Ghiberti and Brunelleschi had presented the best works. Jacopo della Quercia's piece was carefully designed but lacked delicacy of finish. The specimen of Francesco da Valdambrina had beautiful heads, but the composition was confused. Simone da Colle did a beautiful casting, because that was his particular branch of art, but the design was not good. Niccolò d'Arezzo showed the practiced hand of a master, but the figures were stunted and the work not well finished. Lorenzo's alone was perfect in every respect.

Donatello and Brunelleschi drew aside and conferred together. It seemed to them that the work should be given to Lorenzo for the public good, for he was very young, not yet twenty [twenty-three], and would have the opportunity to develop the noble talents of which his beautiful work gave such promise. They declared that, according to their judgment, Lorenzo had executed his relief more perfectly than any other artist.

Lorenzo began to work on the doors. First he prepared a model in wood, making each compartment the exact size it was to be in the metal, complete with framework and ornaments of the angles. On each angle was placed a head. After preparing and drying the mold with infinite care and exactitude in his workshop, he built an immense furnace (which I well remember to have seen), and cast this portion in metal. But it pleased the fates that this should not succeed. Lorenzo promptly prepared another mold, without telling anyone, and cast the piece again, this time with perfect success. In this manner he continued, casting each story and then setting it in place. The arrangement was similar to the design that Giotto had made and Andrea Pisano followed for the first door. The framework about each of the twenty pictures is enriched with foliage and moldings, and at every angle is a male or female head in full relief. These heads, sibyls and prophets, are very beautiful, and their variety shows the master's fertility of invention.

The first story is an Annunciation, in which the Virgin turns from the angel with an expression of terror and sudden alarm in an attitude of infinite grace. The Nativity and the Adoration carry on the series. Next is Christ Disputing with the Doctors in the Temple. Then follow the Baptism of Christ in the Jordan and the Temptation of Christ by the Devil. Next is the Expulsion of the Money-changers from the Temple. They are falling over each other in their fright, in attitudes of grace and beauty. The Shipwreck of the Apostles is followed by the Transfiguration. Beside this is the Resurrection of Lazarus. On the same level, but on the opposite leaf of the door, is the Entrance into Jerusalem; beside it is the Last Supper. The Saviour on the Mount of Olives with the Three Sleeping Apostles and the Kiss of Judas are paired, as are also the Flagellation and Pilate Washing His Hands. Above is Christ Bearing the Cross, a scene so vividly portrayed that those who were present at this mournful spectacle can scarcely have seen it more clearly. Near this is the Crucifixion, with Our Lady and Saint John seated on the earth, overwhelmed with sorrow and indignation. On the opposite side is the Resurrection, the guards lying in deep sleep, like dead men, while the Saviour rises upward, with such grace in his attitude and such perfection of beautiful limbs that he does indeed appear glorified. Finally, in the last compartment appears the descent of the Holy Spirit.

This great work was carried to its completion regardless of cost or effort. The merits of Lorenzo were most honorably acknowledged by his fellow citizens and he received the highest commendations, particularly from artists. This work with its exterior ornaments, which are also metal, cost twenty-two thousand florins, and the door weighed thirty-four thousand pounds.

The guild of merchants considered that they had been extremely well served and commissioned Lorenzo to do a second work. This was a bronze statue of John the Baptist, about eight feet high, for a niche outside Or San Michele. Lorenzo worked steadily until he had completed this figure, which is still highly commended. He engraved his name on the mantle. The modeling of the arm is an early example of the good modern manner.

Lorenzo Ghiberti was now considered the foremost and most ingenious artist in bronze not only in Italy, but in other countries also. Siena called upon him to execute two stories for their baptismal font in their church of San Giovanni, one of the Baptism of Christ with many figures, some naked and the others richly dressed. The other composition represented John led before Herod. Ghiberti's design greatly surpassed the work of Jacopo della Quercia, Donatello, and the Sienese Vecchietta, who had already executed designs for this font.

The masters of the Mint had to furnish a statue for one of the niches of Or San Michele opposite the weavers' guild. This statue was to represent Saint Matthew and was to be the same height as the *Saint John* already in place. They gave the work to Ghiberti, who produced a statue even finer than the other and even more modern in manner. The success of this statue caused the guild of wool merchants to order a figure of their patron saint. Lorenzo completed this *Saint Stephen* to the entire satisfaction of the guild, and it was placed in the niche next the *Saint Matthew*.

After this our artist received important commissions for sepulchers in bronze. Some were ordered by the men whose tombs they were to be; others were ordered by the Medici to house the relics of saints. While the innumerable creations of Lorenzo were increasing his fame (for he continued to work in gold and silver as well as in bronze), a large carnelian fell into the hands of Giovanni de' Medici. This carnelian was said to have served the Emperor Nero for a seal. On it was carved the Flaying of Marsyas. Giovanni confided it to Lorenzo to have a gold frame made for it. The master labored several months, and when the frame was done it was found to be no less beautiful than the antique carnelian itself. The result of this success was a great number of orders for similar work. Among other ornaments, Lorenzo made a gold clasp for the cope of Pope Martin [V], adorned with rare jewels and figures in full relief. He also made a wonderfully rich miter, formed of foliage in gold, the leaves being detached from the surface. Among the leaves were many small figures in full relief, which were considered marvelously fine. From this work the master acquired not only increase of fame but large rewards from Pope Martin.

When Pope Eugenius IV arrived in Florence, in 1438, to unite the Greek and Roman Churches, he saw the works of Lorenzo Ghiberti. As much pleased by the artist as with his art, the Pope commanded Lorenzo to make a miter of gold weighing fifteen pounds, with pearls weighing five pounds and a half, the whole estimated to be worth thirty thousand gold ducats. They say that among the pearls were six the size of filberts, and no one could imagine anything as beautiful as the arrangement of the jewels, with the variety of figures of children which formed the graceful decoration of this work. The master received many favors for himself and his friends, besides the first remuneration.

The city of Florence passed a resolution to give Ghiberti the third door of the Baptistery to do, and they also decided to move Andrea Pisano's door to the side and place the new door in the center. They trusted to the artist's zeal, placed the whole matter in his care, and gave him full permission to proceed with the work as he thought best. They hoped that this door would be the richest, the most highly adorned and the most beautiful that he could contrive or they could imagine. They urged him to spare neither time nor labor.

Lorenzo began the work, calling upon all his knowledge and ability. The folds of the door he adorned with stories from the Old Testament. Animated and exalted by the study of his art, he became more familiar with its difficulties and day by day more bold in experiment. Whether taken in detail or as a whole, we have proof, in this door, of the wonders wrought by the creative power and practiced ability of the sculptor. His mastery of modeling in relief, whether in full, in half relief, or in the lowest relief possible, makes this work the most admirable the world has ever seen—ancient or modern. The justice of this praise of Lorenzo's great work is affirmed by the words of Michelangelo Buonarroti who, standing before these doors, said, "They are so beautiful that they might be the gates of paradise." Here was a tribute from one worthy to judge the work. Well might Lorenzo complete this undertaking successfully, since he labored at it with extreme patience and industry.

In addition to the sum paid for the work Lorenzo Ghiberti received a good farm near the Badia di Settimo as a gift from the Signoria, and was soon made a magistrate of the city.

After this stupendous work Lorenzo undertook the bronze ornaments of another door of the Baptistery, which he did not live to finish. He had nearly completed the model, when he suddenly died. I saw this model when I was still a youth, before the careless descendants of Lorenzo Ghiberti permitted it to be lost.

Lorenzo was one of the first to study the antique. He had made a collection of some very beautiful relics of antiquity, some in marble, some in bronze, and some vases brought from Greece. These were all dispersed and squandered by his descendants, as was also the property he had acquired.

But let us return to our artist. During his lifetime he turned his attention to many branches of art and took delight in painting and working in glass. He made all the windows around the cupola of Santa Maria del Fiore except Donatello's, of *Christ Crowning the Virgin*. Lorenzo was appointed to assist Brunelleschi with the cupola, as will be recounted later, but this arrangement was afterward altered. He also wrote a book in the vernacular [Italian, not Latin]. The only good thing in the book, according to my judgment, is that, after speaking of many ancient painters, particularly those cited by Pliny, he makes a brief mention of Giotto and others of those times, but really only to excuse a discourse about himself, with a minute description of his own works, one after another. Nor will I conceal the fact that he tries to give the impression that the book was written by another, though he forgets and speaks in the first person: "I made," "I said," "I was doing," and "I was saying."

Finally Ghiberti was attacked by a violent and continuous fever, of which he died. He was honorably buried in Santa Croce. The portrait of Lorenzo is on the principal bronze door of the Baptistery, seen in the center when the doors are closed. The head is bald.

Editorial Notes on Ghiberti

WHILE Vasari was whole hearted in his admiration of Ghiberti's skill and devotion to his calling, he disliked the man's character. "Greedy, aggressive, overbearing," thus would Vasari have characterized the sculptor, had he not been so anxious to do the man justice as an artist. We shall hear more of Ghiberti when we read the life story of Brunelleschi.

MASACCIO

Painter, of San Giovanni in Valdarno

« 1401-1428 »

WHEN one great genius is born, it is in the very nature of things that he shall not stand alone. In the same place, at the same time, others live, too, as though to stimulate each other by a rivalry of excellence. Nor does the benefit stop there, for future generations look back with pride to the glorious achievements of that fortunate time and strive to match it by their own zealous effort. This was true when Florence produced at one and the same time Filippo Brunelleschi, Donatello, Lorenzo Ghiberti, Paolo Uccello, and Masaccio, each supreme in his own field and all together leading the way to that grandeur and exalted perfection made manifest in our own times. We are indebted to all, but most especially to Masaccio, who first clearly perceived that painting must be founded on nature both in form and in color.

By perpetual study Masaccio learned to overcome many difficulties. He introduced, in his compositions, many attitudes and movements which had never before been painted. He gave his figures life and force and a certain roundness of relief which makes them perfectly natural. He made his figures stand firmly upon the ground by means of the most skillful foreshortening. It is true that Paolo Uccello had solved some of the problems of foreshortening in his studies of perspective, but Masaccio exhibited his mastery of this point with much greater ability than any artist had done before him. In his painting of flesh tones he harmonized the color with that of the draperies, as is true in nature. Masaccio painted draperies with few and simple folds.

This master was born at Castello San Giovanni, in Valdarno. They say that one may still see things that he painted there as a boy. He was most careless of externals. He had fixed his mind on art and could by no means be induced to care for worldly things, such as his own personal interests and still less for the affairs of others. He gave no thought to his clothing and did not collect debts until he was actually in want. Because of this he was called, not Tommaso (which was his name), but Masaccio [as we would say "Slovenly Tom"]. He was called this without malice, simply because of his negligence, for he was always so friendly and so ready to oblige and do a service to others that a better or kinder man could not be imagined.

Masaccio began to paint when Masolino da Panicale was working in the Brancacci chapel in the church of the Carmine, in Florence. He sought to emulate the excellence of Donatello and Brunelleschi (although, as sculptors, their branch of art was different from his), in giving his figures the greatest animation. His work was so far in advance of that which had been done until his time that it can be compared with the art of any time. Most studious and persevering, Masaccio coped with the problem of perspective, drawing buildings as seen from the sides and angles to reveal the interior as well as the exterior. He showed great facility in foreshortening nude figures, which he drew with the utmost simplicity.

In the church of Santa Maria Novella, he executed a fresco of the Trinity, with the Virgin on one side, and Saint John the Evangelist on the other; they are contemplating Christ crucified. On the side walls are two figures of the donor and his wife; the most beautiful part of the picture is the barrel-vaulted ceiling painted in perspective and divided into square compartments, with a rosette in each, so well done that the surface has all the appearance of being indented. There is another picture by Masaccio in Florence. It represents Our Lady sitting at the feet [in the lap] of Saint Anne holding the Child in her arms. This is in tempera, as is also an Annunciation, perfect in color and design, with a house and a colonnade in admirable perspective.

In Pisa, in the church of the Carmine, is a Madonna and Child with angels at their feet sounding musical instruments. One of them is giving rapt attention to the harmony he is producing. Saint Peter and John the Baptist are on one side of the Virgin, and Saint Julian and Saint Nicholas on the other. On the predella beneath are little scenes from the lives of those saints; in the center is an Adoration of Christ. There are horses in this part of the work which are so beautiful that nothing better could be desired. The persons of the train of the three kings are dressed in the fashionable clothes of that time. Over all are various saints in several compartments, placed around a Crucifix.

When he returned to Florence, Masaccio painted a life-size picture of two naked figures, male and female. But he did not feel at ease in Florence, so he resolved to go to Rome to work and study. There he painted a chapel in the church of San Clemente, with a Crucifixion in fresco and stories from the life of Saint Catherine [of Alexandria]. Many of his works in Rome have been lost, but one remains in Santa Maria Maggiore, of four saints so admirably modeled that they seem like a sculptured relief rather than a painting. In this church there is a portrait of Pope Martin [V] done from life by Masaccio. I was looking at this one day with Michaelangelo Buonarroti, who praised it very highly.

Masaccio went back to Florence to continue the paintings in the Brancacci chapel left unfinished by Masolino. Before he began this work, as a sample to show how he had improved his art, our artist painted the figure of Saint Paul near the bell ropes. It is the portrait of Bartolo di Angiolino Angiolini and has something in it so impressive, so beautiful, and so lifelike that it wants nothing but speech. One who knows nothing of Saint Paul has only to look at this picture to see in the noble bearing of the Apostle his exalted and devout character. While Masaccio was working on this, the church of the Carmine was consecrated. He painted the whole ceremony as it had occurred, in terra verde, over the door within the cloister leading into the convent. In this painting are portraits of a number of the citizens who took part in the procession, clothed in hoods and mantles. Among the figures were Brunelleschi in his wooden shoes, Donatello, Masolino (who had been Masaccio's master), Antonio Brancacci (for whom the chapel was being painted), Niccolò da Uzzano, Giovanni di Bicci de' Medici, and Bartolommeo Valori. Masaccio not only drew the figures from life but the door of the convent is shown as it stood, with the porter holding the keys in his hand. The figures are marshaled five or six deep on the level piazza. He had the wit to make the men not all of a size; and the fat, the slender, the tall, and the stout stand with their feet planted firmly on the ground.

Masaccio then returned to the painting of the Brancacci chapel, where he continued the stories from the life of Saint Peter begun by Masolino. The subjects represent the installation of Saint Peter as the first pontiff, the healing of the sick, the raising of the dead, curing the halt by his shadow falling on them as he approaches the Temple with Saint John. Remarkable above all the rest is the scene where Saint Peter, by the command of Christ, draws the tribute money from the mouth of the fish. Besides the fact that we have in this painting the portrait of Masaccio himself as one of the apostles—done with the aid of a mirror—there is great spirit in the figure of Saint Peter, who looks inquiringly toward Jesus while the Apostles watch with rapt attention. Saint Peter's face is flushed with the effort of drawing the money from the fish's mouth. When Saint Peter pays the tribute money, too, the excessive eagerness of the tax collector is painted with the most vivid truth. In the picture which shows Saint Peter baptizing, there is a very celebrated figure of a naked youth shivering with the cold. This figure has ever been held in the highest reverence and admiration by all artists.

This chapel has, indeed, become a school of art for the most celebrated sculptors and painters, who have constantly gone there to study. Among these may be named Fra Filippo, Filippino [Lippi], who completed the work, Andrea del Castagno, Andrea del Verrocchio, Domenico del Ghirlandaio, Sandro Botticelli, Leonardo da Vinci, Pietro Perugino, and the most divine Michelangelo. Raphael of Urbino also founded his style here. And if I have mentioned only a few who have come here to study, it must be understood that where the leaders go, the masses follow. Great as is the esteem in which these pictures are held, it is the firm belief of many that Masaccio would have done even greater works of art had he not died at the age of twenty-seven. Whether it was the result of envy, or because the best things cannot last, so it was. He died in the fairest flower of his youth and so suddenly that there were some who ascribed his death to poison rather than to any other cause.

It is said that when Filippo di Ser Brunelleschi heard of it, he said, "We have suffered a very great loss in the death of Masaccio."

Editorial Notes on Masaccio

After the time of Giotto the art of painting declined again because everyone imitated the pictures that were already done. Thus it went on from century to century until Tommaso, of Florence, nicknamed Masaccio, showed by his perfect works how those who take for their standard anything but nature—mistress of all masters—weary themselves in vain.

—LEONARDO DA VINCI

WHEN students crowd about a picture to study it, as they have about Masaccio's fresco in the Carmine, what are they seeking? Let us agree that the picture must first have attracted their interest by what Vasari calls the story. For instance, in one part of the Brancacci chapel, Saint Peter counts out the tribute money in a reserved and dignified manner. As the result of a miracle he is able to pay. The tax collector is at a disadvantage and takes the money with an air of bravado. The drama lives today as it lived for Masaccio. Drama is meat and drink to the artist. It is so great a factor in his life and work that the drama is taken for granted. The artist examines the means by which it is expressed. How is it done with line, pattern, form, color, and composition? These are the tools of the art of painting.

Masaccio's skill derived from two sources. On one hand, there was the study of antique sculpture. Forms, in a Roman sarcophagus, fill a three-dimensional space, each shape acting upon every other. The other source—and this was most admired by Leonardo—was an original observation of life. Vasari says that Masaccio used in his pictures "many attitudes and movements that had never before been painted." He saw new gestures to paint; and he employed the new knowledge of anatomy and the science of perspective as well as the understanding of classical form. In all this Masaccio was an innovator.

The interesting and still unsettled problem of the attribution of works to Masolino or Masaccio does not much concern us. The weight of opinion is that Masolino painted the frescoes in San Clemente at Rome, and that Masaccio was the author of all that have survived in the Carmine at Florence, except for Filippino Lippi's portion. The fact that these distinctions are not obvious suggests that Masolino at his height was like Masaccio at the beginning of his career. The Saint Paul in the Carmine is gone, but the description is so fine that I have included it.

FILIPPO BRUNELLESCHI

Florentine Sculptor and Architect

« 1377-1446 »

THERE are many men who, though puny in person and insignificant of feature, are yet endowed with so much greatness of soul and such force of character that, unless they can occupy themselves with difficult, nay, almost impossible, undertakings and carry them to perfection, they can find no peace in their lives. However trifling the task they are given, they find means to lift it into importance. Therefore let no one glance with scorn on any man, however mean his aspect or however lacking he may seem in that grace and beauty that we might expect nature to bestow at birth on those who are to exhibit distinguished talent. For surely, under the clods of earth the veins of gold lie hidden. Force of mind and goodness of heart are often born in men of the most unpromising exterior. If nobility of soul be added to their endowment, nothing short of important and valuable results can be expected from them as they labor to overcome the unsightly exterior by the beauty and brightness of the spirit. Filippo di Ser Brunelleschi was as small a man as Giotto, and of such exalted genius that we may say that he was sent us by heaven to revive architecture, which for hundreds of years had been all but lost. Brunelleschi gave the world the most noble, vast, and beautiful building of modern times and proved that the talent of Tuscan artists, though it had been lost for a time, was not dead. His whole nature was compounded of excellent qualities—kindliness, an incorruptible rectitude of judgment, and serenity. His wit and wisdom were always at the service of his neighbors. He was the confirmed enemy of all vice. He never wasted a minute but was ever working, assisting others in their labors, or helping his friends.

There lived in Florence a worthy man named Ser Brunellesco di Lippo Lapi, who chose for his wife an excellent young woman of the Spini family. With her, as part dowry, he received a house wherein he and his children lived until their death. Here was born to him in 1377 a son to whom he give the name Filippo, after his own father who was dead. This birth he solemnized with all possible gladness. As the boy grew up, his father taught him his letters, which Filippo learned with much ease and intelligence. It surprised some people that the boy, instead of devoting himself to letters, had a natural bent for matters of more obvious utility. This displeased his father, who wished the child to become a notary like himself or a doctor like his great-great-grandfather. But when he saw that his son was forever thinking about art and mechanics, he made him learn arithmetic and then placed him in the goldsmiths' guild, where he might learn design from a friend of his. This was a great satisfaction to Filippo, who soon learned all there was to know about the setting of precious stones. He also executed works in niello, among which were two Prophets for the altar of San Jacopo di Pistoia. He also did reliefs which showed that his genius must overstep the limits of the goldsmith's calling. Then, having made the acquaintance of men of superior intellect, he turned his attention to the computation of time, the adjustment of weights and balances, and the movements of wheels, so that in the end he made, with his own hands, several very good and beautiful watches.

Still unsatisfied, Filippo most earnestly desired to attempt the art of sculpture, and as Donatello, then a youth of great distinction and high promise, was a sculptor, they became fast friends. But Filippo, capable in many fields, turned his attention to architecture, and was soon considered by competent judges to be a good architect. He altered some buildings in Florence, constructing the doors and windows in the antique style, a new thing in Tuscany, where architecture was still in a rude state.

At this time there was a commission going begging for a lindenwood statue of Mary Magdalene for the monks of Santo Spirito. Filippo had done several small sculptures and wished to prove his powers on a larger work, so he undertook to execute this statue. When completed, it was considered a very beautiful thing. It was lost with many other treasures when the church was burned in 1471.

Filippo Brunelleschi spent much time studying perspective, the rules of which were imperfectly understood, and at last discovered the correct method of making a ground plan and sections by means of intersecting lines. He took so much pleasure in this study that he drew the Piazza San Giovanni with all the black and white marble incrustations in perfect foreshortening. Encouraged by this success, he went on to draw groups of buildings. Other artists began to study perspective with great zeal. To the young Masaccio, in particular, Filippo taught this art. He instructed those who work at the inlaying of wood, so that Florence became famous for the craft.

Paolo dal Pozzo Toscanelli [later the friend and counselor of Columbus] returned to Florence about this time and invited Filippo to join him at supper with some friends in a garden. The talk was of the mathematical sciences. Although Filippo had no learning, he became the friend of Toscanelli and acquired a knowledge of geometry. He reasoned so well with the aid of his practical experience that he frequently astonished Toscanelli. Brunelleschi also turned his attention to the Scriptures and never failed to be present at learned discussions. He had such a wonderful memory that his friend Toscanelli used to say that to hear Filippo was like listening to a second Saint Paul. Filippo was also a student of Dante. His mind was never idle. There was no one more to his liking than his friend Donatello. These two artists found perpetual pleasure in each other's society and were forever discussing the difficulties of their art.

Now Donatello had completed a Crucifix in wood, and he asked Filippo's opinion of it. It would have been better if he had not, for Filippo replied, "You have placed a boor upon the cross." Donatello replied—and it became a saying—"Take wood then, and make one yourself." Then Filippo, never irritated, no matter how great the provocation, was silent. For several months he worked on a Crucifix, also in wood and the same size as Donatello's, but most excellent in design and workmanship. At last one morning, Filippo invited Donatello to dine with him. As they were walking together toward Filippo's house, they bought some things in the market which Brunelleschi gave to his friend to carry, saying, "Go on to the house with these. I'll come in a minute." Donatello, entering, saw the Crucifix, which Filippo had put in a good light. Overwhelmed, he let his hand fall, and out of his apron spilled eggs, cheese, and all. Donatello was still gazing when Filippo arrived, who laughingly said, "What have you done? What shall we have to eat now all is spilt?" "I, for my part," replied Donatello, "have had all the dinner I want today. You have represented the Christ. Mine is a common man." This Crucifix is in the church of Santa Maria Novella and is still praised by modern critics.

The talents of these excellent masters were appreciated, and they received commissions from the guilds of the butchers and joiners to prepare statues for the niches assigned to those guilds on Or San Michele. Filippo allowed Donatello to make both of them because he was occupied with other affairs. The statues were done to perfection.

The competition for the doors of the Baptistery took place soon after these events. As we have said in the life of Ghiberti, the final choice was between Ghiberti and Brunelleschi. And, as we have told, Filippo himself persuaded the syndics to give the work to Lorenzo. This was rectitude. Here was talent without envy. Happy spirits! who, while aiding each other, took pleasure in commending the work of a competitor. The syndics asked Brunelleschi to undertake the work in concert with Ghiberti, but he would not. He gave his trial piece to Cosimo de' Medici. Donatello's was given to the guild of the money-changers.

After the commission for the door was given to Ghiberti, Filippo and Donatello decided to go to Rome and spend several years, Filippo in the study of architecture, Donatello of sculpture. Filippo still desired to surpass Donatello and Lorenzo insofar as architecture surpasses sculpture. He sold a small farm that he owned in Settignano, and then they set out for Rome. When he first saw the magnificent ruins and the perfection of the churches of Rome, Filippo was amazed. They immediately set to work measuring ground plans and details of cornices, both working continually, sparing neither time nor money. They left no place unvisited either in Rome or in the Campagna, taking the dimensions of everything in reach. As Filippo had no household cares, he gave himself up wholeheartedly to study, and barely took time to eat or sleep. His every thought was of architecture, not that of the uncouth Gothic manner, but the good old style, which until then had been extinct. Filippo had two things in mind: one was to restore classic architecture and in so doing to be remembered forever as Giotto is; the other was to construct the cupola of Santa Maria del Fiore, which since the death of Arnolfo di Lapo no one had had the courage to attempt. He did not speak of this to a living soul, not even to Donatello, but he was forever pondering the vaulting of the Pantheon. He made careful drawings of all the classic arches and vaults that still stood, and if he found fragments of capitals, cornices, or foundations of buildings buried in the earth, he engaged workmen to unearth them. He and Donatello became known as the "treasure seekers," some color being lent to the popular rumor by the chance finding of an earthenware pot filled with coins. When Filippo's money ran short, he earned what he needed by working at the goldsmith's trade. After Donatello's return to Florence, Filippo worked harder than ever. He never rested until he had drawn every kind of structure: temples, round, square, or octagon; basilicas, aqueducts, baths, arches, the Colosseum, amphitheaters. In every church built of brick he examined all methods of binding and clamping, as well as the turning of vaults and arches. He made notes on how the stones were joined and all the means of securing the equilibrium of the parts. He distinguished the different orders of architecture: the Doric, Ionic, and

Corinthian. He became capable of reconstructing the city entirely, and, in his imagination, beheld Rome as she was before her ruin.

In the year 1407, being somewhat indisposed, he returned to Florence. He found his advice and counsel much needed, for many buildings had suffered by his absence. In the same year a great meeting of architects and engineers was called by the superintendents of the works of Santa Maria del Fiore and by the guild of woolworkers to consider the construction of the dome of the cathedral. Among them came Filippo, who gave it as his opinion that the dome should not be built directly above the piers, as Arnolfo had planned, but that a drum or frieze thirty feet high, pierced by windows, should be erected, on which the cupola itself should be raised. Models were prepared accordingly.

When he had recovered his health, some months after his return to Florence, Filippo was talking with Donatello and other artists in the square before Santa Maria del Fiore when the conversation turned to antique sculpture. Donatello told how, on his way back from Rome, he had gone by way of Orvieto to see the marble façade of the Duomo, a most rare thing. He added that in passing through Cortona, he had seen in the church there a most beautiful, antique marble vase adorned with sculptures. This was then almost unique, since few antiquities had at that time been unearthed. Donatello went on to describe the workmanship of the vase and the delicacy he had remarked in it. Fired by this enthusiasm, Filippo set off as he was, dressed in his working clothes, hood, wooden shoes, and all, and went on foot to Cortona to see the vase. He made a drawing of it in pen and ink and brought it back to Florence before anyone knew he had been away. His friends thought he was at home, drawing or inventing something all the while. When Filippo showed his drawing of the vase to Donatello, the latter was not a little surprised at this evidence of Filippo's love of art.

Brunelleschi spent the next few months secretly preparing models and machines for the erection of the cupola. For relaxation he used to help Ghiberti with the finishing of parts of the doors. One morning, hearing that there was talk of engaging engineers to build the cupola, the fancy took him to go back to Rome. He thought he might have a greater reputation and be more sought after if he were abroad. And so it was. Once he was away, it was remembered that he showed more confidence and courage than any of the other architects, who stood confounded and could not proceed with the work. They were all convinced that the cupola could not be built and that there were no beams strong enough to support the scaffolding for so vast an edifice. The superintendents therefore wrote to

Filippo and asked him to come back. This he was very glad to do. The wardens of Santa Maria del Fiore and the syndics of the woolworkers met with him on his arrival and set before him every difficulty, from the greatest to the smallest. Filippo replied in these words:

"Gentlemen superintendents, there is no doubt that great undertakings are always difficult, and this one even more so than you are fully aware. Not even the ancients raised a vault so enormous as this one will be. Thinking of the required scaffolding necessary both within and without, I am confounded by the breadth no less than the height of the dome. Now if the cupola could be arched in a circular form, we might follow the method the Romans used in the building of the Pantheon, but here we must follow the eight sides of the building, dovetailing the stones, which will be very difficult. Yet, this is a church dedicated to God and the Virgin. I trust that They will inspire the person who does this work with knowledge, strength, and wisdom. But how can I help you, seeing that the work is not mine? I tell you plainly that, if it were mine, my courage and power would overcome all obstacles. I may be able to discover a way to do it without so many difficulties, but I have not yet begun to consider the work in detail, and you will have to tell me how you want it done. But even if you decide to raise the cupola, you ought first to spend some money to obtain the advice of all architects—not just Italians, but German, French, and all other foreigners. After such a council you may decide who has the best plan and ability. This is my best and only advice."

The proposal of Filippo pleased the syndics and wardens of the works, but they would have liked him to prepare a model on which they might decide. But he had no such intention and said good-by, explaining that he had received letters urging him to return to Rome. The syndics saw that he was deaf to their requests and urged his friends to ask him to stay in Florence. Filippo still refused to give in, so the wardens one morning voted him a present of a sum of money. This was on May 26, 1417, and the record may be seen among the expenses of Filippo in the books of the works. Even so, Filippo went back to Rome, where he continued his unremitting study of architecture, for he was convinced that no one but himself could carry out the great work. He had advised the syndics to call in all the architects in order that they might be witnesses of his superior genius. He was sure that the problem of the vaulting of the cupola was beyond anyone but himself. Much time was lost while the architects were being summoned. Orders had been given to Florentine merchants resident in foreign countries—France, Germany, England, and Spain—authorizing them to spend large sums of money for traveling and other expenses of the most experienced and distinguished masters.

In 1420 all these foreign masters were assembled in Florence. Filippo then returned from Rome. They all assembled in the hall of the wardens of Santa Maria del Fiore—the syndics and superintendents and a select number of the leading citizens of Florence. The opinions of all were heard, one after another, and each architect proposed and explained his method. A fine thing it was to hear the strange and various notions they set forth. One said that columns must be built and the supporting arches spring from them. Others suggested the use of sponge-stone to reduce the weight. Several masters agreed that a column must be erected in the center to support the cupola, which was to be in the form of a pavilion. There were even some who proposed building a huge mound of earth with small coins scattered through it; when the dome had been built over this mound, they had only to let people take the earth away, free of cost. Filippo alone declared that the cupola could be built without columns, without huge scaffolding, without a column in the center, without mounds of earth, at less expense than by the use of arches—in fact, without any framework at all.

Hearing this, the syndics, who were prepared to be impressed by some clever method, laughed in scorn, turned away, and begged him to talk of something else, for this was the talk of a fool or a madman. Then Filippo, offended, replied: "But consider, gentlemen, that it is not possible to raise the cupola by any other way than by the use of the pointed arch, and it must be double, one vaulting within and the other without, with a passage between. At the angles of the eight walls, the building must be strengthened by the dovetailing of the stones, and the walls themselves must be girded around by beams of oak. We must provide for lights, for staircases, for watershed, and for that which none of you has remembered —supports for the mosaics. But I, who see the cupola raised, I have thought of all these things, and I know there is no other way."

Becoming more excited as he spoke, Filippo tried to make them see his point of view. The more he explained, the more they doubted, so that instead of believing him, they really took him for a fool. They dismissed him, but he refused to go. Finally, they had the servants put him out bodily. This contemptuous treatment, Filippo said later, made him shy of being seen on the street for fear someone might say, "Look, there goes the fool!" The assembly was confounded, first by the proposal of the others, and then by that of Brunelleschi, which seemed stark nonsense. He seemed to propose the impossible: first, by making the dome double and therefore intolerably heavy; and secondly, by saying it could be done without scaffolding. Filippo, too, was much disturbed, and many times was on the point of leaving Florence. Still he knew that he would need patience if he were to win in the end, and he had seen enough to know that the city administration seldom remained of one mind for very long. He might have showed them a little model he had made, but this he would not do. He knew only too well the imperfect intelligence of the syndics, the envy of the artists, and the fickleness of the citizens with their fads and fancies. And I do not blame him. Everyone in Florence thinks he knows more about these matters than the most experienced masters.

What Filippo could not arrange with the tribunal, he began to do with individuals. He took aside now a syndic, then a warden, then an influential citizen. He showed them parts of his design and finally persuaded them to do something—either to give him a chance or to trust someone else with the work. The judges, encouraged, called another meeting for an open discussion of the plans submitted. Filippo, in the general discussion, discredited them all. The other architects [who had submitted nineteen models altogether] asked that Brunelleschi show his model as they had shown theirs. But this he would not do. Instead, he proposed that any architect who could make an egg stand upright be given the job. Accordingly, each took an egg, and tried his best to stand it up on the smooth marble, but without success. When they gave the egg to Filippo and told him to do it himself, he held it daintily in his hand, and, slightly denting the end, he set it upright. The artists protested loudly, saying they could have done that. Filippo replied, laughing, that they could also build the cupola if they could see his model. Filippo was put in charge of the work, but he was told that he must supply the wardens and syndics with more exact information.

He returned to his house and wrote it all down on a sheet of paper as clearly as he could express it. This is what the tribunal read: "The difficulties of this erection being well considered, magnificent signors and wardens, I find it cannot be made in a perfect circle because the huge span could not bear the weight of the lantern. I propose to build for eternity. I have therefore determined to use pointed arches springing from the eight angles of the walls. When loaded with the lantern, each will help to stabilize the other. The thickness of the base of the vault must be seven feet, and it will diminish like a pyramid toward the top where it must be two feet thick. A second vault must be built as a protective roof for the first. The parts of this shell, lighter than the dome must meet the inner vault at the top, where it will be two thirds as thick as at the base. There must be a buttress at each angle of the octagon base, and each of the walls must have two buttresses, one inside and the other outside, and all sixteen of these buttresses must be eight feet thick at the base. The masonry must be solid. The first and second courses from the base must be strengthened everywhere by long plates of hard stone laid crosswise in such a way that both vaults rest on these stones. Throughout the whole height, at every seventeenth foot, small arches shall be constructed between the buttresses, with strong clamps of oak, to bind and strengthen the buttresses. These are to be built of hard stone, and the walls are to be solid hard stone bound to the buttresses to the height of forty-six feet. Above that the walls should be constructed of brick or some light stone. The rain water shall be carried off through a marble channel a foot wide, and shed by a spout of hard stone. Outside, the segments of the cupola shall have marble ribs tapering to the top. Thus the cupola shall be built to the height of fifty-seven feet. Experience will teach the masters who are building it how to proceed."

Next morning, Filippo gave his paper to the syndics and the wardens. They took it under consideration, though unable to understand it all. But Filippo's self-confidence was so obvious (and there was no other plan worth considering) that at last the work was given to him. They would have liked to see him build a vault without framework, but they formally approved of all the rest. By a lucky chance, Bartolommeo Barbadori asked Filippo to build a chapel in Santa Felicità. He vaulted it without a framework. He made another in Santo Jacopo sopr' Arno. These works convinced Filippo's critics, and he was made principal master of the works by a majority of votes. But they commissioned him to build only to the height of twenty-three feet, but if that much was a success, he would surely be appointed to do the remainder. So much distrust and obstinacy was so surprising to Filippo that, had he not known himself to be the only one capable of the work, he would not have touched it; but magnanimously he accepted the terms. Filippo's letter was copied in a book which was kept by the purveyor of the wood and marble work. An allowance, the same as for any other master of the works, was then made him.

When it became known that Brunelleschi had the commission, some thought well of it and others ill, as always happens when the people give their opinion. While the materials were being gathered to start building, a deputation of artists and citizens went to the syndics and wardens, declaring that the matter had been decided too hastily; that more than one man should be consulted; that the authorities were acting as if there were few men of distinction instead of many, as was the case; and finally, that if any accident happened, they, the wardens and syndics, would certainly get the blame. Considering all things, they recommended that

Brunelleschi should by all means be given a colleague to help keep his feet on the ground.

Lorenzo Ghiberti had a great reputation at this time because of his really wonderful work on the door of the Baptistery, and he had powerful friends in high places who urged the syndics and wardens to appoint him as Brunelleschi's colleague. The bitter vexation of Filippo, the despair into which he fell when he heard of this, may be understood by the fact that he was on the point of flying from Florence. If Donatello and Luca della Robbia had not comforted and encouraged him, he would have gone crazy. The wickedness of envious men! It was not their fault that Filippo did not break his models, burn his designs, and in one half-hour destroy his long labor and ruin the hopes of so many years. The wardens at first tried to smooth things over with Filippo by telling him that he was still the inventor of the noble plan, but they gave Ghiberti an equal salary. The work went on, but with little pleasure to Filippo, who knew he must do all the work and get only half the credit. Encouraged by the thought that he might find a way to end Lorenzo's partnership in the undertaking, he went on with the plan laid out in his letter to the wardens. He began by making a complete working model, aided by a carpenter named Bartolommeo. When Filippo refused to let Lorenzo see the model, Lorenzo set about making one of his own to show that he was earning his salary. Filippo was paid fifty lire and fifteen soldi for his model, as we can read in the account book; but Lorenzo got three hundred lire for his.

This vexatious state of affairs continued. When he heard Lorenzo called his equal in the work, Filippo was kept in a most disturbed state of mind. Improvements and new inventions were occurring to him, and he resolved to get rid of this useless colleague. Filippo had already raised the walls of the cupola to the height of about twenty-four feet in both vaults, but the stone and wood reinforcements to strengthen the whole vault had still to be done. He asked Lorenzo his opinion. But Lorenzo said he would leave it entirely to Filippo, the inventor. This reply was just what Filippo wanted. The builders were waiting for directions. The next step was to build a scaffolding for the workmen, because the height was enough to make anyone giddy. The masons waited, but nothing was determined on either by Filippo or Lorenzo. There arose a grumbling among the builders, who were poor people who lived by their daily labor. They now began to believe that neither architect had the courage to go on. They tried to seem busy by looking over and polishing up the work already done.

One morning Filippo did not appear at the works. He wrapped his head in a towel and stayed in bed, pretending that he had an attack of pleurisy. The builders asked Lorenzo for orders. He replied that the arrangement of the work belonged to Filippo and that they must wait for him. "How," said one, "do you not know what his intentions are?" "Yes," replied Lorenzo, "but I would not think of doing anything without him." Brunelleschi's illness had already lasted two days when the master builders went to him and asked him what to do. "Ask Lorenzo, let him do something for once," replied Filippo. This caused much discussion. Hard words were spoken. Some said that Filippo was sick with grief because he was unable to build the cupola and that he was wishing he had never begun. His friends said he was overworked and really had pleurisy. The work came to a standstill. The masons blamed Lorenzo, saying, "He is good enough at drawing a salary, but he cannot direct the work. If Filippo is ill, is that his fault? If he should be long disabled, what could Lorenzo do?"

The wardens resolved to call on Filippo. First they condoled with him on his illness, told him about the confusion at the works, and then described the troubles which his illness had brought upon them. Filippo replied hotly, "What, is Lorenzo not there? Why does he not do something? I do not blame you for complaining." The wardens answered, "He will not do anything without you." Whereupon Filippo answered, "But I could do very well without him." This acute and significant reply was enough for the wardens and they left, convinced that Filippo was sick of the desire to work alone. With the intention of removing Lorenzo, they then sent certain of Filippo's friends to get him back to work.

But Filippo thought that Lorenzo, favorite that he was, planned to go on taking the salary without doing any work, and he now devised a new way of showing up Lorenzo's ignorance. He said to the wardens, in Lorenzo's presence, "Gentlemen, if we were as certain of life as we are of death, many great works would be completed which are begun but never finished. The illness I have just had might have been fatal. I think it would be better for each of us, Lorenzo and me, to take a portion of the work and carry it through. As your worships have divided the salary, let us divide the labor. There are two difficult problems before us. One is the scaffolding, inside and outside the vault. It must be strong enough to support the men, the materials, and a crane to haul up the stone. The other difficulty is the chainwork to bind and secure the part already constructed, to distribute the weight evenly so that the parts mutually support each other and the whole rests firmly on the foundation." Lorenzo was in honor bound to choose one of these undertakings, and he chose the chain because he remembered that there was a chain in San Giovanni which he could use as a model. The work was begun. Filippo's scaffolding was so ingenious that the men worked up there as if they had been on the ground. The models of the scaffolding were deposited in the hall of the wardens. Lorenzo made the chainwork for one of the eight walls with great difficulty. The wardens asked Filippo to look at it. He said nothing to them, but to his friends he said that it was good money thrown away and no use at all. His remarks getting about, he was called before the wardens to explain what ought to be done. He immediately produced his own models, and the wardens saw the error of trusting Lorenzo. They made Filippo chief and superintendent of the whole fabric for life. They also made him a present of one hundred florins and gave him a pension of one hundred florins for life. From that time on Filippo was so assiduous that not a stone was placed that he had not examined. Lorenzo, though in a manner disgraced, nevertheless, by means of the favoritism he enjoyed, continued to draw his salary for three years.

Filippo prepared the most minute plans for the building and the machines for raising the materials. But he was continually tormented by malicious persons, friends of Lorenzo's, who proposed rival models. When you have perfection you need no officious help.

The chainwork was now completed around all eight sides, and the work went on with speed, but with some discontent on the part of the workmen, who considered themselves unjustly reprimanded concerning the masonry. The chiefs among the workers got up a faction which claimed that the work was so perilous that they would not go on without a substantial raise in salary, which was already above the ordinary rate. This displeased the wardens, and Filippo, too. However, he soon decided what to do. One Saturday evening, he dismissed them all. The men were very sullen. On the following Monday Filippo set ten Lombards to work, and by standing over them and saying, "Do this," and "Put that there," he taught them in a day how to work on for weeks. The masons, seeing themselves out of work, sent a deputation asking for their jobs back. Filippo kept them waiting for several days before he reinstated them at lower wages than they had received at first. They brought the shame and injury on their own heads.

The envious were now silenced, and the genius of Filippo began to obtain due recognition. He was already held to have shown a boldness never before displayed by anyone, ancient or modern. Filippo now brought forth his model and all could see the extraordinary amount of thought that had been put into the design. He had even protected the building from the force of the wind by certain apertures and outlets. The superintendents were almost awe-struck that the mind of one man had been capable of so much forethought. His powers continually increased, and he invented ways of hauling the stones up to the very top, where the work-men were obliged to stay all day, once they were up there. Filippo had wineshops and eating places arranged in the cupola to save the long trip down at noon. When he saw that the building went forward so rapidly, Filippo's confidence increased and he worked incessantly. He supervised the making of the bricks, lifting them out of the ovens with his own hands. He examined the stones for flaws and hastily cut model shapes with his pocketknife in a turnip or in wood to direct the men. He invented hooked hinges and a way to fix them in door posts. In fact, he improved the practice of architecture and brought it to a perfection that it might otherwise not have attained among the Tuscans.

In 1423 Filippo was chosen one of the Signori for the district of San Giovanni, for May and June. Afterward he was appointed to the magistracy of the city and was always most scrupulous in the performance of his duties.

The two vaults were approaching their junction, where the lantern was to begin. Filippo had several designs to choose from. In the meantime he resolved to complete the gallery and made a model, which was not used. Even in our own day, a piece of the gallery was built on only one of the eight sides, but not on Filippo's plan. It was removed upon the advice of Michelangelo Buonarroti [who declared that it looked like a cage for crickets].

Filippo also made a complete model for the lantern, eight-sided, in true proportion to the cupola. He did not omit the stair for ascending the ball, but he closed the entrance with a morsel of wood, and no one knew of it.

His reputation was now very great, but he still had the vexation of finding that all the masters of Florence, once his model had been seen, were setting themselves to make others. There was even a lady, of the Gaddi family, who ventured to place her knowledge in competition with Filippo's. He could not help laughing at their presumption. Some of the masters had used parts of Filippo's model for their own, which made him say, "The next model this person makes will be mine altogether." Every-thing Filippo did was praised, but his model was considered defective because the staircase was not in sight. The superintendents insisted on seeing a model for the staircase. Then Filippo removed the morsel of wood and showed it as it is now seen, within one of the piers, a hollow shaft with rungs on one side. Filippo had now reached an age when it was impossible for him to live to see the completion of the lantern. He left minute directions in his will. Though he could not see it completed, he raised it to the height of fourteen feet and collected all the marble for the building of it. When people saw that amount of stone they marveled that Filippo proposed to lay all this weight on the cupola. They thought of it as tempting Providence. Filippo laughed at these fears and went on with the preparations. He even invented a way to get the marble up there without chipping the edges.

How beautiful the building is, we can see with our own eyes. The ancients never dared so to compete with the heavens as this building seems to do, for it towers above the hills which are around Florence.

While he was working on the cupola, Brunelleschi executed many other buildings, which we shall now name in order. He did the model for the Bussini Palace and the Foundling Hospital. He was called to Milan by Duke Filippo Maria while the hospital was being built. He left the work in the hands of his friend Francesco della Luna. Francesco made the border of the architrave increase from the upper to the lower part, in violation of architectural rules. When Filippo returned and reproached Francesco for doing such a thing, he said he had taken the idea from the Baptistery. "One fault only," answered Filippo, "is to be found in that building, and this thou hast imitated." Filippo also prepared the model for the abbey of the Canons Regulars at Fiesole, for Cosimo de' Medici. He used the slope of the hill, placing the kitchens, laundries, stables, and all below; and the library, the loggia, and the refectory above, with the other apartments proper to a monastery on the same plane. The cost was borne by the magnificent Cosimo de' Medici, partly because of his great natural piety and partly from love of Don Timoteo da Verona, a most excellent preacher of the Augustinian order, whose conversation he valued so highly that he had several rooms reserved in the monastery for his own use. Cosimo spent one hundred thousand scudi on this building, as may be read in the inscription. Filippo also designed the fortress of Vicopisano, the old citadel of Pisa, and the fortifications of the harbor of Pesaro. He then returned to Milan and worked on the plans for the cathedral there.

It was at this time that the church of San Lorenzo in Florence was begun. The prior was chosen superintendent of the work. This person made a hobby of architecture. The building had been begun with columns of brick, when Giovanni Bicci de' Medici, who was contributing some of the funds, invited Filippo to dine with him one day. In the course of the conversation, Filippo was asked to give his honest opinion of the work. He was compelled to point out many faults, which were, he thought, the result of the prior's lack of practical experience. Did Filippo think, Giovanni wanted to know, that a better structure could be made? "Without doubt," he replied, "and I wonder that you, who are the guiding spirit of the undertaking, do not spend a few thousand crowns and make a church worthy of the families whose sepulchers are there. Moreover, if you make a beginning, other families will set about building the chapels to the best of their ability as eternal memorials." Encouraged by these words, Giovanni set about building the sacristy. The roof was not yet completed when he died, but the work was carried on with even more zeal by Cosimo, his son.

While San Lorenzo was being built Cosimo de' Medici engaged Filippo to design him a palace. Filippo set everything else aside. He thanked God for his good fortune. Now he had the chance to build such a house as he had longed all his life to make. His genius and his art were nobly displayed in the plan for the palace. It was to face San Lorenzo, standing entirely isolated in the square. It was so grand and sumptuous that Cosimo feared it might arouse the envy of the populace. He set the plan aside and lived to regret it when he later built his palace on a different model [the Riccardi Palace]. As for Filippo, when he heard of Cosimo's decision not to build it, he broke his model into a thousand pieces in his rage and grief. Whenever Cosimo alluded to Filippo, he would say that he had never spoken with a man of higher intelligence or bolder mind.

For the noble family of the Scolari, Filippo made the model of the fanciful and remarkable church of the Angeli. This was never completed because the Florentines spent the money for the expenses of the building, which was deposited in the Monte [the Treasury], on some emergencies in the city or, as some say, on the war with the city of Lucca. Filippo built, or rather began to build, a palace for Messer Luca Pitti. He completed it to the second range of windows with so much grandeur that no more splendid edifice in the Tuscan manner has yet been seen. The doors are double, each fold being more than thirty feet high and fifteen wide. The windows are similar to the doors, with double vaulting. The whole building is of such high art that more magnificent architecture cannot be imagined.

The machinery for the "Paradise" of San Felice in Piazza was invented by Filippo for the festival of the Annunciation, a pageant like those of the olden days. We have no eyewitnesses left, and the monastery where it was held has changed hands. The weight of the machinery damaged the building, and the machinery itself has been destroyed beyond repair. I will not shrink from the labor of a description of the extraordinary spectacle.

Imagine a heaven full of moving figures and an infinity of lights that go on and off like lightning! Filippo suspended a huge half-globe from the beams of the roof. This was like a barber's bowl, edge down, made of thin planking. Within the outer edge of the rim were fixed brackets exactly the size of children's feet. Two feet above each there was an iron fastening to secure a twelve-year-old child so that he could not fall even though he wanted to. About the rim, were spaced twelve children clothed as angels with gilded wings and wearing wigs of gold thread. They took hands and waved their arms, and so appeared to be dancing while the basin was turning about. Little lamps seemed like stars, and the brackets were covered with cotton wool to look like clouds. Within the globe was a bar ingeniously suspended, which had eight arms, each holding a nine-year-old child, well secured but yet free to turn. In the center of this bouquet of angels was a copper mandorla, which came down, moving softly, to the stage. A boy of fifteen dressed as an angel then stepped from the mandorla and approached the Virgin and made his announcement. Then the entire pageant was drawn up in order. There was, besides all this, a figure of God the Father in a choir of angels fixed near the convex side of the basin. It did truly represent paradise. The whole spectacle was hidden by great sliding doors, which moved very smoothly on a groove, but with a fine noise as of thunder.

Filippo was sent for from Pisa, from Mantua, wherever great works were in progress. But Filippo's most important buildings were in Florence. The plan he made for the church of Santo Spirito would have turned the old church about and cleared a wide approach to the banks of the Arno, so that travelers from Genoa and the Riviera or from Pisa or Lucca should behold the magnificence of this edifice. But the citizens objected to having their houses torn down, and this desire of Filippo's was not carried out. Though it was not completed exactly as it was designed Santo Spirito is still almost the most perfect church in Christendom.

Filippo was very clever at repartee. Lorenzo Ghiberti had bought a farm upon which he spent twice as much money as it returned. At last, he sold it. Filippo was asked, about that time, what he thought was the best thing Lorenzo ever did, and he replied, "To sell his farm."

At length, when he had become very old—he was sixty-nine—Filippo departed to a better life on April 16, 1446, after having labored much and having earned an honored name on earth and repose in heaven. His death was deeply deplored by his country and his fellow artists, more especially by those of them who were poor, whom he had constantly aided and benefited. He left to the world the memory of his excellence and of his extraordinary talents. To me it appears that from the time of the Greeks and Romans to the present there has appeared no greater genius than Filippo. It was he who revived the use of the antique cornices and the orders of architecture. He was unfortunate in some respects, for besides always having to contend with some enemy or other, many of his buildings were not finished in his time, and some not since. He who desires to leave a memorial of his existence, let him complete it in his own lifetime and shun the fate of many of the edifices designed by Filippo Brunelleschi.

Editorial Notes on Brunelleschi

VASARI had before him a life of Brunelleschi by Antonio Manetti (1423-1497) when he wrote this wonderful vita. It could not be more vivid. Though I have not read Manetti, I am sure that Vasari's sympathetic interest gives added color to the drama of Brunelleschi's career. Vasari writes as though he had watched Brunelleschi carve model shapes out of a handy turnip. But the chronology of events is not clear in Vasari's account.

Renaissance architecture was concerned with the same problems as Renaissance painting and sculpture. Given a space, the problem was to use it to the greatest advantage. On the other hand, Gothic architecture serves quite another function. In a Gothic church, the dogma of religion and the stories of the Bible are written, as it were, in every carving, every ornament, every pane of stained glass. The building also serves a function. It houses the congregation assembled before the altar. The Renaissance church of Santa Maria degli Angeli, Florence, was designed about a central focal point. It used a given space, dividing it into ample shapes which contributed to each other. The function of the building was of secondary importance. At least half of the people, for instance, would face the back of the altar.

Steeped in the new lore of the antique, Brunelleschi built modern buildings. He might be compared to a man speaking in Latin to express modern ideas.

As for the Duomo, Leon Battista Alberti said the last word about it. He said it was ample enough to hold all the people of Tuscany in its shadow. There is a saying that when Florentines are too far away from it they are, not homesick, but sick for the Dome. It rises above Florence like a benediction. It looks at once strong and soaring.

DONATELLO

Florentine Sculptor

« CA. 1386-1466 »

THE sculptor Donato, who sometimes signed his works Donatello, was born in Florence in 1386. Not only was he an admirable sculptor, but he had mastered perspective and was considered a very good architect. His work, such was its grace and excellence and masterly design, was considered as fine as the best of Greek and Roman art. Not even in our own day has his work in relief been equaled, much less surpassed.

Donatello was brought up in the house of Ruberto Martelli, and there he was a great favorite. He began producing sculpture while still very young and in such profusion that his early works were not prized. His first notable success was an Annunciation, carved in hard stone. It was for the altar of the Cavalcanti chapel in the church of Santa Croce in Florence. Around it he made a frame ornamented in the grotesque manner [the style of the antique], the base varied and twisted and the pediment a quarter circle. Some figures of little boys, who clutch each other in fear of the height, bear garlands above. But the figure of the Virgin especially displays Donatello's art. Alarmed by the unexpected appearance of the angel, her timidity is overcome by her reverence as she turns with exquisite grace toward the angel, and her face clearly expresses the humility and gratitude due to one who presents an unexpected gift. In the draperies Donatello showed extraordinary ability; he revealed the nude bodies beneath the graceful folds, and proved his determination to discover and restore the beauty of ancient art. In the same church is the Crucifix that Brunelleschi so severely criticized.

In the church of San Giovanni [the Baptistery] in Florence, Donatello made the monument of Giovanni Coscia [Baldassare Cossa], who had been deposed [as Pope John XXIII] by the Council of Constance. The monument was erected at the expense of Cosimo de' Medici, who was an intimate friend of the deposed pontiff. For this tomb, Donatello did the figure of the Pope in gilded bronze, with Hope and Charity in marble.

The figure of Faith was the work of his pupil Michelozzo. Just opposite is a Mary Magdalene, most exquisitely carved in wood. The penitent is seen consumed and exhausted by fasting and abstinence, every part a perfection of anatomical study.

In the Mercato Vecchio [old market] on a granite column, there is a figure of Plenty by Donatello. On the side of Santa Maria del Fiore, which faces the Via del Cocomero, is a figure of an old man, thoughtful, worn with years and labor. It is in the very style of the antique. I must mention again the gallery of singing boys he so freely sketched for the organ loft of the same church. This is a wonderful example of Donatello's skill and judgment. For though many works look well in the studio, they often seem quite different when they are set in place, higher or lower or in a new light. Donatello, on the contrary, treated his figures with such skill that they were not half as effective in his studio as they were when placed in the position for which they had been made. Donatello also designed one of the circular windows beneath the cupola [that is, in the drum which supports the cupola]. The subject is the Coronation of the Virgin.

Donatello made several statues for the outside niches of Or San Michele: *Saint Peter*, an admirable figure full of spirit, which he did for the guild of butchers; *Saint Mark* for the guild of joiners, first undertaken with Brunelleschi but with his consent finished by Donatello alone; and Saint George in his armor for the guild of armorers. The *Saint Mark*, being designed for a high niche, did not look well standing on the floor of the studio. The syndics of the guild were not disposed to accept it, but Donatello begged them to let him set it in position and there work on it. He so placed it and shut it up for a fortnight and then, without having touched it, he uncovered it, to the admiration of all. The *Saint George* is a most animated figure—bright with youthful beauty, generosity, and bravery. His attitude shows a proud and terrible impetuosity. Life seems to move within the stone. It is certain that no modern figure is as lifelike as this marble by the hand of Donatello. On the pedestal which supports the tabernacle enclosing the figure is the story of Saint George and the dragon in relief. The horse has been much admired in this work. In the pediment above is God the Father, in low relief.

Donatello was the sculptor of a tabernacle in classic style for Or San Michele, using the Corinthian order. The tabernacle was intended to house two statues, but these Donatello did not execute because he and the syndics could not agree about the price, so Verrocchio made them after Donatello's death, as will be related. In the façade of Santa Maria del Fiore, which faces the campanile [actually on the campanile, facing the cathedral], there are three figures, each about ten feet high, by Donatello. Two of them are portraits, one of Francesco Soderini as a youth, and the other of Giovanni di Barduccio Cherichini, now called Lo Zuccone [Pumpkin or, as we might say, bald pate]. This is considered the most extraordinary work ever produced by Donatello, who, when he wished to be most emphatic, used to say, "I swear by the faith I have in my Zuccone." While he was working on it, he used to break off and cry, "Speak then! Why wilt thou not speak?" Over the door of the campanile is the portrayal of Abraham about to sacrifice Isaac.

For the Signoria of Florence Donatello cast in bronze a group that represents Judith cutting off the head of Holofernes. This was placed in the Loggia dei Lanzi. This excellent work is a masterly casting in bronze. And the grandeur and simplicity of Judith, her greatness of mind, and her God-given power are made manifest in the liveliest contrast to the sodden figure of Holofernes. The pedestal is very graceful. He signed it *Donatelli Opus*, so great was his own satisfaction in it. In the court of the Palazzo della Signoria is a naked, life-sized David, with one foot on the head of Goliath and a sword in his right hand. It is hard to believe that it is not a cast of a living figure; it is so soft and so flexible. There is another beautiful David in marble with the head of Goliath between his feet and the sling in his hand. The first court of the Palazzo de' Medici is adorned by eight medallions in marble, some copied from antique cameos and some with designs of Donatello's own invention. They are fixed in the frieze between the windows and the architrave above the arches of the loggia. A very fine stone vase with a jet of water for a fountain is among the works of Donatello. Several sculptures in very low relief, in both marble and bronze, in the same palace have extraordinary merit.

Cosimo de' Medici was the perfect patron. He kept Donatello continually at work, and Donatello understood Cosimo so well that he always did exactly as Cosimo desired. There is a story that a merchant from Genoa ordered a bronze bust, life-size. It was a very beautiful thing, and the bronze was made thin and light so that it might be the more easily transported. Cosimo had secured the commission for Donatello, but the merchant balked at the price. Cosimo brought them together to talk it over. The bust was placed on the battlements of the upper court. Cosimo, in an effort to settle the difference, turned to the merchant and remarked that he offered too little. The merchant said that Donatello would have earned half a florin a day if he had worked on it a month. Then Donatello turned in great anger, saying that he had found a way of spoiling the whole labor of a year in the hundredth part of an hour, and he struck the bust a great blow that sent it falling to the street below, where it was dashed to pieces. He said that it was plain that the merchant was more accustomed to bargaining for horse beans than to buying sculpture. The unhappy merchant regretted what had happened and would gladly have paid twice as much to have the head reconstructed, but Donatello refused to do it—even at the request of Cosimo.

In the house of the Martelli are several statues by Donatello. Among them is a Saint John, a most rare thing, which is willed to each generation with the understanding that it can neither be pledged nor sold, nor given away. It is a mute testimony to the affection of the Martelli for Donatello and the gratitude of Donatello for their protection.

At Prato Donatello constructed the marble pulpit from which the girdle of the Virgin is shown. In one compartment of the pulpit is a Dance of Children, which is perfection. Donatello also cast two capitals in bronze to support this pulpit.

At this time the Signoria of Venice sent for him to erect the monument of Gattamelata in the city of Padua. There it stands on the Piazza di Sant' Antonio, the great horse chafing and neighing under his proud rider. In spite of the great size of the casting, it is admirably proportioned and could bear comparison with any antique work for mastery of design, art, and harmony. It continues to amaze those who look at it even today. The Paduans did their best to keep Donatello with them. They gave him the predella of the high altar of the church of the Friars Minor to decorate with stories of Saint Anthony of Padua. These are in low relief and of amazing skill in the composition and handling of perspective. The front of the altar has the *Marys Weeping over the Dead Christ*, an extremely fine work of the master. He made a skeleton of a horse in wood to be used in processions. Whoever examines it will have an idea of the resources and boldness of the artist. The nuns of a convent in Padua brought Donatello a figure of Saint Sebastian, old and very ugly, begging him to make them one like it. He tried to oblige them, but rude as was the figure he had to copy, his own could not be other than excellent. A vast number of works by Donatello are in Padua, where he was so praised that he feared to lose his balance. He said he would be better off in Florence even if he were continually criticized there. He started back to Florence but stopped in Venice, there to leave a John the Baptist in wood, gilded and tinted, and in Faenza to do a Saint John and a Saint Jerome.

After his return to Tuscany he continued to work until he went to Rome, as we have related in the life of Brunelleschi. He studied the antiques and labored to the utmost of his power to imitate them. While he was studying he made a tabernacle for the Sacrament for Saint Peter's. On the way back to Florence, he stopped in Siena to make a bronze door for the

Baptistery. He had completed the wooden frame and had almost finished the wax model when he was persuaded by his intimate friend, the goldsmith Bernardetto di Mona Papera, to return with him to Florence. The work was never really begun, and the only work by Donatello in Siena is a bronze John the Baptist.

Once again in Florence, he worked for Cosimo de' Medici in the sacristy of San Lorenzo. He ornamented the angles of the ceiling with medallions in stucco. He made two doors of low relief of exquisite workmanship, on which he showed the Apostles, martyrs, and confessors. Above these are two shallow niches with Saint Lawrence and Saint Stephen in one and Saint Cosmas and Saint Damian in the other. The bronze pulpits were constructed under his direction, but his great age prevented him from completing them, and the work was finished by Bertoldo.

Over the door of Santa Croce is still to be seen a large statue in bronze of Saint Louis. When Donatello was reproached for making the figure so stupid and clumsy—it is the least meritorious of his works—he said he had done it on purpose because he thought the saint must have been a stupid fellow to forsake his kingdom and become a monk.

For Cosimo de' Medici he portrayed his wife in bronze, and this is preserved in the treasury of our Lord, the duke [Cosimo I], where there are many other works by Donatello, among them a very low relief in marble of the Virgin and Child of matchless beauty. A full account of the life and works of this master would make too long a story, since he gave his attention to so many things, both great and small. He frequently carved coats of arms of families, placing them over chimney pieces or on the fronts of houses. He made a sarcophagus for the Martelli family which is in the crypt of San Lorenzo. Donatello's brother Simone asked him to come to Rome to see the monument of Pope Martin V which he was making before it should be cast in bronze. Donatello happened to arrive just when the Emperor Sigismond came to be crowned by Pope Eugenius IV. So Donatello found himself compelled to give his attention to the sumptuous preparations for the festival.

There is a most beautiful marble head from the hand of Donatello in the treasury of the duke of Urbino; it was said to have been a present from the magnificent Giuliano de' Medici. In fact, Donatello was a master of such merit that he was the first sculptor of his time. And in his day the antiquities now brought to light had not been discovered. Donatello prevailed upon Cosimo de' Medici to make the collection of antiquities in Florence.

Donatello was most liberal, friendly, and courteous to all. He attached little value to his gains, but kept what money he had in a basket, hung by a cord from the ceiling, and his friends could take what they needed without being expected to say anything to him. Donatello grew old serenely, and when he could work no longer, Cosimo and others of his friends took care of him. When Cosimo lay dying he left Donatello in charge of his son, Piero. Piero gave Donatello a farm which brought in sufficient income for an easy life. The artist rejoiced and considered himself secure from the fear of dying of hunger. But within a year he returned to Piero, the deed to the property in his hand. He said he would rather starve than listen to the complaints and outcries of the farmers who came pestering him every third day with calamities of wind, of storms, and of taxes. Piero laughed, but he took back the farm and gave Donatello the equivalent in cash income paid weekly at the bank, an arrangement that pleased the old man greatly. Thus, as the friend and servant of the house of Medici, Donatello lived out his days. When he was eighty-two he had a stroke and became bedridden. He lay in a poor little house in the Via del Cocomero. Day by day he became worse, until he died December 13, 1466. He was buried in San Lorenzo near the tomb of Cosimo, that his body might be near him when dead as his spirit had been near him in life.

Donatello's death was much regretted by all his fellow citizens, almost all of whom accompanied him to his grave. All the painters, architects, sculptors, goldsmiths, and most of the people of Florence were in his funeral procession. It was a long time before they stopped composing verses in his honor.

There is one little story which I think would not be amiss. Shortly before Donatello died, some distant relatives called to offer their sympathy for his illness and to suggest that he leave them in his will a small farm he had. He answered that he proposed to leave the farm to the farmer who had worked it with care rather than to them who had never done a thing for it except to beg for it in this visit. He ended by saying, "Go! And the Lord be with you."

The drawings of Donatello are extremely bold and of a facility and freedom that have no equal. I will not omit to mention that the learned Don Vincenzo Borghini has a book of drawings, both ancient and modern. Among these are, on pages opposite each other, two drawings, one by Donatello and the other by Michelangelo Buonarroti. Under these he has written in Greek: "Either the spirit of Donatello worked in Buonarroti, or that of Buonarroti first worked in Donatello."

Editorial Notes on Donatello

VASARI tells us Donatello's story on many other pages of the Lives. Donatello seemed to him the greatest innovator of his day, "that fortunate age." His achievement ranked with that of Vasari's own time. It is still true, as Vasari said then, that Donatello's work in relief has never been equaled, much less surpassed. No more skillful composition, or figures in swifter motion, or surfaces more alive have ever been done. No wonder that, at Michelangelo's formal funeral, the artists in charge of the decoration of San Lorenzo left Donatello's pulpit in view, when every other surface was decked anew.

Vasari repeats in his life of Donatello all the charming anecdotes concerning him that appear in the life of Brunelleschi. The figure on the Crucifix that Brunelleschi so severely criticized has arms set in sockets so that it could be taken down and set in a coffin when it was used in a mystery play. Donatello was as close as that to the Middle Ages. While his art sprang right out of the inspiration of the antique, it was immediate in its truth to nature. There was a long time during which the world was blinded by this realism. From soon after Vasari's day until about 1860, people shrank from the stark reality of his work. They said his Judith was a female butcher about to carve a slice of Holofernes. They could not bear to look at the emaciated Magdalene. They thought the portrait of Niccolò da Uzzano was actually a death mask and hardly to be considered a work of art. Modern critics, on the other hand, are so impressed by the consummate art of Donatello that the once despised naturalism seems of secondary importance.

PIERO DELLA FRANCESCA

Painter, of Borgo San Sepolcro

《 CA. 1416-1492 》

Unhappy indeed is he who spends a long lifetime in serious study and then is prevented by illness or death from bringing his work to ultimate perfection. Often it happens that the credit is claimed by a presumptuous upstart. Although at long last the truth comes out, for a time at least the laborer is defrauded of his just deserts. Such was the case of Piero della Francesca, who was a master of perspective and mathematics but who first went blind and then died before his books were known to the public. Fra Luca di Borgo [Luca Pacioli], who should have cherished the memory of his master and teacher, Piero, did his best, on the contrary, to obliterate his name, taking to himself all the honor by publishing as his own the work of that good old man. Besides his literary work, which was a series of practical applications of Euclid's propositions, Piero della Francesca was a distinguished painter. He was born at Borgo San Sepolcro and was called Della Francesca because his mother had been widowed before his birth. She brought him up alone and unassisted and helped him to that learning to which his good fortune had destined him. Piero studied mathematics as a boy, and though he was induced to become a painter when he was fifteen, he never deserted the study of that science. He was much employed by the duke of Urbino as a painter. The very beautiful small figures he did have been lost or destroyed in the wasteful wars that have disturbed this duchy. Some of his writings on geometry and the laws of perspective have been preserved. Piero was certainly one of the best-informed men of his time in these subjects, perhaps the equal of any since his day. Among the fine drawings in perspective that illustrate his works, there is one of a vase so treated as to show the front, back, sides, top, and bottom. Each turn of every circle is foreshortened with the greatest delicacy.

Eminent at the court of Urbino, Piero wished to make himself known elsewhere. He traveled about Italy from place to place, working busily. His pictures have suffered damage and even complete loss. Even in Ferrara, where he painted many apartments in the palace, not one of his pictures is still to be seen.

Piero was invited by Pope Nicholas V to Rome, where he painted in the upper rooms of the palace [the Vatican], but these works too are lost. Pope Julius II had Raphael of Urbino paint the *Liberation of St. Peter* and the *Miracle of Bolsena* in the same places. I can only say of the art of this master, so many of whose works have been destroyed, that he painted some portraits in the work we have described that were so beautiful and so perfect that they wanted only speech. Many of these portraits are well known through copies that Raphael caused to be made so that he might have the likenesses of the great personages there represented.

In Milan, over the door of San Sepolcro, I have seen a Dead Christ by this master, which is so foreshortened that, though the picture is not more than twenty-three inches high, the whole length of the body is shown.

Returning to Borgo, Piero della Francesca painted in the deanery there two Saints in fresco which are considered extremely fine. In the Augustinian Monastery he painted the high altar. A Virgin for the Brotherhood of the Misericordia is beautiful, and a Resurrection in the [former] palace of the Conservators is considered his best work in that city. At Santa Maria di Loreto, Piero began a work in company with Domenico of Venice but left before it was done for fear of the plague. It was afterward finished by Luca da Cortona [Luca Signorelli], a disciple of his, as will be related in the proper place.

Piero went to Arezzo to paint the chapel of the Bacci family in San Francesco with the *Story of the True Cross* from the burial of Adam, when the seed of the tree of the cross was placed under his tongue by the forethought of his sons, to the time when the exaltation of the cross itself was solemnized by the Emperor Heraclius, who, walking barefoot, carried it on his shoulders into Jerusalem. This work has many admirable qualities, among others the new treatment of the draperies worn by the attendants of the queen of Sheba. It contains many portraits from life and a range of Corinthian columns, the proportions of which are absolutely perfect. A peasant leans upon his spade as he listens to the discourse of Saint Helena with an attention that is expressed so well that it could not be improved. The dead body restored to life at the touch of the cross and Saint Helena's joy are as well done as the arrangement of the bystanders who prostrate themselves in adoration. But best of all is the treatment of night in the picture of the dream of Constantine. An angel descends, head downward, bearing the insignia of victory to the emperor asleep in his tent and guarded by armed men seen obscurely in the darkness. The light comes from the angel alone. It is very well managed. In this work Piero shows the importance of copying things as they really are. Later artists have been able to profit by his example. There is a picture of a battle, in which fear, rage, and strength are shown in a scene of fearful carnage. Piero has been able to imitate the very glitter of armor. Some war horses are foreshortened with such skill that we may say that they are too beautiful. Piero della Francesca was a master of the then imperfect science of anatomy, as we see in a partly nude figure in an Arabian cloak, seated on a raw-boned horse. He surely deserves the large rewards and the fame which this work brought him.

In the cathedral of Arezzo, Piero painted a Mary Magdalene in fresco near the door of the sacristy. And for the Brotherhood of the Annunziata, he painted the banner that they carry in procession. At Ancona, in the church of San Ciriaco, he told the story of the Marriage of the Virgin in a picture of extraordinary beauty.

He was a most zealous student, using a knowledge of Euclid to demonstrate the properties of rectilinear bodies better than any geometrician. Maestro Luca di Borgo caused the works of his master, Piero della Francesca, to be printed as his own after Piero died.

It was Piero's custom to make clay figures and drape them with soft-textured stuff to use as models.

At about the age of sixty he was attacked by a catarrh which affected his eyes. He became blind and thus lived on until he was eighty-six [seventy-six]. He left a considerable property, part of which consisted of some houses which he had built himself, but they were burned during the embroilments of 1536. He was honorably buried in the cathedral at Borgo. His books, preserved in the library of Frederick II, duke of Urbino, are of such value that they have earned him the title of the first geometrician of his time.

Editorial Notes on Piero della Francesca

PAINTING was the second string to Piero's bow. The drama of the wicked Fra Luca (Luca Pacioli was a respectable man, and not a villain, by the way) proves this to be so. He stole, according to Vasari, the most valuable thing Piero ever achieved—his mathematical treatise. When a geometrician paints pictures that are masterpieces, even when compared with those of his great contemporaries, art must have been indeed the channel through which the age found its expression. It is superfluous to ask if the Renaissance could have been as much the age of scientific and mathematical research as of the plastic arts.

No reproduction that I have ever seen gives the effect of unearthly austerity, clarity, and beauty in the frescoes of the Story of the True Cross in Arezzo. In a black-and-white photograph, the formal arrangement shows up in solemn weight. In a color print, the surface gloss of the paper falsifies the effect. The fresco has a chalky light. The power of the design is veiled by the atmospheric tints. At first glance, the picture is delicately pretty. But study reveals the strength in the organization of the composition. Never before were shapes and colors used in this way. The painters who followed Piero—and in this category come the Florentines—found it easy to master the difficulties of composition, and therefore their work lacked the appearance, so severely noble in Piero's work, of difficulties overcome.

According to Sir Charles Holmes, Piero was the pupil of Domenico Veneziano in Florence.

Of the "very beautiful small figures" that Vasari says he painted for the duke of Urbino, we reproduce a pair that escaped destruction. Each is as minute and exact as a work by Jan Van Eyck. There is no veiling in this oil painting. The distance of the landscape recedes but loses no precision.

FRATE GIOVANNI DA FIESOLE

(Fra Angelico)

Painter, of the Order of
the Preaching Friars

« 1387-1455 »

FRA GIOVANNI ANGELICO DA FIESOLE was no less eminent as a painter and a miniaturist than as an ecclesiastic and on each account deserves to be honorably remembered. He might have made a most comfortable living in the world, having means of his own and the ability to earn as much as he liked by his art. But he chose to enter the Order of the Preaching Friars, the better to serve God and to seek his own salvation. With such an upright purpose, it is possible to find peace and quiet in the cloister, but he who becomes a monk from less worthy motives is bound to make himself miserable.

There are some illuminated manuscripts by his hand in the monastery of San Marco in Florence which are too beautiful for words. Some similar books are in San Domenico in Fiesole, but Fra Giovanni was probably assisted in these by his brother, who was also a miniaturist.

Fra Angelico was so greatly loved and admired by Cosimo de' Medici that the latter had no sooner completed the church and cloister of San Marco than he caused the good father to paint the whole story of the Crucifixion on one of the walls of the chapter house. In this work are figures of all those saints who have founded religious bodies, mourning at the foot of the cross on one side, while on the other are Saint Mark the Evangelist and the Virgin, who has fainted at the sight of the crucified Saviour. Around the Virgin are the Marys, sorrowing with her and supporting her. Near her are Saints Cosmas and Damian. It is said that the Saint Cosmas is the portrait of Fra Giovanni's friend, Nanni d'Antonio di Banco, the sculptor. Beneath this work, on a frieze over the back of the seats, the master painted Saint Dominic standing under a tree, on the branches of which are medallions whereon are all the popes, cardinals, bishops, saints, and masters of theology of the Order of the Preaching Friars, down to his own day. The brethren of his order assisted him by procuring portraits of these personages from different places, so that he was able to make many of them likenesses. All these heads are very graceful and beautiful. In the first cloister he then painted frescoes, of which the most esteemed is the *Dominic at the Foot of the Cross*. He painted in the dormitory a story from the New Testament which is beautiful beyond the power of words to describe, besides many other things in the cells and on the walls.

But exquisite and admirable above all is the picture on the high altar of the church of San Marco. The sight of this Madonna awakens the devotion of all beholders by the pure simplicity of her expression. The saints surrounding her have a similar character. The predella, which tells stories of the martyrdom of Saint Cosmas and Damian and others, is done with such care that figures more delicate or more judiciously arranged can hardly be conceived.

At San Domenico di Fiesole Fra Giovanni painted the altarpiece, which was probably injured at some time, for it has been retouched by other masters. But the predella and the ciborium are much better preserved, and many small figures surrounded by a celestial glory are so beautiful that they seem to belong to paradise. One never wearies of looking at their beauty. In a chapel of the same church is an Annunciation. The Virgin, seen in profile, has a face so delicate, so devout, and so perfectly painted that one can hardly believe it to be the work of a man. In the landscape background are seen Adam and Eve, whose fall made it necessary for the Virgin to give birth to the Redeemer. The predella is extremely beautiful.

The picture in which Fra Angelico surpassed himself and proved the high quality of his powers and his profound artistic intelligence is the *Coronation of the Virgin*. The principal figures are surrounded by a choir of angels and a vast number of saints. The figures are so many, so well done, so varied in attitude, and with the expressions of the faces so diversified, that it is an infinite delight to look at them. It is a most convincing picture of heaven, as if the blessed spirits could not look otherwise, as if, indeed, it had been painted in heaven. There was every reason to call this excellent ecclesiastic Fra Angelico. For my part, I never see this picture without finding something new in it. Nor have I ever seen it enough.

Fra Angelico painted [thirty-six small pictures on] the doors of the armory wherein are kept the silver utensils for the service of the altar, in the chapel of the Annunziata at Florence which Piero di Cosimo de' Medici built. Besides, he painted so many pictures which are now in private dwellings in Florence that I am sometimes amazed that one man could accomplish so much even though he labored for so many years.

Among the best of his works is a Deposition in the sacristy of Santa Trinità, to which he devoted much care. For Santa Maria Novella he painted various reliquaries which it is customary to place on the altar for high solemnities and others which are used at Easter. In the Badia at Florence, he painted Saint Benedict commanding silence. He also painted a picture for the guild of joiners. In Orvieto he began to paint the ceiling of the Lady Chapel, which was afterward finished by Luca de Cortona [Signorelli]. For the Brotherhood of the Temple in Florence, he painted a picture representing the dead Christ, and in the church of the monks of the Angeli, he executed a Paradiso and Inferno. Though the figures are small, Fra Angelico made the countenances of the blessed full of a celestial gladness, but the condemned are sorrowful and conscious of their misdeeds.

These many works and more made Fra Angelico famous throughout Italy. He was invited to Rome by Pope Nicholas V to paint, in the chapel of the palace where the Pope used to hear mass, a Deposition and some episodes from the life of Saint Lawrence. The Pope further commissioned him to paint miniatures for several books. In the palace he decorated the chapel which was afterward destroyed by Pope Paul III, who built a staircase through it. In this fresco, a Life of Christ, Fra Angelico introduced many portraits of eminent persons then living. They would all have been lost to us if Paolo Giovio had not saved some of them for his museum.

And now the Pope, judging Fra Angelico to be, as indeed he was, a most holy, gentle, and modest soul, proposed to appoint him archbishop of Florence. But Fra Angelico begged to be excused, since he did not feel capable of ruling men. He suggested instead a man of the order who was skilled in the art of governing others, a friend of the poor, and one who feared God. The Pope granted him the favor, and thus was Fra Antonino of the Order of the Friars-Preachers made archbishop of Florence. This prelate was most illustrious in learning and sanctity and fully deserved the canonization bestowed upon him in our own day by Pope Adrian VI.

A great proof of excellence was this deed of Fra Angelico's, and a rare one—this renunciation of a dignity so eminent, an office so important, in favor of one whom he sincerely considered more worthy than himself. This ought to be a lesson to the churchmen of our time, and would to God that all ecclesiastics (to speak without offence to the good among them) would follow the example of this excellent father, so well named Angelico, and labor always in the service of God and man. And what more could anyone desire than by living righteously to secure the kingdom of heaven, and by laboring virtuously to obtain everlasting fame in this world? So sublime a gift as that possessed by Fra Angelico should scarcely be conferred on any but a man of most holy life. When sacred subjects are attempted by persons of little faith, they often cause light thoughts to awaken in the beholder and are censured for this, even if they are able works of art. I would not seem to say that rude and inept things are therefore holy, and the beautiful and attractive are licentious, though this is a common error. By some people, feminine and youthful figures are instantly considered licentious. These people wrongfully condemn the sound judgment of the painter, who has made celestial beings so far superior to mere mortals in beauty as heaven is to earth. These critics betray the impurity of their own hearts, which do not aspire to the beauty and perfection of heaven but seek to discover evil. What are we to suppose these people do when they are exposed to living beauty, light manners, and seductive grace, and eyes that cannot but ravish? What then, if they are so troubled by a mere picture? I would not seem to approve of almost entirely nude figures in church. The painter must take into consideration the reserve due to the place, even though he desires to exhibit the extent of his ability.

Fra Giovanni was the most simple of men, and pious in every act of his life. It is told that when he was invited to breakfast with Pope Nicholas V, he scrupled to eat meat without permission of his prior. He disregarded all worldly things and was so much a friend of the poor in life that I believe his soul is now in heaven. He painted incessantly but would not think of doing anything that was not holy. He might have been rich but he did not care to be. On the contrary, he used to say that true wealth was contentment with little. He might have held a position of great authority, but he would not, saying that there was less danger of error in being ruled than in ruling. He declared that he sought no dignity and had no care but to escape hell and to draw near to paradise.

Fra Giovanni was kindly to all. He was moderate in all his habits and held himself apart from the snares of the world. He used to say that painters needed peace and freedom from anxiety, and that one who would do the work of Christ should belong to Christ. He was never seen to display anger, a thing which seems to me almost incredible. If he admonished his friends it was with a gentle smile. If anyone wanted a picture, he answered with the utmost cordiality that they must get the permission of the prior and then he would surely do what they wanted. This father was a most modest, humble, and excellent man in both word and deed, and the saints that he painted so ably have more the air and expression of sanctity than have those of any other master.

It was the custom of Fra Giovanni not to retouch a picture once it was finished. He left it as it was, believing, as he said, that it was the will of God. They also say that he never took up his brush without first humbling himself in prayer. He never painted a Crucifix without tears streaming from his eyes. In the expressions of his figures and their attitudes it is easy to find proof of his goodness and the depth of his devotion to the religion of Christ.

Fra Giovanni died in 1455 at the age of sixty-five [sixty-eight]. He was buried by the brethren of his order in the church of the Minerva [Santa Maria sopra Minerva] at Rome. On his tomb, which is of marble, is the portrait of the master taken from life and an epitaph in Latin, [said to have been composed by Pope Nicholas V himself].

Editorial Notes on Fra Angelico

EVIDENTLY anecdotes about Fra Angelico were popular even in Vasari's day. All the intimate glimpses of the good father, his words, his gentle deeds, have the quality of legend. They are not raw, immediate truth, but truth refined, handled, and reshaped to an ideal reality. The story of the archbishopric of Florence is such a legend.

Here is a description of the last stand of medievalism before the full tide of the Renaissance. Florence was as modern, then, as aggressively progressive, as New York is today. Brunelleschi's dome was being built, Masaccio's frescoes were barely dry on the newly plastered walls of the Carmine. To say, "I am a Florentine," was a proud boast. And yet here the feudal age, the age of faith, found complete expression in the work of Fra Angelico. He, a medieval monk, painted with all the skill of his fellow artists. It was as if a child could express, with the power of maturity, his unclouded sense of reality.

The measure of a work of art depends upon the statement it makes. Benozzo Gozzoli, for instance, so close to Fra Angelico in time, in subject matter, and in use of materials, makes no such impression as the Beato. His compositions are crowded with men and women, actors in a sacred drama, while Fra Angelico peopled his creations with the heavenly hosts.

I have put in the catalogue of Fra Angelico's works, as it appears in Vasari, even the "picture" (though it should rather be called a tabernacle) he painted for the guild of joiners. Each one is a monument of strength, radiant beauty, and heart-calming faith.

LEON BATTISTA ALBERTI

Florentine Architect

« 1404-1472 »

THE knowledge of literature and science is without doubt of great value to every man but especially to the artist. Most of all, sculptors, painters, and architects cannot develop their natural qualities and mature their judgment without the advantage of an education. Even the selection of a site for a building needs careful consideration, as, for instance, in the matter of shelter from dangerous winds, and the question of drainage. The artist must know for himself the theory on which his work is founded, rather than be dependent on others for such knowledge. On the other hand, theory without practice is worth little. For the vocation of the artist nothing can be more suitable than the combination of theory and practice. Science improves art, and the writings of artists have greater weight than those of simple practitioners, who are unable to theorize. Now, Leon Battista Alberti studied Latin as well as architecture, perspective, and painting, and has left books unsurpassed even in our own day, which have shed such a luster upon his practice as an artist that he enjoys a reputation greater than he deserves. As far as fame and fortune go, the written word has the most enduring effect. For books go everywhere and are believed if they are honestly written. We are not surprised that Leon Battista is known more by his books than by his buildings.

He was born in Florence, of the noble family of the Alberti. He studied the history of art, actually examined the antique, and wrote upon this subject—for he was more inclined to be a writer than an artist. Leon Battista was an able mathematician. He wrote ten books on architecture in Latin which were published in 1481. These have been translated into Italian by the reverend Messer Cosimo Bartoli. He also wrote three books on painting and a treatise on practical mathematics containing the rules for taking elevations. He also wrote much prose and verse, and it was he who first applied Latin meter to Italian verse.

At the time when Nicholas V had thrown the city of Rome into utter confusion with his peculiar manner of building, Leon Battista Alberti arrived with an introduction to the Pope from Biondo da Forli. Bernardo Rossellino, the Florentine artist, had begun the restoration of the papal palace. Henceforth he proceeded with the advice of Leon Battista, this being the will of the Pope. Thus the pontiff, with the counsel of the one and the practice of the other, brought many admirable works to conclusion.

Leon Battista then went to Rimini and made a model of the church of San Francesco for Sigismondo Malatesta, which is beyond question one of the most renowned temples of Italy. Within it are six very beautiful chapels, one of which is dedicated to Saint Jerome and is sumptuously adorned. It contains relics from Jerusalem and the tomb of Sigismondo and his wife. This tomb is of marble and has the portrait of Sigismondo upon it. The portrait of Leon Battista appears in another part of the work.

In 1451 [?], when the very useful method of printing books was invented by Giovanni Gutenberg, Leon Battista devised something similar, namely, an enlarging and diminishing machine; all very extraordinary things, useful to art and certainly very fine.

Giovanni di Paolo Rucellai engaged Leon Battista to design the façade for Santa Maria Novella entirely in marble. By 1477 it was finished to the satisfaction of the whole city. The door was particularly admired. This architect also designed the Rucellai Palace and the Loggia [dei Rucellai], which is across from it on the street called La Vigna. In constructing the loggia, Alberti committed a fault in the arching, which was theoretically right but practically unsound. The arches of the internal vaulting could not spring from the tops of the columns without clumsiness. It was simply a question of lack of practical experience.

It is said he also did the palaces and gardens of the Rucellai family in the Via della Scala. There are two very beautiful galleries, or loggie, raised upon columns without arches. This is the method used by the ancients, the architrave resting upon the capitals of the columns. It is impossible to turn a vault from the top of a round column without having the angles awry.

For the same Rucellai family, Leon Battista built a chapel in San Brancazio [Pancrazio]. The ceiling rests on large architraves, supported where the chapel opens into the church by two columns and two pilasters.

This is a difficult mode of procedure, but gives great stability. In the center of the chapel is an oblong tomb of marble, similar, according to the inscription, to the sepulcher of Christ in Jerusalem.

About the same time, Ludovico Gonzaga, marquis of Mantua, determined to rebuild the apse of the Annunziata, the church of the Servites in Florence. He demolished a very old, small, square chapel painted in the ancient manner, to make way for the new. The new chapel has the fanciful form of a circular temple surrounded by nine chapels, each the shape of a niche surmounted by a round arch. But as the arches of these chapels spring from the pilasters which follow the curve of the circular apse, the arches seem to tip backward, though the proportions are correct. The whole effect is an unhappy one, and it would have been better if Leon Battista had avoided this difficult problem altogether. Even the great arch of the entrance to the apse from the church, which is very beautiful from the outside, seems on the other side to be falling backward and is extremely ungraceful. Leon Battista might not have fallen into this error if he had had more practical experience. The work is nevertheless very fanciful and beautiful in itself. Nor can it be denied that it took courage to attempt to build the apse as he did.

The architect was invited to Mantua by the Marquis Ludovico, and there he made a model for Sant' Andrea. Leon Battista's designs were carried out by various Florentine architects. He was fortunate, as I can appreciate from my own experience, in having faithful and friendly assistants who understood his intentions.

In painting, Leon Battista did nothing extraordinary. Yet he knew how to convey an idea by means of a drawing. He designed a roof, a sort of loggia, to cover the bridge of Sant' Angelo, by order of Pope Nicholas V, who died before it was constructed. He painted a few small pictures which were more literary than pictorial. He also did a view of Venice, one of his best paintings, but the figures in it were painted by other masters.

Leon Battista Alberti was a man of refinement and cultivation, a friend of distinguished men, liberal and courteous to all. He lived well, like the gentleman he was, all his life. Finally he departed, content and tranquil, to a better life, leaving a most honorable name.

Editorial Notes on Leon Battista Alberti

LEON BATTISTA ALBERTI seems to have been a man of the world and a scholar of the type of Leonardo da Vinci. He wrote on architecture and on mathematics. His books were designed to elucidate these subjects for the general public, which was cultivated to a high degree. His books were his great contribution and could not be scorned, as Vasari scorned his architecture. In this Leon Battista Alberti made mistakes that were the result of correct theory. For my own satisfaction, I drew a plan of a circular apse and—sure enough—the arches seemed to tip backward.

The invention that Vasari mentions in the same breath with and as comparable to "the very useful method of printing books" of Giovanni Gutenberg was a device for enlarging or diminishing plans or drawings. It was a screen of lines like a network held between the artist and his subject with the help of which the artist could trace exactly the outlines of an object and thus be able to establish the size of his work mechanically.

ANTONELLO DA MESSINA

Painter

« CA. 1430-1479 »

WHEN I consider the improvement in technique in the art of painting in the second period [of the three divisions of this history], I must acknowledge the artists to have been most ingenious. A selfless desire to improve the actual quality of the paint and its lasting properties was always present. The artists continued to use tempera, the method learned by Cimabue from his Greek masters and carried on by Giotto. It was very difficult to lend a grace to the whole design with soft and blended tones in tempera, where the color is laid on with the point of the pencil [brush] only. Many had sought the solution of this difficulty by the use of some liquid varnish, yet none had succeeded. Among the artists who tried were Alessio Baldovinetti, Pesello, and many others, who were still not able to give their work that beauty they had envisioned. And even if they had painted as brilliantly as they desired, there was still the question of durability, of the treatment of the surface so that it could be washed without chipping.

The rest of the world was also thinking about this problem. In Spain, France, and Germany artists were discussing these matters. It happened, when things had come to this pass, that Giovanni da Bruggia [Jan van Eyck] in Flanders set himself to try different experiments in colors, and labored to produce a perfect varnish. Once, when he had completed a picture with extreme care, he varnished it and set it in the sun to dry. The picture cracked deplorably. He decided that what he needed was a varnish that would dry in the shade, and quickly. He finally made a varnish of linseed oil boiled with other mixtures. He mixed this with his colors and found them more easily blended than was possible with tempera. Giovanni began a great number of paintings and, as he worked, his skill increased.

The fame of Giovanni da Bruggia's invention spread all over Flanders and Italy and the rest of the world. Seeing his pictures, artists were anxious to learn his method. They felt compelled to praise him to the skies and to look upon him with a blameless envy. He kept his method a secret until he was very old, when, it is said, he confided it to Ruggieri da Bruggia [Rogier van der Weyden], who gave it to Ausse [Hans Memling?]. Merchants bought these pictures and sold them at great profit in every part of the world, yet the knowledge of oil painting did not extend beyond Flanders, although the pictures kept the pungent odor of oil, especially when they were new, and one would have thought the ingredients of the pigment might have been guessed. At last, certain Florentine merchants sent a picture painted in oil by Giovanni to Alfonso I, king of Naples. The work was greatly prized for the beauty of the many figures and the new type of coloring. Every painter in the kingdom hastened to see it.

Antonello da Messina, a man of lively mind and an experienced painter, hearing that this picture was able to withstand concussion, was washable, and was perfect in all other respects, hastened to obtain sight of the work. He at once laid aside all other business and went to Flanders. On arriving at Bruges, he became an intimate of Giovanni da Bruggia, gave him presents of Italian drawings, and showed him the greatest deference. Nor did Antonello leave Flanders before he had mastered the secret of oil painting. Not long after that, Giovanni died, and Antonello went back to Italy with his valuable knowledge. He settled in Venice where, since he was a man of licentious habits and fond of the pleasures of life, he decided to live out his days in a mode of existence exactly suited to his tastes. Many of his paintings belong to various gentlemen of Venice and many others were sent abroad. At length, he received a commission to paint a picture for the parish church of San Cassiano. Then the magnificent nobles of Venice treated him with even greater consideration, and especially when it was understood that he had brought the new secret from Flanders.

The master executed many pictures for members of the nobility. He was about to begin a painting in the palace of the Signoria of Venice, the [Ducal] Palace, when he fell ill of pleurisy and died. He was honorably buried by his fellow artists, in consideration of the benefit he had conferred on their art by making known the new method of coloring. And certainly he deserves as much credit for bringing this technique to Italy as Giovanni da Bruggia does for inventing it in Flanders. Both have enriched art, and we have since seen masters of oil painting paint with such excellence that their figures are all but alive. No mention of oil painting is found in ancient writers. But as there is nothing new under the sun, perhaps even this was done in times gone by. I will say no more than to commend those who, in addition to drawing correctly, are improving art continually.

Editorial Notes on Antonello da Messina

ONLY a born raconteur, such as Vasari, would dare say that any one individual introduced oil painting into Italy. The fact that painting in oil reached technical perfection first in Flanders is beyond question. Whether Antonello actually journeyed to Flanders, or learned the use of oils at the court of Naples or in Venice is of little importance. There were many Flemish pictures to be seen in both these centers. The Aragonese rulers of Naples brought their Flemish pictures with them from Spain, and both Naples and Venice were profitable markets in which merchants sold these precious wares.

The influence of Antonello's style on the art of Venice was very great. He was an innovator not merely in the technique of handling oil paint (and he was certainly one of the first to master this medium), but also in the organization of the composition of his design. The development of painting in Italy may be traced from Byzantine mosaic. Mosaic seems to emphasize the surface of a wall. The pattern of glittery stone and enamel, whether bronze or purple or pale in tone, impresses the spectator with the physical presence of the wall. The early Sienese and Florentines barely modified this treatment of the picture plane as they painted in tempera on panels prepared with gold leaf or on plastered walls with fresco. It is possible that Flemish painting, on the other hand, was based on Byzantine book illustration. These little pictures within their elaborate and definite borders seem to be windows opening on wide vistas. Long before it was true of Italian painting, Flemish composition gave the illusion of three dimensions. The objects in Antonello's pictures stand in space. His work so closely resembles the Flemish that a portrait in the National Gallery in London for a long time bore the label "Jan van Eyck" and is now attributed to Antonello da Messina. The Bellini were powerfully influenced by Antonello, and even as late as Giorgione we may see traces of his style.

FRA FILIPPO LIPPI

Florentine Painter

« 1406-1469 »

THE Carmelite monk, Fra Filippo di Tommaso Lippi, was born in Florence in a side street called Ardiglione, behind the cloister of the Carmelites. He was left an orphan when but two years old. For some time he was cared for by his aunt, Mona Lapaccia, his father's sister. She brought him up until he was eight. Unable to support him any longer, she placed him with the Carmelites. Filippo was ingenious and showed great manual dexterity but he was proportionately unable to learn his letters. He never did anything but daub his books and those of the other boys with caricatures. The prior, therefore, determined to give him every opportunity to learn to draw. The chapel of the Carmine had been newly painted by Masaccio and pleased the boy greatly. Here he spent his hours of recreation, drawing and practicing with the many other youths who were studying these frescoes. He showed such dexterity and knowledge that it seemed certain even then that he was destined to accomplish some marvelous thing in the course of time. Improving day by day, he followed the manner of Masaccio so closely that there were many who said that the spirit of Masaccio had entered the body of Fra Filippo. Hearing himself so highly praised by all, he threw off the habit of a monk, boldly, when he was seventeen.

Some time after this, while in the March of Ancona, Filippo was out sailing with some friends, when they were all taken by a Moorish pirate and led captive into Barbary, where he was kept in great tribulation for eighteen months. He saw his master often, so it occurred to him to draw his portrait. He took a piece of charcoal from the fire and on the white wall drew a full-length likeness of his master in Moorish garments. The other slaves, to whom this seemed a miracle, told the master. He, though he had the right to punish his captive, instead restored Filippo to liberty because of the glory of that noble art. After painting certain other works for his master, Filippo was conducted safely to Naples. Here he painted a panel for King Alfonso, then duke of Calabria.

Soon Filippo longed to be back in Florence. His first work there brought him to the notice of Cosimo de' Medici, who became his steadfast friend. He painted several highly successful Nativities and other religious subjects. Cosimo sent some of his work to Pope Eugenius IV, and these brought him into favor with the pontiff.

It is said that Filippo was so great a sensualist that he would stop at nothing to gratify his immediate longings. If he could not possibly do so, he drew the object of his desires and endeavored, by discoursing and reasoning with himself, to lessen his inclination. In these periods of dissipation his work was quite neglected. Cosimo de' Medici who knew all this, wished Filippo to execute a picture in his palace; accordingly, he shut him up so that he would not waste his time gadding about. After two days of this confinement, Fra Filippo made a rope of the sheets on his bed and escaped by the window. Then he gave himself up to his amusements. When Cosimo found that his painter had disappeared, he sent men to seek him out. At last Filippo returned to his work. From that time forward Cosimo gave him leave to go and come as he pleased, for he repented of having shut him up and was frightened at the danger Fra Filippo had incurred in climbing out of the window. Painters, Cosimo concluded, were not beasts of burden.

For the church of Santa Maria Primerana, in Fiesole, Fra Filippo painted an Annunciation. The angel is so beautiful (such was Filippo's extraordinary care) that it really seems a celestial messenger. He continued to paint in Florence with great success. And in Arezzo he did a picture for Messer Carlo Marsuppini, a Coronation of the Virgin, for a chapel that belonged to the monks of Monte Oliveto. This work has retained a remarkably fresh color, as if it had just been painted. Here the artist was told to take particular pains with the hands, which had been complained of in many of his works. Ever after he managed to hide the hands in the draperies or otherwise.

There is a wonderful grace in these works; the colors are blended with the most perfect harmony.

Fra Filippo lived for some months in Prato, painting for the whole surrounding district. With him was the Carmelite Fra Diamante, who had been his companion when a novice. He received a commission from the nuns of Santa Margherita to paint a picture for their high altar. He happened to see the daughter of Francesco Buti, a citizen of Florence, who had been sent to the convent either as novice or boarder. After one glance at Lucrezia (for that was her name), Filippo persuaded the nuns to let her sit for him for the figure of the Virgin he was painting for them. The result was that the painter fell madly in love and at last prevailed upon Lucrezia to escape with him on the day she had gone forth to do honor to the girdle of the Virgin, the venerated relic preserved at Prato and exhibited once a year. The nuns were deeply disgraced by this event. But Lucrezia, whether from fear or some other cause, would not return and remained with Filippo, to whom she bore a son who was also called Filippo and who eventually became a most famous painter like his father.

On a small tablet in the capitular church of Prato, Fra Filippo painted the Death of Saint Bernard, by the touch of whose bier many lame persons are restored to health. In this work, there are monks who bewail the loss of their master. The grace of their heads, the truth and beauty of their grief, are marvelous to behold. The hoods and draperies have most beautiful folds, and the whole deserves praise for design, composition, and color, completed, as it is, by the delicate hand of Filippo. He was also appointed by the wardens of that church to paint the chapel of the high altar, and in this work we have evidence of his power. For here he made his figures larger than life and so set an example for future artists in the grand style. The subject was the life of Saint Stephen, to whom the church is dedicated. Saint Stephen, calm and steadfast in the midst of the terrible violence of those who slew him with stones, is seen with his face turned to heaven, imploring the Eternal Father to pardon those who attack him. The variety of expression is very fine. Fra Filippo gave the most earnest attention to this point. In the picture of the Burial of Saint Stephen, the disciples are dejected, drowned in tears, with faces so deeply affected that it is scarcely possible to look at them without feeling sorrow, too. On the other side of the chapel is the history of John the Baptist, his Birth, the Preaching in the Wilderness, his Baptism, the Feast of Herod, and the Decapitation of the Saint. In the picture of the Preaching, the divine spirit animating the speaker is visible in his face, while the crowd of men and women, between hope and anxiety, gladness and sorrow, are charmed and mastered by his words. In the Baptism, beauty and goodness are exemplified. In the Feast of Herod, the banquet is splendid, and the guests display first astonishment and then inexpressible sorrow when the head is presented on a charger. Here are to be seen fine attitudes, splendid draperies, and exquisite expressions of countenance. A self-portrait of Fra Filippo is among the figures of the guests in this scene, while one of the mourners for Saint Stephen is a portrait of Fra Diamante dressed as a bishop. This is Fra Filippo's best work, for, besides the many fine qualities we have mentioned, the figures are larger than life—a foretaste of the manner soon to be developed. The extraordinary gifts and abilities of Fra Filippo outweighed the many circumstances of his life that were blamable. In the work just described is a portrait of Messer Carlo, natural son of Cosimo de' Medici, who was rector of the church.

Fra Filippo was indeed an artist of such power that of his own time there are few better than he. Michelangelo has always praised him and often imitated many things in his work. Among his direct disciples, besides Fra Diamante, who was his zealous imitator to his great credit, were Sandro Botticelli, and several others. Fra Filippo was fond of good company and lived for his own part very joyously. He lived well on what he earned and spent large sums on pleasure, even to the end of his life. He never finished his last picture, in the Lady Chapel of the church in Spoleto, because he died suddenly. Some said he was poisoned by certain persons related to the object of his love.

He left his son in the care of Fra Diamante, who took the ten-year-old boy back to Florence. He placed the boy with Sandro Botticelli, who was then considered an excellent master of painting.

Fra Filippo was buried in a tomb of red-and-white marble in the church in which he was painting when he died. Lorenzo de' Medici afterward sent ambassadors to seek the remains for burial in Santa Maria del Fiore. But the Spoletines replied that, having so few distinguished men, they begged permission to keep this one. And that was all the answer Lorenzo got. Still resolved to honor Fra Filippo, Lorenzo sent his son Filippino to construct a marble sepulcher over the sacristy and beneath the organ. He spent two hundred ducats on this work.

Fra Filippo drew exceedingly well.

*Fra Angelico: The Annunciation (fresco, 7 ft. 6 in. x 15 ft.),
San Marco, Florence.*

Leon Battista Alberti: Façade of San Francesco, Rimini.

Antonello da Messina: Saint Jerome in His Study (oil on wood, 18 x 14½ in.), National Gallery, London.

*Fra Filippo Lippi: Head of the Madonna (wood, 16⅜ x 13⅛ in.).
National Gallery, Washington. (Kress Collection)*

Andrea del Castagno: The Last Supper (fresco), Sant' Apollonia, Florence.

*Gentile da Fabriano: Adoration of the Magi (wooden panel,
9 ft. 10 in. x 9 ft. 3 in.), Uffizi, Florence.*

Pisanello: The Vision of Saint Eustace (tempera on wood, 21 x 25½ in.), National Gallery, London.

Benozzo Gozzoli: Procession of the Magi (fresco), Medici Chapel, Riccardi Palace, Florence.

Desiderio da Settignano: Bust of Marietta Strozzi (marble, life size),
Kaiser Friedrich Museum, Berlin.

*Mino da Fiesole: Virgin Adoring the Child, and Saints (marble),
Cathedral Fiesole.*

Jacopo Bellini: The Annunciation (drawing), Louvre, Paris.

Giovanni Bellini: Madonna Adoring the Sleeping Child (wood,
28½ x 18¼ in.), Metropolitan Museum of Art.

Gentile Bellini: Procession in Piazza of St. Mark (canvas, 12 ft. 1¾ in. x 24 ft.), Academy, Venice.

Ghirlandaio: Birth of John the Baptist (fresco), Santa Maria Novella, Florence.

Editorial Notes on Fra Filippo Lippi

I am poor brother Lippo, by your leave!
You need not clap your torches to my face.
Zooks, what's to blame? You think you see a monk!
What, it's past midnight, and you go the rounds,
And here you catch me at an alley's end
Where sportive ladies leave their doors ajar?

—ROBERT BROWNING, *Fra Lippo Lippi*

I AM tempted to make a comment on commentators. Between Browning's time and ours, there was a whole generation of people who were scandalized by the notion that Fra Filippo Lippi could have been the lusty soul Vasari describes. They were smugly happy to announce that there was no truth whatever in the story of the novice. But since then, I am bound to say, documents have revealed that the story was only too true. Giovanni de' Medici wrote to Bartolommeo Serragli, on May 27, 1458: "And so we laughed a good while at the error of Fra Filippo. . . ."

But the other story, about the pirates, seems to be unsubstantiated. A person like Fra Filippo Lippi apparently attracted romantic legends.

In those days Florence teemed with excellent artists. And what a lucky time it was to be born an artist! The very guardian of an outcast orphan then resolved, as a matter of course, to give "every opportunity" to a gifted child. From the fact that Michelangelo admired his painting, we know that Fra Filippo Lippi was able to assimilate and use the artistic knowledge of his day. But Fra Lippo Lippi's work, charming as it is, falls far short of that of some of his contemporaries. These artists had the power to invent something new, to see new subjects, new shapes and colors.

ANDREA DEL CASTAGNO

Painter, of Mugello

« 1423-1457 »

How reprehensible is the vice of envy (which is intolerable in any man) in a distinguished artist! Above all, what a crime to cloak with a feigned friendship the desire to destroy the fame and honor, and more—even the life of another. In a man capable of such wickedness there dwells an inhuman, a fiendish spirit. It is praiseworthy to wish to surpass others. In fact, progress depends upon this impulse; but once envy is roused, all turns to wickedness, as it did in the case of the unhappy Andrea del Castagno. He was an excellent painter, and a great master of design, but he buried his splendid talent under the rancor and envious hatred of his nature.

Andrea was born on a small farm called Castagno, in the Mugello, a district in Florentine territory, and took that as his surname when he came to Florence. His father died when he was a little child and left him in the care of an uncle, who set him to herd his cattle. He was able and intelligent and so strong that he could keep the cattle in order and defend from attack whatever was placed in his care. One day he sought shelter from the rain in the house of a journeyman painter who was doing a small job for a countryman, an oratory or a tabernacle. Andrea watched in rapt admiration. He had never seen such a thing and he looked attentively at the work and how it was done. A sudden inclination was born in him which became a passionate desire for art, and he began scratching drawings of animals on stones and walls. The report of this reached the ears of a Florentine gentleman, Bernardetto de' Medici, who had the boy called before him and questioned him. He asked him if he would like to become a painter. To this Andrea replied that he wanted this more than anything in the world. So Bernardetto took the boy to Florence and placed him with one of the best masters.

Thereafter Andrea devoted himself to the study of painting. He excelled in design. His coloring was somewhat crude and harsh. His figures moved with great power and the heads had force, whether male or female, and were grave and earnest in expression.

Andrea's earliest works were lost in the siege of Florence; but in the monastery of the monks of the Angeli, he painted a Crucifix. He depicted some famous persons, in one of the halls of the palace at Legnaia [which the Pandolfini bought from the Carducci in 1475]. For the Brotherhood of the Evangelist he painted a banner to be carried in their processions that was considered to be very beautiful. After painting a number of works in and about Florence, he decorated the new cloister of the convent of Santa Croce. This astonishing picture, the *Scourging of Christ*, beautiful in itself, shows a loggia with the columns drawn in perspective. The cross-vaulting and ribs diminish so finely that it is obvious that Andrea knew as much about perspective as about design. The attitudes of the men who are scourging the Saviour are very fine and show great force. Their faces tell their hatred, while the Saviour's expresses patience and humility. Andrea has shown the suffering flesh of the Christ. His noble spirit seems to affect Pilate sitting among his councilors who appears to be seeking an opportunity to set him free. This picture has been marred by children and simple folk who have maltreated the figures of the Jews as if to avenge the injury done the Saviour. Otherwise, it would be Andrea's best work. If he had been able to color as well as he could draw, he would have been one of the most admirable of painters.

In Santa Maria del Fiore, Andrea del Castagno painted Niccolò da Tolentino on horseback. While he was at work, a child who was passing by shook the ladder on which he stood, and Andrea, brutally violent man that he was, got down and ran after him to the corner of the Pazzi. He secured a commission from the Portinari family to decorate the principal chapel of Santa Maria Nuova in collaboration with the famous Domenico Veneziano and Alessio Baldovinetti. Andrea was most envious of Domenico, in spite of his own superiority in design. It irked him that this stranger should be befriended by the Florentines. So powerful were these hateful emotions that Andrea began to plot to remove this competitor. Andrea was quite capable of dissimulation, had a ready tongue, and could assume a cheerful air at his pleasure. He had a sly way of marking another's work with his finger nail when he saw a fault, but, when his own work was criticized by anyone, he would fall upon him with blows and curses. He made it perfectly clear that he was always ready to avenge an injury.

Andrea was jealous of Domenico, as we have said, and plotted to dispose of this rival. He pretended a great friendship for Domenico, and the latter in all simplicity returned true cordiality. He accepted the advances of Andrea, who seemed to him a clever and amusing person. Domenico was very fond of music, and they used to go out in the evening together, sometimes to a party, sometimes to serenade their inamoratas. So affairs stood when Andrea painted the *Annunciation* on his part of the wall. He introduced a charming innovation by showing the angel hovering in the air. The *Virgin Mounting the Temple*, with crowds of beggars on the steps, is an even finer work. One beggar strikes a fellow on the head with his flask, an extremely fine figure, as are all the others. Andrea finished every part with great care, incited by his rivalry with Domenico. In the same picture is an octagonal temple in the midst of a piazza. It is in perspective, and the front is beautifully adorned with statues. Around the piazza are magnificent buildings in great variety, some seen in the shadow of the temple—an admirable effect cleverly handled.

On his part of the wall, Domenico painted the *Meeting of Joachim and Anne* and beneath this the *Birth of the Virgin*, in a splendid chamber. A beautiful child, in this picture, strikes on the door of the room with a hammer in a gesture full of grace. The *Marriage of the Virgin* follows, and in this part of the work there are many portraits from life. A dwarf breaking a staff is an animated figure. There are also several women wearing fashionable clothes. This work, however, remained unfinished for reasons which will be related.

Andrea meanwhile had painted in oil the *Death of the Virgin*, and, whether in emulation of Domenico or from a simple desire to do his best, he did wonders, particularly on the bier with its canopy. Around the bier are the Apostles and angels with lighted torches. These are so well done that it is obvious that Andrea was as able an oil painter as Domenico. He introduced some portraits, one of the superintendent of the hospital of the convent, a figure on his knees which almost seems to breathe. On a sort of medallion, Andrea del Castagno placed his own portrait with a face like that of Judas Iscariot, whom he did resemble both in face and character.

One evening in summer Domenico took his lute as he used to do and strolled out, leaving Andrea drawing. Once Domenico had gone, Andrea disguised himself and posted himself on a street corner. When Domenico passed there on his way home, Andrea fell upon him and with a lead weight crushed the lute and the chest of his victim with repeated blows. As if this were not enough, he struck him over the head with the same weapon and left him for dead. Then he hurried back to his room and went on drawing.

Meanwhile the noise had been heard. When the crime was discovered, the first person to be called was Andrea, who ran to the scene, crying, "Alas, my brother! Alas, my brother!" Domenico died in Andrea's arms and, in spite of every effort to find the murderer, the truth was never known until Andrea himself confessed it on his deathbed.

In 1478, when Giuliano de' Medici was killed and Lorenzo wounded in Santa Maria del Fiore by the Pazzi and the other conspirators, it was resolved by the Signoria that all who had taken part in the plot should be painted as traitors [hanging by their feet] on the façade of the palace of the Podestà. Andrea was chosen and set to work. When finished, this painting was a perfect wonder. They called him Andreino degl' Impiccati [Andrew of the Hanged Men] from that time forward.

This master lived very well. What he earned he spent freely on dress and liberal housekeeping and so left but little property when he died. Soon after his death the impious crime he had committed became known and he was buried with marks of disgrace in Santa Maria Nuova.

Editorial Notes on Andrea del Castagno

ANDREA DEL CASTAGNO's *drawing was as strong as that of Antonio Pollaiuolo, as clear cut as Mantegna's, and had a violent energy that no one could match. Among the strong builders of the fabric of the High Renaissance, he holds an honored place.*

As for his terrible temper, who would not run after a little boy who shakes a ladder? The painter's pet name was Andreino, which suggests that he was a good fellow. For one thing, he certainly did not murder Domenico Veneziano, who lived on after Andrea's death. Perhaps it was another Domenico. For another thing, Andrea died long before the Pazzi conspiracy. He must have painted other hanged enemies of the house of Medici. The name "Andrew of the Hanged Men" he must have earned for painting some luckless Peruzzi and Albizzi in 1435. He was surely a formidable man. That we can see in his work.

GENTILE DA FABRIANO

《 ACTIVE BETWEEN 1408-1427 》

and

PISANELLO DA VERONA

《 1397-1455 》

G REAT is the advantage held by the man who follows in the path of another. The fame and honor won by the exercise of rare gifts and abilities become the property of one who is merely able to follow with discretion. If he had attempted to attain success by his own unassisted efforts, it might have taken much longer and many more pains. A good example of this is the case of Pisano, or Pisanello, of Verona. He studied with Andrea del Castagno for many years in Florence and completed that master's work after his death. He thus acquired so great a reputation that when Pope Martin V came to Florence he took Pisanello with him to Rome. There the Pope caused him to paint some frescoes in San Giovanni Laterano which are very pleasing, especially because of the ultramarine blue that the Pope gave him in richest abundance, a color so deep, so full, and so exquisite in tint that it has never been equaled.

In competition with Vittore [Antonio] Pisano [known as Il Pisanello], Gentile da Fabriano painted some stories on the wall below this fresco. Platina [the papal librarian] mentions these pictures in his *Life of Pope Martin*. He says that the pontiff restored the floor, ceiling, and roof of the church and then engaged Gentile da Fabriano to execute various paintings there, and that the figures of the prophets are the best of all. Gentile worked in the March of Ancona and throughout the whole state of Urbino.

Also in San Giovanni in Siena he did some work. In Florence he painted
an Adoration of the Magi, in which he put his own portrait. In the church
of San Niccolò, at the San Miniato gate, Gentile painted the picture for
the high altar. This seems to me to be his best picture, for (to say nothing
of the Virgin and the saints, which are all extremely well done) the predella, covered with stories of the life of Saint Nicholas, could not possibly
be more beautiful. A picture by Gentile in Santa Maria Nuova in Rome
was held in high esteem by the divine Michelangelo, who used to say it
was like its painter's name: "*gentile.*"

In Perugia this master painted a very beautiful picture for the church
of San Domenico, and a Crucifix which he cut from the wood in silhouette.
He also painted three very beautiful half-length figures which are over the
entrance to the choir.

But to return to Vittore Pisano. We have found, since we wrote the
short account above, that Pisanello was the equal of any painter of his
time. We have this information from the most learned and very reverend
father, Fra Marco de' Medici, of Verona, and from Biono da Forlì's words
on Verona in his *Italia Illustrata*, as well as from the works by this artist,
which may be seen in Verona and which alone are ample proof, although
many are partly destroyed by time. Pisanello was particularly fond of
drawing animals, and in the chapel of the Pellegrini family, in the church
of Sant' Anastasia in Verona, he painted a Saint Eustace caressing a
spotted dog that turns his head as if he had heard a noise—a living dog
could do no better. His signature—*Pisano*—is under this figure. He painted
the whole external front of the chapel. On the inner side he painted Saint
George in silver armor; the saint, having slain the dragon, is sheathing his
sword. His right hand he raises high, the better to slide the sword, which
is very long, into the scabbard held in his left hand. The Veronese, Michele
Sanmichele, state architect of Venice and a very learned man, was often
seen looking at these works with admiration. He used to say that few
better things could be found than the Saint Eustace and the dog, and the
Saint George. In the arch over the same chapel Pisanello depicted Saint
George after he has killed the dragon and in the act of rescuing the
princess who stands near by. He is mounting his horse, and one almost
sees the saint rise to his seat. The horse is admirably foreshortened. The
entire work, correct in design and extraordinary in grace, can never be seen
without admiration and even astonishment, so excellent is it in every part.

In San Fermo Maggiore, at Verona, there is an Annunciation by Vittore Pisano. The Virgin and the angel are partly heightened in gold and
are very beautiful, as are also some buildings in the same picture. There

are, besides, many small animals and birds which are as natural as can be.

Pisanello was also a medalist. In a letter to Duke Cosimo, [Paolo] Giovio wrote, "This master was exceedingly clever in the execution of bas-relief, a work esteemed most difficult by artists, because it holds the mean between the level surface of pictures and the full roundness of statues. There are many highly esteemed medals of great princes by his hand. They are in a large form and of the same proportions as that reverse of the caparisoned and barbed horse which Guidi has sent me. Among the works of this kind in my possession is a portrait of the great King Alfonso, wearing no other headdress than his hair; and on the reverse is the helmet of a general. I have, besides, a medal with the portrait of Pope Martin, with the arms of the Colonna on the reverse. Another is of Sultan Mahomet, who took Constantinople. It is an equestrian figure in a Turkish habit with a scourge in his hand. Of Sigismondo Malatesta, likewise, I have the portrait, with that of Madonna Isotta, of Rimini, on the reverse; and one of Niccolò Piccinino wearing a barret, or cap. . . . In addition to these, I have also a very beautiful medal of John Paleologus, emperor of Constantinople, with that strange-looking hat that he used to wear. This last was made by Pisanello in Florence at the time of the council held by Pope Eugenius [IV], at which the emperor was present; the reverse bears the Cross, held by two hands: that of the Latin Church and that of the Greek."

Vittore Pisano did the portraits on medals of Filippo de' Medici, arch-bishop of Pisa, and many other nobles and personages renowned in arms or in learning. For his reputation as a medalist, Pisanello has been cele-brated by many great men. He was extolled in a poem by his compatriot, the elder Guerino, a well-known writer of that day. Pisanello was also celebrated in a Latin epigram by the elder Strozzi. These are the rewards of a life passed worthily in virtuous labor. Finally, having reached a good old age, he departed to a better life.

Gentile da Fabriano ultimately died from the exhaustion of age, having reached the term of eighty years.

Editorial Notes on Gentile da Fabriano and Pisanello

As for Pisanello, we now know that his name was Antonio, not Vittore, and that he could not have ridden to fame in the wake of Andrea del Castagno, for Andrea was the younger of the two. Nothing could shake Vasari's notion that Florence was the only source of art. Even after he had seen the Pisanellos in Verona and had done them justice, he saw no reason to change his remarks about Pisanello and Castagno.

The large collection of Pisanello's drawings in the Louvre was at one time ascribed to Leonardo da Vinci. Indeed, they are as precise and exact as the studies of Leonardo. It is true, however, that many of his studies of wild animals look as if he had placed the dead beast on the floor in a walking pose, and then had worked with all his might. The famous vision of Saint Eustace of the National Gallery in London, with its wonderful delicacy and precision, reminds us in its static composition of a Persian miniature. He drew his animals as though he were a Flemish artist. No wonder he is listed in the so-called "international" school of painting!

Gentile da Fabriano is a most influential figure in the international school. Luxurious color and jewel-like ornamentation enrich his elaborate, story-telling compositions. Every detail is precisely exact. More primitive than Pisanello, whose teacher he was, he must have pleased the public with his wonderful catalogues of sumptuous clothes and royal regalia. And those who look [in the Adoration of the Magi] beyond the trappings can see, off in the distance, a very real little boat. When the beginning of skill in painting was like this, one wonders how anyone ever moved on in divine discontent from this childlike enchantment to the manipulation of larger forms in greater space.

BENOZZO GOZZOLI

Florentine Painter

« 1420-1497 »

H E W H O climbs, with determination, the steep and thorny path of virtue finds himself at last on a high plateau of happy ease. When he glances back over the way he has come, he thanks God who has preserved him and blesses the pains he has undergone. Well recompensed by his present bliss, he labors without fatigue and he is an example to all that heat and cold, hunger and thirst, borne for the sake of acquiring excellence, are rewarded by freedom from poverty and a life of serene security. Such was the lot of Benozzo Gozzoli.

This artist was the disciple of the well-named angelic master, Fra Giovanni [Fra Angelico], by whom he was much beloved. He was acknowledged by all who saw his work to have great power of invention, facility, ability to draw animals, knowledge of perspective, skill in landscape, and richly varied resources in decoration. Benozzo Gozzoli accomplished so much work in his day that he must have taken pleasure in little else. In comparison with other masters who surpassed him in design, he was not particularly eminent, yet by persevering he left them all behind, and among the multitude of his works are many which are very good.

An early work by Benozzo Gozzoli is an altarpiece for the Brotherhood of San Marco in Florence. For the palace of the Medici, he painted the chapel in fresco with the story of the Magi [*Procession of the Magi*].

Benozzo worked in Rome [his pictures there have been destroyed]. He returned to Florence and then went to Pisa where, in the Campo Santo, he painted stories from the Old Testament on the wall that runs the whole length of the building. This was a formidable undertaking, no less than the representation of the whole creation of the world, day by day. His pictures of the Flood and Noah's Ark are finely composed, with a great variety of figures. Near by are the Tower of Babel, the Burning of Sodom, and stories from the life of Abraham—admirably expressed and worthy of consideration. For though he was not particularly talented in drawing figures, yet in Abraham's Sacrifice, particularly, Benozzo has shown considerable mastery of his art. There is an ass, foreshortened, that is considered very fine. The Birth of Moses follows, with all the signs and prodigies that ensued. He added some other stories of the Hebrew people, for example, those of David and Solomon. He showed infinite perseverance in completing so vast an undertaking with his own hand. Innumerable portraits of living people are scattered through this work, but I mention only those which have authentic records. In the story of the Queen of Sheba there is the portrait of Marsilio Ficino, of Argiropolo, a learned Greek, and of Platina, whose likeness Benozzo had previously done in Rome. The artist also painted himself on horseback, an old man with shaven beard, wearing a black cap, in a fold of which is a white paper where, perhaps, he had intended to sign his name.

In the cathedral of Pisa, behind the seat of the archbishop, Benozzo did a small picture in tempera of Saint Thomas Aquinas disputing with learned men, among whom are Pope Sixtus IV with several cardinals and many chiefs of religious orders. This is the best and most finished work by Benozzo. He also worked in the capitular church of San Gimignano where he painted an altarpiece. In the Hall of the Council he restored figures by an older master [Lippo Memmi]. The best work he did here was the *Life of Saint Augustine*, from his conversion to his death, painted in the chapel of the church dedicated to that saint. In my book of drawings, I have a drawing he made for this work.

Exhausted at length by time and his labors, he departed to the true rest, in his seventy-eighth year. He died in Pisa in a little house he had bought when he had lived there a long time. He was regretted by all the city and buried in the Campo Santo.

Editorial Notes on Benozzo Gozzoli

VASARI evidently voiced a general opinion. Benozzo Gozzoli was able, he was incredibly industrious, but when all was said and done the fact remained that he was a poor sort of artist. There is, however, a compelling reality about the solid figures, the sturdy trees, the firm earth, the bright skies painted by this artist. This quality caught the imagination of those English art lovers who called themselves the pre-Raphaelites. Benozzo Gozzoli was their first discovery. To them he was the prime exponent of the virtues of the art before Raphael.

The contract by which Benozzo was commissioned to paint the altarpiece for San Marco in Florence required him to duplicate the Madonna Enthroned, by Fra Angelico. It said, in part, "The said Benozzo shall, at his own expense, prepare the gesso and diligently gild the panel throughout, both as regards figures and ornaments; and no other painters shall be allowed to take part in the execution of the picture, either in the predella or in any portion of the same."

Though Benozzo was asked to duplicate the work of Fra Angelico, no two artists could be more dissimilar. Each used the same subject matter. While Fra Angelico painted the very arches of the cloister of San Marco as background for his Annunciation—to take this as an example—yet the picture radiates unearthly divinity. Benozzo Gozzoli painted the great men of his day in the Procession of the Magi in the Medici chapel; and the men are so real, so earthly, that we recognize their prototypes on the streets of today. In the constantly shifting emphasis of subject matter and formal manner, Benozzo was the last to tell his tale directly, fact by fact. Masaccio had begun to play form against form, color against color, and to use composition with the force wielded by the artists of the High Renaissance.

DESIDERIO DA SETTIGNANO

Sculptor

« 1428-1468 »

GRATEFUL should they be who are able to work without effort and with a natural grace. For this is a gift from heaven—this loveliness which attracts even those who know nothing of art. It is the air of facility which is so charming and which distinguishes the work of Desiderio.

Many say this artist came from Settignano; others consider him a Florentine—but it is of little consequence, as these places are not more than two miles apart. Desiderio imitated the manner of Donatello though he was gifted with the power of lending every grace and loveliness to his heads. The faces of his women and children have the most charming sweetness and the softest delicacy. As a boy, Desiderio worked on the pedestal of Donatello's *David*. It was he who executed the harpies in marble and the vine leaves and tendrils in bronze. He sculptured the armorial bearings of the Gianfigliazzi family on the façade of their palace, very large and fine, with a lion which is most beautiful. For the church of the Carmine, Desiderio carved an angel in wood in the Brancacci chapel. In San Lorenzo he completed the decorations in marble for the chapel of the Sacrament. Here there was a figure of a child. Now removed from its place, it is used on the high altar at the Feast of the Nativity, because it is such an extraordinary thing.

For the nuns of the Murate he did a small figure of the Virgin to stand on a column in a tabernacle. He made the marble tabernacle for the Sacrament in the church of San Pietro Maggiore which, although it has no figures, is in a very fine manner and has infinite grace. This artist did the portrait in marble of Marietta Strozzi, and, as the lady was exceedingly beautiful, the bust is a very admirable one.

The tomb of Messer Carlo Marsuppini, of Arezzo, was erected in Santa Croce by this master and continues to surprise all who see it. The foliage on the sarcophagus, though somewhat hard and dry, since few antiquities had then been discovered, is a very beautiful thing. Some wings forming part of the ornament seem made of actual feathers rather than of stone, though it is almost impossible to copy hair and feathers with the chisel. There are, besides, several truly beautiful children and angels. The figure of Carlo Marsuppini from life, extended upon the tomb, is excellent, as is a medallion of Our Lady in low relief, after the manner of Donatello. These qualities are to be remarked in other reliefs by Desiderio, some of which are in the collection of Duke Cosimo. At the foot of Messer Carlo's tomb, Desiderio laid a large stone to the memory of Messer Giorgio [Gregorio Marsuppini], a renowned doctor and legist, with the portrait in bas-relief of Messer Giorgio clothed in the robes of a doctor, in the fashion of the times.

Had not death prematurely deprived the world of that powerful mind, Desiderio would doubtless have so profited by experience as to have surpassed all others in knowledge of art, as he did in grace. But the thread of his life was cut short at the age of thirty-six [forty], to the deep grief of all who had hoped to behold the perfection of his maturity. His remains were followed by his relatives and numerous friends to the church of the Servites, and upon his tomb epigrams and sonnets continued to be placed for a long time.

MINO DA FIESOLE

Sculptor

« 1431-1484 »

WHEN artists seek to do no more than imitate some eminent master whose work pleases them—in the attitude of the figures, the carriage of their heads, the fold of draperies—they never attain by these means alone the perfection of their art, since "it is obvious that he rarely presses forward who is content to follow behind" [A saying of Michelangelo's]. The artist should aim to imitate nature rather than that which has already been reduced to a manner by another artist. However truthful and natural the works of any master may appear, it is not possible that they should equal nature itself. It follows that objects taken directly from nature are alone calculated to make sculpture and painting perfect. Many of our artists have left nature out of their view and have thus wronged their own genius. Mino da Fiesole was so enamored of the manner of Desiderio that he preferred it to nature. He became graceful in manner like Desiderio rather than solidly grounded in art.

It was on the hill of Fiesole, a most ancient city now in decay, near Florence, that the sculptor Mino di Giovanni was born. He was placed as a stonecutter with Desiderio da Settignano. While he was busy with the squaring of stones, he imitated in clay the works that Desiderio was doing in marble. His master encouraged him and gave him marble to carve. Mino worked hard and was soon proficient. This pleased Desiderio, and Mino, for his part, was entirely satisfied with his master, whom he found always ready to instruct him. When Mino was thus entering on the path of excellence, it was his ill fortune that Desiderio died. This loss was so great a calamity that Mino left Florence, like one desperate, and went to Rome. There he became assistant to those artists who were making the tombs in St. Peter's which were destroyed when the new building was erected.

Mino was engaged by Cardinal Guglielmo Destovilla [d'Estouteville] to do the marble altar for Santa Maria Maggiore, beneath which rest the bones of Saint Jerome. He put on it the story of the saint, and the portrait of the cardinal done from life.

Pope Paul II, a Venetian, was building his palace of San Marco [the Palazzo di Venezia] and employed Mino to decorate it with armorial bearings. After the death of that pontiff, Mino erected his tomb in Saint Peter's. It was considered the most magnificent sepulcher that had ever been erected to any pontiff. This tomb was cast down by Bramante in the demolition of Saint Peter's and lay buried in the rubbish for several years, but in 1547 it was reconstructed in the old church by the order of some Venetians. There are some who claim this tomb to be the work of Mino del Reame, who lived about the same time, but it certainly is not. It is true that some small figures in the base, different from the rest, are by Mino del Reame (if indeed his name was Mino and not Dino, as some say).

But to return to our artist. When he had won a name for himself, for this and for the sarcophagus of Francesco Tornabuoni, he returned to Fiesole with his earnings and there took a wife. He made a marble taber- nacle for the nuns of the Murate. It was not yet installed when he received another commission of the same sort for the nuns of Sant' Ambrogio. A short time afterward, he portrayed Our Lady with the Child in her arms, in half relief, with Saints Lawrence and Leonard. For the priests of San Lorenzo Mino carved in relief a marble medallion of the Madonna and Child. This was placed over the principal entrance of the church. As it gave universal satisfaction, the artist received the commission for the monument of the illustrious knight, Messer Bernardo de' Giugni. To say nothing of the portrait, a figure of Justice in this work is very much in the manner of Desiderio, but the draperies are wanting in grace and rather commonplace.

This monument caused the abbot to entrust to Mino the tomb of Count Hugo. This tomb in Carrara marble was the most beautiful ever chiseled by this master. The boys who carry the count's arms have much spirit and childish grace. On the wall above the bier is a composition, very carefully grouped and finished, of Charity with children. In a Madonna in a half-circle Mino has imitated the manner of Desiderio to the utmost of his power. If he had improved himself by also referring to life, there is no doubt that he would have become very proficient in his art. He received the commission for another monument on the strength of this success. Mino here presented Bishop Leonardo Salutati in his episcopal robes, a portrait from the life and as close a resemblance as could be imagined. For the same bishop our artist made a life-size bust of the Saviour in marble, which is now cherished as a precious thing by the very reverend

Don Vincenzo Borghini, who takes more pleasure in it than I can express.

Mino constructed a pulpit for the capitular church of Prato and ornamented it with stories of the life of the Virgin, the whole so carefully joined that it seems to be of one piece. He also carved portraits of Piero di Lorenzo de' Medici [father of Lorenzo the Magnificent] and his wife. These marble busts are excellent likenesses. He made the figure of Our Lady in marble for the guild of manufacturers and a tabernacle for the church of San Pietro in Perugia, with Saints John and Jerome in relief. Another tabernacle in the cathedral of Volterra has two angels standing on each side. This work has been deservedly praised by all artists.

Finally, wishing one day to move some stones, and not having any assistance at hand, Mino fatigued himself too violently. An inflammatory disease ensued which caused his death. The artist was honorably interred by his relatives and friends in the canonicate at Fiesole.

JACOPO BELLINI,
GENTILE BELLINI,
GIOVANNI BELLINI

Venetian Painters

« 1424-1470 »
« 1429-1507 »   « CA. 1430-1516 »

WHEN zeal is backed by ability and good character, the greatest distinction is within the reach of any man, however poor and lowly his beginnings. This was particularly true of the Bellini family, who were of humble origin but were devoted to the art of painting.

The Venetian artist, Jacopo Bellini, was a disciple of Gentile da Fabriano and a rival of that Domenico who taught Andrea del Castagno to paint in oil. Although he worked hard, he never acquired any great reputation until Domenico left Venice. But from then on, having no competitor, he increased in fame and was considered the foremost painter of his day. He was fortunate also in having two highly gifted sons, one named Gentile (after Gentile da Fabriano, who had been a kind father to Jacopo in his youth), and the other Giovanni. When the boys were old enough, Jacopo himself taught them the principles of design, and soon they both surpassed their father. He, for his part, was delighted, and encouraged them constantly. He told them he would have them strive, as the Tuscans did, to outstrip each other. He said he hoped Giovanni would surpass him and Gentile vanquish them both, and so on.

Jacopo, with the assistance of his sons, painted the *Miracle of the True Cross* for the Brotherhood of Saint John the Evangelist. This was done on canvas, as was customary in Venice, where they rarely use maple or poplar wood, as is usual elsewhere. In Venice they do not paint on panels or, if they do so occasionally, they then use only fir wood, imported from Germany or Slavonia. Canvas is the preferred material. Perhaps this is so because it does not split, does not suffer from worms, can be of any size, and is easily transported. Whatever the cause, the Bellini painted their first pictures on canvas.

The story in the painting is as follows. A sacred relic of the cross, which is preserved by the brotherhood, fell into the canal; many people flung themselves into the water to rescue it, but it was the will of God that only the principal or guardian of the Brotherhood of Saint John the Evangelist could retrieve it. In this story Gentile painted houses in perspective along the Grand Canal of Venice, the bridge, and the long procession of men and women, a vast number of figures, many of them portraits. He gained great fame from this work.

In time Jacopo withdrew from association with his children, and each painted separately. Of Jacopo I will make no further mention, because his paintings, compared with those of his sons, were not extraordinary. But I will not omit to say that the brothers, though no longer painting together, yet had so great an affection for each other and so much respect for their father that they continually praised and modestly sought to emulate each other in courtesy as well as in excellence in art.

Giovanni painted the altarpiece of Santa Caterina of Siena in the church of San Giovanni. It was a Madonna with the Child in her arms, with saints and three very beautiful boys standing at the feet of Our Lady and singing from a book. This was considered the best work that had been then done in Venice. Giovanni also painted some very fine portraits. These admirable works made certain gentlemen begin to reason among themselves and to declare that it would be well to use these excellent masters to decorate the Hall of the Grand Council with historical paintings. Here should be depicted the glory and magnificence of their most admirable city, her deeds in war, her most important undertakings, and all things worthy of being remembered by all posterity, in order that to the pleasure of reading history should be added the gratification to the intellect in seeing the likenesses of so many nobles and their exploits illustrated. The commission was given to Gentile and Giovanni whose fame increased from day to day. It was further ordered that the work should begin as soon as possible.

Gentile obtained permission to do the work on canvas instead of fresco. In the first picture he showed the Pope giving the doge of Venice a wax taper to carry in the procession. The whole exterior of Saint Mark's appears in this picture, and the Pope is in full canonicals, with many prelates around him. Also shown is the Emperor Frederick Barbarossa [Frederick I, Holy Roman Emperor], with fine views in perspective and numerous portraits. Many times he painted the piazza and façade of Saint Mark's, but the most inventive picture was that of a sea fight with crowds of galleys in all the confusion of battle: the fighting men, the barques shown in perspective, the well-ordered combat, the defenses, the wounded, the dying, an immense diversity of objects. All showed the vast ability of Gentile, for every part was perfect in itself, and the whole was admirably composed.

In another story, the artist has shown the Pope receiving the victorious doge and giving him the golden ring with which he is to espouse the sea, as his successors have done ever since, in token of the dominion over that element which the Venetians so deservedly hold. In this compartment is Otto, Frederick Barbarossa's son, drawn from a living model, kneeling before the Pope. Behind the doge is a retinue of armed men, and behind the Pope are many cardinals and nobles. Only the poops of the galleys appear, and on the admiral's galley is a golden Victory with crown and scepter.

The other part of the hall was given to Giovanni. But as the events that he depicted continue the series begun but not completed by Vivarino [the Vivarini were another family of Venetian painters], I should say something of these first. Vivarino took up the story where Gentile left it. He showed Otto offering himself to the Pope and the Venetians as a messenger of peace between them and his father, Frederick Barbarossa. Vivarino painted a very fine perspective of an open temple with flights of steps and many figures. In another of this series he showed his great ability as a portrait painter in the crowd of nobles who accompany Otto when he is joyfully received by his father. Poor Vivarino could have completed his portion to his great credit had he not become exhausted by his labors and died prematurely. He could not even finish what he had begun, and it was necessary for Giovanni to retouch the work in certain parts.

Giovanni had already begun four stories which carried on the theme we have described. In the first he showed the Pope [Alexander III, actually a portrait of Alexander VI] presenting his foot to Frederick Barbarossa to be kissed. This first picture by Giovanni was for some reason made more animated and beyond comparison better in every way by the most excellent Titian. To follow Giovanni, however. He portrayed the Pope saying Mass in Saint Mark's and afterwards granting plenary and perpetual indulgence to those who should visit the church. The master showed the interior made even more rich and beautiful by the habits of the Pope and cardinals and nobles. In the last picture by Giovanni, Pope Alexander, the emperor, and the doge are seen before Rome, where, outside the gates of the city, the

Pope receives eight standards and eight silver trumpets from the clergy of Rome. Giovanni here showed Rome in a somewhat distant perspective, with many horses and a vast body of soldiers, all gay with banners. These works gave so much satisfaction and were so beautiful that Giovanni received the commission to paint the remaining portion of the hall just before he died, at a ripe old age.

So far we have spoken only of the works in the Hall of the Grand Council, but now we will turn back and tell of other paintings by these same masters. Among them is the picture which is on the high altar of San Domenico [actually in San Francesco] at Pesaro—a most beautiful work. At Venice, in the monastery of the Barefoot Friars, San Francesco della Vigna, there is a picture of the dead Christ which was so beautiful that Louis XI of France begged it as a gift, and so earnestly that the monks were compelled to gratify him, though with great reluctance. Another was put in its place, signed Giovanni, but this was by no means as beautiful. Many believe it was done for the most part by Giovanni's pupil, Girolamo Mocetto. About this time several portraits by this master were taken into Turkey by an ambassador as presents for the Grand Turk. These works aroused such admiration that, although Turks are not permitted by Mohammedan law to own pictures, the sultan accepted them and greatly praised them and their creator. What is more, he asked that the artist be sent to him.

The Senate, considering that Giovanni could ill support the fatigue of the trip on account of his age, and also that he was fully employed in the Hall of the Grand Council, resolved to send Gentile, for they believed he would do just as well for the Turk. Gentile was made ready and carried safely to Constantinople in the Venetian state galleys. The Grand Turk received him very willingly. Gentile was much caressed, as something novel, and Sultan Mohammed could scarcely believe that the very charming picture Gentile gave him could have been made with such exact fidelity to nature by a mere mortal. Gentile soon did a portrait of the Grand Turk so exactly like him that it was considered a miracle. Then the sultan asked him if he had the courage to do a self-portrait. In a few days Gentile produced one with the aid of a mirror. This the sultan could only believe was the work of a divine spirit in Gentile's service. If only this art had not been forbidden by their law, the sultan would never have let him go. But whether the sultan feared popular disapproval, or from some other cause, he one day dismissed the painter with many thanks for the courtesy he had shown and asked him to demand whatever he liked as a parting token. Gentile, modest and upright man that he was, asked only to be given a letter of approval in which the sultan should recommend him to the Serene Senate and Most Illustrious Signoria of Venice. This was written as cordially as possible, and he was dismissed with most honorable presents and the dignity of knighthood. Among the gifts was a chain of gold weighing as much as two hundred and fifty scudi, which was placed around Gentile's neck and which is now in the possession of his heirs at Venice.

After a most fortunate voyage Gentile returned to Venice and was received by his brother and almost the entire city with the utmost gladness. The Signoria granted him a pension of two hundred scudi a year. He worked but little after his return, and when he was almost eighty, he passed to another life and was buried by his brother in the church of San Giovanni e Paolo.

Though deprived of his brother, whom he loved tenderly, the aged Giovanni continued to work a little. He painted portraits from life, and it became the custom that whoever attained a certain degree of eminence should have his portrait painted by him or by some other master. Therefore in all Venetian houses may be seen portraits to the fourth generation back. This is a most praiseworthy custom. For the satisfaction of seeing the effigies of his ancestors, quite aside from the ornamental aspect, is of the greatest value to any man and awakens in him the love of glory.

One of Giovanni's portraits was of a lady loved by Pietro Bembo [later cardinal], done with such truth and animation that it was celebrated in a sonnet by this second Petrarch, even as Simon of Siena was celebrated by the true Petrarch. What greater reward could there be than to be so praised? And was not this same Bellini named among the best painters of his age by the renowned Ariosto? But we would tarry too long if we mentioned all the pictures and portraits by Giovanni's hand in Venice. In Rimini, he painted for Sigismondo Malatesta a dead Christ supported by two children.

Giovanni had many disciples whom he instructed with great kindness, among them Jacopo Montagnana, and most especially, [Niccolò] Rondinelli of Ravenna, who aided him in all his works. Benedetto Coda of Ferrara was also among his disciples. It is said that Giorgione da Castelfranco in his earliest days studied under Giovanni.

Giovanni Bellini died of old age when he had completed his ninetieth year, leaving a deathless memorial in his Venetian works and those he did elsewhere. He was honorably buried in the same church and the same tomb as his brother. There were not a few sonnets written to honor him after his death even as he had done honor to himself and his country during his lifetime.

Editorial Notes on the Bellini Family

WHEN you consider that Jacopo was born at the very beginning of the fifteenth century and that Titian put the finishing touches—and not incongruously—on Giovanni's last picture, you have a vast panorama of development in art.

About the time François Villon in Paris was dedicating his Testament "a mon plus que père," Jacopo was in Florence with "his kind father," Gentile da Fabriano. As the individual emerged from the close-knit web of the feudal family, perhaps he transferred his filial devotion intact to his foster father.

Jacopo returned to Venice to see and to record in a notebook of ninety-nine pages the exact appearance of things—peacocks and antique sculptures, horses and men. In these drawings (which Vasari might have considered of minor interest if he had known of them), we see the Renaissance begun in Venice. The subject of the picture, what Vasari calls the story, is, for instance, an Annunciation, but the real interest is divided among the peacock in the foreground, the classical building drawn in stiff perspective, and a triumphal arch in the distance.

One almost regrets that Vasari was not a Venetian. There was material there, at the crossroads of the world. No one could help but admire Giovanni; did not Dürer write home "He is very old, but still the best of all"? But Vasari does not give us a sense of the unique advantage of being a Venetian. The Orient there met Flanders, while out of the soil of Italy antiquity was being born again. All these strains made up the art of the Bellini family.

Giovanni alone saw the development of the full span of the Renaissance. He learned from his mighty brother-in-law Mantegna and from the Donatellos in Padua. It was certainly not because he was too aged and infirm that the Venetian Signoria decided to send Gentile, older by two years, to Sultan Mohammed. Those Venetian businessmen knew an article of irreplaceable value when they had it.

DOMENICO GHIRLANDAIO

Florentine Painter

« 1449-1494 »

DOMENICO, son of Tommaso del Ghirlandaio, is entitled to an eminent place among the artists of his time because of his talent and the number and importance of his works. He was born to be an artist and followed his bent in spite of the opposition of his guardians. Such impediments often blight genius, but Domenico obeyed his instinct and won high distinction for himself and advanced the art of his age. His father, destined him for the same craft. In fact, the greater part of the votive vessels in silver formerly in the church of the Annunciation at Florence were his father's handiwork. Tommaso del Ghirlandaio invented and made those garlands [ghirlande], whence comes his name. It was not only that he invented them but that he made them better than anyone else, so that none found favor except those that came from his workshop.

Though learning the art of the goldsmith, Domenico drew continually, and since he was intelligent and possessed admirable taste, he acquired extraordinary facility. He was so quick and clever at sketching that he is said to have drawn the portraits of those who passed by his workshop. That he was able to do this we are convinced by the lively portraits throughout his work.

The first pictures painted by Domenico were for the chapel of the Vespucci in the church of the Ognissanti, where there is a Dead Christ with Saints. Here also is a Misericordia wherein Domenico has portrayed Amerigo Vespucci, who sailed to the Indies. In the refectory of the cloister of the Ognissanti, he painted a fresco of the Last Supper. He was commissioned by Francesco Sasseti to paint a chapel in Santa Trinità with stories from the life of Saint Francis. This is a work of great merit, most graceful and tender. In the first compartment of this picture is a miracle

performed by Saint Francis, who hovers in the air over a view of the bridge
of the Santa Trinità and the palace of the Spini, while a child is restored
to life. The women gathered around alternately display grief for his death
and joy at his resuscitation. The burial procession comes from the church
to bury the dead, all with perfect truth to nature. Another picture shows
Saint Francis refusing his inheritance and putting on the habit of penitence, which he girds on with the cord of discipline. Again, in still another
painting, Saint Francis receives from Pope Honorius the confirmation of
his rule and presents the pontiff with roses blooming in January. In this
picture the master has painted the Hall of the Consistory with the cardinals seated. Leaning on a balustrade are half-length figures of various
personages, among them the illustrious Lorenzo de' Medici the Elder.
Saint Francis receiving the stigmata and the death of the saint complete
the series. In the latter, one of the monks kisses the hands of the departed,
and his expression could not be more perfect. There is also a bishop in full
vestments, spectacles upon his nose, chanting the prayers for the dead,
and the fact that we do not hear him alone demonstrates to us that he is
not alive. On the sides of the altar, Domenico painted Francesco Sassetti
kneeling and his wife, Madonna Nera. Their children are portrayed in the
story of the child restored to life. On the vaulted ceiling are four sibyls.
To these works Domenico added a picture in tempera of the Nativity that
astonishes everyone who knows about art. This contains the master's self-
portrait and some heads of shepherds that are wonderfully fine.

For the order of the Ingesuati, Domenico painted the altarpiece for the
high altar with saints about the Virgin. He deserves to be commended for
painting an imitation of the borderings and ornaments of gold and doing
away with those flourishes and scrolls made of gilt gypsum which are more
suitable for tapestry than for the paintings of good masters. Most beautiful
of all is the figure of Our Lady with the Child in her arms and four little
angels around her. Nothing better could be done in tempera. This picture
was moved to San Giovannino when the church was destroyed.

Ghirlandaio executed a great number of pictures for churches about
Florence. In the Ognissanti, he painted, in competition with Sandro Botticelli, a Saint Jerome surrounded by learned books and various instruments.
When the monks made alterations in the choir, they moved this work and
that of Botticelli into the center of the church. This was done at the
moment when these *Lives* were going into their second edition.

Ghirlandaio was invited to Rome by Pope Sixtus IV to paint part of
his chapel [the Sistine]. He depicted Christ calling Peter and Andrew
from their nets. The rich and eminent merchant, Francesco Tornabuoni,

Domenico's friend, commissioned him to paint the wall behind the tomb of his wife, who had died in childbirth. Tornabuoni was so pleased with all he had done that when the master returned to Florence, he bore letters of recommendation to Giovanni Tornabuoni. These letters declared that the Pope, too, was highly satisfied.

It chanced at this time that the principal chapel of Santa Maria Novella, painted by Orcagna, was ruined in many places where the rain had leaked through the roof. Many citizens had offered to restore the chapel, but the Ricci family, who owned it, could not afford the expense and did not want to lose their right to the chapel or to see their ancestral arms removed. But Giovanni Tornabuoni wished to employ Ghirlandaio on this magnificent site on a memorial to himself and at the same time to bring renown to the artist. He set to work on the problem. At length he promised the Ricci not only to bear the whole expense himself, but to have their arms emblazoned in the most honorable and conspicuous place in the chapel. A solemn contract was drawn up and signed. Then Domenico undertook to paint the chapel, retaining the subjects used by Orcagna. He was to earn twelve hundred gold ducats, and two hundred more if Giovanni were pleased with the finished work. Domenico set to work and did not cease until the end of the fourth year, when he had entirely finished it to Giovanni's great satisfaction. Giovanni said that Domenico had earned the additional two hundred ducats but confessed, ingenuously, that he would be glad if the painter would be content with the first price. Ghirlandaio immediately remitted the remainder, declaring that he had it much more at heart to give satisfaction than to get rich.

Giovanni Tornabuoni had two large escutcheons made in stone, one for the Tornaquinci and the other for the Tornabuoni, and erected on the two pilasters outside the chapel, and in the lunette he placed armorial bearings belonging to different branches of the family. Finally Domenico painted the altarpiece. Beneath an arch in the gilt framework, Giovanni placed a most beautiful tabernacle for the Sacrament. On the pediment of the tabernacle a small shield, about five inches across, bore the arms of the Ricci.

But the best was to come, for when the chapel was opened, the Ricci sought in vain for their arms. Enraged, they hurried off to the magistrate with their contract. Then the Tornabuoni proved that they had placed the Ricci arms in the most honorable part of the whole work, nearest the Holy Sacrament, and so the court decided. And if anyone thinks this has little to do with the life I am writing, let him be calm, for it just ran off my pen. If it is good for nothing else, this story will show how poverty becomes the prey of riches and how prudent wealth may attain its ends without blame.

But to return to the beautiful works of Ghirlandaio. This chapel contains the life of the Virgin and the life of John the Baptist. In the picture of the Birth of the Virgin, painted with extraordinary care, we may mention the window that lights the room, deceiving all who look at it. A faithful scene of a nativity is shown—women busy caring for the mother, bringing water, washing the baby, bringing swaddling clothes. But of all the stories we have by Ghirlandaio, the best is certainly the Massacre of the Innocents, which is executed with great judgment, ability, and art. In the animated contest between the mothers and the soldiers, every sort of passion is displayed—rage, despair, cruelty. All is done in the manner of a deeply thinking philosopher rather than in that of a mere painter.

In the *Life of John the Baptist* on the opposite wall, Ghirlandaio pictured the offering of Zacharias, and to show that in those old days the offering of sacrifices was made by the most honorable people, he has painted the most distinguished citizens of Florence, most particularly the members of the Tornabuoni family, old and young. And wishing to make it obvious that his age abounded in talent, Domenico painted a group of four half-length figures in the foreground, all portraits of the most learned men of Florence. The first is Marsilio Ficino in the dress of a canon; then comes Cristoforo Landino; and turning toward him are the Greek Demetrius, and Angelo Poliziano—all most animated portraits. In the Visitation scene there are several women dressed in the style of the times, among them Ginevra de' Benci, then a most beautiful maiden.

Domenico did not live to finish the altarpiece, but it was completed by his brothers, Davide and Benedetto.

This chapel was considered to be an extremely fine work, majestic and beautiful, charming in color and of admirable craftsmanship as a mural painting, to say nothing of the invention and composition. The master deserves infinite commendation on all accounts but mostly because of the many vivid portraits of distinguished persons.

Ghirlandaio took such pleasure in his work that he told his students to accept every commission brought to his workshop, even though it were only to paint hoops for women's baskets, saying that if they would not paint them he would do them himself—no one was to be sent away unsatisfied. But when household cares were laid upon him, he complained bitterly, saying to his brother Davide, "Leave me to work, and do thou provide. Now that I have begun to get into the spirit of this art, I wish they would give me the walls of Florence to paint the whole circuit with stories." Besides this resolute and invincible character of mind, Domenico possessed so accurate an eye that, when drawing the antiquities of Rome— triumphal arches, baths, columns, colossal figures, obelisks, amphitheaters, and aqueducts—he drew all by eye alone, but afterward he measured what he had done and found every part to be correct.

For the abbey of Passignano Domenico executed some work in company with his brother Davide and Bastiano [Mainardi] of San Gemignano. The latter found themselves ill treated and ill fed before the arrival of Domenico. They complained to the abbot that it was not decent that they should have hod carrier's fare. The abbot promised to better affairs and excused himself by blaming an ignorant monk. But it was no better when Domenico came, and Davide complained again. He apologized for pressing the abbot, but he insisted that a man of Domenico's distinction deserved more consideration. In the evening the same porringers appeared again, the same coarse meat. Thereupon Davide rose in a rage, dumped the soup over the friar, and beat him with a great bread loaf, which he used for a club. The abbot, who had already gone to bed, heard the clamor and thought the monastery was falling down. The monk was in bad condition, and the abbot began to reproach Davide. But the latter flew into a fury and ordered the abbot out of his sight, shouting that the talents of Domenico were worth more than all the hogs of abbots who had ever lived in the monastery. The abbot, thus brought to his senses, did his best thereafter to treat them as the honorable men they were.

Among those who studied under Domenico was Bastiano Mainardi of San Gemignano. These two together painted the chapel of Santa Fina and produced a work of much beauty. The fidelity and kindliness of Bastiano led Domenico to give him one of his sisters in marriage. In Santa Croce Bastiano painted an Assumption for the chapel of the Barincelli and Bandini. This is an admirable fresco, but the cartoon for it was prepared by Domenico himself. They also worked together in Siena and Pisa. But at the very moment when Domenico had many great works in hand, he fell sick of a pestiferous fever which killed him in five days. The Tornabuoni heard that he was ill and sent him a hundred ducats as a proof of their friendly consideration.

Domenico Ghirlandaio lived forty-four years and was borne to his grave in Santa Maria Novella by his brothers and his son, Ridolfo, with sorrowing hearts and many tears. His loss was a great grief to his friends, and many foreign painters sent their condolences to his relations.

Editorial Notes on Ghirlandaio

IN THE history of art Ghirlandaio's painting occupies the last page before the chapter entitled the High Renaissance. It has gravity, direct reality in details, and great dignity. And yet for all its order and skill, it has a coltish grace. It is oddly appealing. "Never again," we think as we look at the still grace of the figures. Never before, either! In the picture from Santa Maria Novella, the persons in the "story" take their ordered places in a well-proportioned room. A graceful figure (one of those rich Tornabuoni, doubtless) poses for her portrait. Like a breeze, like a ripple in still water, a handmaiden runs in, bearing a basket of fruit on her head.

Even then Michelangelo was there, working as an apprentice paint boy—he who was to carve and paint the grandest forms in mightiest movement in the deepest space in all art.

ANTONIO and PIERO POLLAIUOLO

Painters and Sculptors of Florence

« 1429-1498 »   « 1443-1496 »

THERE are many who begin tentatively with unimportant works and then, gathering courage as they grow in facility and power, mount ever higher until their thoughts reach almost to heaven itself. Haply they encounter some liberal prince who, satisfied in all his expectations, is compelled to reward their services most liberally. Such men live out their lives with honor and leave memorials which awaken the admiration of the world. Such were Antonio and Piero Pollaiuolo, who in their time were highly esteemed for their rare abilities.

These artists were born in Florence within a few years of each other. Their father was a poor man, and humble, but he recognized the clear and just intelligence of his sons. Not being in a position to give them a liberal education, he apprenticed Antonio to Bartoluccio Ghiberti [*stepfather of Lorenzo*], as a goldsmith, and Piero to Andrea del Castagno as a painter. Antonio set jewels and worked at the preparation of silver to be enameled and was held to be the best who worked with the chisel in that vocation. Lorenzo Ghiberti, then engaged on the Baptistery doors, employed Antonio with many other young men to assist him. He set Antonio to work on one of the festoons, where the youth produced a quail which may still be seen and which is so perfect that it wants nothing but the power of flight. Antonio had not spent many weeks at this occupation before he was known as the best of all the assistants. His ability and reputation increased together, and he left Bartoluccio and Lorenzo and opened his own shop in the Mercato Nuovo [New market]. Here he worked for several years continually preparing new designs and making chandeliers in relief and other fanciful works which caused him to be known as the best in his craft.

There lived at the same time a famous goldsmith called Maso Finiguerra who surpassed all other masters in the skillful grouping of a number of figures. In competition with Maso, Antonio executed various stories which surpassed those of his rival in beauty of design. The syndics of the guild of merchants engaged him, because of the success of this work, to make some silver reliefs for the altar of San Giovanni. Of all the silver for that altar, done at different times and by a great variety of masters, his was acknowledged to be the best. The subjects chosen were the Feast of Herod and the Dance of Herodias. But most beautiful of all was the *Saint John* for the center of the altar, which was done entirely with the chisel. Antonio was then commissioned to do the silver chandeliers, about six feet high, with a cross in proportion. Antonio took the greatest pains with everything he undertook, whether in gold, enamel, or silver, and these works for San Giovanni he brought to such a degree of perfection that they have been admired by all: his own countrymen and foreigners alike.

Antonio taught Mazzingo and Giuliano del Facchino, tolerably good masters, and Giovanni Turini of Siena, who was the best of all Antonio's pupils. From Antonio di Salvi, who did the large silver cross for the abbey of Florence, down to the craftsmen of our own day, there has been little done that is extraordinary. But many of the works of Antonio di Salvi, as well as those of the Pollaiuoli, have been melted down for the use of the city in times of war.

Realizing at last that the art of the goldsmith brought little assurance of immortality, Antonio joined his brother in the career of painting. He found this a very different art and possibly regretted his hasty resolution. But perhaps from a sense of shame, he set himself to master the processes of painting in a few months' time, and did, indeed, become an excellent master. He joined Piero and they collaborated on many paintings. Among them was one in oil for the altar of the chapel which belonged to the cardinal of Portugal in San Miniato al Monte. And in Or San Michele, the brothers painted an oil of the angel Raphael with Tobit. In the Mercatanzia of Florence, in the tribune where the court sits, they depicted the virtues [Faith, Hope, Charity, Justice, and Temperance]. For the Pucci chapel in the church of the Servites [the Annunziata] Antonio painted the altarpiece. This remarkable work [*Saint Sebastian*, now in the National Gallery, London] has numerous horses, many undraped figures, and singularly beautiful foreshortenings. The picture contains the portrait of Gino di Ludovico Capponi in the figure of Saint Sebastian. Antonio has evidently copied nature to the utmost of his power. One of the archers is bending over and exerts all the force of his strong arms—the veins swelling, the muscles taut—to prepare his weapon. The other figures are as well done. Antonio Pucci paid three hundred scudi and said that he knew he was barely paying for the colors. This picture was finished in 1475.

Antonio's courage now rose to new heights, and in San Miniato-fra-le-Torri he painted a Saint Christopher almost twenty feet high and in the modern manner of correct proportion. In the Medici Palace he painted three pictures of Hercules, each almost ten feet high. In the first, Hercules is strangling Antaeus; he uses every muscle and nerve in his body to destroy his opponent. His set teeth are as expressive as the rest of the figure down to the toes, on which he lifts himself in his effort. Antaeus is seen sinking, gasping for breath. In the second picture Hercules kills the lion by pressing his knee against the animal's chest, rending the lion's jaws by main force while the beast claws at him and tears his arm. The third, in which the hero destroys the hydra, is indeed an admirable work. The reptile itself and its fire and ferocity are so effectually displayed that the master merits the highest praise and deserves to be imitated by all good artists. This master treated his nude figures almost in the modern manner. He dissected many human bodies to study anatomy and was the first who investigated the action of the muscles by this means. Antonio engraved on copper a combat of nude figures and later produced many other engravings which are a great advance over other works of his time.

Antonio was invited to Rome by Pope Innocent VIII after the death of Pope Sixtus IV. He made a bronze tomb for Pope Innocent with the pontiff seated and giving the benediction. This monument is in Saint Peter's near the chapel in which the lance of Christ is preserved. He also made the tomb of Pope Sixtus, which is richly decorated and stands clear of the wall. The figure of Sixtus, very finely executed, lies extended on top of the tomb. It is wrongly asserted that this artist designed the palace of the Belvedere.

Finally the brothers died within a short time of each other and were buried in San Pietro in Vincoli. Their monument consists of two portraits, medallions in marble.

Antonio made a bas-relief in bronze which was sent into Spain, the subject being a combat of nude figures. After his death a model for an equestrian statue of Francesco Sforza, duke of Milan, was found. There were two designs: one showed the city of Verona beneath him; and in the other, he is in full armor on a pedestal covered with battle pieces and is forcing his horse to leap upon an armed man. I could never discover why this was not executed. There are also several very beautiful medals by the Pollaiuoli.

Antonio left many disciples. He was a most fortunate man and led a

Antonio Pollaiuolo: Ten Fighting Nudes (drawing). Uffizi, Florence.

Botticelli: Saint Augustine (fresco, 6 ft. x 3 ft. 8 in.), Ognissanti, Florence.

Botticelli: Portrait of a Youth (wood, 16⅛ x 12 in.), National Gallery, Washington. (Mellon Collection)

Verrocchio: Colleoni (bronze, over life size), Venice.

Mantegna: Madonna della Vittoria (canvas, 9 ft. 2¼ in.
x 5 ft. 5½ in.), Louvre, Paris.

Mantegna: Saint James Led to Execution (fresco), Church of the Erimitani, Padua.

Filippino Lippi: Virgin Appearing to Saint Bernard (wood, life-size figures), Badia, Florence.

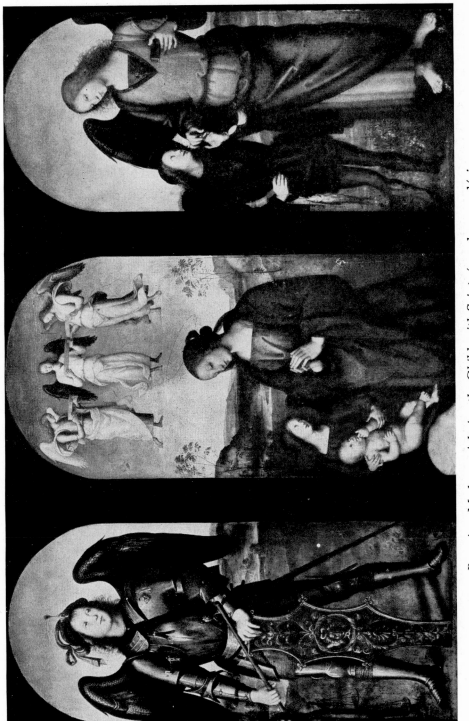

*Perugino: Madonna Adoring the Child, with Saints (wood, 50 x 25½ in.
center, 22½ in. edges), National Gallery, London.*

Pinturicchio: Journey of Moses to Egypt (fresco), Sistine Chapel, Vatican, Rome.

Francia: Portrait of Federigo Gonzaga (tempera on canvas transferred from wood, 19 x 14 in.), Metropolitan Museum, New York.

Carpaccio: Saint Ursula and the Prince (oil on canvas, 9 ft. high), Academy, Venice.

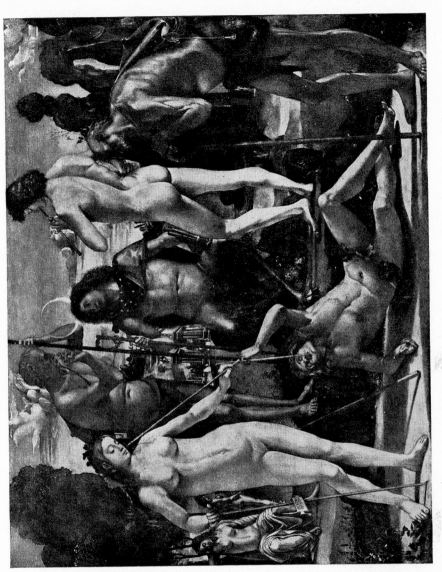

Signorelli: The School of Pan (canvas, 6 ft. 4 in. x 8 ft. 5 in.), Kaiser Friedrich Museum, Berlin.

very happy life. He had the patronage of rich pontiffs and lived when his native city was at the summit of its prosperity and remarkable for its love of talent. Had he lived in less favorable times he might not have produced the rich fruits which we derive from his labors, for the cares of life are the deadly enemies of that disinterested study so necessary to those who profess the arts.

He designed some vestments for San Giovanni in Florence which were embroidered with the most subtle mastery by Paolo da Verona, who took twenty-six years to do the work. They were done wholly in close stitch, which gives the effect of actual painting. This art is now all but lost. Modern embroidery, done with a longer stitch, is less durable and much less pleasing.

Editorial Notes on the Pollaiuoli

PIERO and Antonio were the students of anatomy of the generation just before the High Renaissance. They were the forerunners and teachers of the greatest artists the Renaissance produced, but they were hardly painters at all. They explored the muscles and sinews of men and animals. The searching intensity of their studies matched the types they drew: thin, energetic, straining, or swaggering. In this way, their figures epitomize the Florentine spirit. Of all who paved the way for Michelangelo and Leonardo, Piero Pollaiuolo and his brother Antonio made the most essential contribution.

SANDRO BOTTICELLI

Florentine Painter

« CA. 1444-1510 »

IN THE time of the illustrious Lorenzo de' Medici the elder, truly an age of gold for men of talent, there flourished Alessandro, called after our custom Sandro, and surnamed di Botticello. His father, Mariano Filipepi, brought him up carefully and gave him a good schooling. But though the boy learned readily what he wished to learn, he was always discontented and took no pleasure in reading, writing, or accounts. His father, troubled by this eccentric behavior, turned him over to a friend of his, the goldsmith Botticello, to be taught that art.

There was a close connection between the goldsmiths and the painters, and Sandro resolved to devote himself to design. He so informed his father, who well understood the force of his son's inclinations and took him at once to the Carmelite monk, Fra Filippo, a most excellent painter of that time, and placed him there to study.

Sandro followed directions and imitated the manner of his master so closely that Fra Filippo came to love him. He instructed him so effectually that Sandro surpassed all expectations. While still a youth he painted the figure of Fortitude in the series of the virtues that Antonio and Piero Pollaiuolo were executing in the Mercatanzia in Florence. After doing a picture for the chapel of the Bardi family in Santo Spirito as well as some others, he painted a Saint Augustine for the Vespucci family in the church of Ognissanti. He strove particularly to surpass Domenico del Ghirlandaio, who had painted a Saint Jerome there. In this work of extraordinary merit, the saint's countenance is marked by the power of his thought and the acuteness of perception of those who think long and constantly on abstruse and exalted subjects.

Honored because of this work, Sandro was appointed by the guild of Porta Santa Maria to paint a Coronation of the Virgin for San Marco. Our Lady is surrounded by a choir of angels, and the whole picture is finished with infinite care. For the elder Lorenzo, Sandro also did some works for the Medici Palace. Besides these religious subjects, for private houses he painted many pictures of undraped women. Two of these depict the Birth of Venus and the Allegory of Spring [Primavera] wherein Venus is crowned with flowers by the Graces.

For the monks of Castello this master painted an Annunciation in one of their chapels. In the church of San Pietro he made a picture for Matteo Palmieri which contained a large number of figures. It is an Assumption of Our Lady, and the zones of heaven are painted in their order. Patriarchs, prophets, apostles, evangelists, martyrs, confessors, doctors, virgins, and the hierarchies—all are here executed from a design furnished by the learned and able Matteo. At the foot of the picture are the portraits of Matteo kneeling and of his wife. This exceedingly beautiful picture should have put envy to shame, but there were certain malevolent persons who declared that Sandro and Matteo had fallen into grievous heresy. Now, whether this is true or not, let no one ask me to judge. The whole work is entirely worthy of praise: the figures, the circles of heaven, the angels, and all. [This picture is in the National Gallery, London, labelled Botticini.]

About this time Botticelli painted a small picture of the Adoration of the Magi, which was placed between the doors of Santa Maria Novella. The face of the oldest of the kings has the liveliest expression of tenderness and satisfaction. This figure is the most faithful and animated likeness of Cosimo de' Medici. The second king is a portrait of Giuliano de' Medici, and he presents his gift to the divine child with the utmost sincerity. The third, who is also kneeling, apparently in thanksgiving as well as adoration, is the likeness of Giovanni, the son of Cosimo. The beauty that Sandro has given to these heads cannot be described, and all the figures are wonderfully varied in attitude, whether seen full face or in profile, or bent down, young or old. The followers of each king are distinguished from each other so that it is easy to see which belong to one court and which to another. This work won such fame for the master that Pope Sixtus IV appointed Sandro superintendent of the work of decorating his [Sistine] chapel. Among Botticelli's pictures there, are the *Temptation of Christ, Moses Slaying the Egyptian, Moses and the Daughters of Jethro,* and the *Sacrifice of the Sons of Aaron,* with several figures of Popes in the niches above. Botticelli was highly praised for these works and received from the Pope a considerable sum of money which he squandered during his residence in Rome, where he lived immoderately, as was his habit.

Botticelli returned to Florence and, being whimsical and eccentric, spent his time illustrating the *Inferno* [Dante] and making prints over which he wasted much time and neglected his true vocation. He also engraved many of his own works, but not well, for the plates were ill cut. His best attempt of this kind was the *Triumph of Faith*, by Fra Girolamo Savonarola, of whose sect our artist was so zealous a partisan that he abandoned painting and, since he had no other means of livelihood, fell into great difficulties. He became what was then called a piagnone [mourner or kill-joy] and abandoned all labor. Old and very poor, he might have died of hunger had he not been supported by Lorenzo de' Medici for whom he worked at the small hospital of Volterra. Lorenzo assisted him while he lived, as did other friends and admirers.

In San Francesco, near San Miniato, Botticelli painted a Madonna, life size, which was considered a very beautiful picture. Sandro was fond of a jest and often amused himself at the expense of his disciples and friends. One of his pupils copied this picture very exactly for the purpose of selling it. Sandro sold it for him to a citizen for six gold florins. To his pupil he said, "Well, Biagio, I've sold thy picture at last, but the buyer wishes to see it in a good light. Fetch him tomorrow morning that he may see it in place. He will then pay thee the money." "Oh, master," quoth Biagio, "how well you have done!" And he hung the picture and went his way. Thereupon Sandro and another disciple named Jacopo made paper caps like those that are worn by the citizens of Florence and pasted them on the heads of the angels that surrounded the Madonna. In the morning Biagio appeared with the citizen, who had been warned of the jest. Biagio raised his eyes and saw his Madonna, not surrounded by angels but seated among the Signoria of Florence. He was about to make a great outcry, but the buyer made no comment except to praise the picture, so he kept still. At last the citizen took him home and paid him the six florins. By the time he returned to the shop, the caps were off. Altogether astonished, he turned to his master and said, "Master mine, was I dreaming or did I see red caps on the angels' heads? What may this mean?" "Thou art out of thy wits. Would the citizen have bought thy picture if it had been so?" "He certainly said nothing," replied Biagio, "but for all that, it seems a very strange matter." And they soon convinced him that he had imagined it all.

A weaver set up eight noisy, clattering looms in the house next to Sandro's. The painter could not work; he could not even stay at home. When he asked for an end of the disturbance, the reply was that the weaver both could and would do as he liked in his own house. Sandro then balanced an enormous weight of stone on the roof of his house that was higher than his neighbor's. This stone threatened to fall when the wall was shaken, and had it done so it would have crushed the weaver's roof, floors, looms, and workmen. The man hastened to Sandro in terror, but got the same reply he himself had given: that Sandro both could and would do as he liked in his own house. Thereafter the weaver became a less troublesome neighbor.

The master loved zealous students of art. He is said to have made a great deal of money and to have spent it all, being a very bad manager. Finally, very old and unfit for work, he went about on crutches and so died in his seventy-eighth [sixty-seventh] year after long illness and decrepitude.

Sandro Botticelli drew remarkably well, and artists have cherished his drawings. His stories are exceedingly rich with figures. This master deserves the highest praise for all the works that he chose to execute with care. A small picture, *Apelles' Calumny*, was presented by Sandro himself to his most intimate friend, Antonio Segni, and nothing more perfect could be imagined.

Editorial Notes on Botticelli

His portrait by *Filippino Lippi* in the Brancacci chapel of the *Carmine* shows a sullen, sensual man with deep-set eyes and a heavy jaw. Who could have predicted that this man, among the painters of his day—*Pollaiuolo, Ghirlandaio, Benozzo Gozzoli, Perugino,* should have been all but forgotten? Such emotional force, passionate strength, and infinite fantasy to be submerged by the flood of the High Renaissance and ignored for more than three hundred years! Yet this was so. The present great popularity of Botticelli's truly beautiful work dates from about 1890.

I have chosen the Saint Augustine as an illustration, instead of the often reproduced Birth of Venus or the Nativity, because it shows another side of Botticelli. Behind this strong and ascetic picture, we can see the painter as a religious fanatic, a follower of Savonarola. Could Savonarola have had, too, one wonders, another side? Did he love the jewels and furbelows he tore with moral force from the women of Florence? Botticelli, for his part, had his cake and ate it, too! Venus and the Virgin, the pagan and the Christian, riotous living—and yet he was one of Savonarola's piagnoni. He packed them all into his life.

ANDREA VERROCCHIO

Painter, Sculptor, and Architect

« 1435-1488 »

T HE Florentine, Andrea del Verrocchio, was at once a goldsmith, a
master of perspective, a sculptor, a carver of wood, a painter, and a
musician. His manner in sculpture and painting was somewhat hard and
crude, as if he had learned these arts by means of infinite labor and study.
Had he been as gifted as he was industrious, Andrea Verrocchio would
have been among the most excellent of masters. These arts demand both
talent and zeal in supreme degree, and where either fails, the artist rarely
attains first rank in his profession. Yet study will conduct him to a certain
eminence, and Andrea, more industrious than all others, is numbered
among the distinguished masters.

When a boy he was interested in science and especially in geometry.
As a goldsmith he made the brooches for the copes used in the cathedral
of Florence, and some larger things. There is a vase with garlands and
animals and various fantasies, a work which is known to all goldsmiths,
and another with a dance of children. These gave proof of his ability,
and Andrea was appointed by the guild of merchants to do silver reliefs
for the two ends of the altar of the Baptistery. These brought him high
praise and a very great reputation.

At that time Pope Sixtus [IV] wished to complete the ornaments of his
chapel [the Sistine], the large silver figures of the Apostles, which stand
upon his altar. The Pope commissioned Andrea to finish the whole work.
This Andrea did with great good judgment and diligence. Meanwhile, as
he perceived the value set upon the antique statues discovered in Rome,
and saw that the Pope placed the *Bronze Horse* [the equestrian figure of
Marcus Aurelius] in St. John Lateran, and that even such fragments as were
daily found were cherished, Andrea resolved to devote all his time to
sculpture. Some small figures that he cast in bronze were well received, and
this gave him courage to begin to work in marble.

Just then, the wife of Francesco Tornabuoni died in childbed. Her husband, who had loved her dearly, wishing to do her all honor after her death, commissioned Andrea to make her monument. The master portrayed the lady on the stone which covered her tomb, with the birth of her infant, in bas-relief, and her departure to another life on the sides. He added three figures of virtues which were considered very beautiful. This was his first work in marble.

Andrea Verrocchio returned to Florence with money, fame, and honor and was appointed to make a figure of David in bronze about five feet high, which was placed, to the great credit of the master, on the summit of the stairway where the chain formerly was [in the Palazzo Vecchio]. While he was working on this, he made the figure of Our Lady in marble for the tomb of Leonardo Bruni in Santa Croce. He also did a relief of a Madonna and Child, which was once in the Medici Palace but which is now placed, as being a very beautiful thing, over a door in the apartment of the duchess of Florence. The master portrayed Alexander the Great and Darius on two medals, after his own fancy, and in profile. These were sent to Matthias Corvinus, king of Hungary, by the illustrious Lorenzo de' Medici.

Verrocchio had won fame for his casting in bronze and was given the monument of Giovanni and Piero, sons of Cosimo de' Medici, to execute in bronze in full relief. The sarcophagus is of porphyry supported by four bronze consoles decorated with foliage of great beauty. He showed his skill in architecture when he placed the tomb within the embrasure of a window, and constructed a grating in bronze made in the form of a network of ropes, which he adorned at intervals with festoons and other fancies, to close the aperture above the tomb.

Donatello had erected a tabernacle in Or San Michele for the Council of Six of the guild of merchants and there was also to have been a Saint Thomas, but, because some of the guild wanted Ghiberti and some wanted Donatello, the affair remained undecided while those artists lived. Now the work was entrusted to Andrea Verrocchio. Our artist cast the figures and they came out firm, complete, and beautiful. Andrea then set about polishing and finishing and brought his work to the perfection in which we now see it. The incredulity of Thomas, his too great desire to prove the truth of what has been told him, and at the same time his tender love for the Christ are all obvious. The Christ raises his arm with much freedom, and with grace and divinity, so to speak, disperses the doubts of his incredulous disciple. The handling of the draperies also shows that Andrea was as learned in his art as Donatello and Ghiberti and the other masters who preceded him. The work truly deserved its niche in a tabernacle made by Donatello.

Since Andrea's reputation could not be improved in sculpture, and as he was one who ever strove for new triumphs, he turned his attention to painting. By diligent study he produced a cartoon of a combat of nude figures in pen and ink, which was designed to be used later for the decoration of the façade of a building. He prepared other cartoons and even began to carry them out, but for some reason or other these remained unfinished. He made many drawings of female heads which, because of their exceeding beauty, were later imitated by Leonardo da Vinci in expression, arrangement of the hair, and features. There are also, in my book of drawings, two horses drawn with the correct measurements so that they could be reduced or enlarged. A relief in terra cotta of a horse's head, a copy from the antique and a singularly beautiful thing, is also in my possession.

Andrea made for Lorenzo de' Medici a figure in bronze of a boy strangling a fish [Boy with a Dolphin] on the fountain of the villa at Careggi. Duke Cosimo has placed it in the court of his palace. The figure of the boy is truly admirable.

When the cupola of Santa Maria del Fiore was finished, it was decided after many discussions that the copper ball which, according to Brunelleschi's plans, was to top the edifice, should be prepared by Andrea. He made it about eight feet high, fixed it on a disk, and chained it securely in order that the cross could be erected on it. When it was put up there was great public rejoicing. The work required much skill because the ball had to be fashioned so that it could be entered from below.

Andrea Verrocchio never stopped working; he was always painting or doing sculpture, changing from one to the other. A picture for the nuns of San Domenico was such a success that he painted another for the monks of Vallombrosa. The subject was the Baptism of Christ. Leonardo painted one of the angels. It was obvious that this was the best part of the picture, and Andrea resolved never to paint again because he had been outdone by one so young.

In the Medici collection of antiquities there was a Marsyas fastened to a tree and about to be flayed. This was just within the door of the garden. Lorenzo wished to see it balanced by another Marsyas in pietra rossa— the torso and head of which had come into his hands, a work of high antiquity and much more beautiful than the first one. Lorenzo gave it to Andrea Verrocchio to restore. He completed it perfectly by adding legs, thighs, and arms in red marble. Lorenzo was highly satisfied and placed it facing the other.

The Venetians at this time wished to honor their victorious general, Bartolommeo [Colleoni] of Bergamo, and also hoped thereby to encourage other leaders. They invited Andrea to Venice to execute an equestrian statue to be placed in the Campo San Zanipolo. The master prepared his model and was taking the necessary measures for casting it in bronze when, by favoritism, it was decided that Vellano of Padua should do the figure of the general and Andrea that of the horse only. Andrea no sooner heard this than he broke the head and legs of his mold and returned to Florence in great anger without saying a word. The Signoria of Venice gave him to understand that, if he ever dared to show himself in Venice, they would have his head off. In reply to this threat, the master wrote that he would take care not to come to Venice, for, if they once took off his head, they could not replace it any more than they could put as good a one on his horse as the one he had broken. Andrea was induced to return to Venice in spite of this reply, which did not displease those rulers, and his fee was doubled. He restored his first model and cast it, but did not live to see it finished. In the heat and fatigue of casting the work he caught cold and died after a few days' illness. Another work was left incomplete, the tomb of Cardinal Forteguerra in Pistoia.

Andrea Verrocchio died when he was fifty-three. His death was a great sorrow to his many friends and disciples, but most of all to the sculptor Nanni Grosso, a very eccentric person. It is told of this artist that he insisted, especially when he was working for monks, that the door to the wine cellar be left open so that he might drink without asking leave. Once, when Nanni Grosso came home from a hospital cured, his friends asked him how he felt. "Ill, very ill," said he. "Ill!" they replied, "Why, you are perfectly cured." "That is just the trouble," said Nanni, "for want of a little fever, I can no longer stay in the hospital, well attended and at my ease." When he was at the point of death, which happened at this hospital, they placed a clumsy wooden crucifix before him. He implored them to take it away and bring him one by Donatello, declaring that if they did not he would die despairing, so greatly did the sight of ill-executed works offend him.

Among the disciples of Andrea Verocchio were Pietro Perugino and Leonardo da Vinci and the Florentine Francesco di Simone, whose work was so exactly like Andrea's that it might be taken for his. More beloved than all the others was Lorenzo di Credi, who brought Verrocchio's remains from Venice to Florence and deposited them in the church of Sant' Ambrogio.

Andrea enjoyed making plaster casts of things he wanted to keep for study—life masks, hands, feet, the knee, the torso, and death masks. From this beginning the *miracoli* [figures for religious purposes], which had formerly been made of silver, were cast in wax and were very lifelike.

In addition to all that we have told, this master made Crucifixes in wood and various works in terra cotta. In the latter he was an excellent artist, as may be seen from some very beautiful figures of children and a bust of Saint Jerome. He also made the boy on the clock of the Mercato Nuovo [new market], the arm of which is free to strike the hours with a hammer. In those times this was considered a beautiful and fanciful work.

And here shall we end the life of the excellent sculptor, Andrea Verrocchio.

Editorial Notes on Verrocchio

VASARI's attitude toward Verrocchio is astonishing. Though in every instance giving him all praise for the skill and beauty of his work, Vasari knows that Verrocchio was really no good, just a hard worker. And when Andrea took up sculpture, it was only because sculpture was a good bet— a sound investment!

This preposterous notion might have been dispelled, one would think, by a glance at the David—I fancy that "where the chain formerly was" was at the head of the stairs in the courtyard of the Palazzo Vecchio—or the inexhaustibly beautiful Boy with a Dolphin or the Colleoni. This sculpture has not the vigor of Donatello, that quality of discovery which belongs to the older artist's works; but it is so alive! The forms are fine, strong, springing, and they have great style. In David's head, we see the first expression of that peculiarly Florentine type, full in form and yet drawn so fine, the type which Leonardo carried to perfection in his La Gioconda. David and Mona Lisa smile the same smile.

This David is a stripling, still. The statue of a fiery boy defying a giant seems to express the Florentine's idea of his position in the world. When Michelangelo made his David, as we shall see, the stripling became a giant too.

Vasari was too dramatic in his anecdote of the Leonardo angel in Verrocchio's Baptism. Of course Verrocchio continued to paint. The pictures that came from his shop were usually composite works, designed by the master to order and executed by his workmen. Vasari's anecdote serves to emphasize the obvious fact that the group of angels is the best part of the picture.

ANDREA MANTEGNA

Painter, of Mantua

« 1431-1506 »

THE stimulating effect produced on talent by reward is known to every man who has been well paid for his work. He who can expect honor and reward feels no inconvenience, suffers no pain, admits to no weariness. Every day brings new power to his talents. It is true that merit is not always fortunate in finding those able to appreciate it. But Mantegna was so exalted by a kind fate and his own abilities that though his beginnings were lowly (a shepherd on the hills), he became a knight. When he was almost grown, he was placed in the household of Squarcione, of Padua, who appreciated his remarkable abilities and soon adopted him as his son. But since Squarcione knew himself to be not the most distinguished painter in the world, and wished Andrea to know more than he could teach him, he set the boy to drawing from casts of antique statues. From these studies Andrea Mantegna learned much and he was stimulated also by his fellow pupils, Marco Zoppo, Dario, and Niccolò Pizzolo.

Mantegna was not more than seventeen when he painted the high altar of Santa Sofia, in Padua, a work of mature excellence. Squarcione, who was commissioned to paint a chapel in the church of the Eremite Brothers [the Eremitani] in Padua, gave the work to Niccolò Pizzolo and Andrea Mantegna. For his share Niccolò painted God the Father Enthroned between the Doctors of the Church, and this part of the work was considered as meritorious as that done by Andrea. Mantegna was left to do the rest by himself. He painted the four Evangelists, which are considered very beautiful. Great things were expected from the young artist and high hopes were raised for his future, which were in fact fulfilled. Jacopo Bellini, father of Gentile and Giovanni and rival of Squarcione, offered Andrea Mantegna the hand of his daughter in marriage. When Squarcione heard of this, he was so displeased that he became Mantegna's enemy. Instead of praising Andrea's work, Squarcione censured it bitterly and found fault even with the Eremitani frescoes, saying that they had been

155

copied from the antique and could have nothing good in them because stone must always be rigid. He added that Andrea would have done better not to have colored those figures but to have left them the white of marble, and so forth.

Andrea was deeply wounded by these disparaging remarks, but they were of great service to him. For he began to draw from life and improved his style. But he always held that the antique was more perfect than nature. He also thought that the very muscles, veins, and nerves were more clearly marked in statues than in life, where the softness of the flesh clouds the outline. It is obvious from his work that he always held to this view, for his manner recalls the idea of stone rather than that of living flesh. However, his last works in the Eremitani chapel gave the highest satisfaction. He painted Squarcione and many of his intimate friends, clothed in glittering armor, among the figures. Among the portraits was that of a certain Hungarian bishop, a man altogether witless, who rambled about Rome all day and at night slept in any stable with the beasts. This work obtained a very high reputation for its author.

In Verona, Andrea painted several altarpieces, among them a Crucifixion for San Zeno. While he stayed in Verona he painted many pictures which were sent to different places. One, a half-length figure of Our Lady with the Child in her arms, framed among heads of singing angels, was painted with infinite grace. This picture was sent to the abbot of Fiesole, Mantegna's friend and relative.

Mantegna had been employed by the Marquis Ludovico Gonzaga in Mantua. The nobleman had him paint a small picture for the chapel in the castle of Mantua. The figures in this work are not very large but are exceedingly beautiful. The foreshortening has been much extolled. And, though the draperies are somewhat hard and the work has a certain dryness of manner, the whole is done with much art and great care. For the same marquis Andrea painted the *Triumph of Caesar* in a hall of the [duke's] palace of San Sebastiano in Mantua [now in Hampton Court]. This is the best work ever executed by his hand. Here are seen in most admirable arrangement: the triumphal car, the figure who is cursing the hero, the kindred, the incense bearers, the booty, the spoils, the well-ordered phalanx, the elephants, the spoils of art, the victories, cities, and fortresses in models borne on huge cars, the trophies carried aloft on spears, an infinite variety of helmets, corselets, and arms of all kinds, with ornaments, vases, and rich vessels innumerable. Among the spectators there is a woman who holds a child by the hand. The boy has a thorn in his foot which he shows to his mother, weeping in a very natural manner.

The master displayed much forethought on the perspective of this work. The plane on which the figures stand is above eye level, so that the figures in the foreground stand on the first line of the plane and those in the back recede so that their feet and legs are lost to view in the exact proportions required. We perceive, then, that these excellent masters imitated life with studious care. As for this work of Mantegna's, it couldn't be better. If the marquis was pleased before, he now valued Mantegna more than ever.

When Pope Innocent VIII sent for him to come to Rome to adorn the Belvedere with paintings, Mantegna bore with him the favor of the marquis, who had made him a knight. Andrea was immediately given a small chapel in the Pope's palace to decorate. This he accomplished with so much care that the walls and ceiling seem to be painted in miniature rather than in fresco. We are told that the Pope, busy as he was, neglected to pay Mantegna as often as the artist could have wished. Among the figures in this work, there were several Virtues and one day the Pope inquired what a certain one might be. To this Mantegna replied, "That is Discretion." The pontiff answered, "If thou wouldst have her well accompanied, set Patience beside her." The painter understood, and never afterward uttered a word of complaint. When the work was finished, the Pope dismissed Mantegna with much favor and honorable rewards.

Mantegna painted a small Virgin and Child in a landscape of mountains with caverns where stonecutters are at work [Madonna of the Quarries]. All is so elaborately drawn and so highly finished that it is hard to believe it is done with the pencil [brush] point. This picture is now in the possession of the illustrious Signor Don Francesco de' Medici, who values it among the rarest of his treasures. There is a drawing of Judith placing the head of Holofernes in a wallet held by a Negro slave. The manner of handling the lights is no longer used. The artist left the white paper to serve for the high light. It is done with so much delicacy that hairs are distinguishable, and one might call this a painting rather than a drawing.

Andrea Mantegna found great pleasure, as Pollaiuolo also did, in engraving on copper. He engraved his Triumph of Caesar and did it better than any engraving ever done before. One of his last works was a picture for the church he designed, Santa Maria della Vittoria, which was built for the Marchese Francesco to commemorate his victory on the river Taro. The picture [Madonna della Vittorie, now in the Louvre, Paris] shows the Virgin and Child on a pedestal, and at her feet are the archangel Michael, Saint Anne, and Joachim. They are recommending the marquis, portrayed from life so admirably that he seems alive, to the protection of Our Lady who extends her hand to him. This work, which then pleased everyone (as it still continues to please all who see it), satisfied the marquis so entirely that he rewarded Andrea most liberally. Well recompensed by princes for all his works, Andrea was able to maintain his status as a cavalier honorably to the end of his days.

This master built and adorned with paintings a most beautiful house in Mantua which he enjoyed while he lived. He departed to a better life and was buried in Sant' Andrea.

Andrea Mantegna was so kindly, and in every way so estimable, that his memory must ever be held in cordial respect. The purity of his life and his gentle courtesy matched the excellence of his paintings. He well deserved the distinction of being celebrated by Ariosto, who names him among the most illustrious painters of his time: "Leonardo, Andrea Mantegna, Gian Bellino."

One of his greatest contributions was the reproduction of his works by means of engravings on copper. For, thus the whole world has been able to see his work, as, for example: the *Bacchanalia*, the *Battle of Marine Monsters*, the *Deposition*, the *Entombment*, and the *Resurrection of Christ*.

Editorial Notes on Mantegna

MANTEGNA *is comparable to Masaccio. These are the greatest painters of the early Renaissance. Like Masaccio, he remains unsurpassed. When twelve hundred years had elapsed, as they did between Greek and Roman art and the Renaissance art, the rediscovery of the mechanics of classical composition and, with it, something of the Greek attitude of mind made something entirely new.*

Mantegna's clear and strong use of form in composition greatly influenced European art. Dürer studied his engravings to advantage and was on his way to pay him homage when he was turned back by the news of Mantegna's death. In the seventeenth century, Rembrandt studied him with the keenest insight. Mantegna engraved a Madonna and Child, a noble, impersonal, monumental figure draped in statuesque folds, holding the divine infant to her breast. Rembrandt used every shape and form, built his pyramid from foot to knee, to brow, folding the robe at the same place, following the line of the Mantegna shape by shape. Then he transformed it. His Madonna sits in a carpenter's shop, croons over her heavy, human baby, hushes him to sleep in cradling arms while Joseph peeps in at the window. To see what Rembrandt used of the Mantegna is to understand the importance of form in art.

The Triumph of Caesar, which Vasari calls "the best work ever executed" by Mantegna, was bought for Charles I of England. This series of nine pictures was reserved by Cromwell for the adornment of Hampton Court Palace. How they must have suited the austerity of his mind!

Though all must agree that Mantegna's engravings are among his greatest contributions, Vasari seems to be in error when he says that he engraved his own pictures. These were reproduced by other artists. The engravings Vasari mentions are all original designs. It was these whose influence was literally world-wide.

FILIPPO (or Filippino) LIPPI
Florentine Painter

« 1457-1504 »

THERE lived at the same time as Mantegna a painter of fine genius and great powers of invention. He was Filippo [also called Filippino], son of Fra Filippo del Carmine. He followed his late father in the art of painting. He was brought up and instructed by Sandro Botticelli, though his father on his deathbed had entrusted him to Fra Diamante, who was his most intimate friend, almost his brother.

Filippino was very original. He displayed the most copious invention in his paintings, adding new ornament so richly varied and so fanciful that he ranks first among the moderns in the new method of giving variety to the dress of his figures. He dressed them in the manner of the antique. Filippino was also the first to ornament his frames with masks as the ancients did. His work displayed a more finished grace than that of any of the masters who had preceded him. It was a wonderful thing to see the wealth of fancy displayed by this artist. What is more, he never did any work whatever without using Roman antiquities, which he studied diligently. He drew helmets, banners, trophies, vases, temple ornaments, headdresses, draperies, mantles, buskins, armor, the toga, swords, and scimitars —all so varied and so beautiful that those who follow him are under perpetual obligation to Filippino for all the rich embellishment that he added to this department of art.

While still a youth this master completed the Brancacci chapel in the Carmine, which had been begun by Masolino and carried on, but not entirely finished, by Masaccio. Filippino carried it to ultimate perfection and completed the unfinished picture of Saint Peter and Saint Paul restoring the emperor's nephew to life. In the figure of the nude youth Filippino drew the features of the painter Francesco Granacci, then very young. The other portraits are of Soderini, Antonio Pollaiuolo [in the picture of St. Peter condemned to death], and others, and, finally he drew himself as the boy he then was—our only portrait of him [also in the same picture as the

portrait of Pollaiuolo]. In the next picture he painted Sandro Botticelli
with many other distinguished friends, among them the broker Raggio, a
very witty man who had carved in relief upon a shell the whole *Inferno* of
Dante with all its circles and divisions and every other minutia in exact
proportion as it had been imagined by the great poet. At that time it was
considered an admirable performance.

Filippino afterward painted a Saint Bernard for the chapel of Francesco
del Pugliese in the abbey at Campora [but now in the Badia]. The saint
is seated in a wood writing, and Our Lady appears to him surrounded by
angels. This work has been much admired for the accessories: the rocks,
trees, books, and so forth. The portrait of Francesco also in the picture is
so truly natural that it seems almost alive.

Filippino painted many successful pictures for churches in Florence and
in the neighborhood. In a tabernacle at Prato, there is a very beautiful
fresco of the Virgin in the midst of a choir of seraphim surrounded by a
bright light. Among the extraordinary things about this picture we may
remark the dragon beneath the feet of Saint Margaret, a loathsome monster,
the very abode of venom, fire, and death. The whole work merits the
highest praise for its fresh and animated coloring. Filippino also worked in
Lucca, in one of the chapels of San Ponziano which contains a very beautiful relief of that most excellent sculptor, Andrea Sansovino.

Filippino Lippi was invited to visit Hungary by King Matthias, but he
declined and instead sent two very beautiful pictures, one of the portrait of
Matthias as he appears on the medals. Filippino also sent various works to
Genoa, and to Bologna a Saint Sebastian worthy of the greatest praise. He
painted one small picture with such art and care that when he was asked
to make another like it for another client, he said he could not even attempt
to duplicate it.

Filippino then undertook an important work in Rome for Cardinal
Caraffa, a friend of Lorenzo de' Medici. On the way to Rome he passed
through Spoleto and made the arrangements for the tomb of his father Fra
Filippo, which Lorenzo determined to erect at his own expense since the
people of Spoleto refused to give up the remains of Fra Filippo Lippi for
burial in Florence. Filippino designed it, and Lorenzo caused the monument to be handsomely constructed. After his arrival in Rome Filippino
painted a chapel in the church of the Minerva with events from the life of
Saint Thomas Aquinas, poetically illustrating these with compositions
of his own naturally abundant fancy. Here, then, is Faith with Infidelity a
prisoner, Despair is vanquished by Hope, and other Virtues subjugate the
Vices which are their opposites. In one compartment is Saint Thomas in a

professor's chair defending the Church against the heretics. The draperies
of all these figures are graceful and appropriate. There is also a picture of
Saint Thomas being addressed by the Crucifix, which said to him, *Bene
scripsisti di me Thoma* [Thou hast written well of me, Thomas]. A companion who hears this stands utterly confounded. The altarpiece bears an
Annunciation, and on the principal wall is an Assumption. The whole work
was and is considered extremely fine.

After his return to Florence, Filippino undertook to paint at his leisure
the Strozzi chapel in Santa Maria Novella, but, when the ceiling was done,
he was obliged to return to Rome. Here he constructed a tomb with ornaments in stucco for the same Cardinal Caraffa, in the church of the
Minerva. Some of the figures upon the tomb were done by his disciple,
Raffaellino del Garbo. The chapel of the tomb was estimated by two of
the best painters then in Rome as being worth two thousand gold ducats,
exclusive of the cost of the ultramarine and the expenses of the master's
assistants.

When Filippino had received this sum, he returned to Florence and
completed the Strozzi chapel to the astonishment of all who behold it.
It is admired not only because of the admirable design, but also on account
of the novelty and variety of the fanciful objects in it—men in armor,
trophies, spears, banners, draperies, and so on. In the picture of the Resurrection of Drusiana by Saint John the Evangelist, the amazement of the
surrounding people is expressed with force and truth. A priest or philosopher—for he may be either—shows the very extremity of astonishment
in his face. He is dressed in the antique manner and bears a vase in his
hands. There is a small boy, too, frightened by a little red-and-white
spaniel, who hides himself in the folds of his mother's garments, as much
possessed by his fear as his mother is by her dread and horror as she
watches the resurrection of Drusiana. Near this is another painting in
which Saint John is seen boiling in oil. The expression of rage in the
countenance of the judge is very fine, and the flames are reflected in the
face of him who blows the fire. Saint Philip, in another picture, is in the
temple of Mars where he calls forth the serpent from beneath the altar.
The master here painted a cleft in one of the steps of the altar through
which the serpent crawls, and the fracture is so natural that one evening
a student of Filippino's, wishing to hide some trifling thing when he heard
someone come knocking, ran in haste to this hole, but was foiled. The
serpent is just as real. The invention in the picture of the crucifixion of
Saint Philip has been much commended. The artist has imagined that the
saint must have been fastened to the cross while it lay on the ground and

then dragged aloft by means of ropes, cords, and stakes; and the ropes looped around fragments of old buildings, pillars, basements, and the like. It could not have been better done.

At San Donato, near Florence, Filippino painted an Adoration for the Scopetine friars. It contains portraits of members of the Medici family as well as Moors and Indians in fancy dress. In a loggia at Poggio a Caiano he began a Sacrifice in fresco for Lorenzo de' Medici, but this was not finished. The painting in the hall of the palace of the Signoria where the Council of Eight hold their sessions was done by Filippino. He made the drawings for another large picture to be placed in this hall, but it was never carried out. He began a Deposition and had finished the figures from the middle up when he fell ill of angina and died in a few days.

Ever courteous, obliging, and friendly, Filippino was lamented by all, especially by the noble youth of Florence, who often availed themselves of his readiness and generosity in the creation of masks and festivals. Filippino quite effaced the stain—to whatever extent it existed—attached to him at birth by his father. He was buried by his sons, and while the funeral was passing all the shops were closed, as is usually done for princes only.

Editorial Notes on Filippino Lippi

THE *High Renaissance was not so much a period of time as an exaltation of the human spirit. Leonardo was living—was, in fact five years older than Filippino Lippi—and yet Filippino belongs to one era and Leonardo to another. Vasari, as we have seen, divides his history into three parts. It was obviously more difficult for him to decide where to put Donatello, who lived so long before the time of the creative giants of the late fifteenth and the early sixteenth century, than to place this charming artist.*

In the story of Leonardo, Vasari will tell that Filippino and Leonardo came very near together in the commissions they did. The altarpiece for the Hall of the Eight in the Palazzo Vecchio was first given to Piero Pollaiuolo to do, then to Leonardo, who made a cartoon for it; it was finally executed by Filippino. Again, in 1499, Filippino surrendered to Leonardo "with great courtesy" an order to paint a picture for the high altar of the church of the Servites, the Santissima Annunziata. If this was actually so, and Vasari states it as a fact, the contrast between Filippino and Leonardo could not be more dramatic, since the picture Leonardo did was the matchless Virgin and Child and St. Anne.

PIETRO PERUGINO

Painter

« CA. 1450-1523 »

How powerful the benevolent influence of early poverty may be, is
to be perceived in the history of Pietro Perugino. This artist fled
Perugia to earn his fortune by his abilities in Florence. There he
remained many months, with never a bed to lie on. He slept upon a chest,
or oftener turned night into day, laboring without intermission to learn
his profession. Continual toil became the rule of his life and he knew no
other pleasure and therefore painted perpetually.

Having the terror of poverty ever before his eyes, Pietro undertook
work for gain which he would not have touched if he had had other
means of support. On the other hand, wealth might have closed the path
to the eminence his talents deserved. His poverty spurred him on to a
mighty struggle against mere want. He disregarded cold, hunger, fatigue,
and privation; nor was he ashamed to undertake any sort of work. It was
his habit to say, as if it were a proverb, that after bad weather good must
come; and that in fair weather one must prepare for a rainy day.

But I must begin at the beginning and tell his story. According to a
common report, there was born in Perugia, to a poor man called Christo-
fano [Vannucci] of Castello della Pieve a son whom they named Pietro.
This child, brought up in dire poverty, was given by his father to be the
shop drudge of a not very distinguished painter of Perugia, but one who
held his calling in reverence and continually told the child to study art.
He kindled in Pietro's mind the desire to be a great master, to earn the
rewards and the honors of the successful artist. The boy often asked where
the best painters were to be found. From his instructor he always got the
same reply: Florence was the place above all others where men attain
perfection in all the arts, but especially in painting. He gave three
reasons: first, there were so many good critics there, for the air of the city
makes men quick and perceptive and impatient of mediocrity; next, to
succeed in Florence a man must work hard, be rapid and ready, and able

to earn money, since living in Florence is expensive; and the third reason is the most important of all, that the rivalry between men of talent is there most keen. In fact, the Florentines wish to surpass their rivals so whole-heartedly that they are apt to be thankless for favors, harshly critical of their competitors, and in many ways evil-minded unless they are endowed with an innate sense of justice. It is, however, true that, if a man wishes to earn more than the bare necessities by which to live from day to day as do the beasts that perish, he must market his works and his reputation else-where. For the city of Florence treats her artists as Time treats his works, which, having perfected, he destroys and little by little consumes.

Therefore Pietro went to Florence, determined to attain excellence, and he succeeded well, for in his time his type of work was held in high esteem. He studied under Andrea Verrocchio and began painting for the nuns and monks of Florence. In a few years his reputation was so great that his works were dispersed not only throughout Florence and all Italy, but also were found in France, Spain, and other countries whither they had been sold for large sums, merchants buying and selling them to their great profit.

For the nuns of Santa Chiara, Pietro painted a Pietà, the coloring of which was so beautiful that it foreshadowed the excellence he was destined to attain. In this work there are admirable heads of old men, and the Marys contemplate the departed Saviour with an expression of love and reverence that is singularly fine. The landscape is beautiful, though the true method of treating landscape had not then been discovered. It is said that Francesco del Pugliese offered the nuns three times what they had paid for the picture and also to replace it with another by Pietro's hand, but they would not sell it when Pietro told them that he did not think he could equal the one they had.

In the cloister of the Frati Gesuati, which was destroyed in the siege of Florence, only two panels by Pietro Perugino were saved, one a Pietà and the other an Agony in the Garden. Pietro here shows how wonderful a refuge is sleep from the cares and pains of life. The disciples lie in atti-tudes of perfect ease and repose. A picture of the Saviour on the Cross with the Magdalene, Saint Jerome, Saint John the Baptist, and the blessed Giovanni Colombini is executed with infinite care. These pictures have cracked badly in the darks because the color was laid on in coats before the first undercoat was dry. This was an understandable mistake at that time when painting in oil was imperfectly understood.

The prior of this cloister was skillful in the preparation of ultramarine blue and wished that Pietro should use it frequently. At the same time he was so niggardly that he did not trust Pietro with the color, but doled it out little by little, and took care to be present when the master was using it. The master took this distrust much to heart and resolved to make the prior ashamed of it. He placed a bowl of water beside him and called for blue, which the prior took grudgingly from his little bag; Perugino washed his brush after every other stroke. The prior, who found his bag empty and the picture going slowly, cried, "O, what a quantity of ultra-marine is swallowed by this plaster!" "You see for yourself how it is," replied Pietro. The prior went away. When he was gone the master gathered the blue from the bottom of the bowl and returned it to the prior, saying, "This belongs to you, Father; learn to trust honest men who would not deceive those who confide in them, though they might circumvent distrustful persons like yourself."

Pietro Perugino's reputation was now so great that he was almost compelled to go to Siena, where he did two important works. He showed himself able to manage color in fresco and in oil, and most able artists are much indebted to his skill and knowledge, especially in the painting of light.

Cardinal Caraffa commissioned him to paint an Assumption for the cathedral in Naples. For the abbot of Borgo San Sepolcro, he painted a large picture which was transported [from Florence], on the backs of porters at very heavy cost, to the church of San Gilio at Borgo. To Bologna he sent a picture of two figures standing upright, with the Virgin appearing to them in heaven.

Because of the wide fame of these works, the master was invited to Rome by Pope Sixtus IV, to his great glory, to work on the Sistine Chapel together with other eminent artists. Some of the works were destroyed during the pontificate of Paul III, when the divine Michelangelo painted the Last Judgment there. Pietro painted a ceiling in the Torre Borgia [in the Vatican] with some stories from the life of Christ, with ornaments of foliage in chiaroscuro. He did other works in Rome, all of which brought him a very large sum of money. So he returned to Perugia with the good will of all the [papal] court.

In his native city of Perugia Pietro worked with his customary diligence. Here he painted the Hall of Audience in the Exchange entirely in fresco. The ceiling he did in the old manner, with the seven planets, each drawn in a kind of chariot by different animals. On the side wall, he painted figures in his own style—classical characters balancing biblical characters, and added some sibyls. Beneath each figure is a sentence, a sort of motto, taken from the writings or sayings of the persons represented.* Here he placed his own portrait, a most animated head. This fine work is still held in great estimation by the people of Perugia.

Pietro had worked so much, under such pressure of demands for his services, that he frequently used the same object or figure in several different pictures, and his work had become so mannered that he gave all his figures the same expression. Now Michelangelo was becoming important and Pietro earnestly desired to see his works. But as he felt his own great name beginning to suffer an eclipse, he became very caustic in his criticisms. Several artists had resented Pietro's criticism, and, as for Michelangelo, he told him publicly that he was a dolt and a blockhead in art. Pietro could not endure such an affront, and the two artists appeared before the Council of Eight. Pietro withdrew, however, with very little honor.

Meanwhile the Servite monks of Florence, who had given Filippino Lippi their altarpiece to do when Leonardo da Vinci left for France, confided the work to Perugino when Filippino died and left it unfinished. Filippino had done the upper part, and Perugino continued the work by painting the Swooning of Our Lady. The altarpiece was to consist of two pictures, one turned toward the choir, and one toward the body of the church. The monks proposed to have the *Deposition* toward the choir and the *Assumption* toward the church, but Pietro executed the latter in so ordinary a manner that the monks put the *Deposition* in front. I find it related that when the artists blamed Pietro for using the same figures over and over again, Pietro replied, "I have painted in this work the figures you formerly admired—what more can I do?" This did not prevent the artists from attacking him with satirical verses, and being offensive to him in public, so that he left Florence altogether and returned to Perugia.

Pietro, who confided in no one, used to carry all his money about with him. He was waylaid one night and robbed of all he had, but at his earnest entreaty the robbers spared his life for the love of God. His friends helped him to recover a great part of the money, but he almost died of grief over this misfortune. Pietro had little religion and did not believe in immortality. He rejected all good counsel with stubborn, hardheaded folly. He trusted only in fortune and would do anything for money. He became very rich and bought, as well as built, several great houses. He married a beautiful young wife who bore him children. He is said to have arranged her headdresses himself, so great was his pleasure in her appearance. Finally he finished the course of his life and was honorably buried.

* He was required to do this in his contract.

Pietro formed many masters, of whom the most excellent was the wondrous Raphael Sanzio of Urbino, who very greatly surpassed his master.

But of his other disciples, none equalled Pietro Perugino himself in the remarkable amount of work or the grace with which it was done. His manner pleased so in his day that artists came from France, Spain, Germany, and other countries to study his methods. His work was sold as merchandise, as we have said, and was exported before Michelangelo's manner became known.

We shall soon, in the third part of this work, treat of the perfection of the arts—the good and true path made manifest by Michelangelo.

Editorial Notes on Pietro Perugino

FOR us, Perugino is important primarily as the master of Raphael. If there had been no Raphael, we might value Perugino more highly than we do. Vasari says that, in Perugino's day, "the true method of treating landscape had not been discovered." One understands Vasari's meaning. Landscape was at first a mere backdrop. There is a stratification, a cameo quality of definite planes, in Perugino's landscapes. However, the land in his pictures stretches back and back, bathed in light; the sky soars to the zenith, without a hint of paint. It is clear, lovely, melting light. (And if anyone thinks this is easy, let him take brush and do it!)

Perugino invented a formula for graceful figures. The pose is an easy swing with the head upturned. The eyes roll to carry on the line of the whole gesture. Little tendrils of hair, angels' robes, banners continue and prolong the flowing sweep. Even the trees contribute a precise grace. When these things were new, they must have been delightful. But Perugino used his formula too often, and even his own age tired of it. A too perfect formula can defeat itself, it seems.

BERNARDINO PINTURICCHIO

Painter, of Perugia

« 1454-1513 »

MANY of the undeserving are aided by fortune while numbers of able men have persistent hard luck. It seems that fortune's favorites are those who must depend on her alone, unaided by any ability, and of this we have an instance in Pinturicchio of Perugia, whose reputation was far greater than his deserts. Pinturicchio had great facility in mural painting and plenty of practice and he constantly employed many assistants. In his youth he worked under Pietro Perugino, his master, and received a third part of what Perugino earned. Then Pinturicchio was invited to Siena by Cardinal Francesco Piccolomini to paint the library erected by Pope Pius II [Aeneas Sylvius Piccolomini] in the cathedral of that city. It is indeed true that all the cartoons for the stories were drawn by Raphael of Urbino, who had been his fellow in Perugino's studio. One of these cartoons is still in Siena, and sketches for them are still preserved.

In this work of ten compartments, Pinturicchio had the help of many assistants, all of the school of Pietro Perugino. The pictures tell the story of Pope Pius II from birth to the moment of his death while he was preparing an immense sea expedition against the Turks, at which time a holy hermit of Camaldoli saw his soul being borne to heaven by angels. The whole of this work is rich in portraits from life, and beneath each story is a Latin inscription explaining the picture above. In the center of this library the cardinal nephew of Pius II placed a beautiful marble group, the *Three Graces*, one of the first antiques to be held in esteem. Before the library was quite finished, Cardinal Francesco was himself elected Pope and took the name of Pius III in memory of his uncle. Pinturicchio then painted the coronation of Pius III over the door of the library which opens into the cathedral.

While Pinturicchio was working in Rome with Perugino, during the pontificate of Sixtus [IV], he was also in the service of Domenico della Rovere, who engaged him to decorate his very fine palace in the Borgo Vecchio. Pope Innocent VIII had Pinturicchio paint some of the halls and loggias in the palace of the Belvedere. After the manner of the Flemings he painted a loggia entirely with landscapes of Rome, Milan, Florence, Venice, and Naples. This was a new thing and gave great satisfaction. In Santa Maria del Popolo he painted two chapels, one for Domenico della Rovere and one for Cardinal Innocenzio Cibò. He placed a portrait of each cardinal in his chapel. In the palace of the Popes [the Vatican], Alexander VI caused him to decorate the rooms used by the Pope as well as the whole of the Torre Borgia. Here the artist painted allegories of the Liberal Arts in one of the rooms. He adorned the ceilings with stucco work and gold, but much of it has fallen into ruin. Over the door of one of the rooms of the palace, Pinturicchio portrayed Pope Alexander adoring the Virgin, the Signora Giulia Farnese being represented as the Madonna.

Pinturicchio used to decorate his pictures with ornaments in relief, gilded to make a great show, for the delectation of the ignorant. In the apartment we have mentioned [Torre Borgia], in a story of Saint Catherine, he made the triumphal arches of Rome in relief. The perspective is all wrong—a grievous heresy in our art.

At Monte Oliveto, in Naples, there is an Assumption by Pinturicchio. In fact, he painted a large number of works in different parts of Italy, but, because they are not very distinguished, though of great facility, I pass them over in silence. This artist also worked in Perugia.

When he was fifty-nine he received a commission to paint the Birth of the Virgin for San Francesco in Siena. He desired that the monks should give him a bare room to work in. They left therein an old chest, too heavy to move, and Pinturicchio so continuously made such a clamor that they resolved in desperation to carry the chest away. In dragging it out, one of the sides was broken, and out fell five hundred ducats in gold. This discovery vexed Pinturicchio so, and he took the good fortune of these poor friars so much to heart, that he could think of nothing else. He finally died of vexation.

And this shall be the end of the life of Pinturicchio. Among other qualities he possessed the power of giving satisfaction to princes and nobles because he worked fast and delivered the pictures promptly. Such works may be, however, less excellent than those of masters who proceed more slowly and with greater deliberation.

Editorial Notes on Pinturicchio

PINTURICCHIO was the foreman of Perugino's shop. Could it be "indeed true" as Vasari says, that an experienced painter, aged about fifty, would have followed the designs of a boy of twenty for Cardinal Piccolomini's library? My notion is that the pictures are so good that it would have spoiled Vasari's whole story to have credited the design to Pinturicchio. Something like this certainly happened with the so-called "Sketchbook of Raphael." It contains a drawing for the kneeling Virgin in the Adoration that Pinturicchio painted for Donemico della Rovere in Santa Maria del Popolo, the year Raphael was born. The drawings are so beautiful that they have been ascribed to Raphael.

Pinturicchio is obviously an example of a man of great talent spoiled by too great a worldly success.

FRANCESCO FRANCIA

Goldsmith and Painter, of Bologna

« 1450-1517 »

FRANCESCO FRANCIA was born in Bologna of parents who were of the working class, but respectable people. As a youth he was destined to be a goldsmith, and his skill and ability grew as he himself increased in stature. His behavior and conversation were so gentle and obliging that he kept everyone about him in good humor. He was beloved by all who knew him, and as time went on he obtained the favor of many princes and nobles, Italian and others. While still a goldsmith Francesco applied himself to design with the greatest pleasure. He made extraordinary progress, as may be seen in his native city of Bologna from the many works he did in silver, in niello. Francesco often grouped as many as twenty well-proportioned and beautiful figures together within a rectangle measuring approximately two inches. He also did much enameled silver, but this was destroyed when the Bentivogli were ruined and exiled. In a word, he did the most beautiful work in that art, more perfect than that of any other master.

What Francia liked to do most was to cut metal dies. In this craft he was highly distinguished, and his works are most admirable as may be seen from a medal bearing the head of Pope Julius II, which will bear comparison with the work of Caradosso. His medals of Signor Giovanni Bentivoglio are speaking likenesses. A number of distinguished princes, passing through Bologna, stopped long enough for him to take their portraits in wax, which he later cast in metal. He not only became famous, but also received very handsome presents.

During most of his life Francesco Francia was director of the mint at Bologna and prepared all the dies for coins in the time of the Bentivogli and, after their rule, for Pope Julius II. We may mention, particularly, the money coined by the Pope when he entered the city. These coins bore the likeness of His Holiness on one side and the inscription *Bononia per Julium a Tyranno Liberata* on the other. Francia's work was considered so excellent that he continued to make dies for the coinage down to the time of Pope Leo [X]. His dies are so valued that they are now rare and impossible to buy.

But Francia wished for even greater glory. Having made the acquaintance of Andrea Mantegna and many other painters who had become rich and famous through their art, he resolved to try his hand at color, because he already could draw as well as many of them. He attempted a few portraits and other small things and entertained artists at his house so that they might teach him the methods and processes of coloring. Francia had remarkable intelligence and judgment and soon learned by these means. The first work he did was of no great size, commissioned by Messer Bartolommeo Felicini, who placed it in the Misericordia, a church just outside the gate of Bologna. The subject is a seated Madonna with many figures about her, among them Messer Bartolommeo drawn from life. In oils and finished in 1490, it brought Francia a commission from Bentivoglio, who wished to have his chapel in San Jacopo adorned with the works of this new painter. Here he painted a Madonna who appears in heaven with a figure on each side and two angels playing musical instruments below. Francia was much praised and well rewarded for this admirable picture. Bentivoglio ordered another picture to be placed over the high altar of the Misericordia. This is a Birth of Christ. The drawing is very fine, and the monsignore is portrayed as a pilgrim wearing the garb in which he returned from Jerusalem. For the Annunziata outside the gate of San Mammolo Francesco painted an Annunciation, and this work is thought to be very well executed.

Francia, finding that he was earning much honor and profit, decided to try fresco, too. Messer Giovanni Bentivoglio had just had his place decorated with paintings by masters from Ferrara, Bologna, and Modena, but when he saw Francia's work, he gave him his own apartments to decorate. Here the master painted the camp of Holofernes with sentinels watching the tents. While they look the other way, a woman, dressed as a widow, is seen approaching the sleeping Holofernes. She has seized his hair, heavy with the damps of sleep and the heat of wine, in her left hand, and with the right she is striking the blow that is to destroy her enemy. Beside her stands a wrinkled old handmaid whose face is a perfect model of fidelity as she watches her mistress and holds a basket in which to receive the head of the sleeping lover. This was considered one of Francia's best pictures, but it was destroyed when the Bentivogli were exiled. All these works brought Francia the esteem of all Bologna.

Francia became so facile that he executed numberless paintings of which I can only name the most celebrated. Nor did his painting interfere with his work in medals or in the affairs of the mint. The exile of the Bentivogli caused Francia much sorrow, yet like the prudent, modest man that he was, he continued to work away. He painted three pictures which were taken to Modena: a Baptism of Christ, an Annunciation, and the third, a Madonna in the heavens with many other figures, which was placed in the church belonging to the Observantines.

By such works the fame of the master became noised abroad, and various cities competed for his art. Parma, Cesena, Ferrara, and Bologna, all acquired pictures for their churches. Of the paintings scattered throughout Bologna in the houses of the citizens, I will not speak, still less of the vast number of portraits by this master, or I should become too prolix.

While Francia was living in so much glory and peacefully enjoying the fruits of his labors, Raphael was working in Rome and attracting admirers from all over Italy, among them many gentlemen from Bologna. These Bolognese told Raphael about Francia and soon so much friendship was established between these two masters that they exchanged letters. Francia desired to see Raphael's work, but he was now old and taking his ease in his beloved Bologna. It so happened that Raphael painted a Saint Cecelia in Rome to be sent to Bologna for one of the chapels of San Giovanni in Monte, where the tomb of the Blessed Elena dell' Olio is to be seen. Raphael sent it in care of Francia whom, as his friend, he asked to see that the picture be placed. This was an office which pleased Francia greatly because he was at last about to see a work of Raphael. The letter begged him to repair any scratch or blemish and to correct anything he saw that was wrong, so Francia had the picture unpacked in a good light. But such was the astonishment it caused him, and so great was his admiration, that he was struck with his own folly and with presuming to believe in his own superiority. So he fell ill and died.

The picture of Raphael was indeed divine—not painted, but absolutely alive. He had executed and finished it to such perfection that among all his works, though every one is beautiful, this may be called the most exquisite. Comparing it to his own work, Francia felt as one terrified and utterly confounded. Nevertheless he had the picture placed. But a few days afterward he took to his bed. He now thought himself almost nothing in art when compared to what he had believed himself and to what he had always been considered. Thus he died and, as many believed, from grief and vexation at having looked on the living picture of Raphael.

There are, however, many who say his death was caused by poison or apoplexy rather than anything else. Francia was a prudent man who led a regular life and had a robust constitution. At his death his sons had him honorably buried at Bologna.

Editorial Notes on Francia

THE only fault anyone could find with Francia was that he had nothing very original to say in painting. He thought it, as Vasari clearly points out, merely a sound policy to become a painter. No one would ever blame a person for taking up carpentry without having a novel attitude toward it. And painting, not so long before Francia's day, had been a craft. But times were changing. With Raphael, Leonardo, and Michelangelo in the world, it was no longer enough to turn out merely respectable work. Francia's pictures were not at all bad. They certainly did not merit Michelangelo's scorn or even Francia's own fatal dismay. There is no doubt in my mind that Francia died of the shock to his self-esteem. It would be enough to kill any man to come too suddenly upon a work of dazzling genius when he expects only a familiar and sound piece of workmanship.

VITTORE SCARPACCIA

(Carpaccio)

Painter

《 CA. 1455 BETWEEN 1523 AND 1526 》

IT IS well known that masters of our arts, wherever they are established, attract many followers. Emulation and rivalry, as well as the connection these artists may happen to have with different great masters, combine to excite their competitive zeal. Even if they derive from one master, they soon divide when different tendencies develop, and each one seeks to become pre-eminent. Of the many who flourished about the same time and in the same place, but about whom I could not discover every particular, I now propose to make mention. I would not neglect any who have labored to adorn the world by their works. But, I repeat, I have been unable to gather the entire history of their lives, or their portraits, except that of Scarpaccia, whom I have, on that account, made head of the others.

There were many painters who belonged to the school of Gentile and Giovanni Bellini, but Vittore Scarpaccia was without doubt the most important. The earliest pictures by this master were painted on canvas in the Scuola di Sant' Ursula and were of the life and death of that saint. His reputation as an able and experienced master was established by his skill in this work.

For the altar of the Resurrection of Christ in the church of Sant' Antonio this master painted the Appearance of the Saviour to Mary Magdalene and the other Marys. This picture has a landscape background that diminishes very finely in perspective. In another chapel, he painted the History of the Martyrs, with more than three hundred figures, large and small, and with many horses and numerous trees. The opening heavens, the variety of attitude of the figures, both clothed and nude, the foreshortenings and the multitude of other objects represented in this painting, prove that the master could not have executed the work without extraordinary labor.

For the altar of Our Lady in the church of Saint Job, Vittore painted the *Presentation in the Temple*. The Virgin is standing upright, and Simeon, in the cope, is between two ministering priests dressed as cardinals. Behind the Virgin are two women, one of whom holds a pair of doves. Beneath are three boys sounding musical instruments: a lute, a woodwind instrument of spiral form, and a lyre or kind of viol. The color is exceedingly pleasing and graceful.

Carpaccio was without doubt a very diligent and able master, and many of his pictures in Venice and other places, besides the numerous portraits by him, are held in high esteem.

Editorial Notes on Carpaccio

I HAVE extracted this account from a general chapter on lesser Venetian masters. It does not do Carpaccio justice—he has been called the Signorelli of Venice—but we must praise our Florentine Giorgio for noticing him at all.

LUCA SIGNORELLI
Painter, of Cortona

« 1441-1523 »

THE excellent painter, Luca Signorelli, of whom in orderly sequence we are now to speak, was in his day highly renowned throughout Italy, and his work was more valued than that of any other master of whatever time. In his painting he introduced the nude and proved that it could, though not without consummate art, be made to seem as real as life. He was the disciple of Pietro dal Borgo San Sepolcro [Piero della Francesca] and labored much in his youth to imitate and surpass his master. While working with the latter in Arezzo, he lived in the house of his uncle, Lazzaro Vasari [the author's great-grandfather]. Luca copied the manner of Pietro so exactly that it was difficult to distinguish the work of one from the other.

Luca's early works in Arezzo were processional banners which have disappeared. In Perugia, he did many works and, among others, one in the cathedral, painted at the command of Bishop Jacopo Vannucci of Cortona. It is a Virgin and Saints with a very beautiful angel tuning a lute. In San Francesco in Volterra, he painted a fresco, a Circumcision of Christ, which is considered a wonderfully beautiful picture except that the child had been repainted. Truly, it would often be better to leave the work of excellent masters, though half ruined, than suffer them to be retouched by less capable artists. In Città di Castello, in Cortona, his native city, and at Castiglione, he painted famous pictures. He worked also in Siena.

From Siena, Luca Signorelli went to Florence to see the works of the living artists as well as those of the old masters. He there painted nude figures of the gods [*Pan and the Gods*, now in Berlin] for Lorenzo de' Medici and a picture of Our Lady with two prophets. He presented both of these works to Lorenzo, who never let himself be surpassed in generosity by any man. The master also painted a round picture of Our Lady which is exceedingly beautiful. At Chiusuri, in one of the houses of the monks of Monte Oliveto, Luca painted one side of the cloister with events from the life of Saint Benedict. From Cortona he sent certain works to Monte-pulciano, others to Foiano, and others elsewhere in the Valdichiana.

In the Madonna of Orvieto, which is the principal church of that city, Luca Signorelli finished the chapel begun by Fra Angelico. There he painted the Last Judgment, a most singular and fanciful invention. Angels, demons, earthquakes, ruins, fires, and miracles of antichrist are in this work, with nude forms in foreshortening and many beautiful figures. Here the artist has imagined all that shall add to the terror of that last, tremendous day. This work was a source of enlightenment to all who came after him. Nor am I surprised that the works of Signorelli were ever praised by Michelangelo or that for the divine Last Judgment in the Sistine Chapel Michelangelo should have courteously availed himself to a certain extent of the inventions of Signorelli, by making use of angels and demons and the division of the heavens, as everyone may see for himself.

It is related of Luca Signorelli that his son, a youth of singular beauty in face and person whom he had tenderly loved, was killed in Cortona. In his deep grief the father had the child undressed, and with extraordinary constancy of soul, uttering no complaint and shedding no tear, painted the portrait of his dead child so that he might still be able to contemplate that which nature had given and fate taken away.

Signorelli was invited by Pope Sixtus IV to work in the Sistine Chapel in competition with many other masters, and there he painted two pictures which are considered, even among so many, as the best of all.

Finally, having worked for almost all the princes of Italy and having grown old, Luca returned to Cortona. There he worked for his pleasure since he could not resign himself to a life of idleness. In his old age, then, he painted a picture for the nuns of Santa Margherita in Arezzo and one for the Brotherhood of San Girolamo. The latter was partly paid for by Niccolò Gamurrini, doctor of laws, who appears in the picture kneeling before the Madonna, to whom he is recommended by Saint Nicholas. There are also figures of Saint Donatus, Saint Stephen, and Saint Jerome, undraped, beneath. David sings to a psaltery while two prophets seem, by the scrolls they hold in their hands, to be discussing the conception of the Virgin. This work was transported from Cortona to Arezzo by members of the brotherhood, who bore it on their shoulders. Luca, also, old as he was, determined to go to Arezzo to see the picture in its place and also to visit his friends and relations.

During his stay in Arezzo, Luca Signorelli lived at the Casa Vasari, where I was then a little child eight years old. I remember that the good old man, who was most courteous and agreeable, when he heard that I paid attention to nothing in school but drawing figures, turned to my father, and said, "Antonio, let Giorgino by all means learn to draw, for even though he should afterward devote himself to learning, yet the knowledge of design, if not profitable, cannot fail to be honorable and advantageous." Then he turned to me, standing immediately before him, and said, "Study well, little kinsman." He said many other things about me which I refrain from repeating because I know I have not lived up to the expectations of the good old man. When he heard that I suffered from severe nosebleed, he bound a jasper round my neck with his own hand and with infinite tenderness. This recollection of Luca I shall cherish while I live. After he had seen his picture placed, Luca returned to Cortona, escorted by many citizens as well as by his family and friends. This honor he well merited, for he always lived in the manner of a gentleman rather than in that of a painter.

About this time Silvio Passerini, Cardinal of Cortona, wished to adorn his new palace with a picture from the hand of Luca. Although he was very old and afflicted with palsy, Luca painted the *Baptism of Christ* in fresco on the chapel wall. But he could not entirely finish it, because while he was still working on this picture, he died, in the eighty-second year of his age.

Luca Signorelli was a man of the most upright life, sincere in all things, affectionate, mild, and amiable in his dealings with all, and most especially courteous to everyone who desired his works. He was a very kind, efficient instructor to his disciples. He lived very splendidly, dressed handsomely, and was always held in the highest esteem for his many good qualities both at home and abroad.

And now, with the close of this master's life, we bring the second part of our work to an end. We terminate this part of the book with Luca, who, in the fundamental principles of design, his treatment of the nude, and his composition, laid open to succeeding artists that path to the ultimate perfection of art which those who followed him—and of whom we are about to speak—were able to attain.

Editorial Notes on *Signorelli*

THE survival of a work of art might be called accidental, if by that word we mean the action of forces not implicit in the work itself. Signorelli, the austere, kindly, and magnanimous artist, saw many of his works effaced in his own time. He was great enough to be called to decorate important buildings. And he was followed immediately by men much greater than he. His work had not time to become traditional, so quickly did progress tread upon his heels. Orvieto was a backwater, and there we see Signorelli's power. Sir Charles Holmes, in his notes on the Italian Schools, says, "Indeed, in his hands the complete achievement of the Renaissance is time after time foreshadowed."

PART III

VASARI'S
Introduction to Part III

GREAT strides toward perfection in the arts of painting, sculpture, and architecture were made by the excellent masters whose work we have described in the second part of these Lives. Rule, order, proportion, design, and manner were added by them to the characteristics of the art of the first period, if not to perfection, yet with so near an approach to the truth, that the masters of the third period have been enabled by their light to reach the very summit.

To make this more clearly understood, it may not be out of place for me to define these five distinctive properties of art and to declare the origin of that truly good manner which surpassed the older period and has rendered the modern era so glorious. Rule in architecture is the exact study of the measurements of antique buildings. Order refers to classification of all art and to the orders of architecture: Doric, Ionic, and Corinthian. Proportion is the relationship of the members within the form and applies to sculpture and painting as well as to architecture. Design means the imitation of the most beautiful parts of nature, and this requires that the hand and mind of the artist be capable of reproducing them exactly upon the flat surface of the picture or bas-relief. Manner requires a more minute selection and combination of parts—beautiful legs added to perfect torso in order to invest one figure with every beauty in highest perfection.

These things neither Giotto nor the other early masters accomplished, though they made great strides in their approach to nature, harmony in color, and good composition. The masters of the second period improved in all the characteristics mentioned above, but they lacked a certain freedom within the rules which may exist without disturbing the order. This freedom demands a rich variety of invention, a sure perception of beauty, even in the smallest details. In proportion they still lacked that rectitude of judgment which could be right without measurements and which lends a surpassing grace to all works. In drawing, the summit had not been reached, for though the arm was made round and the leg straight, still, where the muscles were displayed, they were somewhat crudely overemphasized, producing a displeasing effect and giving a hardness to the manner. This was particularly true of their representation of women and children, which ought always to be done as naturally as possible without ever bordering on coarseness, as sometimes happens in life. All should be ennobled and refined by the artist's judgment. Variety in drapery was lacking, too. The charm of color, the diversity of buildings, and the space and depth of landscape in which, though a beginning had been made, for example, by Andrea Verrocchio and Antonio Pollaiuolo, perfection had not yet been attained. The restored Marsyas of Verrocchio, offer us a comparison between this second period and the antique. There is a certain delicacy of finish wanting in the parts Verrocchio did.

The perfection and bloom of art is a power, a boldness, a lightness, beauty, and grace. This we do not find in the second period, though we see diligent endeavor. Nor can this ultimate perfection be reached by studious effort. It was the sight of the antique, of the Laocoön, the Hercules, the mighty torso of the Belvedere, the Venus, the Cleopatra, the Apollo, that made success possible. Softness and power are visible; freedom from distortion, flexibility, and ease of nature are everywhere exhibited. These statues caused the banishment of the hard, dry sharpness of manner of Piero della Francesca, Andrea del Castagno, Giovanni Bellini, Ghirlandaio, Botticelli, Mantegna, Filippo Lippi, and Luca Signorelli.

These masters of the second period labored continually to produce the impossible in art, especially in foreshortening and in the rendering of ugly things, which are as difficult to do as they are unattractive. Francia of Bologna and Pietro Perugino began a new treatment. People rushed like madmen to see their works, so lifelike in their beauty. They believed that it would be impossible for future artists to do better. But then came Leonardo, who, besides the power and boldness of his drawing and the exactitude with which he copied the most minute particulars of nature exactly as they are, displays perfect rule, improved order, correct proportion, just design, and a most divine grace. Abounding in resource, and deeply versed in art, Leonardo may be said to have imparted to his figures not beauty only, but life and movement.

LEONARDO DA VINCI

Florentine Painter and Sculptor

« 1452-1519 »

THE most heavenly gifts seem to be showered on certain human beings. Sometimes supernaturally, marvelously, they all congregate in one individual. Beauty, grace, and talent are combined in such bounty that in whatever that man undertakes, he outdistances all other men and proves himself to be specially endowed by the hand of God. He owes his pre-eminence not to human teaching or human power. This was seen and acknowledged by all men in the case of Leonardo da Vinci, who had, besides the beauty of his person (which was such that it has never been sufficiently extolled), an indescribable grace in every effortless act and deed. His talent was so rare that he mastered any subject to which he turned his attention. Extraordinary strength and remarkable facility were here combined. He had a mind of regal boldness and magnanimous daring. His gifts were such that his celebrity was world-wide, not only in his own day, but even more after his death, and so will continue until the end of time.

Truly admirable, indeed, and divinely endowed was Leonardo da Vinci, the son of Ser Piero da Vinci. He might have been a scientist if he had not been so versatile. But the instability of his character caused him to take up and abandon many things. In arithmetic, for example, he made such rapid progress during the short time he studied it that he often confounded his teacher by his questions. He also began the study of music and resolved to learn to play the lute, and as he was by nature of exalted imagination, and full of the most graceful vivacity, he sang and accompanied himself most divinely, improvising at once both verses and music.

Though he divided his attention among pursuits so varied, Leonardo never abandoned his drawing, and also continued to model in relief, occupations which attracted him more than any others. His father, Ser Piero, observing this and taking into account the extraordinary character of his son's genius, took some of Leonardo's drawings to Andrea del Verrocchio, his intimate friend. He begged Andrea to tell him whether the boy showed promise. Verrocchio was amazed at these early efforts of Leonardo's and advised Ser Piero to see to it that his son become a painter. Leonardo was therefore sent to study in the shop of Andrea, whither he went most willingly. He studied not one branch of art only, but all. Admirably intelligent, and an excellent geometrician besides, Leonardo not only worked in sculpture—certain terra-cotta heads of smiling women and others of children done in early boyhood seem to be the work of a master—but, as an architect, designed ground plans and entire buildings; and, as an engineer, was the one who first suggested making a canal from Florence to Pisa by altering the river Arno. Leonardo also designed mills and water-driven machines. But, as he had resolved to make painting his profession, he spent most of his time drawing from life. He sometimes modeled clay figures on which he draped soft cloth dipped in plaster, and from these he made careful drawings on fine linen. He drew on paper also with so much care and so perfectly that no one has equaled him. Leonardo, imbued with power and grace, was endowed with so marvelous a facility, and his mind, his memory, and his hand were so efficient in the service of his intellect, that he confounded every antagonist.

Leonardo was frequently occupied in the preparation of plans to remove mountains or to pierce them with tunnels from plain to plain. By means of levers, cranes, and screws, he showed how to lift or move great weights. Designing dredging machines and inventing the means of drawing water from the greatest depths were among the speculations from which he never rested. Many drawings of these projects exist which are cherished by those who practice our arts. Besides all this, he wasted not a little time designing curiously intertwined cords made into a circle. A very curiously complicated and exceedingly difficult specimen of these coils may be seen engraved about the words *Leonardus Vinci Academia*. Among Leonardo's models and drawings is one by means of which he sought to prove to the ruling citizens of Florence, many of them men of great discernment, that the church of San Giovanni could be raised and mounted upon a flight of steps without injury to the building. He was so persuasive that it seemed feasible while he spoke, although every one of his hearers, when he was gone, could see for himself that such a thing was impossible. Indeed, he was so pleasing in conversation that he won all hearts.

Though his patrimony was a mere pittance, and though he worked very little, Leonardo kept many servants and horses, taking extraordinary delight in the latter. He was fond of all animals, and it is told that he used to buy caged birds only to set them free. Leonardo, in mind and spirit, gave evidence of such admirable power and perfection that whatever he did bore an impress of harmony, truthfulness, goodness, sweetness, and grace, beyond all other men.

Leonardo, with his profound comprehension of art, began many things that he never completed, because it seemed to him that perfection must elude him. He frequently formed in his imagination enterprises so difficult and so subtle that they could not be entirely realized and worthily executed by human hands. His conceptions were varied to infinity. In natural philosophy, among other things, he examined plants and observed the stars— the movements of the planets, the variations of the moon, and the course of the sun.

While he was in Andrea Verrocchio's shop, that master was engaged on a picture of Saint John Baptizing Jesus Christ. Leonardo painted an angel holding some vestments, and, although he was then but a youth, the angel was the best part of the picture. This caused Verrocchio never to touch color again, so much was he chagrined to be outdone by a mere child.

Leonardo was commissioned to prepare a cartoon for a tapestry which was to be woven in silk and gold in Flanders for the king of Portugal. The subject was the Fall of Adam. Here the artist drew a meadow in chiaroscuro, with an immense variety of vegetation and many animals. For careful workmanship and fidelity to nature, no genius in the world, however godlike, could match it. In the fig tree, for example, the leaves are foreshortened and the branches drawn with inconceivable patience. There is a palm in which the roundness of the fanlike leaves is done to perfection. Nothing short of the genius and patience of Leonardo could have done it. But the work for which the cartoon was made was never carried out, and the drawing remained in Florence and is now in the fortunate house of the illustrious Ottaviano de' Medici, to whom it was presented not long since by Leonardo's uncle.

There is a story that a peasant on Ser Piero's country place brought a homemade shield, a piece of a fig tree he had cut down, and asked that Ser Piero have it painted for him in Florence. As the countryman was a very able huntsman and a great favorite with his master, the latter willingly promised to have it done. He took the wood, therefore, to Leonardo, not telling him for whom it was, and asked only that he paint something on it. Leonardo took the shield in hand, but since he found it crooked, coarse, and badly made, he straightened it before the fire and sent it to a turner, who returned it smooth and delicately rounded. Leonardo covered it with gypsum [gesso] and prepared it to his liking. He then considered what to put on it and thought of the head of Medusa and the terror it struck in the hearts of those who beheld it. He, therefore, assembled in a room that no one entered but himself a number of lizards, hedgehogs, newts, serpents, dragonflies, locusts, bats, glowworms, and every sort of strange animal he could lay his hands on. He fashioned a fearsome monster, hideous and appalling, breathing poison and flames and surrounded by fire issuing from a rift in a rock. He labored on while the room filled with a mortal stench, of which Leonardo was quite unaware in his interest in his work. When it was done, long after both his father and the countryman had stopped inquiring for it, Leonardo went to his father and told him he might send for the shield when he liked. Ser Piero went himself to fetch it. When he knocked, Leonardo asked him to wait a little. He darkened the room and placed the shield where a dim light would strike it, and then asked his father in. Ser Piero drew back, startled, and turned to rush out, but Leonardo stopped him, saying, "The shield will serve its purpose." The work seemed more than wonderful to Ser Piero, so he bought another shield, which was decorated with a heart transfixed with an arrow, and this he gave to the peasant who cherished it all his life. Leonardo's shield he secretly sold to a merchant for a hundred ducats. It subsequently fell into the hands of the duke of Milan, who paid three hundred ducats for it.

Leonardo next did a very excellent Madonna which afterward belonged to Pope Clement VII. Among other things, it contained a bowl of water holding dewy flowers, as real as reality. For his good friend, Antonio Segni, he drew a Neptune on paper, who seems alive. The sea is rough, and the chariot is drawn by sea horses. There are sprites, monsters, the heads of the winds and other fine sea creatures. The drawing was given by Antonio's son Fabio to Giovanni Gaddi with an epigram: "Virgil and Homer both described Neptune driving his sea horses through the rushing waves. The poets imagined, but Vinci saw him, and so vanquished the poets."

Leonardo had the fancy to paint the head of a Medusa in oil paint, with hair of twining serpents, a most strange and extravagant idea. But it was never finished. This head is in the collection of Duke Cosimo where there is also a half-length angel, with one arm raised, foreshortened from shoulder to elbow, and with the other arm laid on the breast. This great genius desired to give the deepest form to his works and sought constantly to find a black darker than any known black to serve as contrast to the lights and to render them even more brilliant. He finally produced that totally dark shade in which there is no light left so that the objects have the appearance of things seen by night rather than by daylight. All this was

done to give greater relief to the forms in his work, and to attain the ultimate perfection of art.

Leonardo used to follow people whose extraordinary appearance took his
fancy, sometimes throughout a whole day, until he could draw them as
well by memory as though they stood before him. Of heads thus drawn
there exist many. Among them is the head of Amerigo Vespucci, a very
beautiful old man, done in charcoal. Another was of the gypsy Scaramuc-
cia. A picture of the Adoration was begun by Leonardo and is among the
best of his works. This also remained unfinished.

When Ludovico Sforza became duke of Milan in 1493, he invited
Leonardo most ceremoniously to come and play the lute before him.
Leonardo took an instrument he had himself constructed of silver in the
shape of a horse's head, a form calculated to render the tone louder and
more sonorous. Leonardo was one of the best *improvisatori* in verse of his
time. He surpassed all the musicians who had assembled to perform and so
charmed the duke by his varied gifts that the nobleman delighted beyond
measure in his society. The duke prevailed on him to paint a Nativity for
an altarpiece to be sent as a present to the Emperor [Maximilian I]. For
the Dominican monks of Santa Maria delle Grazie at Milan, Leonardo
painted the *Last Supper*. This is a most beautiful and admirable work.
The master gave so much beauty and majesty to the heads of the Apostles
that he was constrained to leave the Christ unfinished, convinced as he
was that he could not render the divinity of the Redeemer. Even so, this
work has always been held in the highest estimation by the Milanese and
by foreigners as well. Leonardo rendered to perfection the doubts and
anxieties of the Apostles, their desire to know by whom their Master is to
be betrayed. All their faces show their love, terror, anger, grief, or bewilder-
ment, unable as they are to fathom the meaning of the Lord. The spectator
is also struck by the determination, hatred, and treachery of Judas. The
whole is executed with the most minute exactitude. The texture of the
tablecloth seems actually made of linen.

The story goes that the prior was in a great hurry to see the picture
done. He could not understand why Leonardo should sometimes remain
before his work half a day together, absorbed in thought. He would have
him work away, as he compelled the laborers to do who were digging in
his garden, and never put the pencil down. Not content with seeking
to hurry Leonardo, the prior even complained to the duke, and tormented
him so much that at length, he sent for Leonardo and courteously en-
treated him to finish the work. Leonardo, knowing the duke to be an
intelligent man, explained himself as he had never bothered to do to the

prior. He made it clear that men of genius are sometimes producing most when they seem least to labor, for their minds are then occupied in the shaping of those conceptions to which they afterward give form. He told the duke that two heads were yet to be done: that of the Saviour, the likeness of which he could not hope to find on earth and had not yet been able to create in his imagination in perfection of celestial grace; and the other, of Judas. He said he wanted to find features fit to render the appearance of a man so depraved as to betray his benefactor, his Lord, and the Creator of the world. He said he would still search but as a last resort he could always use the head of that troublesome and impertinent prior. This made the duke laugh with all his heart. The prior was utterly confounded and went away to speed the digging in his garden. Leonardo was left in peace.

The head of Judas, as we see it finished, is indeed the image of treachery and wickedness. The nobility of this painting, in composition and in high finish, made the king of France [Francis I] wish to remove it to his own kingdom. He attempted to find architects to frame it in wood that it might be transported without injury. He was not deterred by any consideration of cost, but as the painting was on the wall, he had to forgo his desire, and the Milanese kept their picture.

While engaged on the *Last Supper*, Leonardo painted Duke Ludovico with his eldest son, Maximilian, in the left foreground of an old painting of the Crucifixion in this same refectory and, on the other side, Duchess Beatrice with Francesco, their second son.

Leonardo proposed to the duke to make a colossal equestrian statue of the duke's father [Galeazzo Maria Sforza]. This he began on so large a scale that there were many who said that Leonardo had no intention of finishing it. Such is the malice of envy. Insuperable difficulties presented themselves when the question of casting came up. Obviously it could not be done in one piece, and this lent color to the malicious gossip. But the truth seems to be that it was the greatness of his exalted mind always striving after more than could be accomplished. It was the desire to heap excellence on perfection that was the hindrance, so that "desire outran performance," as Petrarch says. Those who saw the large model in clay declared that they had never seen anything more beautiful or majestic. This model was destroyed by the French under King Louis [XII] when they came to Milan. A small model of the statue was also lost, together with Leonardo's studies of the anatomy of the horse which he made for his own use.

Leonardo afterward gave his attention to human anatomy, in company with Messer Marcantonio della Torre, an eminent philosopher. Messer Marcantonio was then lecturing in Pavia and writing on anatomy, a subject which had, until that time, been lost in the darkness of ignorance. Leonardo filled Marcantonio's book with drawings in red crayon outlined with the pen. These were drawn with the utmost care from bodies dissected by his own hand. He set forth the structure, arrangement, and disposition of the bones. Later he added the nerves in their due order, and then the muscles. He wrote an explanation, left-handed and backward, that can be read only with a mirror. A great many of these drawings are in the possession of Messer Francesco Melzi, who, in the time of Leonardo, was a beautiful child, much beloved by him, and is now a handsome and amiable old man, who treasures these drawings as relics, together with the portrait of Leonardo of blessed memory. It seems almost incredible that this sublime genius could discourse, as he had done, of art, and of the muscles, nerves, veins, and every other part of the frame. There are besides, other writings of Leonardo's, also written with the left hand. They treat of painting and design in general and his theory of color. The manuscript is in the possession of an artist of Milan who came to see me in Florence lately and said he intended to publish the work. He took it with him to Rome, and what was the end of the matter I do not know.

But to return to Leonardo. During his time the king of France [Charles VIII] came to Milan, and Leonardo was asked to prepare something extraordinary for his reception. He constructed a lion which advanced a few steps, then opened its breast which was entirely filled full of lilies. In Milan, Leonardo took Salai for his disciple. This youth, of singular grace and beauty, had curled and waving hair, a feature of personal beauty by which Leonardo was always greatly pleased. He taught Salai to paint, and certain works in Milan are said to be by Salai, though retouched by Leonardo.

When he returned to Florence, Leonardo found that the Servites had commissioned Filippino to paint their altarpiece, which Leonardo was still anxious to do. Filippino heard this and, like the amiable man he was, withdrew, and the monks gave the task to Leonardo. To help him on with it, they lodged him and all his household. He kept them attending on him a long while. At last he made a cartoon with the Madonna, Saint Anne, and the infant Christ so admirably depicted that not only were artists astonished, but the chamber where it stood was crowded with men and women for two days, all hastening to behold the wonders produced by Leonardo. And with reason, for in the face of the Virgin is all the simplicity and loveliness which can be conceived as giving grace to the Mother of Christ as she contemplates the beauty of her Son whom she holds on her lap. Saint Anne, at the summit of delight, looks upon the group with a smile of happiness, rejoicing to see her earthly progeny become divine. Leonardo then painted the portrait of Ginevra, the wife of Amerigo Benci, a most beautiful thing, and abandoned the commission entrusted to him by the Servite monks. They once more confided it to Filippino who died before he could complete it.

For Francesco del Giocondo, Leonardo undertook to paint the portrait of Mona Lisa, his wife [La Gioconda], but, after loitering over it for four years, he left it unfinished. It is now in the possession of Francis, king of France. Whoever desires to see how far art can imitate nature, may do so by observing this head wherein every subtlety and every peculiarity have been faithfully reproduced. The eyes are bright and moist, and around them are those pale, red, and slightly livid circles seen in life, while the lashes and eyebrows are represented with the closest exactitude with the separate hairs drawn as they issue from the skin, every turn being followed and all the pores exhibited in the most natural manner. The nose with its beautiful and delicately red nostrils might easily be believed to be alive. The mouth, admirable in outline, is rose tinted in harmony with the carnation of the cheeks, which seems not painted, but of flesh and blood. He who looks earnestly at the pit of the throat must fancy he sees the beating of the pulse. It is a marvel of art. Mona Lisa was very beautiful, and while he painted her, Leonardo had someone near at hand to sing or play to her, or to amuse her with jests, to keep from her that look of melancholy so common in portraits. This picture, on the contrary, has so pleasing an expression and a smile so sweet that one must think it rather divine than human. It has ever been esteemed a wonderful work.

All men who delighted in the arts, in fact, all the people of Florence, were anxious to have some great public work by Leonardo, that the commonwealth might have the glory and the city the ornament imparted by his genius, grace, and judgment. It was decreed that Leonardo should paint something for the newly completed Hall of the Grand Council. He began a cartoon of an episode in the story of Niccolò Piccinino, in which he depicted a group of horsemen fighting around a standard, a masterly composition. It is an odd thing to see that not only do the men show rage, disdain, and the desire for revenge, but the horses, too, are attacking each other with their teeth, and fight no less fiercely than the knights. One of the combatants has seized the standard with both hands and strives to tear it with main force from the hands of four others. An old soldier in a red cap has also seized the standard with one hand and is raising his scimitar in the other, uttering cries of rage as he deals a blow to sever the hands of two of his opponents. Under the feet of the horses two men, hurled to the ground, are engaged in a death struggle. One brings his dagger down with all his might to the throat of his enemy. It is scarcely possible to do justice to the skill of this drawing, the beauty of the details of the helmets, crests, and other ornaments or to the wonderful mastery which the artist shows in the forms and movements or the horses. Their muscular development, the animation of their action, and their exquisite beauty are rendered with the utmost fidelity.

They say that Leonardo had a scaffolding made for his use for working on this cartoon, which could be made higher by drawing it together, or lowered by making it wider. It was his intention to paint the picture in oil on the wall, but he made his ground so coarse that the paint began to sink in very soon after he put it on, and so he abandoned the whole project.

Leonardo da Vinci was a man of very high spirit, generous in all his actions. It is told of him that when he went to the bank to collect his salary, which Piero Soderini, the gonfaloniere of justice, ordered to be paid to him every month, the cashier was about to pay him in small coins. Leonardo refused them, saying, "I am no penny painter." When he did not finish the picture, he was reproached for deceiving Piero Soderini. Leonardo persuaded his friends to make up the sum he had received and took the money to Soderini, but he would not accept it.

When Leo X became pope, Leonardo went to Rome with Duke Giuliano de' Medici. The pontiff was interested in philosophical inquiry and especially in alchemy. Leonardo made some fanciful figures of animals out of a wax paste, hollow and very light, which floated in the air when they were inflated, but fell to the ground as the air escaped. A gardener of the Belvedere one day brought in a curious lizard for which Leonardo made wings from the skins of other lizards. In these wings he put quicksilver, so that, when the animal walked, the wings moved with a tremulous motion. He then made eyes, horns, and a beard for the creature, which he tamed and kept in a cage. He showed it to his visitors, and all who saw it ran away terrified. More than once, he had the intestines of a sheep cleaned and scraped until they were so fine that they could be held in the hollow of the hand. Then he fastened one end to a pair of bellows in another room and blew them up so that they filled the whole room, which was a very large one. Anyone who was there had to take refuge in a corner. He made numbers of these follies and occupied himself with mirrors and optical instruments. He also made experiments in oils and varnishes for painting. Leonardo received a commission for a picture from Pope Leo and immediately began to distill oils and herbs for the varnish, whereupon the pontiff remarked, "Alas! this man will do nothing at all, since he is thinking of the end before he has made a beginning."

There was constant discord between Michelangelo Buonarroti and Leonardo. Michelangelo even left Florence because of it, and Duke Giuliano excused him by saying that the pope had summoned him to Rome. When Leonardo heard of this, he departed for France to the court of the king [Francis I] who already owned several of his works and wished him to paint the cartoon of Saint Anne. Leonardo kept him waiting, according to his custom, a long time. Finally, being old, he lay sick for many months. When he found himself near death he made every effort to acquaint himself with the doctrine of the Catholic ritual. Then he confessed himself with great penitence and devoutly received the sacrament, sustained, because he could not stand, by his servants and friends. The King, who used to visit him often, came immediately afterward to his room. Leonardo was lamenting to him his fear that he had offended God and man, since he had not labored in art as he should have done, when he was seized with a violent paroxysm, the forerunner of death. The king rose and supported his head to assist him, in the hope of alleviating his pain, and Leonardo departed this life in the arms of the monarch.

The death of Leonardo caused great sorrow to all who had known him. Nor was there ever an artist who did more to honor the art of painting. The radiance of his countenance, which was splendidly beautiful, brought cheer to the most melancholy. He was most persuasive and could make a man say "yes" or "no" as he desired. He was physically so strong that he could bend a horseshoe as if it were lead. His generous liberality offered hospitality to rich or poor, provided only that his guest was distinguished by talent or excellence. The poorest or most insignificant abode was adorned by his presence, and as the city of Florence was blessed by his birth, it suffered grievously by his death. To the art of painting he contributed a mode of deepening the shadows which the moderns have used to give force and relief to their figures. His ability in sculpture is proved by three figures in bronze over the north door of San Giovanni. These were cast by Giovan Francesco Rustici, but under the direction of Leonardo, and are, without doubt, most beautiful in design and finish. We are indebted to Leonardo for a work on the anatomy of the horse and for a still more valuable one on human anatomy. For his many admirable qualities, with which he was so richly endowed, although he talked of more things than he actually accomplished, his fame can never be extinguished. Messer

Giovan Battista Strozzi wrote this in his praise:—"He alone vanquished all others: he surpassed Phidias, surpassed Apelles and all their proud followers."

Editorial Notes on Leonardo

LEONARDO, the complete man of the Renaissance, paces forth, as far removed from medieval man as imagination can conceive. Think of the rigid mold of medieval society, with its infinite stratification of cast. There was no escape from a man's inherited social position except into that other mold of the Church. Then consider Leonardo, the illegitimate son of a village squire, and follow him as he moved freely about the world. He went at will from Florence to Milan, to Rome, to France, unhampered by loyalties.

And in the realm of the intellect, Leonardo's mind was seemingly open to everything. Varied as his studies were, they were carried in every instance as far as though each one were his sole interest. Vasari has described his anatomical studies. But in Leonardo's observations on the movements of the planets, he wrote, "The sun does not move." Vasari was a man of the world, and born fifty years or more after Leonardo, and yet he still writes blandly, "in all the years the sun has been going round." It staggers the imagination to think of the intellectual power possessed by the men who were pioneers of our concept of the solar system.

In painting, the problem of giving the surface of the canvas the illusion of form is enough to baffle an artist for a long lifetime. Leonardo did something that revolutionized the treatment of form in pictures. Instead of treating his picture as if it were a bas-relief, more or less freely modeled in depth, he conceived the object as bathed in space. He modeled the edges of his masses to give the quality of the air around the corner. The Italians called this procedure lo sfumato.

In the epigrams about Leonardo, there is an untranslatable play upon the word Vinci. Vinci: vanquished. Those elaborate knots, endless scrolls of elaborate design, also, according to Ludwig Goldscheider (Leonardo da Vinci, Phaidon Press, London, 1941), are another kind of pun, a knot being also a vinci.

Leonardo wrote a celebrated letter to Ludovico Sforza, in which, after recommending himself as an inventor and military engineer, he says: "I can execute sculpture in marble, bronze, or clay, and also I can do in painting whatever any man can do, be he who he may."

GIORGIONE OF CASTELFRANCO

Venetian Painter

« CA. 1478-1510 »

WHILE Florence was gaining so much fame from the works of Leonardo, Venice obtained no small glory from the excellent talents of one of her citizens who surpassed the Bellini and all others who had practiced painting up to that time. This was Giorgio of Castelfranco, afterward called Giorgione, as much from the character of his person as the exaltation of his mind. He was of lowly birth but had a very pleasing manner and an estimable character. Brought up in Venice, he was an amorous gallant, fond of the music of the lute to the accompaniment of which he sang to perfection. He was often invited to musical assemblies and festivals by the most distinguished personages. He chose painting as his profession and was so favored by nature that he devoted his life to the rendering of her beauties, and not only excelled Gentile and Giovanni Bellini, but was able to compete with the originators of the modern manner who were working in Tuscany.

Giorgione selected for his pictures the most beautiful objects that he could find. He painted, whether in oils or fresco, with a high degree of life, softness, and harmony. He was particularly successful in the shadows, in which he was influenced by the work of Leonardo. The most eminent artists declared that he was born to bring new spirit to painting and to copy the freshness of the living form more exactly than any other painter in Venice or anywhere else.

In his youth, in Venice, Giorgione painted many very beautiful pictures of the Virgin, with numerous portraits from life. These are dispersed throughout various parts of Italy. One, a likeness of Doge Leonardo Loredano, I saw when it was displayed on Ascension Day, and I almost believed I was seeing that illustrious prince himself. Another of these fine works is at Faenza. The colors are blended with such perfect harmony that it seems rather to be a relief than a painting.

Giorgione enjoyed fresco painting, and one of his frescoes covers the entire façade of the Soranzo Palace. Here also is an oil painting done right on the plaster, which has weathered remarkably well. Also there is a picture of Spring that seems to me to be Giorgione's best work in fresco, but it is a lamentable fact that it has been cruelly injured by time. For my part I believe that nothing injures frescoes as much as the south winds, which bear a most noxious saline humidity.

In the year 1504 there was a terrible fire in the Fondaco de' Tedeschi [German Exchange], near the Rialto Bridge. It was burned to the ground. The Signoria of Venice commanded that it should be rebuilt. This work was begun at once and accomplished in due time with great magnificence. Giorgione was commissioned to paint the building in fresco to please himself, provided only that he produce a work of adequate excellence for one of the finest sites in the whole city. He set to work immediately, but thought only of executing fanciful figures which would show his ability. There is in this work, indeed, no arrangement of events or even single episodes of Venetian history. I, for one, have never known what his pictures mean, and no one has ever been able to explain them to me. Here is a man, there a woman; one has the head of a lion beside him; near another is an angel that looks rather like a cupid—it is impossible to tell what it all means. On the whole, nevertheless, it is apparent that the work is well composed, well designed, and colored with great animation. This work is highly extolled in Venice.

It is related that Giorgione was in conversation with certain sculptors when Andrea Verrocchio was working on his bronze horse [part of the Colleoni statue]. They claimed that sculpture was better than painting because you could walk around it and see all sides. Giorgione said that painting was better because you did not have to walk around it—you could see it all at a glance. To prove his point, he painted a nude figure with its back toward the spectator. At the feet of the figure a limpid stream reflected the front, while a mirror on one side and a burnished corselet on the other reflected the profiles. By this beautiful fancy, Giorgione wished to prove that painting is the superior art, requiring more talent and greater effort.

Giorgione painted the portrait of Caterina, queen of Cyprus, which I saw in the possession of the illustrious Giovanni Cornaro. In my book of drawings there is a head in oil, a portrait of a member of the Fugger family, one of the German merchants trading in Venice. This head is wonderfully beautiful.

While he was laboring to his own honor and that of his country, Giorgione was much in society and delighted his many friends with his admirable performances in music. At this time he fell in love with a lady, who returned his affection with equal warmth. They were immeasurably devoted to each other. But the lady fell ill of the plague. Giorgione, unaware of this, continued his visits and was also infected. He died in a very short time. This shocking event grieved the many friends to whom he was endeared by his excellent qualities. It was also greatly to the loss of the world, which was thus prematurely deprived of his talents. Amid these regrets, there was, however, the consolation of knowing that Giorgione had left behind him two worthy disciples in Sebastiano del Piombo and Titian of Cadore, who not only equaled but surpassed him greatly.

Editorial Notes on Giorgione

GIORGIONE and Titian. Where does one leave off and the other begin? In the constantly shifting appraisal of works of art by connoisseurs, pictures have been attributed first to one and then to the other.

There are other instances of pairs of painters, the first short-lived and brilliant, the second more slowly paced and long-enduring, whose work seems the expression of a single impulse. While he lived, Giorgione enjoyed a more splendid reputation than Titian did in his lifetime. Nobles cherished Giorgione's paintings as treasures. And besides his followers, Titian and Sebastiano, he had a host of imitators. As time went on, the near-Giorgiones tended to be labeled Giorgiones. Modern authorities are still disputing the merits and the attribution of many enchanting little pictures.

The reason that there are few unquestioned pictures by Giorgione is that much of his work was in fresco on the walls of Venetian palaces, at the mercy of the damp sea wind. How sad that we cannot see and enjoy, without understanding the allegory, the frescoes on the Fondaco de' Tedeschi, "here a man and there a woman."

ANTONIO DA CORREGGIO

Painter

« 1489-1534 »

I AM NOT willing to take leave of the land wherein our great Mother Nature, in her impartiality, presented to the world extraordinary men, comparable to those with whom she had for so many years adorned Tuscany. Of the masters of this vicinity, then, was Antonio da Correggio, an excellent painter in the new manner. In a few years and by means of diligent study, he became a most remarkable and excellent artist. Timid and overanxious, he subjected himself to severe and continuous labor for the support of his family. While he bore this oppressive burden, he afflicted himself further by resisting even the temptations common to all mankind. Antonio's melancholy shows in his work, which he carried out with zealous study of all its difficulties. Of his success we have proof in the vast multitude of figures executed in the cathedral of Parma. These paintings in fresco are in the cupola of the church, and the foreshortening is managed with the most extraordinary ability.

Correggio was the first modern painter of Lombardy, and it is thought that, if he had gone to Rome, he would have performed wonders and would have been a dangerous rival to many who, in his day, were called great artists. The quality of his work, as it is, is such that it could only have been even better had he seen the masterpieces of the antique and the best works of the modern masters. In any case, we may say that no artist has used color more effectually than he, nor has any painted in a more charming manner, or given more form to his figures. He used exquisite softness of color and finished his works with the most attractive grace. In the cathedral of Parma, he also painted two large pictures in oils which have been highly praised. In the church of San Giovanni, in the same city, he painted a tribune in fresco, a picture of Our Lady ascending to heaven among a multitude of saints. It seems almost impossible that a man could have conceived such a work as this is, and more impossible still, that he should have done it with human hands. It is extraordinary in its beauty, so graceful is the flow of the draperies, so exquisite the expression on the faces.

Some of the sketches for this work are in my book of drawings, done in red chalk. He has drawn a kind of border of figures of beautiful children and other ornaments, some of them being fanciful representations of sacrifices in the manner of the antique. Indeed, if Antonio had not finished his work as admirably as he did, his drawings, though they show the practiced hand of a master, would scarcely justify his reputation. Art is so difficult and has so many ramifications that an artist often finds himself unable to master them all. Some draw well, but can not paint in color; others work wonderfully with color but can not draw with equal success. All this depends on youthful training. Before perfection can be reached, the ability to color perfectly what is first well drawn must be acquired. To Correggio belongs the great praise of having reached the highest point of coloring, whether in oil or in fresco.

For the church of San Francesco in Parma Correggio painted an Annunciation in fresco, a work of extraordinary beauty. When, later on, it was necessary to demolish the wall, the friars framed the picture in woodwork secured with irons, and cut it away little by little, in such a way that they saved their picture and afterward built it into a more secure place in another part of the convent.

Over one of the gates of the city of Parma, Correggio painted a Virgin and Child. This picture, of astonishing beauty and exquisite coloring, has brought the master infinite praise from those strangers and travelers who have seen no other of his works than this fresco. In Sant' Antonio, a church of the same city, our artist painted a Virgin with Saint Mary Magdalene. Near them is a little boy angel with a book in his hand, who is smiling so naturally that all who look at him smile, too. No one, no matter how sad, can behold him without a sensation of pleasure. There is also a Saint Jerome, so admirably painted that artists praise it as a wonder, saying that it would be impossible to paint better.

Antonio painted a number of pictures for many Lombardy nobles. Two of them were for Federigo II [duke of Mantua]. He sent them to the emperor [Charles V] as gifts worthy of such a prince. Giuliano Romano saw them and said he had never seen such perfection of coloring. One was a nude Leda, the other a Venus, both painted with such softness, and with shadows treated so admirably, that they seemed to be of living flesh. The landscape was beautiful, and indeed no other Lombard could equal Correggio in this respect. An added charm in the picture of Venus was a limpid stream which bathed the feet of the goddess, but scarcely concealed their dazzling whiteness. For these works Antonio deserved all praise and honor in his lifetime and the utmost glory after his death.

There is a Virgin by Correggio in Modena, which is said to be the best picture in that city. In Bologna, likewise, there is a very beautiful thing, a Christ Appearing to Mary Magdalene. Another delightful work was formerly at Reggio, but recently Messer Luciano Pallavicini, a great admirer of fine paintings, happened to see it and bought it regardless of cost, as one buys a precious jewel, and sent it to his house in Genoa. In Reggio there is another picture by this master, a Nativity. The light from the divine child throws its splendor on the shepherds and on all the figures contemplating the divine infant. A woman who longs to look upon the Saviour has to shade her eyes from His radiance. Over the cabin wherein the divine child is lying hovers a choir of angels that seems to have been showered down from heaven rather than painted by the hand of a mortal.

A small picture, not more than a foot high, an Agony in the Garden, is one of the most extraordinary of Correggio's works. The angel who appears to the Saviour illumines him in the splendor of his rays. On a plain at the foot of the mountains are the three Apostles asleep. The shadow of the eminence on which the Saviour prays falls upon these figures and imparts to them a force impossible to describe in words. The day is just breaking in the distance, and Judas approaches from one side with soldiers. Tiny though it is, this work is so admirably conceived and so finely executed that no work can bear comparison with it, whether in beauty and depth of thought, or in the patience with which it has been done.

Much more might be said of the works of this artist, but, since everything he has done is cherished as something divine by the most eminent masters of our calling, I will not expatiate further. Correggio held himself in very slight esteem, for he perceived the difficulties of his art and could not credit himself with approaching the perfection he sought. He was a man who was content with little, and he always lived like a good Christian.

He became very penurious. They say he was paid sixty copper scudi in Parma. Since he wished to meet some particular demand in Correggio, he loaded himself with the money and set out for home on foot in the blazing sun. He drank water to refresh himself. When he reached home, a raging fever compelled him to take to his bed, and he never raised his head again, but departed to another life.

Correggio handled his colors like a true master. More than one fine genius among his countrymen has followed in his steps, and some have produced commendable works. The Lombards were induced by his example to open their eyes.

Editorial Notes on Correggio

WHAT did Vasari mean by saying, "Antonio's melancholy shows in his work"? If Correggio's pictures show strain or sadness, we may no longer believe our eyes. This is the painter of ecstatic joy. Here is a man who is drenched in rapture. Titian said, of the dome of the cathedral of Parma, that if you turned it upside down and filled it with gold, you would not equal the value of Correggio's fresco.

PIERO DI COSIMO

Florentine Painter

« 1462-1521 »

WHILE Giorgione and Correggio were earning honors for Lombardy to their own great praise and glory, Tuscany also had her men of genius. Not the least important was Piero, the son of a certain Lorenzo, a goldsmith. He was the godson of Cosimo Rosselli, after whom he was always called—Piero di Cosimo. And it is only right that his teacher, to whom he owed the better part of his being, should be honored as much as his natural father from whom he simply derived his existence. Piero's father, recognizing his inclination toward the arts, entrusted his son to Cosimo Rosselli, who accepted the charge more than willingly and bore a fatherly affection to the boy.

Piero was naturally high-minded and was an odd and thoughtful person. He often became so self-absorbed that, if a conversation was going on, as often happens, it was necessary to go back to the beginning and tell it all over for him. He loved solitude and knew no greater pleasure than building castles in the air, alone and uninterrupted. His master, Cosimo, found his confidence in Piero's powers quite justified and used him often as his assistant. In fact, he often trusted Piero with works of the utmost importance, for he knew that this disciple had a better manner than he himself had. This was why he took Piero to Rome when he was summoned by Pope Sixtus [IV] to do the historical pictures in his [Sistine] chapel.

Piero painted extremely well from life and was much employed in Rome executing portraits of distinguished persons, among whom were Virginio Orsino and Ruberto Sanseverino. He painted the duke of Valentinois [Cesare Borgia], son of Pope Alexander VI. In Florence this master did many portraits now in private houses. I have seen many that are very good. He undertook commissions of various kinds. One is a Visitation, in which Our Lady is accompanied by Saint Nicholas and by Saint Anthony, who is reading with his spectacles on his nose, a figure of great animation. In the same work our artist painted a book, bound in parchment, which really looks old and much handled. It is more like a real book than a painting. Some balls, the attribute of Saint Nicholas, shine and reflect the light one upon another; they show the pleasure the artist took in tackling difficult problems.

After Cosimo's death Piero's peculiarities became more pronounced. He kept himself shut up, would not permit anyone to see him at work, and lived the life of a wild beast rather than of a man. He never allowed his room to be swept and ate only when he was hungry; nor would he have his garden weeded or his fruit trees pruned, but let the vines grow wild. He preferred to let everything run wild and said that it was better to leave all to nature. He sometimes searched for oddities among animals and plants, such as nature produces by chance or from caprice. He took indescribable pleasure in these things, and, quite carried away by his own interest, he would describe them until even interested listeners grew bored. From stains of filth thrown against a wall, he would conjure strange scenes, combats of horses, curious cities, and the most extraordinary landscapes. He also did this with cloud shapes.

Piero devoted much time to oil painting. He imitated some highly finished and harmonious work by Leonardo Da Vinci. Piero was far from approaching Leonardo and was, in fact, entirely unlike him. His manner was most original, extravagant, and peculiar; and he often changed it and adopted a new one for every work that he did. Had he been less eccentric, had he been more restrained during his long life, he might have developed the genius he certainly had. As it was, by his extravagance he made himself a laughingstock. In the end he harmed no one but himself, while his works have been valuable to art. Yet men may learn from his example that life should not be spent without purpose and direction.

In his youth Piero di Cosimo was very imaginative and in Carnival time was often called upon by the young nobles with whom he was a favorite, to help design masquerades to which he imparted great pomp and variety. Piero is said to have been the first to give these maskings the character of a triumphal procession. Not only did he compose words and music for the events chosen as the subject of the show, but he caused the procession to be accompanied by large trains of men and horses in vast numbers. The effect was exceedingly rich and beautiful and most ingenious in detail. There was a grandeur to the whole which was certainly imposing. To see at night, by the light of innumerable torches, twenty-five or thirty pairs of horses, richly caparisoned, with their riders splendidly arrayed, was, without doubt, to behold an attractive and beautiful spectacle. Six or eight attendants in livery accompanied every cavalier, and each carried a torch; sometimes there were four hundred of these. Next followed the triumphal chariot, elaborately decorated with trophies and fanciful ornaments. These spectacles served to sharpen the wits of their contrivers and gave infinite pleasure and delight to the people.

Among all these ingenious spectacles, I am inclined to describe one which was, for the most part, invented by Piero when he reached maturity. This was not a pleasing or attractive show; on the contrary, it was altogether strange, terrifying, and unexpected. It gave no small pleasure to the people, nevertheless. For, just as they sometimes prefer sharp and bitter food, so in their pastimes, they are attracted to horrible things, provided the presentation is artful. With a similar pleasure do we listen to tragedy. The spectacle was called the Triumph of Death. The chariot was prepared in the hall of the Pope by Piero himself, and with such secrecy that not a whisper got abroad. The completed work was disclosed and presented at one and the same moment. The triumphal car was draped in black cloth, with skeletons and crosses painted on it. It was drawn by coal-black buffaloes. Within the car stood a colossal figure of Death, scythe in hand, while around him were covered tombs which opened when the procession halted. The figures in the procession chanted lugubrious songs, while there stole forth figures clothed in black, with white bones painted to represent ribs, arms, and legs, which gleamed horribly on the black beneath. At a distance appeared figures bearing torches and wearing death's-head masks. At the sound of a wailing summons, moaned through trumpets, the figures of the dead raised themselves half out of their tombs and seated their skeleton forms thereon while they sang the words: "*Dolor, pianto, e penetenzia.* . . ." [Woe, lamentation, and penitence. . . .]

Before and after this chariot rode a train of the dead on the most miserable horses that could be found, all draped in black covered with white crosses. Each was led by four shrouded attendants who bore black torches and a large black standard, and sang in trembling voices and in dismal unison the psalm of David called the *Miserere*.

The novelty and the terrifying character of this singular spectacle filled the whole city with awe and admiration. Although at first sight one would not have thought it appropriate for a Carnival, yet, because it was novel and within the grasp of every man's comprehension, it brought high praise to Piero, and set a fashion for this sort of display in Florence where such pageants were produced as were never equaled by any other city. The old people who saw it still have the most lively recollection of the scene and are never weary of extolling it. I remember having heard Andrea di Cosimo, who assisted Piero in preparing it, and Andrea del Sarto, who was

Piero's disciple and took part in it, say that the spectacle was meant to signify the return of the exiled Medici, who were, so to speak, dead, but might be expected to rise again. Or, it may have been that this significance was attributed to it because that illustrious house did soon return from exile. The human intellect is prone to apply words previously spoken to succeeding events.

But we will now return to the art of Piero. He received a commission to paint a picture for the chapel of the Tebaldi family in the church of the Servites, who there preserve the vestments and a pillow used by Saint Philip [Benizi], who was a brother of their order. The subject of this work is Our Lady, who stands on a slight elevation and holds a book in her hand. She looks toward heaven where the Holy Spirit is seen. No other light appears in the picture except that which comes from the dove, which shines upon the Virgin and the company of saints surrounding her. Piero added a fanciful landscape of strange trees, caves, and grottoes. There are many beautiful parts in this picture, and the color has great merit. Piero certainly understood the method of painting in oil. In the predella of this work there is a Santa Margherita escaping from the stomach of the dragon, a monster of fantastic deformity with venom darting from its eyes. Fire and death are in its aspect. I do not believe any master could produce more extraordinary effects than Piero di Cosimo. He presented a picture of a marine monster to the illustrious Giuliano de' Medici. The deformity of this animal is so extravagant that I do not believe anything so hideous and repulsive could be found in nature. Duke Cosimo has this picture, and also a book filled with animals of different kinds, some singular, some beautiful, but all carefully done with the pen.

For Filippo Strozzi the elder, Piero di Cosimo painted a picture, with small figures, of Perseus delivering Andromeda. This is one of the best and most agreeable pictures ever executed by him. A more fanciful sea monster could not easily be conceived, and Perseus lifts his sword with a menacing gesture as he prepares to destroy the beast. Andromeda is seen bound and trembling between hope and fear, and her countenance, which exquisitely expresses these emotions, is very beautiful. In the foreground are numerous figures, oddly dressed, and singing to the music of strange instruments. Some of the heads are divinely beautiful. The landscape is very fine and the colors are blended in perfect harmony. The whole work, in short, is done with exceeding care.

This master painted a picture of Mars and Venus, both nude, with troops of Loves hovering around them and carrying off the helmet and armor of Mars. A grove of myrtles forms part of the landscape, and here is

Leonardo: Madonna of the Rocks (canvas, 6 ft. 5¾ in. x 4 ft. ½ in.),
Louvre, Paris.

Leonardo: Study for a Madonna's Head (drawing), Louvre, Paris.

Giorgione: Concert Champêtre (canvas, 43¼ x 54¼ in.), Louvre, Paris.

Correggio: Madonna of the Day (wood, 7 ft. 4½ in. x 4 ft. 7½ in.),
Picture Gallery, Parma.

Piero di Cosimo: Death of Procris (tempera on wood, 25½ x 72 in.), National Gallery, London.

Bramante: Tempietto, cloister of S. Pietro in Montorio, Rome.

Raphael: Fire in the Borgo (fresco), Vatican, Rome.

Raphael: Baldassare Castiglione (canvas, 32¼ x 26⅜ in.), Louvre, Paris.

Andrea del Sarto: Self-portrait (wood, 40½ x 29½ in.), Pitti, Florence.

Titian: Pope Paul III and His Nephews (canvas, 6 ft. 10½ in. x 5 ft. 8½ in.),
National Museum, Naples.

Michelangelo: Holy Family (marble, about 4 ft. in diameter),
Uffizi, Florence.

Michelangelo: Moses (marble, 8 ft. 4½ in.),
San Pietro in Vincoli, Rome.

a cupid alarmed at the sight of a rabbit. Venus' doves are also depicted, with other emblems of love. This picture is at Florence in the house of Giorgio Vasari, who cherishes it in memory of Piero di Cosimo, in whose singular caprices he has always taken much pleasure.

The superintendent of the Foundling Hospital, a great friend of Piero's, gave him the commission for a picture for the chapel of the Pugliese family, near the entrance of the church. Piero completed it at his leisure. But, long before it was done, he had driven the superintendent nearly mad, for he would not let him see the work until the whole was finished. His refusal seemed all the more extraordinary to the superintendent, not only because they were friends, but because he was constantly paying money to Piero di Cosimo on account. At length he declared, in his vexation, that he would pay no more until he had seen the work. Piero threatened to destroy the whole picture, and the superintendent was compelled to give him the remainder of the sum due him, and also—though more displeased than ever—to wait for the work to be completed. And a worthy work it is.

For Giovanni Vespucci this master painted bacchanalian scenes in one of the rooms of his house with fauns, satyrs, and sylvan deities of various kinds, and children and bacchantes and the grace and truth of the deer, goats, and other animals are all wonderful to behold. In one of the stories, Silenus is mounted on his ass, surrounded by a group of children who support him and give him to drink. A spirit of mirth and gladness is seen throughout this company.

Piero studied nature with a zeal that made him oblivious of time or labor. No effort was too severe; he endured any hardship willingly for the mere love of study. Piero was indeed so earnestly devoted to his vocation that he forgot himself and his convenience. He allowed himself, for instance, no other food but hard-boiled eggs, and these he cooked only when he had a fire to boil his glues and varnishes. Nor did he cook them six or eight at a time, but by fifties. He kept them in a basket and ate them when he felt hungry. This mode of existence suited him perfectly; any other seemed to him the merest slavery.

He was much disturbed by the cries of children, the sound of bells, the singing of monks, and even the coughing of men. When the rain was coming down in torrents, he loved to see the water pouring off the roofs, but lightning frightened him. When it thundered, he wrapped his head in a blanket and crouched in a corner until the storm had passed. Piero di Cosimo was most amusing to talk to and said such original things that his listeners were ready to die of laughing. But, when he grew old, he became so capricious that no one could bear him. Not even his pupils would he suffer to be with him, so that he was without aid in his helplessness. Sometimes, when he wanted to work and could not because of his palsy, he would fall into fits of rage. The maulstick would drop from his grasp, or the pencils themselves would fall from his fingers, in a way that was pitiful to behold. The flies on the wall sometimes made him angry. Even shadows were an offense to him.

The few friends who still visited him urged him to make his peace with God, but he put them off from day to day; not that he was an unbeliever (for he was a zealous Christian), but he did not know he was near his death. He sometimes discoursed largely of the torment of death by lingering disease. He would then abuse doctors, apothecaries, and nurses, who, he said, starved their patients to death. Next he would expatiate on the wretchedness of having to take sirups or potions of any kind and would talk of the cruelty of being awakened to take medicine when a man preferred to sleep. He spoke of the torment of making a will, of seeing wailing relatives about, of being shut up in a dark room. Of death by the hand of justice, on the contrary, he would speak in glowing terms. It must be so fine a thing to be led forth, to see the clear, bright open air and all the mass of people, to be comforted with sugar plums and kind words, to have priest and people praying for one and to enter paradise with the angels. He thought the man who died suddenly most fortunate. Thus he would discourse, forsaking common sense.

Living thus, Piero brought himself to such a pass that he was found, one morning, dead at the foot of a staircase. This happened in the year 1521. He was buried in San Piero Maggiore.

The disciples of this master were very numerous and among them was Andrea del Sarto, a host in himself.

Editorial Notes on Piero di Cosimo

VASARI thought Piero was much older than he was. Piero was born in 1462 instead of 1441 as Vasari wrote.

There is a constant element in almost every artist's style, which is recognizable from first to last in his career. This quality is the specific gravity, as it were, of the objects within the picture. Compare a Masaccio with a Ghirlandaio to appreciate the greater weight of the Masaccio and to recognize that neither of these artists would have been capable of painting like the other. Piero di Cosimo's pictures vary widely even in this respect. This clever, unstable man painted few pictures alike.

The glue Piero was making, when he boiled his eggs, was for gesso. This thin mixture of plaster of Paris and glue was applied to the surface of both wooden panels and canvas as a preparation for the paint. Each artist, or his assistants in his studio, made their own materials. Colors were ground in a mortar and mixed with white of egg for tempera or with oil for oil paint, as they were needed. It was still another eccentricity of Piero's that he would have no apprentice to do this menial task.

BRAMANTE

Architect, of Urbino

« 1444-1514 »

THOUGH it was Filippo Brunelleschi who revived the antique style in architecture, Bramante in our own age preserved what Brunelleschi did, adapting it to the uses of modern life. A greater genius than Bramante could not be imagined. He possessed determination, power, and profound knowledge that at once was theoretical and practical. Devoted to the principles of his art, and firm in his respect for proportion, he also invented a profusion of rich decoration. Under Julius II, a prince of daring ideas and one most bent to leave great monuments behind him for future ages, all Bramante's skill and power came into play. Both the artist and the people were most fortunate in this. Rarely does an artist find a patron at whose expense he may display all his resources and develop to the full the power with which he is endowed. The extraordinary merit of this architect is obvious, not only in the design of whole buildings but also in the details of cornices, shafts of columns, graceful capitals and bases, the finish of angles, vaultings, staircases, buttresses, ressaults, and other supports. Every architectural work he designed is a surprise and a delight. It seems to me that we should be as grateful to Bramante as we are to the ancients; for, if the Greeks invented what the Romans copied, Bramante not merely imitated—he also embellished.

Bramante was born at Castello Durante, in the duchy of Urbino, of well-born but poor parents. He learned to read and write and delighted in the study of arithmetic. But it was necessary that he should earn his living, so his father urged him to take up painting. He studied zealously, but soon found that it was architecture that interested him most. He went to Lombardy and traveled from city to city, in each of which he obtained work as best he could. That he might improve himself he went to Milan to examine the Duomo. He was so inspired by what he saw that he resolved to devote himself entirely to architecture. He went to Rome, where he arrived at the beginning of the Holy Year of 1500. Introduced by some friends, fellow countrymen who lived in Rome, he received the commission to paint the armorial bearings of Pope Alexander VI in fresco over the holy door of Saint John Lateran, which door is opened only on the occasion of the Jubilee. He added several angels and other figures as supporters of the escutcheon.

Bramante had brought some money with him, and he earned more by the execution of certain works in Rome; and these funds he spent as frugally as possible, because he wished to study the ancient buildings and to make accurate measurements of them entirely at his leisure. With the greatest possible concentration he set to work, quite alone. Before long he had examined and measured, not only structures in the city of Rome, but those in the Campagna, too. He even went as far as Naples and searched out and visited all the places where ancient edifices were to be found. At Tivoli he studiously measured Hadrian's Villa. His studies brought him to the notice of the cardinal of Naples [Oliviero Caraffa]. While Bramante was continuing his studies, the cardinal thought of rebuilding a cloister of the monks of the Pace and committed the work to Bramante. Ambitious to advance himself and to please the cardinal, Bramante set to work with the greatest zeal and brought this work quickly to a most successful conclusion. It is true that the building is not particularly beautiful, but it brought fame to the architect because there were few masters then in Rome who devoted themselves to architecture with such zealous study and prompt execution.

Bramante served as under architect to Pope Alexander VI when that pontiff was constructing the fountain in the Trastevere and another which he built in the Piazza of Saint Peter's. Bramante's reputation increased. He was invited, among other eminent architects, to take part in the consultation about the palazzo di San Giorgio and the church of San Lorenzo in Damaso, which the cardinal of San Giorgio, Rafaello Riario, was going to build in the Campo di Fiore. Although better works may have been done since, this palace, if only for its size, has always been considered, and still continues to be thought, a splendid and commodious habitation. He was consulted about the enlargement of San Jacopo degli Spagnuoli, and the building of Santa Maria dell' Anima. He also designed a palace for Cardinal Adriano da Corneto. The enlargement of the principal chapel in Santa Maria Maggiore was done from Bramante's designs. He began to be considered the best architect in Rome. The most distinguished personages of the city now employed him in all their important undertakings, so that when Julius II came to the pontifical chair, Bramante was at once engaged in his service.

A project had been formed in the mind of that pontiff for covering the space between the papal palace and the Belvedere, thus enclosing a small valley. The intention of Julius was to build corridors on each side of the valley, so that he could go from the palace to the Belvedere under a loggia and return without exposure to the weather. The ascent was to be effected by a flight of steps.

Bramante, with great good judgment and most ingenious fancy, divided the lower part into two ranges, one over the other, the lower being a loggia in the Doric order. It resembled the Colosseum of the Savelli [the Theater of Marcellus] except for the substitution of pilasters for the half-columns and the fact that it was all built of travertine. Over this was a second range, in the Ionic order, on the first-floor level of the palace but reaching only to the ground-floor level of the Belvedere. It formed a loggia of more than four hundred paces facing toward Rome, with another of equal length facing toward the forest. Between them was the valley, which was to have a magnificent fountain at its lowest point.

Such was the plan. Bramante constructed the first corridor and laid the foundation of the second, but the death of Julius II interrupted the work. All applauded the plan and said that nothing better had been seen in Rome since the time of the ancients.

Bramante also built the cupola to cover the Hall of Antiquities and the range of niches for the statues: the Laocoön, the Apollo, and the Venus.

When not hindered by the niggardliness of his patrons, Bramante was a wonderfully prompt builder. He hurried the building of the Belvedere with a zeal to match the eagerness of the Pope, who would have had it done when thought of rather than await the slow process of erection. The earth was dug for the foundations in daylight and was carted away by night, and without further precautions the foundations were laid. The result of this haste is that it has cracked and is in danger of ruin.

There are many beautiful staircases in the Belvedere, rich and varied. Bramante's model for the building is said to be of the most imposing beauty. Among other features, there is a winding stair, between columns, the idea for which was borrowed from San Niccolò, in Pisa, as we have mentioned in the account of the lives of Giovanni and Niccolò Pisano.

The master proposed to make a fanciful inscription in which he intended to use pictorial symbols, after the manner of hieroglyphics: Julio II Pont. Maximo. A profile of Julius Caesar was to be followed by a bridge of two arches, for Julio II Pont.; then an obelisk of the Circus Maximus to signify Max. But the Pope laughed at this fancy and made him change it to letters, two feet high, as we now see it. The Pope declared that Bramante had borrowed that absurdity from a gate in Viterbo where Maestro Francesco, the architect, had carved a St. Francis with an arch (*arco*), a roof (*tetto*) and a tower (*torre*) to mean *architettore*.

Pope Julius valued Bramante highly, and gave him the office of clerk of the signet. While he held this appointment, Bramante constructed a building for the business of the office and made a press for the printing of the papal bulls.

This master prepared many designs for buildings, of fine proportions and consummate art. Bramante taught Raphael the rules of architecture and drew for him the buildings which Raphael afterward painted in perspective in the hall of the papal palace. Raphael placed Bramante in one of the pictures, with a compass in his hand, drawing.

Pope Julius, among his other undertakings, determined to unite all the public offices in certain buildings along the Via Giulia which Bramante had thrown open and straightened. It would have been most convenient. Bramante began with the construction of the Palazzo di San Biagio, on the Tiber, but the plan was never completed. It is a great pity that so honorable, useful, and magnificent an edifice should have failed of completion.

In the first cloister of San Pietro in Montorio, Bramante built a round temple [the *Tempietto*] of travertine, most graceful and beautiful in arrangement, proportion, and variety. If the whole cloister had been completed, it would have been much more noble than it now is. In the Borgo, he designed the palace that Raphael built of brick and cast stucco. Bramante's design and arrangement of the decorations for Santa Maria at Loreto were carried out by Andrea Sansovino.

This admirable artist was most enterprising. He proposed to restore and even to rearrange the Pope's palace. Hearing His Holiness speak of demolishing Saint Peter's to build it anew, Bramante made innumerable plans. Among these there was one that astonished everyone by its magnificence and beauty. It is indeed peerless in art and perfect judgment. Two towers flank the front of the building, as we see it on the medals struck by Caradosso. The Pope determined to undertake that stupendous building and had half of the old building torn down. He resolved that in art, invention, arrangement, and beauty, as well as size, magnificence, and splendor of decoration, Saint Peter's should surpass the buildings of republican Rome. With his usual promptitude, Bramante laid the foundations and before the death of the Pope he had raised the height to the cornice over the arches of the four piers. He completed the vaulting of this part and also finished the vaulting of the principal chapel and of another chapel called that of the king of France. For this chapel he invented the method of constructing vaulted ceilings by means of a strong framework of beams in which the decorations were carved and afterward covered with castings in stucco. The cornice is most elegant and graceful. The capitals, formed of olive leaves, and all the external work, which is in the Doric order, show the boldness of Bramante's genius. We have clear proof that, had he had means to match his conceptions, Bramante would have performed work never before imagined.

But, after his death, the work was altered by each succeeding architect, and except for the piers that support the cupola, we may say that nothing of Bramante's original plan remains. Raphael began to make alterations as soon as he was appointed architect, along with Giuliano da Sangallo, after Julius II died. At last, Michelangelo, having set aside all the varying plans, has given the building a high degree of beauty. Michelangelo often remarked to me that he was carrying out the design and arrangements of Bramante and that Bramante should have sole credit. The original plan was of almost inconceivable vastness. If he had begun this stupendous edifice on a smaller scale, neither Sangallo nor the other masters, not even Michelangelo himself, would have been able to make it more imposing, though they proved themselves abundantly able to diminish the work.

We find it asserted that Bramante, in his haste to see the building arising, permitted the destruction of many admirable works of art in the old Saint Peter's. Tombs of popes and paintings and mosaics were lost, as were the portraits of many great personages which were scattered about in this, the principal church of all Christendom. The altar of Saint Peter's and the ancient choir were all that Bramante retained, and these he enclosed within a rich balustrade of the Doric order. The enclosure is large enough to hold the Pope and all his court when he goes to perform high mass.

Bramante was a most cheerful and amiable man. He was the friend of all men of talent, and helped them to the utmost of his power. An instance of this is his conduct toward the graceful Raphael. Bramante lived in splendid style and delighted in poetry and music. He enjoyed hearing and practicing improvisations on the lyre. He would occasionally compose a sonnet, perhaps not so polished as might be, yet always earnest and entirely free from errors of style. He was a favorite with prelates and nobles. He enjoyed great renown during his life and even more after his death. Bramante lived to the age of seventy and when he died he was borne to the grave with most honorable ceremonies, attended by the papal court, as well as by all the sculptors, architects, and painters at that time in Rome. He was buried in Saint Peter's in the year 1514.

Editorial Notes on Bramante

"WHY did the ancients give a round shape to coins except that they should roll more easily? . . . I have banished from myself as far as possible all melancholy, and I have tried to feed my soul on gaiety and pleasure. Did not God give to man what you call free will? Man then is free to live freely."

(Bramante is talking to Saint Peter at the gate of heaven in this pamphlet, Simia, by Andrea da Salerno, which imagines a meeting between Saint Peter and the destroyer of his sanctuary.)

Here is the true Renaissance expressed in buildings for power, pleasure, and religion! Tear down the old Saint Peter's! Make way for a building "più bello e più magnifico." Disturb the tombs of Gregory the Great, Leo the Great, and so many other heroes of the faith, even the very tomb of Saint Peter! The whole preoccupation of Julius II and his architect Bramante—they seem to have been made for each other—was to make something stupendous, new, something that would challenge even the grandeur of imperial Rome.

Vasari says ". . . resolved to devote himself entirely to architecture. He went to Rome. . . ." Between these two sentences we must imagine an interval of eighteen years. Bramante worked in the court of Lodovico il Moro as engineer, architect, and sometimes painter. The architecture of Lombardy has Scandinavian elements. There we find buildings that have broken profiles with fanciful projections, airy domes, and airy galleries, and ornaments of terra cotta and stucco on a construction of brick. The lack of marble and stone was a large factor in the development of the Lombard style. When brick and stucco are the materials, there is a temptation to trifle with technical difficulties, even with the fundamental rules of architecture.

With this freedom for a background, Bramante plunged into the study of the classic. This revolution in his art took place when he was fifty-six years old and had an established reputation behind him. "Sole e cogitativo," says Vasari. So, alone and pondering, he absorbed the rules that governed classical architecture. In the Tempietto he created what has been called the first classical building in twelve hundred years. Severely classical though it is in detail, here is something entirely new in the use of shapes. A series of recesses, alternately rectangular and semicircular in the cella, together with the ring of columns, gives an atmosphere of light and shade. Bramante's plan was to have a circular portico surrounding the Tempietto and, in each corner of the courtyard, a chapel with a curved niche. The circular principle would have been repeated and re-echoed. The effect is the same as that of fluting on a column, but carried out on a large plan. This rhythmic scheme of supports and niches, applied within as well as outside, was later to become the conception of the design of Saint Peter's.

RAPHAEL SANZIO

Florentine Painter and Architect, of Urbino

« 1483-1520 »

HEAVEN sometimes showers infinite riches on one sole favorite—treasures which are usually distributed over a long period of time and among many individuals. This is clearly shown in the case of Raphael Sanzio of Urbino. As excellent as he was graceful, Raphael was modest and good. Gentle and always ready to conciliate, he was considerate of everyone. At the moment when nature was vanquished by the art of Michelangelo, she deigned to be subjugated by Raphael, who combined art and nature. Till then, artists often had been rude, eccentric, uncouth, or fantastic, sometimes even stained by vice. In Raphael the rarest qualities of the heart shone forth; his character was perfected by diffidence, application to study, and an excellence of life that was quite exceptional. We may not call such men as Raphael common men. They are rather mortal gods who leave such fame on earth that they may hope for sure rewards in heaven hereafter.

Raphael was born at Urbino, that renowned city, on Good Friday, 1483, at nine o'clock at night. His father was Giovanni de' Santi, a painter of no great eminence, but an intelligent and cultivated man. He insisted that his son should not be given to a wet nurse, but be nourished by his own mother. He also desired to bring up his own child rather than let him be sent where he might learn unrefined habits and manners. As the child grew older, Giovanni began to instruct him in the first principles of painting.

At length, Giovanni realized that he was not able to teach his son as he should be taught. This good and kind parent resolved to place the boy with Pietro Perugino, who was considered the first painter of his time. Giovanni went to Perugia but found Pietro absent from the city. While he waited for him, Giovanni painted certain works for the church of San Francesco. After Pietro returned, Giovanni made his acquaintance, and when the opportunity presented itself, made his request in the most suitable manner. Pietro, with equal courtesy, agreed to accept the care of

Raphael. So Giovanni went back to Urbino to fetch the boy. Raphael's departure for Perugia was not made without many tears from his devoted mother. As soon as Pietro saw Raphael's drawings and his pleasing deportment, he conceived that opinion of him which was in time so amply confirmed.

While he studied with Perugino, Raphael imitated his master's manner so exactly that one cannot tell their works apart. This is proved by an Assumption in San Francesco at Perugia. Anyone would take it for a Perugino, but it is certainly a Raphael. In Città di Castello Raphael painted several pictures which, were it not for his signature, would certainly be supposed to be by Perugino. But here he also painted a small picture of the Marriage of the Virgin [the famous *Sposalizio*, now in the Brera, at Milan] which shows the beginning of his own style and surpasses the work of Pietro. There is a church in the background, drawn in perspective with amazing skill.

While Raphael was earning fame by these labors, Pinturicchio, a friend of his, was commissioned to paint the library of Pius II in Siena. He took Raphael along with him. Raphael made some of the cartoons for the decorations and would have continued to work there had he not heard reports of Leonardo's cartoon for the great hall of the palace in Florence and the cartoon of the *Nude Bathers* by Michelangelo Buonarroti. Fired by the desire to see these drawings, Raphael set aside his own interests and convenience and at once proceeded to Florence.

Once there, Raphael liked the city as much as the art he had come to see which seemed to him to be divine. He decided to stay and soon made friends with several of the young painters. His best friend was Taddeo Taddei, a great admirer of talent, who constantly invited him to dine at his house. Raphael, not to be surpassed in generosity and kindness, painted for him two pictures [one of these is the *Madonna in the Meadow*, Kunsthistorisches Museum, Vienna] which show traces of his early manner and also the beginning of his mature style. Another friend was Lorenzo Nasi, for whom Raphael painted a Virgin and Child with Saint John. The little Saint John is offering the infant Christ a bird to the delight of both the children [*Madonna of the Goldfinch*]. The childlike simplicity of their attitudes is perfectly lovely and wonderfully real. Equally good is the Madonna with her air of grace, and even divinity, while all the rest of the picture, both foreground and landscape, is exceedingly beautiful.

After this, Raphael was compelled to go back to Urbino to arrange his affairs which were in confusion because of the death of both his mother and father. While there, he painted two Madonnas for Guidobaldo

Montefeltro, then captain-general of the Florentines. These are both small pictures, but they are beautiful examples of Raphael's second manner. He also painted, for the same nobleman, an Agony in the Garden, which is as carefully finished as a miniature.

After arranging his affairs, Raphael returned to Perugia, where he painted a number of religious subjects, among them a Virgin and saints for the chapel of the Ansidei family [now in the National Gallery, London], in the church of the Servites, and a Virgin for the nuns of Sant' Antonio of Padua [now in the Metropolitan Museum of Art, New York]. In it the infant Christ is on his mother's lap, fully clothed, as it pleased those simple and pious ladies that he should be. On each side are saints, Peter and Paul, Cecilia and Catherine, to whom the master has given lovely features and graceful poses and—what was at that time most unusual—varied and fanciful headdresses. In a lunette above is the Almighty Father and on the predella are three scenes from the life of Christ. The first is the Agony in the Garden [Metropolitan Museum of Art, New York], the second the Bearing of the Cross [the National Gallery, London] —here the attitudes are most beautiful—and the third is the Pietà [Gardner Museum, Boston]. This work is full of devout feeling and is held in great veneration by the nuns for whom it was painted.

I must not fail to mention that Raphael so much improved his manner after his visit to Florence that he seemed to be an entirely different and much greater artist.

While Raphael was living in Florence, Agnolo Doni, who disliked spending money on anything but sculpture or painting, in which he greatly delighted and for which he spent willingly but as frugally as possible, commissioned him to paint portraits of himself and his wife [Pitti, Florence]. Both were done as we now see them.

In a Madonna and Child Raphael painted for Domenico Canigiani, the infant Christ is caressing the little Saint John brought to him by Saint Elizabeth. She looks at Saint Joseph with a most animated countenance, while Saint Joseph, leaning upon his staff, bends toward her with an expression of astonishment and reverence to God who has given this mother, so advanced in years, a child. All appear to be amazed at the behavior of the cousins; one shows reverence, and the other, tender affection. Every brushstroke creates the illusion of life itself rather than the mere colors of the painter.

While in Florence, this most excellent painter studied the ancient works of Masaccio. This and what he saw in the work of Leonardo and Michelangelo helped him to make great progress in art. He formed a close intimacy with Fra Bartolommeo di San Marco and imitated his coloring. He, for his part, taught the good father the rules of perspective, to which the monk had not previously given his attention. But just when this intercourse was most frequent and intimate, Raphael was recalled to Perugia. Here the first work that he performed was a painting in the church of San Francesco, the cartoon for which he had prepared while he was in Florence. The Dead Christ Borne to the Sepulcher, is the subject. It was painted with such care and freshness that it seems only just completed [Borghese, Rome]. Raphael had imagined all the grief and pain of the nearest and most affectionate relatives for one who has been most dear to them, upon whom, indeed, the honor and the welfare of the family have depended. Our Lady is sinking in a swoon. Saint John clasps his hands with an expression which can not but move the hardest heart to compassion. This work rouses admiration in all who behold it, not only for the expression of the heads, but for the beauty of the draperies—in short, for its perfection in every part.

Upon his return to Florence, Raphael began to paint the altarpiece for the chapel of the Dei family in the church of Santo Spirito. He prepared, at the same time, a picture for Siena, which had to be left with Ridolfo Ghirlandaio so that an azure vestment, which was still lacking when Raphael left Florence, could be finished.

Raphael left Florence because Bramante of Urbino, who was then in the service of Pope Julius II and who was a remote kinsman as well as a fellow townsman of Raphael's, wrote to say that he had persuaded the Pope to entrust Raphael with the decoration of some new rooms in the Vatican. Gratified by this proposal, he left his works in Florence unfinished and proceeded to Rome. There he found many of the rooms already painted, or in the process of being painted, by different masters. For example, there was a historical picture by Piero della Francesco, and one side of another room had a painting by Luca da Cortona [Signorelli], and there were others.

Pope Julius received Raphael with much kindness. Raphael began a picture, in the chamber of the Segnatura, of the reconciliation of Philosophy and Astrology with Theology [the *School of Athens*]. Here are depicted all the sages of the world. Diogenes with his cup is lying on the steps rapt in his own thoughts, a well-imagined figure, much to be commended both for the beauty of the form and the characteristic negligence of the garments. Aristotle and Plato are the center of the circle of philosophers. The dignity of those astrologers and geometricians who are drawing with the compasses on a tablet is not to be described. A youth of the most graceful beauty, who extends his arms and inclines his head in admiration, is the portrait of Federigo, Duke of Mantua, who was then in Rome. The figure stooping to draw with compasses on the ground is said to be Bramante. Next to him a figure turns his back to the spectator and holds a globe. This represents Zoroaster, and near him stands Raphael himself, a youthful head most modest in expression, wearing a black cap —the whole infinitely pleasing and graceful.

It would not be possible to describe the beauty and nobility of character that the master has imparted to the heads and figures. There is a most convincing air of meditative thought and attentive consideration in the faces, especially of those who are writing. An old man has placed his paper on his knee and is copying from another. Intent on his occupation, he stretches out his head and his chin as if he would thus make his pen larger and longer. To say nothing of these well-considered details, the composition is so perfect in every part that the master proved his supremacy over all painters. The whole was finished in a manner so delicate and harmonious that Pope Julius resolved that the other pictures, old or new, should be destroyed at once, and that Raphael alone should have the glory of seeing his work preferred above all others.

Raphael retained the compartments of the ceiling as he found them. There were four circular divisions in which he placed figures depicting Philosophy, Theology, Poetry, and Justice. In the angles of the ceiling he executed four historical pictures which exhibit much thought and feeling, but the figures are not large. The subjects are the Fall of Adam, Science placing the stars and planets, Marsyas and Apollo, and the Judgment of Solomon.

At one end of the room, the master depicted Mount Parnassus as a deeply shaded laurel grove, the foliage so finely painted that the spectator fancies he sees every separate leaf trembling in the gentle breeze. Innumerable figures of naked Loves hover in the air, gathering branches of laurel and weaving garlands which they scatter on the mount, over which the Spirit of Divinity does, of a truth, seem to breathe. It is amazing that with imperfect colors and the help of excellent drawing a human mind and mortal hand could make a picture which appears to be alive. The figures of the poets on the mount are most truly animated—standing, seated, speaking, singing, conversing in groups—as it seemed best to arrange them. There are portraits of the most renowned ancient and modern poets, including some who lived in Raphael's own time. The older poets were drawn, some from statues, some from medals, and many from old pictures. Here we see Ovid, Virgil, Aeneas, Tibullus, Catullus,

Propertius, and Homer, who, blind, his head lifted, pours forth his verses while a youth at his feet writes them down as he sings. Apollo and the Muses have an air of such divinity that grace and life breathe from every feature. The learned Sappho, the most divine Dante, the graceful Petrarch, and the gay Boccaccio are all most lifelike.

On the other side of the hall [opposite the *School of Athens*], is heaven with Christ and the Virgin, Saint John the Baptist, the Apostles, Evangelists, and martyrs—all enthroned in the clouds. Above is God the Father, who sends his heavenly Spirit over them all, but especially on a vast company of saints celebrating the mass below. The four Doctors of the Church are here, as are many saints, and Dante and Savonarola, and all the Christian theologians. Four children hold the gospels open above the altar on which is the Host. The saints are seated in a circle in the air, the coloring giving them the appearance of life and the foreshortening so judicially managed that they seem to stand out in relief. The vestments are richly varied and arranged in graceful folds, and the expression of the countenances is celestial rather than human. This is particularly true of the Saviour, all mildness and clemency. Raphael had the power of giving his faces the most exquisite expression and the most graceful character to the heads. The Virgin, her hands crossed on her bosom, is regarding her divine son with a look of perfect assurance that He will not refuse forgiveness. The patriarchs have the reverence of age, the Apostles are earnest and simple, and the martyrs are radiant with the faith that is in them. Still more richly varied are the resources of art displayed in the holy Doctors engaged in disputation, eager to discover the precise truth. This is manifest in the action of the hands, in the way they lend an ear intently or knit their brows in thought, with looks of surprise or other emotion as the contending propositions are presented. Distinguished from the rest are the four Doctors of the Church who are illuminated by the Holy Spirit and who explain all the difficulties presented by the gospels.

On the last wall, which has a window looking upon the court, Raphael painted the virtues of Temperance, Fortitude, and Prudence above the window, and Justinian giving the laws to the Doctors for revisal below it on one side, and, on the other, the Pope delivering the Decretals. In the figure of the pontiff, Raphael has painted the portrait of Julius II.

The Pope was very well satisfied with all that was done. He commissioned Raphael, whose powers were now developed to the utmost, to paint a second room in the Vatican. At this time our artist painted another portrait of Pope Julius which impresses all beholders with a sense of awe, as if it were the Pope himself. A Nativity is preserved together with this portrait, which shows the Virgin covering the Child with a veil while Saint Joseph leans upon his staff and contemplates the Queen of Heaven with the adoration of a most righteous old man. Both these pictures are exhibited to the people on occasions of solemn festival.

Raphael, famous as he was, and familiar with the antique, had not yet formed his grand style. One day Bramante, who had a key, let him in to see the unfinished Sistine Chapel, while Michelangelo was absent in Florence. Instantly, Raphael repainted the figure of the prophet Isaiah, which he had finished in the church of San Agostino, and in this work he profited so greatly by what he had seen in the work of Michelangelo that his manner was inexpressibly enlarged and received henceforth an obvious increase in majesty.

But when Michelangelo afterward saw the work of Raphael, he thought that Bramante had wronged him in order to enhance Raphael's fame.

Soon after this, Agostino Chigi, a very rich merchant of Siena, gave Raphael a commission to paint a chapel, because the master had recently done a fresco of Galatea in a loggia of his palace [the Farnesina] showing the nymph drawn by dolphins and surrounded by tritons. The chapel is in the church of Santa Maria del Pace, on the right as you enter. Raphael painted it in his new manner and put in it some of the prophets and sibyls before Michelangelo had thrown open the Sistine Chapel. These figures are considered to be the best, and among so many beautiful, the most beautiful that Raphael ever executed.

A chamberlain of Pope Julius most earnestly begged Raphael to paint an altarpiece for the chapel of the Ara Coeli. He did a Madonna on the clouds of heaven [Madonna di Foligno, the Vatican, Rome], with Saint John, Saint Francis and Saint Jerome robed in the vestments of a cardinal, with a beautiful landscape beneath. This Virgin has an expression of modesty and humility worthy of the mother of Christ. The Child is playing with the mantle of Our Lady. The form of Saint John gives clear proof of fasting, and one can read in his face the sincerity of his soul and the serenity which comes from his exalted devotion to truth. The head of Saint Jerome is raised as he gazes fixedly at the Virgin, and in his eyes is written all the learning and wisdom to be found in his writings. With a movement of both hands he is recommending the chamberlain to the protection of Our Lady, and the figure of the chamberlain in real life is hardly more real than the one here painted. Nor is Saint Francis less true to life. A glow of pious affection in his countenance shows that he is receiving comfort from the gentle and beautiful mother as well as from the sovereign loveliness of the divine child. In the center of the picture is an unimaginably beautiful boy holding a tablet. There is also a landscape of singular beauty.

Raphael then continued his work in another chamber of the Vatican, painting *The Mass of Bolsena*. In this story, the priest who is reading the mass has the aspect of a man utterly confounded as he sees the Host bleeding as a reproof for his want of faith. The spectator can almost see his hands tremble in his confusion. Around the priest are many figures of varied character, some kneeling in beautiful attitudes on a flight of steps and all moved by the extraordinary event. Some show that they wish to acknowledge their error, and this is seen in the men as well as in the women. One of these women is seated upon the ground and turns with an attitude full of wonder and feminine grace to listen to a speaker. On the other side, the Pope, who is hearing the mass, is an admirable portrait of Julius II; there are also a number of portraits from life. Raphael has used the break caused by the window of this room most cleverly, so that it seems as if the window were not there. No artist ever showed such readiness, resourcefulness in invention, and grace of composition. The architectural details in the *St. Peter in Prison* on the opposite wall are handled so simply and with such ingenuity that the works of other artists, when compared to Raphael, seem utterly confused. Raphael tried to tell his story exactly as it was, and he used only the most appropriate objects, as in the picture before us he has revealed the wretchedness of the prison. The resplendent light that shines from the angel illuminates the most minute particulars of the scene, the burnished armor of the sleeping guards, and the aged Saint Peter bound with chains. No less remarkable is the other part of the picture, where the Apostle walks forth from his prison with the angel. He looks like a man in a trance. Equally well expressed is the dismay of the guards when a sentinel with a torch in his hand awakens them. Where the torch does not shine, the scene is lit by moonlight. This admirably conceived picture Raphael placed over a window in the darkest part of the room. When the spectator looks at it, the light from the window dazzles him, and he fancies he sees the smoke from the torch, the splendor of the angel, and the shadows of the night. Never had a painting of night been so true to reality. We cannot but declare Raphael to be the master of all masters.

On an unbroken wall of the chamber Raphael painted the worship of God as practiced by the Hebrews [*Heliodorus Driven out of the Temple*]. Here also is the figure of Julius II, in the form of him who drives the avaricious intruders from the temple. This work is as beautiful as the night piece described above. Heliodorus is overthrown by an armed man on horseback accompanied by two men on foot. Seeing Heliodorus struck down by these figures invisible to them (for they were but a vision), his followers scatter in confusion and horror. Raphael has placed figures about the building who cling to columns in their efforts to get a better view to see what is going on. The mass of people watch amazed, waiting to see what will happen. The very cartoons for this work were treasured as masterpieces. The ceiling above these works was painted with four subjects from the Old Testament.

And now, when Raphael was doing such wonders, the pontiff, protector and support of his talent, died. Julius died but he was succeeded by Leo X, who forthwith commanded that the work should continue. The genius of Raphael was now exalted to the skies. Encouraged, he devoted himself with all his heart to the work. On another wall he painted the march of Attila on Rome, as he is met by Pope Leo, who repulsed him by his word alone [*Attila Turned away from Rome*]. Saint Peter and Saint Paul appear in the air, sword in hand, come to defend their Church. History, it is true, does not mention this occurrence, but poets and painters are permitted a certain freedom which they may use without changing the original thought. Attila is riding a most beautiful fiery black horse with a star on its forehead, which is turning, about to bolt with fright. There are other magnificent horses, among them a Spanish jennet ridden by a figure whose armor was copied from Trajan's column. The Pope's retinue is painted with extraordinary animation, as are their mounts. The Pope is on horseback in full pontificals, most truthfully portrayed. The whole scene is a beautiful spectacle in which everything is finely appropriate to its place.

About this time, Raphael painted a picture for Naples, for the chapel in the church of San Domenico, wherein is the Crucifix that spoke to Saint Thomas Aquinas. In this work [*Madonna del Pesce*, Prado, Madrid] are our Lady and Saint Jerome dressed as a cardinal, with the angel Raphael leading the youthful Tobit.

When Lorenzo Pucci, cardinal of the Quattro Coronati, was created high penitentiary, he had Raphael paint him, for the church of San Giovanni in Monte, in Bologna, a Saint Cecilia listening in ecstasy to celestial music. The musical instruments and the cloth of gold and silver veil and vestments of the saint are painted with admirable reality. The other figures are marked with the power and thought of the master. Saint Mary Magdalene in the group seems to rejoice in her conversion. The attitude of this figure is singularly graceful, as is the turn of her head. I do not think it would be possible that any work of this kind could be more perfectly done. Other masters paint pictures, but Raphael paints life itself. His figures all but breathe.

In Rome Raphael painted a good-sized picture of Pope Leo X, Cardinal Giulio de' Medici and Cardinal de' Rossi [Pitti Palace, Florence]. The figures seem to be in the round, even to be living. The textures of skin, of glossy damask, of fur, and of silk are copied to the life. There is a parchment book with miniatures and, among other accessories, there is a ball of burnished gold which reflects the Pope's shoulder and the divisions of the opposite window. I do not believe any master has ever done or ever can do, any better. The Pope richly rewarded Raphael for his work. His fame and the rewards conferred on him increasing largely, Raphael built a palace in the Borgo Nuovo which was decorated with stucco work by Bramante. His renown had reached France and Flanders, and Albrecht Dürer, a most admirable German painter and the engraver of the most beautiful copperplates, sent a tribute of respect to Raphael. It was Dürer's own portrait drawn on very fine linen, so that the drawing showed on both sides. The lights were transparent and painted in water color. Raphael then sent to Dürer a number of his own drawings.

Dürer's engraving prompted Raphael to have his own works engraved by Marcantonio Raimondi of Bologna. It was such a success that Raphael commissioned him to engrave many of his earlier works. A number of these engravings were given by Raphael to his disciple, Il Baviera, who was the guardian of a certain lady to whom Raphael was attached until the day of his death. He painted her portrait to the very life [La Donna Velata?]. It is now treasured as a relic for the love he bears to art and most especially to Raphael, by the good and worthy Botti, a merchant of Florence.

For the monks of Monte Oliveto, Raphael painted a Christ bearing his Cross [Prado, Madrid]. It is altogether admirable and is remarkable for the force with which the master has rendered the cruelty and rage of the executioners. This picture was entirely finished and shipped for Palermo, when a frightful tempest drove the vessel on a rock, where all perished except this picture, which, secure in its packings, was carried by the sea into the Gulf of Genoa. Here it was picked up without spot or blemish, for even the fury of the elements had had respect for so noble a work. The fame of this event reached the ears of the monks to whom the picture belonged. They recovered it, at last, though not without great difficulty, and only by the aid of the Pope, and by giving large rewards to those who had rescued it from the waves. The picture was ultimately landed in Sicily where it has more reputation than the Mount of Vulcan [Mt. Etna] itself.

While he was engaged on all these works, which he could not well refuse since the orders came from great and important personages, Raphael did not neglect those he had begun in the Vatican. He kept people working on them, drawing from his drawings, and he inspected every part and did the more important portions himself. Soon, therefore, the room called the Torre Borgia was opened. One of the pictures is the *Fire in the Borgo*. This fire was extinguished entirely by the benediction of Pope Leo IV. Many perilous incidents are represented by the ingenious and most admirable artist. Other historical pictures in this room tell the stories of Pope Leo IV and the Turks at Ostia [*Battle of Ostia*], of the coronation of Charlemagne by Leo [III], though the figures are portraits of King Francis [I] and Leo X, and of another event in which Charlemagne and Pope Leo III take part. The ceiling of this apartment had been painted by Pietro Perugino, and this Raphael would not destroy, out of respect to his memory and the affection that he bore him.

So comprehensive was Raphael's interest in all things relating to his work that he kept people employed for him gathering material in all parts of the world and even in Greece.

He went on with the work in the Vatican, painting, ornamenting, and designing stairways and loggias. He was placed in charge of all the works that were to be executed in the palace. It is said that Raphael was so courteous and obliging that he had the masons leave apertures and spaces for storage room, for the convenience of certain friends. But these spaces weakened the walls and have since had to be filled in.

He designed several palaces, some in Rome and some in Florence.

Raphael painted many pictures to be sent into France, one particularly, for King Francis I: a Saint Michael in combat with the archfiend [Louvre, Paris]. The work was performed so admirably at all points that Raphael obtained the large reward he merited. He also painted the portrait of Beatrice of Ferrara and of other ladies, his own inamorata especially.

Raphael was much disposed to the gentler affections and delighted in the society of woman. He permitted himself to indulge too freely in the pleasures of life. We find it related that his intimate friend, Agostino Chigi, commissioned him to paint the first floor of his palace, but Raphael was so engrossed in his love for the lady of his choice that Agostino, in despair of seeing the work finished, prevailed upon the lady to come and live in his house. Then the work was at last brought to a conclusion. For these pictures Raphael prepared the cartoons and painted many of the figures with his own hand in fresco. The subjects were from mythology: a Council of the Gods, the Marriage of Psyche, Mercury with his flute, and a Jupiter of the most sublime dignity. The whole work, whether as painting or poetry, is eminently beautiful. Raphael caused Giovanni da Udine to surround it all with festoons of fruits and flowers in the richest variety. All is as beautiful as can be.

Raphael also designed the stables of his palace for Agostino Chigi and his chapel in the church of Santa Maria del Popolo. This he painted and made, as well, the preparations for a magnificent sepulchral monument, which was completed, after both Raphael and Agostino had died, by Sebastiano Veniziano.

Raphael was now at the summit of his fame, and Leo X commanded him to begin the painting of the upper hall of the Vatican. The Pope also had him prepare the cartoons for some very rich tapestries to be executed in silk and gold. They were sent to Flanders to be woven, and when the cloths were finished, they were sent to Rome. They are amazing. One can hardly believe they are woven, not painted. They cost 70,000 crowns and are preserved in the papal chapel.

For Cardinal Colonna, Raphael painted a Saint John on canvas. It was much prized by the Cardinal, but he gave it to his doctor, Messer Jacopo da Carpi, for he believed himself to be infinitely indebted to this physician for his recovery from a dangerous illness.

For Giulio de' Medici [later Pope Clement VII], Raphael painted the *Transfiguration*, which he brought to the highest perfection by laboring continually at it with his own hand. In this work the master has produced heads and figures of such extraordinary beauty, so new, so varied, and in every way so admirable, that of all his works, this is considered by all artists the most excellent, the most divine. Whoever desires to see how Christ should be represented as he is transformed into the Godhead should see this picture. The Saviour floats, foreshortened, between Moses and Elias, who awaken into life in the splendor of his radiance. Prostrate on the earth are Peter, James, and John, in attitudes of great and varied beauty; one bends his head to the ground, another shields himself from the immense light which proceeds from the splendor of Christ, who is clothed in snowy white, his arms thrown open, his head raised toward heaven. The essence of the Godhead, the Trinity in one Person, is made apparent in utmost perfection by the divine art of Raphael. But, as if that sublime genius had gathered all the force of his powers into one effort, whereby the glory and the majesty of art should be made manifest in the countenance of Christ, he, having completed that, as one who has accomplished his destined task, touched his pencils no more, being shortly afterward overtaken by death.

I must say something about Raphael's style for the benefit of those who practice our calling, before I tell what remains to be told about his life. As a child, he imitated Perugino but improved upon him in every way. Then, when he saw the work of Leonardo, he set himself to study it with the utmost zeal, for it pleased him more than anything he had ever seen. But whatever he did, and in spite of his best endeavor, he could not surpass that master. Many think Raphael surpassed Leonardo in tenderness and in a certain natural facility, but he was surely by no means superior in that force of conception which is so noble a foundation of art, and in which few masters have equaled Leonardo. Raphael had drawn from the nude only after the manner of Perugino and found himself unable to master the freedom of Michelangelo, as shown in the cartoon in the Hall of the Council. After having been a master, he became again a disciple and compelled himself to learn in a few months what would have taken years of boyhood. He devoted himself to the study of anatomy by dissecting and studying the articulation of the bones and the muscles, the sinews, the nerves, and the veins. He knew, nevertheless, that he could never equal Michelangelo, but he considered, like the sensible man he was, that painting does not embrace merely the nude, but has a much wider field. He saw that he who could express a thought clearly and compose without confusion may also be reputed an able master. Raphael rightly thought that art should be enriched by inventions in perspective, by landscapes, and by the skillful use of light and shadow. He learned also from Fra Bartolommeo a grace of design and coloring.

I have thought proper to make these remarks at the close of his life to show to what labor, study, and care this artist subjected himself.

I will now return to the life and death of Raphael. Cardinal Bibbiena, Raphael's intimate friend, wished the master to marry. Raphael did not refuse, but he put the matter off. At last he accepted Bibbiena's niece, but he continued to put off the marriage from time to time. His motive was an honorable one. For Leo X, so they intimated, intended to reward him for his labors and honor his talents by bestowing upon him the red hat. The painter, in the meantime, did not abandon the light attachment by which he was enchained. One day, returning from one of these secret visits, he fell ill of a violent fever which was mistaken for a cold. The doctors bled him, which exhausted him at the very time when he needed to be strengthened. Thereupon he made his will, and like a good Christian he sent his love from the house, but left her enough to live on, and divided his property among his disciples. He then confessed, and in much contrition, completed the course of his life on the day whereon it had com menced, which was Good Friday. The master was then thirty-seven, and, as he embellished the world by his talents, so it is to be believed that his soul is now adorning heaven.

After his death the body of Raphael was placed in the hall where he had last worked, with the *Transfiguration* at the head of the corpse. Any man who looked at the living picture and then turned to consider the dead body, felt that his heart must burst with grief. Not an artist in Rome but bewailed his loss. His death was bitterly deplored by all the papal court. Oh, most happy and thrice blessed spirit, of whom we are all proud to speak, whose deeds are praised by all men, and the least of whose works is admired and prized! When this noble artist died, well might painting have departed also. But now, to us who remain, is left his example while we keep ever in our hearts the remembrance of his great merit and maintain his memory in high honor in our speech. He brought invention, coloring, and execution to that point of perfection for which few could have dared to hope, nor has any man aspired to pass before him.

Among his many extraordinary gifts, there is one of such value and importance that I can never sufficiently admire it and I always think of it with astonishment. This was his heavenly power of bringing all who came near him into harmony, inconceivably surprising in the nature of an artist, and true only in his presence. This was because all were surpassed by him in friendly courtesy, all confessed the influence of his sweet and gracious nature. Even the very animals followed his steps and always loved him.

They say that whenever any other painter, whether known to Raphael or not, asked for his help with a drawing or for anything else, he would leave his own work to do him service. He employed a large number of artists, whom he assisted and instructed rather as a father than as artist to artist. He was never seen at court without some fifty painters, all men of ability and distinction, who attended him as a mark of their respect. He did not live the life of a painter, but of a prince. O happy art of painting! One artist with his virtues exalted thee to heaven, and thy disciples in following him, learned how to live, as well as how to paint. Raphael had the force to constrain the greatness of Julius II and to awaken the generosity of Leo X, both of whom, high as they were in dignity, selected him as their most intimate friend and treated him with every kind of familiarity. Their favor assisted him to do the utmost honor to himself and to art. Happy those who worked under his eye, for all of them have done well. Also, those who try to emulate his art will be honored on earth, as it is certain that all who resemble him in virtue will receive their reward in heaven.

Editorial Notes on Raphael

"Among so many beautiful, the most beautiful . . ."
—VASARI on Raphael

RAPHAEL wrote to Baldassare Castiglione: "With respect to Galatea, I should think myself a great master if it were half as fine as you say, but in your words I cannot fail to see your partiality to myself. To paint a truly beautiful figure, I should have to see beautiful women and to have you there to select the best, but as good judges and beauties are scarce, I use the ideas that come to mind. Whether I am excellent in art or not, I do not know, but I do my best."

Raphael, the gracious, Raphael, loved even by animals: this we get from Vasari. There are rare souls, harmonious in every fiber, flexible, receptive, creative, at ease, and uninhibited. What we do not gather from Vasari's account of this radiant life is the great strength of Raphael's art. True, it is veiled in beauty and always will be.

Vasari did not go to the Vatican often, but how hard he must have looked at the new pictures when he was there! In his description of the two great frescoes, the Dispute of the Sacrament and the School of Athens, he mixed them up a bit as if he had tried to see everything at once. Even if he had had more time and had been less concerned with the great personages who were probably present when he was, he was so close to the tradition that provided the form for these compositions that he might not have described what we see in them from our greater perspective. I have not changed the meaning of what he said, but I have left out, in charity, the names of Christian saints that he applies to figures in the School of Athens. For us, the Disputà is the crowning expression of the Christ in judgment familiar from the west portals of French cathedrals. The subject is traditional, the new variations, like sprung rhythm in music, point up the well-known pattern of thought and form. The floor of the scene is the ground plan of the new Saint Peter's in Rome, Bramante's creation. The altar bears the inscription: "Julius II Pontifex Maximus." Imagine flattery of this magnitude! God the Father, Jesus Christ, the Holy Ghost, Adam, and the greatest figures of the Old Testament alternating with the greatest of the New Testament (Adam, the first man, to Saint Stephen, the first martyr). Below are the Doctors of the Church and the saints, gathered together at the laying of the cornerstone of the church Bramante was building to the eternal fame of Julius II.

Then, on the other side of the room, the School of Athens is the traditional summing up of the seven arts: grammar, logic, rhetoric, music, geometry, arithmetic, astronomy. These abstractions are represented by famous personages. Arithmetic here has a turbaned Moor looking over his shoulder. The Plato, who points upwards as though to say, "The ideal!" is said to be a portrait of Leonardo. Aristotle points with a powerful gesture, as though to take the earth to witness. Wisdom is thus contrasted with science. The setting for this epitome of culture is the new Saint Peter's, not yet built, but drawn from the plans of Bramante.

Raphael was made art dictator of Rome. It was he who applied the word "Gothic" to everything not classic, and therefore to everything worthless. He proposed to clear away all the Gothic remains in Rome and restore the Rome of the Empire.

Michelangelo and Raphael, these names are coupled in time and place. They worked in the Vatican for Julius II. The incongruity is bound to strike us. On one hand there is the long-enduring might of Michelangelo, his severe intellectual majesty, contrasted with the grace, the loveliness, and the early death of Raphael. But it is not only weighty matter that makes art great; another factor is the form of the work of art itself. Raphael's form is supreme. He took it from Masaccio, Leonardo, and Michelangelo, and added to it his own luster. He was before his fellows in some respects. In the Mass of Bolsena, he made a noble wall decoration out of realistic portraiture. Thus, in 1512, long before Titian had matured, he achieved a masterpiece in a course parallel to Titian's.

ANDREA DEL SARTO

The Most Excellent Florentine Painter

« 1486-1530 »

A⊤ LENGTH we come, after having written the lives of many artists— some, great colorists, others, great draftsmen, and some notable for imagination; we come, I say, to the truly excellent Andrea del Sarto, in whom all these qualities combine. Had this master possessed a somewhat bolder mind, had he been a more distinguished man, qualified by character as he was by artistic skill, he would have been without an equal. But there was a lack of force in his nature which took all the ardor and animation out of his work. Nor did he show at any time one particle of that magnanimity which would have rendered him a truly divine painter. His works lack grandeur, richness, and force. His figures are well drawn; they are entirely free from errors and perfect in all their proportions, and are, for the most part, simple and chaste. The expressions of the heads are graceful in women and children and, in men, full of animation. The draperies of this master are beautiful to a marvel. The nude figures are admirably executed with simple drawing, and the coloring is exquisite; nay, it is truly divine.

Andrea was born in Florence in 1486. His father was a tailor, so the boy was always called Andrea del Sarto [Andrew the Tailor's son] by everyone. At seven he was taken from school and placed with a goldsmith, where he preferred drawing to working with the chisel. It chanced that Gian Barile, a Florentine painter of rather coarse and plebeian taste, noticed that the child drew well, and took him over to train him as a painter. Andrea began to enjoy himself and in a very short time was doing things with color that astonished Barile and the other artists of the city. After three years the boy had done so well that Barile spoke to Piero di Cosimo, who was then considered one of the best artists in Florence, and put Andrea in his care. Andrea studied without ceasing, and this perpetual labor and his natural talent produced so great an effect that one might have thought he had been painting for fifty years.

Piero was very fond of his disciple and heard with pleasure that whenever Andrea had any free time he spent it drawing from the cartoons of Michelangelo and of Leonardo da Vinci in the hall of the Pope, and he surpassed all the other students, natives as well as strangers, who worked there.

But of all his fellow students Franciabigio was the one Andrea liked best. They became fast friends. Andrea confessed that he could no longer bear the eccentricity of Piero and had determined to live by himself. Franciabigio had determined to do the same thing because his master, Mariotto Albertinelli, had abandoned the art of painting. They decided to live together and hired a place on the Piazza del Grano, where they executed many works in company. They painted some altar curtains for the church of the Servites, a commission which they received from the sacristan, a relative of Franciabigio's. One of the curtains had on it a Deposition similar to the picture by Filippino and Pietro Perugino in the same church.

Members of the Barefoot Brotherhood of Saint John the Baptist used to meet in a house built by several Florentine artists at the end of the Via Larga. The house had an outer court with a loggia on rather low columns. Some of the members, perceiving that he would someday be an important artist, engaged Andrea to paint twelve stories from the life of Saint John around that cloister. Andrea won honor and fame by these works, and received many orders from people who were sure that he would become a great artist.

Among this artist's early pictures is a Christ Appearing to Saint Mary Magdalene, which he did for the Augustinian monks. The coloring of this work is so good, and there is so much softness, harmony and delicacy in it that it brought Andrea two more commissions from the same church, as will be recounted later.

Then Andrea and Franciabigio moved to rooms near the cloister of the Annunziata, where Andrea became intimate with Jacopo Sansovino, who was then a boy studying sculpture under Andrea Contucci. They became such friends that they were never apart, night or day. They always discussed the difficulties of their art, and it is therefore no wonder that they both became excellent.

In the monastery of the Servites there was a monk, the sacristan, Fra Mariano del Canto alla Macino by name, who sold the tapers. He heard everyone praising Andrea's progress and thought of a scheme to gratify his own desires. He began to cultivate Andrea who was a kind man of gentle manner, by telling him that he would assist the painter to gain fame and fortune.

Many years before Alesso Baldovinetti had painted a Nativity in the first cloister of the Servites and Cosimo Rosselli had begun but never finished the story of Saint Philip [Filippo Benizzi] the founder of the Order of the Servites. The sacristan told Andrea that, if he finished the series of pictures of Saint Philip, he would become famous and that everyone would see his work in such a public place, Florentines and strangers alike. He added that, far from expecting payment, Andrea ought to be glad of the opportunity to show his prowess on such a site. He further-more added that, if Andrea did not do it, Franciabigio certainly would jump at the chance.

Andrea had no intention of undertaking the task, but the mention of Franciabigio who had become his rival decided him, and he wrote a con-tract that stipulated that no one else should be permitted to interfere in the work. And all he got in payment was ten ducats a picture from the sacristan, who told him that the money came out of his own pocket. In a little while he was able to show three pictures. The first is Saint Philip clothing the naked. Another is of the saint reproving a group of gamblers, who mock him for his pains, when suddenly, a flash of lightning blasts the tree under which they are sitting and kills two of them. Terrified figures flee the spot with gestures so true that they seem to be alive. A horse rears up. The whole scene shows Andrea's fine imagination. In the third, a woman is delivered from evil spirits. All these pictures were very well done.

Encouraged by praise, the artist continued the series with two more pictures. In the first Saint Philip is lying dead, mourned by the brethren of his Order, and a dead child is revived by the touch of the bier upon which the saint has been laid. The boy is shown twice, first dead and then revived, and very natural it all is. In the last picture, our artist showed several monks laying the vestments of the saint on the heads of some children. In this work Andrea has painted the portrait of Andrea della Robbia, a bent old man dressed in red, holding a staff. There is also the portrait of Luca [della Robbia] his son.

One side of the cloister was now finished. Andrea thought the reward too little and the honor rated too high and determined to do no more. The monk complained bitterly and held the artist to his agreement. They compromised on Andrea's doing two other pictures at an increased pay.

Andrea was now much better known, and received many commissions. Among others was one from the monks of Vallombrosa for a Last Supper. It was to be painted on a wall of the refectory of the convent of San Salvi, and on the vaulting of the ceiling he painted four Saints about a circle in the center. This circle has three aspects which represent one only, to signify the Trinity. All these pictures gained him the reputation of being a most excellent master of fresco.

I cannot discourse at length of the many pictures this artist painted in Florence. But, about this time, the sacristan of the Servites commissioned Franciabigio to paint one of the stories still wanting in the cloister we have already mentioned. Andrea was apprehensive lest he be surpassed by Franciabigio, who seemed to him to paint with a greater facility than he, so he prepared cartoons for two stories and proposed to execute them immediately. One is the Birth of Our Lady, a composition of well-proportioned figures in groups. A child warming himself before the fire is very natural; and an old man reposing upon a couch is a figure of great merit. The second picture is of the Magi led by the star. The kings are followed by their courts in Florentine dress, with carriages and baggage, and attended by numerous followers, three of whom are portraits. The full-length figure looking at the spectator is Jacopo Sansovino; the second, leaning on him, is Andrea himself; and the head in profile behind Jacopo is the musician Aiolle. There are boys climbing the walls to get a view of the show and to see the strange animals which form a part of the train. The whole is admirably painted. The master surpassed himself in both these works.

These labors, and many more, secured so great a name for Andrea that he was considered one of the best artists in Florence. He found himself able to render assistance to his family and, for his own part, to be free from oppressive poverty. But he fell in love with a young woman, whom he married when she became a widow, and found that he had his work cut out for him for the rest of his days. He was obliged to toil harder than ever. His wife delighted in snaring men and worked her wiles on Andrea by her beauty and fascination. He soon became jealous and found that he had fallen into the hands of an artful woman who made him do in all things as she pleased. He abandoned his father and mother and took in his wife's parents instead. All who knew the facts were sorry for him, but the respect and affection his friends had borne him soon changed to disgust. His disciples remained with him, it is true, in the hope of learning something useful, yet there was not one of them, great or small, who was not maltreated by Andrea's wife through evil words and spiteful actions. Although Andrea lived in the midst of all this torment, he thought himself most blessed.

But—to return to the works of this master—they were very numerous and also very beautiful. He painted Our Lady for the Franciscan nuns. The Madonna is standing upright on a pedestal of eight sides, and at each angle are figures of harpies adoring the Virgin. The draperies are most beautiful. It was one of Andrea's excellencies that their flow was ever ample, while he contrived, by a certain flexible turn of the forms, to show the outline of the figure underneath. This work is now considered one of Andrea's best and is indeed of singular and wonderful beauty.

The merchants' guild decided to have triumphal chariots made of wood, to be used in the procession of San Giovanni instead of canopies of cloth borne in token of subjection and tribute by men representing the different cities and fortresses, as they pass before the duke and the principal magistrates. Ten of these chariots were prepared, and Andrea painted several of them. It was proposed that a number of these chariots be made every year until each city and town should possess one. They would certainly have made a fine show, but nothing has been done since 1527.

While Andrea was thus adorning his native city with these and other works, and at the same time adding to his own glory, the Barefoot Brethren decided to have him finish their cloister. The master recommended his work with great good will, adding two very beautiful figures of Justice and Charity as ornaments to a door. In a picture of Saint John preaching, the artist has given the saint an expression that shows his inspiration and his contemplative habits. There is also much variety in the faces of his hearers who listen with amazement and emotion to this new doctrine. Still more wonderful is the picture of the saint baptizing. Every man, as he pulls off his garment, shows his eagerness to receive the sacred rite. They are so admirably painted in chiaroscuro that they resemble lifelike marble statues.

I will not omit to mention that, while Andrea was occupied with these pictures, many engravings by Albrecht Dürer were brought out, and that Andrea used them freely, copying certain figures and adapting them to his own purposes. This has made some people complain, not that it is wrong to make use of the good in others' work, but that Andrea lacked power of invention.

At this time Baccio Bandinelli, well known as a draftsman, wished to learn the art of painting in oil, and, because he was aware that no one knew more than Andrea, he engaged Andrea to paint his portrait. Baccio watched him carefully but never used the knowledge he gained, perhaps because it was too difficult or because he was not sufficiently attracted to painting. He stuck to sculpture as the art which suited him best.

The merchant Puccini, a particular friend of Andrea's, caused him to paint some religious pictures for the export trade to France. They were so well received that Andrea considered going to France himself.

But, in the meantime, the Florentines heard that Pope Leo X [Giovanni de' Medici] planned to do his native city the honor of paying it a visit, and they prepared the most magnificent decorations. A very sumptuous array of ornaments, triumphal arches, temples, and colossal statues were accordingly made ready, and the fronts of buildings were richly decorated. The like had never before been seen, as there were then, more distinguished artists in Florence than ever. Most beautiful of all was the façade of Santa Maria del Fiore, made of wood and decorated in chiaroscuro by Andrea del Sarto. The architecture of this work was by Jacopo Sansovino. The Pope declared that it could not have been finer had it been made of marble.

Andrea was now asked to paint another picture for the king of France. In a short time he finished one, which was sent immediately into France, where it brought four times the sum it had cost in Florence. At this time Pier Francesco Borgherini had Baccio d'Agnolo carve some handsome furniture for a bed chamber, and desired the paintings to be as fine. He asked Andrea to paint him the story of Joseph, in competition with Granaccio and Jacopo Pontormo. Andrea exerted extraordinary effort and spent a great deal of time, in order to surpass his rivals, and he did so with the greatest possible success. At the siege of Florence, an attempt was made to remove these pictures to send them to the king of France, but they were so firmly fastened that they could not be loosened without the destruction of the whole work. So they were allowed to remain.

Andrea rarely painted a woman without using his wife as a model. It was not only that she was always before him, but, what is more, that he carried her image in his heart. There is something of her in all his women. But Andrea now began to feel, not that he was tired of the beauties of his wife, but that his life was too oppressive. His wife's family devoured everything he earned, and, although he was used to it, it became too great a burden. Some friends who still loved him, though more as an artist, perhaps, than as a man, advised him to move and to leave his wife in some secure place until his fortunes might improve. Hardly had he decided that something had to be done than an opportunity presented itself. The two pictures that had been sent into France pleased the king [Francis I]. He gave orders that money should be sent to Andrea in Florence to defray the expenses of the journey into France, and Andrea accordingly set out most gladly.

He arrived in due time at the French court, was very well received, and given, not only a present of money, but some fine clothes. He began his service with so much success that he soon thought of his departure from his native land as the best of good fortune. One of his first works was a portrait of the dauphin, a babe in swaddling clothes. When he took this painting to the king he received three hundred ducats in gold.

He continued his labors and painted an exceedingly beautiful picture of Charity for King Francis. From that time the monarch had an annuity settled on Andrea and did everything he could to induce the painter to remain at his court. Andrea was so prompt and so pleasant that he gave great satisfaction.

Now if Andrea had only considered what he had escaped and the advantages he now enjoyed, he might have become, I will not say only rich, but famous as well. But one day when he was painting a picture of Saint Jerome doing penance, which was intended for the king's mother, he received letters from Florence. He had left his wife well provided for, she wanted for nothing. He had even ordered a house to be built for them and had given her hopes that he might return at any moment. Yet, as she could not give money to her kindred and connections as she had formerly done, she wrote bitter complaints, and declared that she never ceased to weep and was in perpetual affliction over his absence. And she dressed this up with sweet words, well calculated to move the heart of the luckless man who loved her only too well. She drove the poor soul half out of his wits. She said that if he did not come soon, he would certainly find her dead. That settled it, and he resolved to go back to his chains, for he preferred to live in wretchedness with her than to live in ease with all the glory his art might bring. He was then so handsomely dressed, so decked out in finery that he could hardly wait to show himself to his wife. He took some money from the king to buy statues and pictures. He promised on his Bible oath to return in a few months, saying he was going only to arrange his affairs in Florence.

Andrea del Sarto arrived safely in Florence, where he enjoyed the society of his beautiful wife and of his friends for several months. But, when the time was up, and he should have returned to France, he found himself without funds. What with building, indulging in various pleasures, and doing no work, he had spent the king's money, too. He was determined, nevertheless, to return to France, but the prayers and tears of his wife had more power over him than his promise to the king. He stayed in Florence, and the king was so angry that he declared that if Andrea ever fell into his hands he would do him more harm than he had before done him good. Andrea stayed in Florence, and from an eminent position, he sank to the very lowest, earning his livelihood and passing his time as best he could.

Andrea did a number of pictures in and about Florence. He sighed, sometimes, when he thought of how he had behaved to the French king, and would have gladly received pardon for his fault. He painted a Saint John the Baptist expressly to send to France, but for some reason it never went and was sold to the illustrious Ottaviano de' Medici, always a protector of artists and a patron of the arts. Ottaviano, by the command of Pope Leo [X], was placed in charge of the decorations of the great hall in the Poggio a Caiano, a palace of the Medici. This whole undertaking was at first given to Franciabigio, but Ottaviano now ordered that he should do only a third, and divided the rest between Andrea del Sarto and Pontormo. But no matter how Ottaviano tried to forward this work, no matter what sums he promised or even paid to the artists, he could not get the decorations done. Andrea finished one part, but this was all. His picture showed Caesar receiving a tribute of all kinds of animals. The rich invention and great diversity of the figures of those presenting the animals were not enough; he adorned the flight of steps that led up to the throne of Caesar with statues admirably arranged. On these steps is a dwarf holding a box, or case, in which is a chameleon so well done that it would be impossible better to imagine the deformity of that strange creature. But the whole work, as I have said, was never finished.

In 1523, the plague broke out in Florence. Andrea retired to Mugello, and took with him his wife and some of her family. There he painted a picture for the nuns of San Piero. It was a Pietà with Saint John the Evangelist and Mary Magdalene, figures so full of life that they seem to have soul and spirit. When he had finished this work, Andrea stayed on, for the plague had not passed. This was all the more agreeable as the venerable ladies had been so friendly and kind to his wife and his whole party. Not to be idle, he painted several pictures which will bear comparison with the best painting of our time.

Upon his return to Florence, Andrea painted two more stories for the cloister of the Barefoot Brethren. Then it chanced that Federigo II, duke of Mantua, passed through Florence on his way to pay his respects to Pope Clement VII [Giulio de' Medici] in Rome and saw Raphael's portrait of Pope Leo [X] between Cardinal Giulio de' Medici and Cardinal Rossi. Much impressed by it, he begged it as a gift from Pope Clement, who gave it to him. Orders were sent to Ottaviano de' Medici to have it packed and sent to Mantua. Ottaviano was displeased, and marveled that the Pope [his kinsman] should have granted this request. He replied, nevertheless, that he would do it, but that the frame needed regilding. Then Messer Ottaviano, to "have his cake and eat it too," went secretly to Andrea del Sarto and asked him to make an exact copy. When it was done, not even Ottaviano could tell which was which. The duke of Mantua received his picture with great satisfaction. Even Giulio Romano, the disciple of Raphael, would always have believed it to be the work of Raphael, if Giorgio Vasari, who had seen Andrea at work on it, had not told him the truth when he later went to Mantua. Giulio was showing Vasari the duke's treasures, and pointed out this picture as the best of all. Giorgio said, "It is indeed a beautiful picture, but it is not by Raphael." "How!" exclaimed Giulio, "not his! Why, I recognize the very marks I made on it when it was being done." "You are mistaken," replied Giorgio, "for this was painted by Andrea del Sarto, and as a proof there is a mark on the back so that one could be told from the other." Giulio had the picture turned around and discovered the countersign. He shrugged his shoulders and said, "I value it none the less, for it is a most amazing feat."

Enough of this but it shows how capable Andrea was, and how, by his skill and the prudence and judgment of Messer Ottaviano, the duke was satisfied and Florence still preserved this most admirable work.

Later, Messer Baldo Magini, who wished to present a picture to the church of the Madonna delle Carceri in Prato, prepared a magnificent marble frame for it. Andrea was asked to do the picture, but a certain Niccolò Soggi of Sansovino was also proposed and so well recommended that he was given the job. When Andrea arrived with his associates to begin work, Soggi had the boldness to say before Messer Baldo that he would put up any sum and wager that he could paint the better picture in competition with Andrea. With unusual spirit, Andrea replied, "I have a young disciple here who might compete with you, but I will not. If I won, it would be no triumph, and, if you won, it would be to my eternal shame." Then he told Baldo that it would be a good idea to give the work to Niccolò, who would be sure to please the market folk. And with that, Andrea returned to Florence.

Now, a monk of the Servites had commanded a woman, by way of commutation of a vow, to have a picture of Our Lady painted over the side door of the Annunziata. The monk told Andrea that he had this money to spend, and there was little of it, but he thought it would be better if Andrea rather than another did it. Andrea was an obliging person and agreed, partly for the money and partly for the fame. He painted a very beautiful Madonna in fresco [the Madonna del Sacco]. This work is so beautiful in the drawing, grace of the figures, color, and force of the relief, that it proves Andrea to have surpassed all painters. The painting speaks for itself as a wonderful and extraordinary work.

Only one more picture was needed to complete the series in the cloister of the Barefoot Brethren. Andrea resolved to paint it. His manner was by now much enlarged by the sight of Michelangelo's figures in San Lorenzo. His improvement shows clearly in this picture of the Birth of John the Baptist. The figures are in much finer relief. Admirable is an old woman on a stool, who smiles to see so old a mother giving birth. Her attitude and expression are exactly as they would be in life.

Andrea continued to paint for eminent patrons. Many years had passed since the monks of San Salvi had commissioned him to paint the Last Supper in the arch. At last there came an abbot, a man of sense and judgment, who determined that the picture should be completed. Andrea began it and worked when the spirit moved him. At length it was finished, and all agree that it is the most lively in design and color of all our artist's works. All who see it are struck with astonishment. It is not surprising that, when in the siege of Florence the suburbs were razed to the ground as a measure of safety, this refectory was spared, only because of this wonderful painting.

When Andrea had finished a portrait of the intendant of the monks of Vallombrosa, he found he had some colors left. He called his wife, Lucrezia: "Come, wife, and I will paint you, and all may see how handsome you still are, yet how changed from what you were." But the woman would not sit—perhaps she had other things on her mind—so Andrea, as though he knew his end was near, drew himself instead. This most natural portrait [illustration], which seems almost alive, is in the possession of Madonna Lucrezia, who still survives.

Giovanni Battista della Palla was buying whatever great paintings he could lay his hands on, and was actually despoiling Florence by sending these treasures to the French king, for whom magnificent apartments were being prepared. This Giovanni Battista was anxious to have Andrea return to the service of the French king and had him paint two pictures. One is the Sacrifice of Abraham, his most perfect work, and the other is a figure of Charity with three children, an admirable performance.

The illustrious Ottaviano de' Medici wished to own a picture by Andrea, who was only too anxious to please that nobleman. He painted a Madonna playing with the child, with Saint Eizabeth and a young Saint John. Power and knowledge, beauty of design, and delicacy of finish make this a work of indescribable excellence. Andrea took the picture to Ottaviano, but Florence was under siege, and Ottaviano thanked him in the most friendly way but suggested that he dispose of the picture as best he could in those troubled times. Andrea only said, "The work was done for you and no one else shall own it." "Sell it," replied Messer Ottaviano, "sell it and use the money, for I know what I am talking about." Andrea carried the painting home and refused all offers for it, and there were many. When the siege was lifted and the Medici returned to Florence, he once more took the picture to Messer Ottaviano, who received it gladly and paid double the price.

During the siege some officers of the troops fled the city, taking funds entrusted to them for the soldiers' pay. Andrea was asked to paint their pictures on the palace of the Signoria, facing the open square. He did not want to be called, like Castagno, Andrea degl' Impiccati, so he said that one of his disciples would do the work, but actually he himself glided behind the boarding which had been put up, and painted them secretly at night. They were whitewashed over, many years since.

When the siege was over and everyone expected affairs to take a turn for the better, some of the soldiers were found to have contracted the plague. Great was the alarm in Florence, and this terror was quickly followed by the plague itself. Whether it was anxiety that affected Andrea's health, or whether he ate too much after the long privation of the siege, he fell mortally ill one day. No remedy was found, nor much care taken of him, for his wife fled, in fear of the pest. Thus he died, almost without anyone being aware of it, and was buried with little ceremony by the Barefoot Brethren in the church of the Servites near his house.

The death of Andrea was a great loss to his native city and to art, for at the age of forty-four he was still improving his manner. The longer he had lived the better artist he would have become. If he had stayed in Rome longer, he would have enriched his style by studying the marvels there, and some say he would have surpassed all the artists of his time. Some think that Andrea was awed by the antique in Rome as well as by the school of Raphael. So he went back to Florence and painted admirable pictures, which since his death have sold for three times what he asked for them. Two reasons for this posthumous success may have been his timid disposition and the shrewdness of his employers, who made good use of his desperate need for money when he would work for the meanest price. This had nothing to do with the value of his paintings, which are held in highest estimation. Andrea was certainly one of the greatest and best masters that the world has yet seen.

Editorial Notes on Andrea del Sarto

VASARI *tells this story in even greater detail. He was one of those disciples who stuck to Andrea in spite of Lucrezia and in spite of Andrea's degrading passion for his wife. Some of the revealing and intimate details of Andrea's domestic tragedy were omitted in the second edition, 1568, which contains the complete Lives. I have restored them to this story, for Browning has fixed our attention for all time on the "faultless painter . . . whose Virgin was his wife."*

> *But had you—oh, with that same perfect brow,*
> *And perfect eyes, and more than perfect mouth,*
> *And the low voice my soul hears, as a bird*
> *The fowler's pipe, and follows to the snare—*
> *Had you, with these the same, but brought a mind!*

It is a savage indictment Browning makes, but there is a difference in Vasari's. Lucrezia was a thoroughly worthless person, but it was Andrea his fellow artists despised, while they pitied him for his lack of character. His ability was so great that Michelangelo said to Raphael: "There is a little fellow in Florence who would make you sweat, if he ever got a great commission to do."

I like the fine distinction between a Raphael partly painted by Giulio Romano—the genuine article—and the perfect and spurious exact copy by Andrea del Sarto. It illustrates the futility of the expertising which adds "and followers" to an attribution. "Raphael and Giulio Romano" would be silly. If the picture could not be painted without Raphael, it is a Raphael, no matter who wields the brush. After Raphael's death Giulio Romano painted no more Raphaels.

TITIAN

Painter, of Cadore

« 1477-1576 »

TITIAN was born at Cadore, about five miles from the foot of the Alps. He was of the family of the Vecelli, one of the most noble of those parts. The intelligent boy was sent to Venice at the age of ten to stay with an uncle who placed the child with the excellent and famous Gian [Giovanni] Bellini. Titian soon proved himself a gifted painter. Now Gian Bellini and the other masters of that country were not accustomed to study the antique but copied what they saw before them, and that in a dry, hard, labored manner, and this Titian also acquired. But in 1507 Giorgione da Castelfranco began painting in a very beautiful manner. He did not neglect to work from life, or to use natural color, and he painted directly in color without a drawing. He held that this was the best way, shading with colder or warmer tints as the living object might demand.

But, in doing this, he failed to perceive that it is impossible to arrange a composition intelligibly without first sketching the forms and grouping them in different ways, for the fancy needs actually to see the design, to form a correct judgment. The nude also must be studied to be understood, and drawing on paper is essential. To be compelled to have a model for every picture is a great restraint. Facility in designing and painting comes from a store of knowledge, a host of ideas garnered in many drawings, so that the artist can draw upon his own imagination for natural objects to put in his pictures. He who can draw need not rely on color alone to hide the lack of design as many of the Venetians do.

Titian began at once to imitate the manner of Giorgione, and with such success that his pictures were sometimes taken for those of that master. As he grew older and matured in judgment and facility, our young artist painted many frescoes. He did a portrait of a gentleman of the Barberigo family, who was a friend of his, the coloring most true, the texture of the satin doublet very natural, and the hair so distinctly painted that each one could be counted. It was so well and carefully done that it would have been taken for a picture by Giorgione, if Titian had not signed it.

Giorgione, meanwhile, had painted the façade of the German Exchange [the Fondaco de' Tedeschi]. Barberigo used his influence to have Titian appointed to paint another part of the same building. Then Titian painted a Flight into Egypt, the figures being life-size. Our Lady is in a great wood where there are various animals so naturally painted that they seem alive. Titian owed the excellence of the landscape in this picture to his studies with some German painters whom he had entertained in his house for several months. He painted several pictures for a Flemish gentleman and merchant, Messer Giovanni Danna. One was a portrait that seems to breathe, another an *Ecce Homo*, considered by Titian as well as by others to be a very good work, and a third was a picture of Our Lady surrounded by portraits of men and children of the Danna family.

Titian painted the angel Raphael with Tobit and the dog, in the church of San Marciliano. In the distance, in this picture, Saint John the Baptist is seen at prayer in a wood. He is looking to heaven and a light shines upon him. Some believe that this picture was done before the fresco on the German Exchange was begun. Now it happened that certain gentlemen congratulated Giorgione on what they supposed to be his latest painting on the Exchange. They said the last picture was even better than the first. This vexed Giorgione so that he hardly showed himself in public until the whole work was completed and Titian known generally to be the painter. Nor would he speak to Titian again, and they were no longer friends.

In 1508, Titian published a wood engraving of the *Triumph of Faith*. It showed a vast number of personages, from our first parents to the Doctors of the Church and the holy confessors—all displayed in a fine manner and an improved facility. I remember Fra Sebastiano del Piombo saying that if Titian had gone to Rome and seen the Michelangelos and Raphaels and the antique, he would have produced works of the most astonishing perfection, as he already deserved to be called the most perfect imitator of nature in our time as far as coloring went. Had he gone to Rome, he would then have equaled Michelangelo and the Urbinese [Raphael] in design—the great foundation of all art.

In the church of San Spirito, Titian painted a small picture in oil of Saint Mark seated among other saints, whose faces are portraits from life. This picture has been taken for a Giorgione.

An unfinished picture in the Hall of the Grand Council, which shows the Emperor Frederick Barbarossa kneeling before Pope Alexander III, who plants his foot on the emperor's neck, was finished by Titian. He altered many parts of it and introduced portraits of his friends. For this work he received an office with an income of three hundred crowns on condition that, from time to time, he paint the portrait of the newly elected doge at the price of eight crowns, which the doge must himself pay. The portrait is then preserved in the Palazzo di San Marco as a memorial of that doge.

In 1514 Duke Alfonso of Ferrara had a small apartment painted by Dosso and Bellini. The subjects were classical, that by Giovanni Bellini being a bacchanal with satyrs and dancing figures both male and female, all inebriated, and with a Silenus on an ass, a very beautiful figure. Around this group are crowds of figures bearing grapes and other fruits. This is one of the finest works of Giovanni Bellini, although there is a certain stiffness in the draperies, which he had imitated from a picture by Albrecht Dürer lately brought to Venice. On a vat of red wine, in the picture, Giovanni Bellini wrote the following words: "*Joannes Bellinus Venetus, p. 1514*" [Giovanni Bellini, Venetian, painted it in 1514]. This picture was not finished because of the great age of the master. Titian, more eminent than any other artist, was summoned to complete it. Titian also painted in that apartment two other pictures, one of a river of red wine with singers and musicians, all half inebriated, and a very beautiful figure of a sleeping woman, a nude. The second picture is a Garden of Love, with a crowd of children, the most beautiful of whom is fishing in the river and is reflected in the water. The children are gathered about an altar on which is a statue of Venus with a shell in her hand. This greatly pleased Duke Alfonso, as did also the first picture. On the door of a press, Titian painted a torso of Christ, a most beautiful and admirable work, in which a wicked Hebrew is showing the coin of Caesar to Jesus. Other pictures of about the same time are thought to be the best ever produced by Titian. He was largely rewarded by the duke. Titian painted the duke leaning against a large cannon, and also Signora Laura, who afterward married the duke. This, too, is an admirable work. It cannot be denied that the liberality of princes is a great stimulus to the energy of those who toil for art.

About this time Titian formed a friendship with the divine Messer Ludovico Ariosto, who praised him as an admirable painter in his *Orlando Furioso.**

On his return to Venice, Titian painted a nude shepherd to whom a peasant girl offers a flute. This group is set in a beautiful landscape. For the high altar of the Ça Grande this artist painted Our Lady ascending into heaven, with the twelve Apostles beneath. In the same church, in the chapel of the Pesaro family, Titian painted a Madonna and Child with saints and

* This epic poem by Ariosto has been called an "immortal work wherein the pleasing and the grave, the gracious and the terrifying, are blended with inimitable art."

donors. These are all Pesaro portraits, among them the bishop of Paphos and his brother, who had just returned from the victory over the Turks. In the little church of San Niccolò in the same convent, Titian painted four saints in a picture: Francis, Nicholas, Catherine, and Sebastian. This last figure is nude and has been exactly copied from life without the slightest art or any effort to beautify any part, so that it might seem to be a sort of cast from life. It is, nevertheless, considered very fine. Titian himself drew this on wood, but it was engraved and painted by others.

Then our artist painted a Christ Bearing his Cross for the church of San Rocco. Many have thought this to be a work by Giorgione. It has become an object of the utmost devotion in Venice and has received more money in offerings than Titian and Giorgione made in their whole lives. Titian had done the portrait of Bembo, then secretary to Pope Leo X, and was invited by him to come to Rome to see the city and to meet Raphael of Urbino and other distinguished persons. But the artist delayed his visit until 1520, and by that time both Pope Leo X and Raphael were dead, so he put it off, for that time, altogether.

For the church of Santa Maria Maggiore Titian painted a Saint John the Baptist in the Wilderness, a wide landscape with most graceful trees on the banks of a river. An angel in the picture appears to be living. He painted portraits of Prince Grimani and of Loredano, and, not long after, of King Francis, who was leaving Italy to return to France.

When Andrea Gritti was elected doge, our artist also made his portrait, and a beautiful thing it is. The likeness is in the figure of Sant' Andrea, who is one of a group composed of Our Lady and Saint Mark and himself. Titian painted portraits of other doges, for that was his office, as we have said.

The renowned poet, Pietro Aretino, who left Rome before the sack of that city and went to Venice, became the intimate of Titian and Sansovino. This was very useful to Titian, since he became widely known by the writings of this author and was brought to the notice of some powerful princes, as will be related in due time. The celebrated altarpiece of Saint Peter Martyr is the best and most perfectly finished picture that Titian has yet done. Saint Peter, a figure larger than life, is lying outstretched in a wood of very large trees. He is fiercely attacked by a soldier who has already wounded him so severely that the shadow of death is on his face. A monk flying from the scene has an expression of the utmost terror. In the air are two nude angels descending from heaven in a blaze of light by which the picture is lit. This is the best, as well as the most famous, of Titian's pictures. When Gritti saw it, he procured Titian the commission to paint a

great battlepiece for the Hall of the Grand Council, representing the rout
of Chiaradadda [actually, of Cadore]. The soldiers are fighting furiously
while heavy rain falls on them. The work is considered the best, most
animated, and most beautiful picture in the hall.

Titian's picture of Our Saviour at Table with Cleophas and Luke was
presented to the Signoria by a gentleman of the Contarini family, who
thought it deserved to be seen in public, as it certainly does. About the
same time our artist painted the Virgin ascending the Steps of the Temple,
in which picture the heads are all portraits.

In 1530, when Charles V was in Bologna, Cardinal Ippolito de' Medici
invited Titian, on Pietro Aretino's suggestion, to come to that city. Titian
painted a magnificent portrait of His Majesty in full armor. This gave such
satisfaction that he received a present of a thousand crowns, half of which
he had to give to Alfonso Lombardi. This artist had asked Titian's leave to
act as an assistant preparer of colors while the emperor posed. Alfonso
stood right behind Titian and modeled a medallion and finished it just in
time. He slipped his work into his sleeve so that Titian would not see it,
but the emperor said, "Show what thou hast been doing." Charles examined
it and asked him if he could do it in marble. "Yes, your sacred Majesty,"
replied Alfonso. "Do it then," said the emperor, "and bring it to me in
Genoa." And the most singular part of the story is that when Titian
received the one thousand crowns, he was instructed to give five hundred to
Alfonso.*

Returning to Venice, Titian found that many gentlemen had begun to
favor the artist Pordenone and had engaged him to paint a small picture in
the church of San Giovanni Elemosinario to match one already there by
Titian. But try as he might, Pordenone could not equal or even approach
the work of Titian. Titian was then appointed to paint an Annunciation,
but his price of five hundred crowns was thought too high, so Titian sent
this picture, on the advice of Pietro Aretino to Charles V as a gift. The
emperor made him a present of two thousand crowns. The place where
the picture was to have hung was then filled by a work by Pordenone.

When the emperor, some time later, returned with his army from
Hungary and was in Bologna to hold a conference with Pope Clement VII,
he had Titian paint his portrait again. Titian also painted Cardinal Ippolito
de' Medici, both in Hungarian costume and in full armor. He painted
Alfonso Davalos, and Pietro Aretino, at the same period. These works
brought him to the notice of Federigo Gonzaga, duke of Mantua, who
engaged him in his service. At Mantua, our artist made a portrait of the

* This story of high-pressure salesmanship is taken from Vasari's life of Lombardi.

duke which seems to breathe, and afterward of his brother, the cardinal. He painted twelve beautiful heads of the twelve Caesars, to decorate one of the rooms Giulio Romano was building.

When Pope Paul III came to Ferrara and Bologna, Titian painted a very fine portrait of him and another of Cardinal Santa Fiore. Many copies have been made of these. A portrait of Francesco Maria, duke of Urbino, is so wonderfully beautiful that Messer Pietro Aretino has celebrated it in a sonnet in which he compares Titian to Apelles.

In the collection of the duke of Urbino, there are two heads of women which are very pleasing, and a reclining Venus partly covered with flowers and transparent draperies which is exceedingly beautiful. Also in this collection are a very lovely Mary Magdalene, all disheveled, and portraits of Charles V, King Francis as a youth, and Duke Guidobaldo II, Popes Sixtus IV, Julius II, and Paul III, the old cardinal of Lorraine, and [Sultan] Soliman.

In 1541 Titian painted the picture for the high altar of Santo Spirito in Venice, the *Descent of the Holy Spirit*. The Almighty is represented as a flame, and the Spirit as a dove descending upon the Apostles. The picture showed signs of deterioration in a very short time, and Titian was obliged to repaint it. He painted the high altar in the church of San Nazzaro in Brescia in five divisions. Also in 1541, the master painted Don Diego di Mendoza, then ambassador from Charles V to Venice. That beautiful portrait is full-length, the first of many that Titian painted. Francesco Marcolini ordered a portrait of Pietro Aretino, but this is not as fine as the first one which Aretino sent to Duke Cosimo de' Medici as a present. He also sent a likeness of the duke's late father [Giovanni delle Bande Nere], which was painted from a death mask.

The productions of Titian, especially in portraiture, are so numerous that it would be almost impossible to make a record of them all. He painted Charles V a number of times and with such success that the emperor would allow no other to paint him and finally invited Titian to his court. Each portrait earned Titian a thousand crowns. The artist was made a knight, with an income of two hundred crowns payable by the treasury of Naples and attached to his title. When Titian painted King Philip of Spain, the son of Charles, he received another annuity of two hundred crowns, which, added to the three hundred from the German Exchange, made a fixed income of seven hundred, even if he were not to work at all. He also painted Ferdinand, king of the Romans [Charles V's brother], who was afterward emperor, and his children, Maximilian, now emperor, and Maximilian's brother. He also painted Queen Maria and the duke of Saxony.

But what a waste of time this is! There is hardly a noble of high rank, scarcely a prince or lady of great name, whose portrait has not been painted by Titian.

That year Giorgio Vasari was in Venice painting the decoration of a ceiling for Messer Giovanni Cornaro. Sansovino, who was directing the construction of Santo Spirito, ordered three designs for the ceiling. When Giorgio left without doing them, Titian painted the ceiling most admirably: Abraham's Sacrifice, David taking off the head of Goliath, and Cain killing Abel. About this time Titian painted a self-portrait as a memorial for his children. In 1546, Titian was invited to Rome by Cardinal Farnese and recommended to the care of Vasari, who kept him faithful company in his visits to the remarkable objects in Rome.

After a few days' rest, Titian received rooms in the Belvedere and began another portrait of Paul [III] full length, and the portraits of Farnese and Duke Ottavio. These patrons prevailed upon him to paint a half-length Christ in the manner of the *Ecce Homo*, as a present for the Pope. But this work, whether Titian lost courage in the presence of the paintings of Michelangelo and Raphael or from some other cause, did not seem to the painters to be as good as his usual work. Now it chanced that Michelangelo and Vasari went to see Titian one day in the Belvedere. They looked at the nude *Danaë* he had just painted. Many of those present began to praise the work, as people do when the artist stands near, but when the others had gone, Michelangelo said that the coloring was very pleasing but that it was a pity that the Venetians did not study drawing more. "For if this artist," said he, "had been aided by art and knowledge of design, as he is by nature, he would have produced works which none could surpass, especially in imitating life, since he has a fine genius and a graceful, animated manner."

It is quite true that without much study of drawing and of the best works both ancient and modern, one can never give complete grace to a work of art.

Titian enriched Rome by many works. When he reached Florence, he was as amazed at the sight of the fine works in that city as he had been by Rome. He visited Duke Cosimo and offered to do his portrait, but the duke did not give himself much trouble in the matter, perhaps because he had no intention of slighting the many noble artists of his own dominions.

Titian continued to produce a host of works. In Venice, for example, he painted an altarpiece of the Trinity Enthroned. Charles V ordered this work, and its composition, which contained the figures of the emperor and empress kneeling in prayer. His Majesty was then considering his retirement from the world and took the picture to the monastery where he lived until his death.

For Queen Maria Titian painted a Prometheus torn by the eagle of Jupiter, a Sisyphus in hell, and one of Tityus devoured by the vulture. These were on canvas and in oil paint and were sent to her Majesty. Titian then painted the *Venus and Adonis* and the equally large *Perseus and Andromeda*. A more beautiful painting could not be imagined. This could also be said of another, of Diana and her nymphs, and of still another, depicting Europa borne over the sea by the bull. These pictures are in the possession of the Catholic King [Philip II].

It is true that Titian's manner in these works is very different from his youthful style. His early work is careful and delicate and may be seen at a distance or examined closely. His later work is done in bold strokes and dashes and, if seen too near, the effect is confusing, but at a distance it is perfect. This manner has been widely imitated and is responsible for many wretched pictures. His imitators evidently labor under the delusion that it is easy to paint loosely. Actually, Titian's great expense of time and labor is most obvious. This method of his is a judicious, admirable, and beautiful one which makes the paintings seem alive and is done with a profound art, which is nevertheless concealed.

On a canvas six feet wide by eight feet high, Titian painted the *Adoration of the Magi* with numerous figures. It is very good, and so is the copy he made to give to the cardinal of Ferrara. Another work of this master, *Christ Crowned with Thorns*, was placed in a chapel of Santa Maria delle Grazie in Milan. For the high altar of San Domenico in Ancona, Titian painted a Crucifixion with the Virgin, Saint John and Saint Dominic, a very beautiful thing in his bold manner. The picture on the altar of San Lorenzo in the church of the Crucicchieri ["at the Crossroads," as the church of the Jesuits is called] at Venice is by Titian, the *Martyrdom of Saint Lawrence*. It shows a building crowded with figures and in the midst of them lies the foreshortened figure of Saint Lawrence on the gridiron, beneath which is a fire. The executioners stand about. It is a night scene; two stewards hold torches which illumine the picture beyond the glow of the fire, but the greatest light in the picture is a flash of lightning which cleaves the clouds and shines brightly over the head of the saint. At the windows of the building gleam candles held by those within. All this produces a fine effect.

On the altar of Saint Nicholas at Saint Sebastian's, there is a small very animated picture by Titian of Saint Nicholas seated on a marble throne, with an angel holding his miter.

Our artist painted a half-length figure of Mary Magdalene for the Catholic [Spanish] King. Her hair falls about her shoulders, and her tearful eyes give evidence to her sorrow for her past sins. This most beautiful picture moves all those who see it to compassion. A Venetian gentleman named Silvio was so much taken with it that he gave Titian a hundred crowns for it, and Titian had to make another, no less beautiful, for the Catholic King.

Among his portraits were those of Messer Paolo da Ponte and his daughter, a most beautiful girl and a friend of Titian's; and also that of the Signora Irene, another lovely and accomplished maiden celebrated by the pens of most of the Italian writers. In the house of the lawyer, Messer Francesco Sonica, a friend of Titian's, is the gentleman's portrait and also a large picture of the *Flight into Egypt*. The Madonna has dismounted from the ass and is sitting by the wayside. Saint Joseph stands near, and the little Saint John offers to the Saviour some flowers gathered by an angel from a tree in the wood, wherein are numerous animals. This picture is very graceful. For the Florentine Giovanni della Casa, both learned and well born, our artist painted the portrait of the lady he loved while he was in Venice. Giovanni wrote an exquisite sonnet in praise of Titian and the picture.

There are a number of important pictures, besides many sketches, still in Titian's studio; one of Our Saviour Appearing to Mary Magdalene, an Entombment, and a Madonna with, it is said, a self-portrait, done about four years ago, which is very beautiful and natural. All these works and many others that I omit in order to avoid prolixity have been executed by our artist up to his present age of seventy-six.* Titian has always been healthy and happy. Luckier than most men, he has received from heaven only favors and blessings. Every distinguished man who has visited Venice or lived there has sought him out. To say nothing of his excellence in art, he has always distinguished himself by courtesy, goodness, and rectitude.

Titian has had some rivals, but none who could challenge him. He has always been well paid. It might have been better, these latter years, if he had painted only for his own amusement and not risked his high reputation by works of inferior merit done at a time of life when nature tends inevitably to decline.

In 1566, when Vasari was in Venice, he went to pay a friendly call on Titian and found him, although very old, busy painting. Vasari had great pleasure in looking at his works and in talking to the master.

* Titian indicates in a letter that he was born in 1477. Vasari thought he was born in 1480.

Titian has adorned Venice, or rather all Italy, even all the world, with excellent paintings and deserves to be loved and respected by artists and admired and imitated as one who has produced and is still producing works of infinite merit, which must endure as long as the memory of man.

Many young men went to Titian to learn painting, but he has few disciples, since he never gave much instruction. Yet, all may learn from the master once they have understood his art. Among those about Titian was Giovanni, a Fleming [Johann Calcar], who is most honored for his anatomical studies. But Titian's most successful imitator was Paris Bordone.

Editorial Notes on Titian

WE MUST take it for granted that Vasari could not be truly appreciative of Venetian art, so different from that of the Florentines. However, Vasari's succinct observation that the Venetian painters, since Giorgione, modeled their forms with warmer or cooler tones of color shows that he had lost none of his critical faculty among these "foreigners." His observation is accurate and discerning. This use of color distinguishes Venetian painting from the Florentine, the Sienese, and the Umbrian schools. Perhaps Venetian painting had another and a fundamental distinction of which Vasari was not aware. It lies in the structure of Venetian composition.

Elsewhere, in Italy, the form in painting developed from the surface of the picture, what we call the picture-plane. The first paintings were done in flat patterns. Then, at the very beginning of the Renaissance, the figures and objects on the picture-plane were modeled deeper step by step, as if the picture were a bas-relief sculpture. From Duccio to Giotto to Masaccio we can follow this progress. In Venice, on the other hand, there seems to have been another structural principle. With Antonello da Messina the objects in the picture begin to stand on a well defined floor almost as if they were conceived as sculpture surrounded by space. Giovanni Bellini carried this principle to a monumental strength. We look at his Madonnas on a stage, as it were. The throne is set upon a triple platform. The Virgin sits directly under a semidome. From the apex of the dome a censer hangs by a slender chain right over the Virgin's head. The Madonna's attendant saints and cherubs are ranged around like monoliths.

Giorgione took the structure of Bellini's sense of composition and modeled upon it by the use of color. Titian developed Giorgione's innovation. In form, as in color, Titian is unexcelled. There is a swift whirl to his compositions. The very surface of his canvases seems alive. The ample shapes all but move in a golden haze.

Vasari has collected, in this life, an amazing catalogue of Titian's works. The mere naming of these masterpieces will be thrilling to those who admire Titian—and who does not?—and the incidental gossip about how the pictures came to be painted is interesting. The chronology of the catalogue is confused because Vasari lumped whole collections of this most prolific master's work together, just as he must have seen the pictures on his travels about Italy. The experts have taken Vasari's material and have salted it down. Vasari's unique contribution consists in having brought to life the painter and the subjects for his portraiture—his princely, his regal, his imperial, his pontifical patrons.

The whole drama of a life is placed before us, in our portrait of Paul III. Those obsequious and dangerous courtiers attend an old man whose power may make itself felt at any moment. In the portrait of Alfonso d'Este, an example of which is in the Metropolitan Museum of Art in New York, the duke of Ferrara stands resting one hand possessively on the barrel of his cannon (the Julia, made of bronze melted down from Michelangelo's statue of Pope Julius II), and looks at us with an almost frightening vitality. I have heard a doctor say that Alfonso suffered from high blood pressure. Titian knew Alfonso through and through. Titian's insight is as great as that of any portraitist. In spite of Michelangelo's slighting remarks, "good at imitating reality . . . if only he knew more . . ." it is certain Titian saw deep into character, beyond the mere scope of imitation.

Between the galleries of the Uffizi and the Pitti Palace in Florence runs a long corridor which is hung with other portraits of the personages of the High Renaissance. The very men who posed for Raphael and Titian are here portrayed by lesser artists. Though the features and costumes are recognizable, these men are but common clay. Great men, it would seem, shine brightest in the eyes of all posterity when they are painted by great artists.

While Titian's reputation as a portraitist is unassailable, he is equally superior in another field. No one has ever done more than he in the realm of emotion. The figures in the Entombment, in the Louvre, are bent in the very shape of grief as they lower the solemn weight of Christ into the grave.

MICHELANGELO BUONARROTI

Painter, Sculptor, and Architect

« 1475-1564 »

WHILE the artists who came after Giotto were doing their best to imitate and to understand nature, bending every faculty to increase that high comprehension sometimes called intelligence, the Almighty took pity on their often fruitless labor. He resolved to send to earth a spirit capable of supreme expression in all the arts, one able to give form to painting, perfection to sculpture, and grandeur to architecture. The Almighty Creator also graciously endowed this chosen one with an understanding of philosophy and with the grace of poetry. And because he had observed that in Tuscany men were more zealous in study and more diligent in labor than in the rest of Italy, He decreed that Florence should be the birthplace of this divinely endowed spirit.

In the Casetino, therefore, in 1475, a son was born to Signor Lodovico di Leonardo di Buonarroti Simoni, a descendant of the noble family of the counts of Canossa. The child's mother was also of a very good family. Lodovico was then mayor of Chiusi-e-Caprese, near the spot where Saint Francis of Assisi received the stigmata.

Moved by compelling impulse, he named the boy Michelangelo.

When his term of office was over, Lodovico returned to Settignano near Florence. Michelangelo was given to a stonecutter's wife to nurse. In that place stone quarries provide most of the employment. Talking to Vasari one day, Michelangelo said, "Giorgio, if I am good for anything, it is because I was born in the good mountain air of your Arezzo and suckled among the chisels and hammers of the stonecutters."

Because Lodovico had many children and was far from rich, he placed his boys as apprentices in the weaver's trade. At school, Michelangelo did more drawing than studying. A friend of his, Granacci, who, though just a boy, was working for Domenico Ghirlandaio, used to bring Michelangelo drawings made by his master, who was then one of the foremost painters of all Italy. The result was that Michelangelo became apprenticed to Ghirlandaio by the time he was fourteen years old.

He made great progress. One day he corrected the drawing of another and older disciple by a few strong lines. It is wonderful to see what a difference he made. I have the very sheet of paper, which Granacci gave me and which I treasure as a relic. I showed it to Michelangelo in Rome in the year 1550. He was most interested and pleased to see it and modestly remarked that evidently he knew more as a boy than now that he was old. One day when Ghirlandaio was painting the chapel in Santa Maria Novella, he went out, and while he was gone Michelangelo drew the scaffolding, trestles, pots of paint, brushes and the apprentices at their tasks. When he returned, Domenico Ghirlandaio was amazed at the power and originality of the lad's work. "This boy knows more than I do!" he exclaimed.

But it was no wonder that Michelangelo was so able. He studied continually. He copied a copper engraving by the German Martin Schongauer. The subject was Saint Anthony tormented by devils. First he drew it in pen and ink and then he painted it. He studied actual fish scales to make the devil's scales more real. He also copied drawings of the old masters so perfectly that his copies could not be distinguished from the originals, since he smoked and tinted the paper to give it the appearance of age. He was often able to keep the originals and return his copies in their stead. He did this only because of his admiration for the old masters.

Lorenzo the Magnificent at about this time engaged the sculptor Bertoldo (once the pupil of Donatello), not so much to be curator of his great collection of antiquities in the Medici gardens, as to form a school for sculptors. It is true that Bertoldo was old and could no longer work, but he was an excellent craftsman, especially in bronze. Lorenzo was concerned because there were no sculptors comparable to the many able painters of the day. He asked Ghirlandaio to recommend and bring to the school any promising young sculptors.

Michelangelo and Granacci, among others, were sent to the Medici gardens. Torrigiano was already there working on some terra-cotta figures in high relief. Michelangelo, with great enthusiasm, tried his hand at it, and was so successful that he was given a piece of marble to work on. He began to copy the head of a marble faun, a Roman work. He changed it, opening the mouth wider to show all the teeth. The Magnifico [Lorenzo] was delighted with it. He said that he did not think a faun as old as that would have such a perfect set of teeth. Michelangelo, in his simplicity, took him seriously and set to work again. He broke out a tooth and even filed down the gum to make it look shrunken. Lorenzo was much amused.

Lorenzo sent for Lodovico, Michelangelo's father, and formally arranged to receive Michelangelo into his princely household. The lad was then fifteen or sixteen. He stayed there four years, until the death of Lorenzo, receiving for himself an allowance of money and a purple cloak to wear, while his father, Lodovico, was made an official of the customs.

At this time Michelangelo carved a relief of the Battle of Hercules and the Centaurs. It is incredible that so young a man could have made anything so beautiful. He also did a plaque of the Virgin in very low relief so exactly in Donatello's manner that it really looks like a Donatello, except that it is more graceful and better designed. Michelangelo made the most of the unusual opportunity for study which the Medici collection afforded. He also studied Masaccio's frescoes in the church of the Carmine. Here in a brawl, the jeering Torrigiano gave him that blow on the nose which disfigured him for life.

When Lorenzo died, Michelangelo, in great sorrow for the loss of his patron, returned to his father's house. Piero, Lorenzo's heir, often sent for Michelangelo when he was buying antiques, and once sent to have him make a snow statue in the courtyard when the snow fell heavily in Florence. Lodovico could see that his son was really a personage among the rich and mighty and so he began to give him more stately clothes.

The prior of Santo Spirito permitted the artist to use a room in which he dissected many dead bodies. To show his gratitude for this opportunity to study anatomy, Michelangelo carved a Crucifix in wood and gave it to the prior.

A few weeks before the Medici were driven from Florence, Michelangelo, afraid to be connected with such obviously bad government, went to Bologna. He went on to Venice, but, finding no work there, returned to Bologna. Here he stayed a year. He cut two marble figures to complete the tomb of Saint Dominic which had been begun by Giovanni [Niccolò, rather] Pisano and continued by Niccolò del Arco. But he felt he was wasting his time in Bologna and returned to Florence where the Medici were again in power.

Michelangelo made a Saint John in marble for Lorenzo di Pier Francesco de' Medici. He carved a sleeping cupid, life-size. A friend said, "I am certain that, if you bury this statue for a time and then send it to Rome as an antique, you will get more for it than if you sell it here in Florence." This Michelangelo is said to have done, though some say that the friend took it to Rome and buried it there. In any case the Cardinal of San Giorgio bought it for two hundred crowns. Others say that the friend delivered only thirty crowns to Michelangelo and told him that was all he could get and kept the difference. In the meanwhile the cardinal discovered that the cupid was no antique, and had, in fact, been made in Florence, and insisted on getting his money back. He was well laughed at, and even blamed for not being able to appreciate the merit of the work, which was really perfection. What matter, they laughed, whether it were modern or not? But there will always be men who value fashion rather than real worth. The whole affair increased Michelangelo's reputation. He was invited to Rome by Cardinal San Giorgio and stayed a year with him. But the cardinal had no understanding of art and did nothing to further Michelangelo's career.

The cardinal's barber, who had been a painter and did tolerably well in fresco, made the acquaintance of Michelangelo at this time. Michelangelo drew him a cartoon of Saint Francis receiving the stigmata. This the barber painted very carefully. The beauty of the design showed through and was so clearly seen by the discerning Jacopo Gallo that he commissioned Michelangelo to carve a Bacchus. In the execution of this group Michelangelo revealed his ability to surpass all modern masters, especially in the treatment of the almost feminine softness of the young god's form and the sharp, rough, little satyr that nibbles at the grapes.

In Rome Michelangelo made such great progress in both conception and facility of execution that even the uncultivated were impressed and saw that his work was beyond comparison with any other. The cardinal of St. Denis, a Frenchman, wished to leave a memorial of himself in Rome and one done by the hand of this most famous artist. He arranged to have Michelangelo carve a Pietà. No sculptor, no matter how distinguished an artist, could add a single grace or improve this marble masterpiece in any way either in elegance or strength. In the body of the dead Christ, to say nothing of the admirable draperies, is shown the absolute perfection of research in anatomy; every vein, every muscle, every nerve is perfectly rendered as it appears in death. Besides, there is the beauty of the face, the exquisite expression. It is a marvel that the hand of an artist, in so short a time, can transform shapeless stone into a perfection of beauty seldom achieved by nature in the flesh. The love and care which Michelangelo lavished upon this group were such that he carved his name upon it, on the ribbon that crosses the Virgin's bosom. This is the only work he ever signed. Michelangelo had happened to find a large group of strangers from Lombardy looking at the Pietà one day. They were admiring it and one said that the artist was "Our Hunchback of Milan." Michelangelo came back that night with a lantern and carved Michelangelo Buonarroti where all could see. He gained great fame from this work. I have heard dull-witted folk object that the Virgin is too young. They have not been able to understand Michelangelo's ideal conception of the nature of the Madonna's virginity.

Michelangelo now received letters from friends in Florence telling him that, if he came back, he might have the big piece of marble that Pier Soderini, then gonfaloniere of the city, had talked of giving to Leonardo da Vinci, but was now proposing to present to Andrea Sansovino, an excellent sculptor, who was making every effort to get it. Few people were courageous enough to attempt to carve this eighteen-foot block of stone, which had remained in the workshop of Santa Maria del Fiore ever since a certain Maestro Simone da Fiesole had marred it thirty-five years before.

No sooner had Michelangelo arrived in Florence than he set about securing the stone. He begged it of Soderini and received it as a worthless thing. He measured the mass and accommodated his design to the injury that had been done to it. He made a little model in wax of David, sling in hand. Then he built a boarding about the marble which hid it entirely from view. He let no one look at it until he had finished it.

The problem of moving the statue [the *David*] from Santa Maria del Fiore to the Piazza de' Signori now confronted him, but Giuliano da Sangallo and his brother Antonio made a stout framework of wood about it and suspended the figure by means of a clever slipknot that became tighter under tension. They moved it forward, gradually, by means of beams and windlasses.

Soderini was very pleased with it when it was in place. He watched Michelangelo retouch it and said he thought the nose too short. Michelangelo saw that Soderini was badly placed to view the head, but, to satisfy him, he took his chisel and a little loose marble dust in his hand and climbed the scaffolding. As he tapped lightly on the chisel, he let the marble dust drift down. "I like it better now," said Soderini, "you have given it life." Michelangelo came down, not without compassion for those who wish to appear good judges in matters about which they know nothing.

Then Michelangelo showed the statue. And we may say that it surpasses all others, both ancient and modern. Not even the treasures of Rome—the *Nile* and the *Tiber* in the Belvedere, or the *Giants* of Monte Cavallo—can compare with it. The whole form is divine. The outline of the legs is most beautiful. The connection of each limb to the body is faultless. Never since has a statue been produced with so fine an attitude, so perfect a grace, such beauty of hand, of foot, of brow.

Michelangelo now began but did not finish two medallions of the Virgin and Child and Saint John. He also roughed out a Saint Matthew for the superintendents of Santa Maria del Fiore. This piece could serve as a model of workmanship to show sculptors how to draw a figure in the stone.

About this time Michelangelo cast a Madonna in bronze for certain influential Flemish merchants. They paid him one hundred crowns for the work, which they sent to Flanders [Bruges].

Agnolo Doni commissioned Michelangelo to make him something. The master painted him the *Holy Family* in a tondo [within a round frame]. This composition, unlike the bas-relief medallions, he completed. The Virgin in this most beautiful work turns tenderly, and with gravity, to offer the divine child to Saint Joseph, who receives the baby with infinite reverence.

Michelangelo sent the picture to Agnolo Doni's house by messenger with a note asking for sixty ducats. But Agnolo, who was a frugal man, objected to spending so much for a picture. He said forty ducats was enough. Michelangelo sent the messenger back to collect either one hundred ducats or the picture. Doni at once offered the sixty at first demanded. But Michelangelo, offended, now demanded one hundred and forty, and so compelled him to pay more than double.

The renowned painter, Leonardo da Vinci, was now working on his cartoon for the Great Hall of the Council, and Michelangelo was given a part of the hall to do. He chose as his subject an incident of the war with Pisa, when Florentine soldiers were surprised while bathing in the Arno. To draw groups of men, hurriedly dressing and arming, gave him every opportunity to show his skill in anatomy and action. This cartoon became a veritable school of art in itself. It seems that any artist who has studied it has himself become excellent in art. Afterward the cartoon was removed to the great hall of the Medici Palace, where it was torn to pieces during Giuliano's illness. Fragments are preserved in Mantua in the house of Messer Umberto Strozzi and treasured as they deserve.

Michelangelo's fame, because of the *Pietà*, *il Gigante* [David], and the Cartoon was so great that in 1503, when he was twenty-nine years old, he was invited to Rome by Pope Julius II. His Holiness commissioned him to make his tomb. Months passed before the design was finally approved. Indeed, it outdid any monument, even the imperial tombs, in magnificence of superb ornament and wealth of figures. When it was accepted, Julius determined to rebuild the choir of Saint Peter's to make it a fit setting.

Michelangelo set to work with all his might excavating the marble at Carrara. He was provided with a fund of one thousand crowns and was assisted by two disciples. He toiled at Carrara for eight months without receiving any additional money or supply. He amused himself with the plan for a vast monument to himself that might be carved from the living rock. Finally he selected the blocks he needed and sent them to Rome by ship. There they filled fully half the piazza near Santa Caterina and all the space between Saint Peter's and the Castello where he had his studio. To make it easier for the Pope to watch him at work, a bridge was built from the corridor of the Vatican across to the studio. This intimacy between the Pope and his favorite made others envious and caused Michelangelo a great deal of trouble.

He finished four statues and began eight others of the whole monument so magnificently planned. The tomb was to stand clear of the wall, a rectangle eighteen by twenty-three feet. The lower part was to be composed of a series of alternating niches and figures to support the cornices. In the niches were to be bound captives, some to symbolize provinces brought by Julius II to obedience to the Apostolic Church, others to represent the Fine Arts and Liberal Sciences languishing because of the death of their great patron the Pope. The feet of these figures were to rest upon the foundation of the base. The second stage was to have four large figures: Active Life and Contemplative life, Saint Paul and Moses. Above, the mass was to diminish gradually. There was to be a frieze in bronze, with figures of angels and other ornaments. Over all were to be two figures, one of heaven, smiling to receive the Pope, the other of Cybele, or the earth, weeping at his loss. It was planned in such a way that the spectator could walk between the niches to reach the central part. This resembled a temple and was designed to receive the dead body of the Pope. Finally, there were to be added forty statues in marble, to say nothing of the ornaments, cornices and architectural decorations.

Michelangelo sent some of the marble to Florence so he could work there in the summer and escape the malaria of Rome. In fact, he finished one whole side of the monument in Florence. In Rome he finished two statues of the Captive Arts [the *Slaves*] and better work has never been seen. But, since they were not used for the tomb, Michelangelo gave them to Signor Roberto Strozzi, who later gave them to King Francis of France. Our artist also began eight statues in Rome and five others in Florence. And he completed a Victory, now in the possession of Duke Cosimo. It stands in the great hall of the Medici palace, which has been painted by Vasari.

The Moses, ten feet high, was also completed. No modern work will ever approach it in beauty, no, nor ancient either. Seated in imposing dignity, the lawgiver rests one arm upon the tablet. With his other hand he restrains his flowing beard that descends so softly, hair by separate hair, as though the chisel had become a pencil. The countenance, sacred and mighty, is of the most sublime beauty. Dazzling in splendor, the lawgiver radiates his divinity. The draperies are beautifully handled and turned at the edges. The anatomical development, the muscles, and the veins of the hands are exhibited to the utmost perfection. The same may be said of the legs and feet. This Moses seems indeed the friend of God. Nay, Jews are to be seen every Saturday (which is their Sabbath), hurrying like flights of swallows, men and women, to visit and worship at this figure, as though it were something divine.*

Michelangelo set up one portion of the tomb; that is the shorter sides of it. While he was doing this, more of his marble arrived from Carrara. Because Michelangelo found His Holiness engaged with important news just received from Bologna, he advanced the money out of his own pocket. A few days later he sought an audience with the Pope but was told to have patience by a groom of the chambers who added that he had orders not to admit him. A bishop who stood near observed that possibly the groom was unacquainted with the person whom he refused to admit. The groom replied that he knew him only too well. "I, however," he added, "am here to do as my superiors command, and to obey the orders of the Pope." Displeased with this reply, the master left, bidding the attendant tell His Holiness, when next he should inquire for Michelangelo that he had gone elsewhere. He went at once to his dwelling, where he left instructions that all his belongings should be sold to the Jews. He took horses that very night and left Rome.

Once in Poggibonsi, in Florentine territory, he made a halt. Five couriers followed him, one after another, with orders from the Pope for him to return to Rome. No threat or entreaty could induce him to go back. But at last he wrote a letter, in which he complained of the treatment he had had and added that the Holy Father might seek for someone who would serve him better.

In Florence, Michelangelo worked on the cartoon for the great hall. The Signoria received three briefs in which the Pope requested that he be sent back to Rome. But the very eagerness of these requests alarmed the artist, who is said to have considered placing himself in the service of the Grand Seigneur of Constantinople [the sultan]. Piero Soderini urged Michelangelo to go to the Pope, but finally prevailed by making him ambassador from the Florentine Republic and placing him in the care of his brother, Cardinal Soderini, and sending them both to Bologna, where the Pope then was.

* A preposterous but diverting notion.

When he arrived in Bologna, scarcely was his foot out of the stirrup before attendants hurried him to the Pope's presence. Michelangelo was accompanied by a bishop because Cardinal Soderini was ill. He knelt before the Pope, who merely glanced at him, saying angrily, "It seems that you would not come to us, but were waiting for us to come to you!" (He thus alluded to the fact that Bologna is nearer Florence than is Rome.) Michelangelo excused himself and admitted that he had acted in anger, but said that he could not bear to be ordered away. If he was wrong, he hoped the Pope would forgive him.

Now the bishop, in an effort to smooth things over, said that one should not expect artists to know anything outside their vocation, ignorant as they always were. This remark threw the Pope into a furious rage. He rushed at the bishop with a stick he happened to have in his hand, crying, "It is you who are the ignoramus, with your impertinences such as we would never think of uttering!" And he drove him out, the ushers hurrying the bishop along with blows. His rage thus spent upon the prelate, the Pope bestowed his benediction on Michelangelo. He then commissioned him to begin at once a bronze figure of himself, ten feet high. Of this figure we must say that the attitude was majestic and graceful, the draperies were rich and magnificent, and the countenance showed animation, force, resolution, and an imposing dignity. It was placed in a niche over the entrance of San Petronio in Bologna.

There is a story that the celebrated goldsmith and painter, Francia, begged permission to see the statue while Michelangelo was still working on it. He was immensely impressed by it, but said only that it was a fine casting and a beautiful material. Said Michelangelo, "I am as much obliged to the Pope who gave it to me, as you are to the shopkeepers who sell you the colors you paint with." And he added in the hearing of everyone that Francia was a dunce. He also said on this occasion to a beautiful young son of Francia's, "The living figures your father makes are handsomer than those he paints." One of the gentlemen present asked which was the larger, the statue of the Pope or a pair of oxen. "That depends," replied the artist, "for, if they are Bolognese oxen, it is certain that our Florentine cattle are not such great brutes as they are." When the statue was almost finished in the clay, the Pope went to see it before he left Bologna. The Pope said he could not tell whether the figure was blessing or anathematizing the people. Michelangelo replied that he was admonishing the Bolognese to behave discreetly, and asked if he should not put a book in the left hand. "Put a sword," said the Pope, "for of letters I know but little."

The Pope left a thousand crowns on account with a banker for the completion of the figure, and after sixteen months of work it was set in place, as we have said. It was later torn down by the Bentivogli, and the bronze was sold to the duke of Ferrara, who made it into a cannon called the Julia.

The Pope returned to Rome; and while Michelangelo was still working on the statue, Bramante, who was the friend and kinsman of Raphael and hostile to Michelangelo, influenced the mind of the Pope to drop the work on the tomb and to employ Michelangelo instead on the painting of the chapel of Pope Sixtus [Sistine Chapel] in the Vatican. Bramante told the pontiff it was an invitation to death to build a tomb while one lived. Bramante and Michelangelo's other rivals hoped to thwart Michelangelo in his sculpture, in which he was perfect, and compel him to paint in fresco, in which they expected him to prove himself inferior to Raphael. Or, should he succeed at painting, it was almost certain that he would be so enraged as to secure the success of their main purpose, which was to be rid of him.

Michelangelo returned to Rome, therefore, and found the Pope no longer disposed to have the tomb finished. He was asked instead to paint the ceiling of the chapel, a great and difficult labor. Our artist, aware of his own inexperience, excused himself from the undertaking. He proposed that the work be given to Raphael. The more he refused, the more the impetuous Pope insisted. A quarrel threatened. Michelangelo saw that the Pope was determined, so he resolved to accept the task. His Holiness ordered Bramante to prepare the scaffolding. This he did by suspending the ropes through perforations in the ceiling. Michelangelo asked how the holes were going to be filled in when the painting was done. Bramante replied that they could think about it when the time came. Michelangelo saw that the architect was either incapable or unfriendly, and he went straight to the Pope to say that the scaffolding would not do and that Bramante did not know how to construct one. Julius, in the presence of Bramante, replied that Michelangelo might make it his own way. This he did by the use of a method that did not injure the walls, and which has since been pursued by Bramante and others. Michelangelo gave the ropes that were taken from Bramante's scaffolding to a poor carpenter, who sold them for a sum that made up his daughter's dowry.

Michelangelo now began to prepare the cartoons for the ceiling. His Holiness ordered that the paintings by the older masters of the time of Pope Sixtus should be effaced. Michelangelo's fee was put at fifteen thousand ducats, an estimate made by Giuliano da Sangallo. But the extent of the work compelled Michelangelo to seek assistance. He sent to Florence for Granacci, Giuliano Bugiardini, Jacopo di Sandro, and the elder Indaco, with Agnolo da Donnino, and Aristotile da Sangallo. These men were experienced in fresco-painting. Michelangelo, stimulated by the challenge, resolved to prove his pre-eminence. He finished the drawings but deferred beginning the painting until his assistants should arrive.

The masters reached the city and the work was begun. Michelangelo gave them a portion to do by way of sample. What they did came far from approaching his expectations or fulfilling his purpose. One morning he decided to destroy the whole of it. He then shut himself up alone in the chapel and not only refused them admittance there, but would not see any of them at his house. Finally, ashamed and mortified, they returned to Florence. Michelangelo made arrangements to do the whole thing himself. He avoided everyone for fear of being asked to show the work. A more and more earnest desire to see it grew day by day. Now, Pope Julius always enjoyed seeing the progress of the works he had undertaken, the more if he was thwarted. Thus it happened that he went to see the chapel one day. Michelangelo did not recognize him and rushed out upon him with a plank of the scaffolding and drove him out in a fury.*

Michelangelo told me that he refused to show the painting because of spots that had appeared on the wet plaster. In fact, he was in despair and refused to continue the work until Giuliano da Sangallo told him how the spots might be removed.

When it was half done, Pope Julius, who had gone more than once to see the work, mounting ladders with Michelangelo's assistance, insisted on having a public showing. Hasty and impatient, he would not wait for the finishing touches. In fact, when all Rome came hurrying to see the chapel, the Pope was the first to enter. He hardly waited for the dust from the removal of the scaffolding to settle. Then it was that Raphael of Urbino, who was very prompt in imitation, instantly changed his style and painted the *Prophets* and the *Sibyls* in the church of Santa Maria della Pace. Bramante tried to make the Pope give the second half of the chapel to Raphael. Hearing of this, Michelangelo complained of Bramante to the Pope. He spared no pains to point out faults in Bramante's life as well as errors in his work. Julius commanded that Michelangelo should continue the work. He completed it in twenty months, without even so much help as a man to grind his colors. It is true that Michelangelo sometimes complained that the Pope hurried him constantly by asking when it would be finished. Once Michelangelo answered, "It will be done when I believe I have satisfied art." "And we command," rejoined the pontiff, "that you

* This is one of those silly stories that has an irresistible appeal. It is palpably absurd.

satisfy our wish to have it done quickly," adding that, if it were not at once completed, he would have Michelangelo thrown from the scaffolding.

When he heard this, our artist, who feared the Pope's fury, and with good cause, instantly removed the scaffolding without retouching the painting a secco [on dry plaster], as the older masters had done. He had wanted very much to add some gold and ultramarine to the draperies to enrich the whole. The Pope, too, heard from all who praised the chapel highly that these things were still wanting and would fain have had Michelangelo do it. But Michelangelo knew it would have been too great a labor to put up the scaffolding, so the pictures remained as they were. The Pope, who saw Michelangelo often, would sometimes say, "Let the chapel be enriched with bright colors and gold, it looks poor." Then Michelangelo would answer, "Holy Father, these were poor folk and holy men, besides, who despised riches and ornament."

For this work Michelangelo was paid three thousand crowns by the Pope. He may have spent twenty-five for colors. He worked under great personal inconvenience, constantly looking upward, so that he seriously injured his eyes. For months afterward he could read a letter only when he held it above his head. I can vouch for the pain of this kind of labor. When I painted the ceiling of the palace of Duke Cosimo, I never could have finished the work without a special support for my head. As it is, I still feel the effects of it, and I wonder that Michelangelo endured it so well. But, as the work progressed, his zeal for his art increased daily, and he grudged no labor and was insensible to all fatigue.

Down the center of the ceiling is the History of the World, from the Creation to the Deluge. The Prophets and the Sibyls, five on each side and one at each end, are painted on the corbels. The lunettes portray the genealogy of Christ. Michelangelo used no perspective, nor any one fixed point of sight, but was satisfied to paint each division with perfection of design. Truly this chapel has been, and is, the very light of our art. Everyone capable of judging stands amazed at the excellence of this work, at the grace and flexibility, the beautiful truth of proportion of the exquisite nude forms. These are varied in every way in expression and form. Some of the figures are seated, some are in motion, while others hold up festoons of oak leaves and acorns, the device of Pope Julius.

All the world hastened to behold this marvel and was overwhelmed, speechless with astonishment. The Pope rewarded Michelangelo with rich gifts and planned still greater works. Michelangelo sometimes remarked that he was aware that the pontiff really esteemed his abilities. When the Pope was sometimes rude and rough, he always soothed the injury by gifts and favors. Once, for example, Michelangelo asked leave to go to Florence for the festival of San Giovanni and begged also for some money for the journey. Pope Julius said, "Well! but when will this chapel be finished?" "When I can, Holy Father," said the artist. At that the Pope, who had a staff in his hand, struck Michelangelo and exclaimed, "When I can—when I can! I'll make thee finish it, and quickly." But no sooner had Michelangelo returned to his house to prepare for the journey, than the pontiff's chamberlain brought five hundred crowns to pacify him. The chamberlain excused the Pope, declaring that these outbursts must be considered marks of His Holiness' favor. Michelangelo knew the Pope and was, after all, much attached to him. He laughed at what had happened, the more readily because things of this kind always turned out to his profit, and he saw that the Pope was anxious to keep him as a friend.

Pope Julius, before he felt the approaches of death, enjoined his nephews to see that his tomb should be constructed after a simpler design than that at first adopted. Michelangelo set to work with a will and he hoped to bring it to a conclusion without further obstacles. But Pope Julius died, and under Pope Leo [X] the work was laid aside. This pontiff was no less splendid in his undertakings than Julius. He was the first Florentine pope and he wished to leave some great memorial of himself and of that divine artist, Michelangelo, his fellow citizen, in his native city. He therefore commissioned Michelangelo to execute the façade of the church of San Lorenzo, which had been built by the house of Medici in Florence. He required Michelangelo to act as superintendent of the works. Michelangelo resisted as much as he dared, urging that he was pledged to do the tomb. But the Pope procured Michelangelo's release from the nephews of Pope Julius by promising that the artist should continue his preparations for the tomb by working on the figures for it in Florence, as he had formerly done. All this was much to the dissatisfaction of the cardinals [the nephews of Pope Julius] as well as to Michelangelo, who left Rome with tears in his eyes.

There was endless discussion about the façade of San Lorenzo, which ought certainly to have been confided to many persons instead of to one. Among the artists who applied to the Pope for the direction of this work were Baccio d' Agnolo, Antonio da Sangallo, Andrea and Jacopo Sansovino, and the graceful Raphael of Urbino. But Michelangelo determined to do the whole thing himself. He had a grant of a thousand crowns to be given him by Jacopo Salviati. When he presented himself for the money, Jacopo happened to be closeted with certain citizens on matters of importance, and Michelangelo refused to wait. He set out immediately for Carrara.

When Salviati heard that the master had been in Florence, he sent a messenger with the money to Carrara. The messenger asked for a receipt. Michelangelo replied that the money was the Pope's and not his own, and that the messenger could take it back if he liked, but that he, Michelangelo, was not accustomed to sign receipts for others. Whereupon the man became alarmed and went back to Jacopo Salviati without any receipt.

While Michelangelo was at Carrara, excavating marble for both the tomb of Julius and the façade of San Lorenzo, he got a letter from Pope Leo saying that there were equally beautiful marbles to be had in Florentine territory, at Serravezza. Now, Michelangelo knew this already, but he was the friend of the Marchese Alberigo, lord of Carrara, and perhaps he thought Serravezza inaccessible. The Pope would not hear a word of objection. A road had to be built over mountain, over mire. Years were lost, but at last Michelangelo procured five columns of fine proportion from these quarries. One of them is now on the Piazza of San Lorenzo in Florence, while the others lie on the shore. And the Marchese Alberigo became the bitter enemy of Michelangelo, although the latter was so little to blame.

Other marbles were afterward procured at Serravezza, where they have been lying more than thirty years, but the road lacks two miles of being complete. Michelangelo also found another quarry of very beautiful hard marble. He thus wasted many years. It is true that he prepared models for these undertakings, but the money appropriated for the work was spent in the Lombardy wars. At the death of Leo all was left incomplete, with nothing accomplished but the foundations of the façade and one great column transported to the Piazza of San Lorenzo.

The death of Leo X was a staggering blow to the arts and the artists both of Florence and of Rome. While Adrian VI ruled, Michelangelo worked on the tomb of Julius II in Florence. Adrian died, and Clement VII was elected in his place. The latter proved himself as anxious as Leo to leave great memorials of his fame in painting, sculpture, and architecture. It was at this time that Giorgio Vasari, then a boy, was taken to Florence by the cardinal of Cortona and placed to study art with Michelangelo. But because Michelangelo was called to Rome to consult with the Pope about the library of San Lorenzo, it was determined that Giorgio should go to the workshop of Andrea del Sarto. The master went with the boy to recommend him to the care of Andrea.

Michelangelo went straight to Rome. The duke of Urbino [nephew of Julius II] harassed and threatened him and complained that the artist had received sixteen thousand ducats for the tomb and still loitered in Florence instead of completing it. Pope Clement advised Michelangelo to square his accounts with the duke. The Pope would gladly have had the master's time at his own command, and suggested that the duke was probably Michelangelo's debtor. Thus the matter was left, but the Pope and Michelangelo agreed that the sacristy and the new library of San Lorenzo should be entirely completed.

Back in Florence, the master erected the cupola [of San Lorenzo]. He had the goldsmith Piloto make a ball of seventy-two facets. His friends advised him to take care to have his lantern very different from Filippo Brunelleschi's. Michelangelo said, "Brunelleschi's would be difficult to imitate and impossible to surpass." He made monuments for the inside of the sacristy, for Giuliano and Lorenzo de' Medici. Michelangelo wished to imitate the old sacristy of Brunelleschi, but with new ornaments, and composed a decoration richer and more varied than any ever seen before. He boldly departed from the accepted rules. The unfortunate result has been that other artists have been encouraged to an injudicious imitation outside the wholesome rules of ornamentation. Artists, however, owe a great deal to Michelangelo, who freed them from the beaten path of convention. Boldness and grace are conspicuous in every part of his design, and the whole building is so unlike the usual treatment that one stands amazed at the sight of it.

Then came the sack of Rome and the exile of the Medici from Florence. Those who governed the city appointed Michelangelo to rebuild the fortifications. He prepared numerous plans to add to the defenses, fortifying San Miniato with bastions constructed after he had inspected the fortifications at Ferrara. While he was in Ferrara, Duke Alfonso I begged the master to execute some work of art for him at his leisure. This Michelangelo promised to do. He returned to Florence and proceeded with the fortifications. Yet he found time to paint a Leda, in tempera, for the duke of Ferrara, a divine performance. He also worked secretly on the statues for the tombs in San Lorenzo. He remained for six months at San Miniato, hastening the defenses, for the city would have been lost if the enemy had mastered that point. The sacristy was progressing and Michelangelo occupied a portion of his time in making seven statues for that place; one was a Madonna with the Infant astride her knee who turns as if entreating the breast, while the Virgin holds him with one hand and supports herself with the other, bending forward to give it to the babe. The figures are not finished in every part, but in the imperfection of the sketch, perfection clearly shows. Still more amazing are the tombs of the dukes Giuliano and Lorenzo de' Medici. As though the earth itself were not enough to be their burial place, Day and Night and Dawn and Twilight overshadow the sarcophagi. All are beautiful in form and attitude, and the knowledge displayed is so great that, if the art of sculpture were lost, it might be restored from these figures alone. The statues of the princes in their armor form part of the ornament. Duke Lorenzo, in deep thought, has a form of immortal beauty. Duke Giuliano is erect and haughty. The head, the throat, the profile of the nose, the chiseling of the mouth—all is truly divine. The spectator is never satisfied with gazing. The very buskins and cuirass seem not of this world. But what shall we say of Aurora? The nude female figure awakens deep melancholy in the soul, in her own unchanging beauty bewailing the bitterness of the death of the great prince. Or what shall I say of Night? This statue is not rare, it is unique. Where in the world's history has any statue shown such art? This is the Night that blots out those who expect not to surpass, but to equal Michelangelo. A weight of sleep hangs upon this figure, seemingly molded by nature herself. Many verses were composed in praise of our artist's work, as for example these by an unknown author:

> The Night that here thou seest, in graceful guise
> Thus sleeping, by an Angel's hand was carved
> In this pure stone; but sleeping, still she lives.
> Awake her if thou doubtest, and she'll speak.

Michelangelo replied as follows, speaking in the person of Night:

> Sweet is my sleep, but more to be mere stone,
> So long as ruin and dishonor reign;
> To hear naught, to feel naught, is my great gain;
> Then wake me not, speak in an undertone!
> —Translated by JOHN ADDINGTON SYMONDS

If the enmity between fortune and genius had but allowed this work to be completed, art might have surpassed nature on every point.

Then came the siege of Florence, and Michelangelo turned all his attention to the defenses of the city. He lent the Republic a thousand crowns and was one of the Council of War. But, when the enemy had closed round the city, and hope of aid faded, Michelangelo felt himself in a position not suited to him and he resolved to save himself by going to Venice. He departed secretly, accompanied only by his disciple, Antonio Mini, and his good friend, the goldsmith Piloto. Each of them had a sum of money sewed into his clothes. When they reached Ferrara they halted to refresh themselves.

Because of the state of war, Alfonso of Ferrara kept strict watch and was secretly informed of the presence of all foreigners. He was aware of Michelangelo's arrival and rejoiced at it. That magnanimous prince delighted in works of genius all his life. He sent an invitation to Michelangelo to come and stay at the palace. His courtiers were ordered to conduct the artist thither. Michelangelo saw that he had no choice; he went, though without taking his baggage. The duke received him graciously but complained of his reserve and secrecy. He did his utmost to persuade Michelangelo to remain in Ferrara. But to this Michelangelo would not agree. The duke then offered to serve him to the best of his ability. Not to be outdone, Michelangelo said the duke was welcome to the twelve thousand crowns he had brought with him. Then the duke showed Michelangelo the palace with all the fine works of art, among others his own portrait by Titian, which Michelangelo praised highly. He could not be persuaded to accept rooms in the palace but returned to the inn. The duke sent various supplies to the inn, and instructed the host to refuse any remuneration when his guest should depart.

Our artist went on to Venice, where many of the most distinguished people wished to make his acquaintance. He had a poor opinion of their judgment in artistic matters. They say he prepared a design for the bridge of the Rialto, at the entreaty of the Doge Gritti. Meanwhile he was begged to return to Florence and a safe conduct was sent him. He did return but not without danger to his life. It is furthermore related that Michelangelo at that time obtained the eighteen-foot block of marble that Pope Clement had promised to Baccio Bandinelli. The stone now belonged to the commonwealth, and Michelangelo asked the gonfaloniere for it. He made a very fine model, but the war ended and the Medici were restored, so the stone was returned to Bandinelli. Michelangelo even had to hide for a few days from a threat of arrest and imprisonment. But when the first bitterness of resentment had subsided, Pope Clement remembered the ability of Michelangelo and gave orders that he should proceed with the works of San Lorenzo. Reassured Michelangelo began a figure of Apollo drawing an arrow from his quiver, and though it was never quite finished, it is a work of extraordinary merit.

About this time a gentleman sent by Duke Alfonso sought out Michelangelo to ask for the beautiful work he had made for the duke. The master received him courteously and showed him the *Leda*. The duke's messenger expected something much grander and remarked, "Oh, this is a trifling thing." Whereupon our artist asked him what his vocation was. He replied, with some sort of slighting jest about the industry of the Florentines, "I am a merchant." "Indeed!" answered Michelangelo, "then you are about to make a bad bargain for your master. Please get out of my sight!" And he presented the *Leda* to his disciple Antonio Mini, who had two sisters to marry, a noble gift indeed. When Mini went to France he took the painting with him and there it was sold to King Francis.

Michelangelo thought it time to go to Rome and receive the commands of Pope Clement. His Holiness forgave all and commanded that he should complete San Lorenzo. Some of the statues were given to other sculptors to do, though Michelangelo made rough models in clay for all of them. Michelangelo worked on the library. The ceiling and shelves and the stucco work were done by good masters in their vocations. Michelangelo wished to complete his statues, too, but he was summoned to Rome by Pope Clement to paint the *Last Judgment* on the wall behind the altar in the [Sistine] Chapel.

While this work was in progress, not a day passed but agents of the duke of Urbino accused Michelangelo of receiving sixteen thousand crowns for the tomb of Julius II. He most earnestly wished to remain in Rome and work on the tomb. An agreement was finally reached to make the tomb with a single façade, with only six statues carved by Michelangelo himself. By the terms of this contract the duke of Urbino allowed Michelangelo to work four months a year for the Pope. Michelangelo now felt assured of peace, but the Pope hurried on the painting of the Last Judgment. Yet Michelangelo did work secretly on the tomb.

In 1534, Pope Clement died, and the work in San Lorenzo was at once laid aside. Michelangelo now believed himself free to give all his attention to the tomb of Pope Julius. But Pope Paul III soon summoned him, received him with great favor, and said he wished the master to enter his service. Michelangelo excused himself, saying he was under contract to the duke of Urbino to finish the tomb. Paul was much displeased. "For thirty years I have wished this! And now that I am Pope, will you disappoint me? That contract shall be torn up. I will have you work for me, come what may." Michelangelo was tempted to flee Rome and contrive to work on the tomb elsewhere, but he resolved to try to pacify the Pope, already so old, until something new happened.

Pope Paul, meanwhile, went with ten cardinals to Michelangelo's house to see the statues for the tomb of Julius. The cardinal of Mantua remarked that the *Moses* was sufficient of itself to do honor to the late pontiff. They also examined the cartoons for the wall of the chapel and

were amazed at their beauty. His Holiness promised to persuade the duke
of Urbino to be satisfied with three statues on condition that the other
three be executed after Michelangelo's designs by other artists. But Michelangelo offered to pay for these three statues in order to be rid of this long
and vexatious labor.

Michelangelo resolved, as he needs must, to enter the service of Pope
Paul III and continue the painting of the chapel. The pontiff held the
genius of Michelangelo in great respect and loved and admired him
besides. The Pope wished to place his arms beneath the prophet Jonas
where those of Julius II were, but he yielded at once with a good grace,
when he saw that the suggestion gave Michelangelo pain.

I do not propose to describe this work [the Last Judgment], which has
so often been reproduced. It will be enough to say that the purpose of the
master was to render the human form in the absolute perfection of proportion and the greatest variety of attitude and to express the passions with
force and truth. With this in mind he gave little attention to coloring
or to minutiae.

When it was three quarters done, Pope Paul went to see it. Messer
Biagio da Cesena, the master of ceremonies, when asked to give his
opinion, said that he thought it very improper to have so many nude
forms, shameless in their nakedness, in that sacred place. He added that
such pictures were suited to a bath or a wineshop. Messer Biagio had no
sooner left than our artist drew his portrait from memory, with a serpent
wound around him surrounded by devils in hell. Nor could Messer Biagio
persuade the Pope to have the portrait removed.*

Michelangelo fell from the scaffolding and hurt his leg, but would not
allow a surgeon to come near him. Messer Baccio Rontini, his great friend
and admirer, went to his house and knocked. Getting no answer he finally
forced his way in and found the master in a desperate state. Baccio never
left his bedside until the leg was cured.

When he was well, Michelangelo completed the painting. This great
work may be described in the words of Dante, "Dead are the dead, the
living seem to live." Michelangelo surpassed himself. The seated figure of
Our Lord, terrible in his anger, turns toward the condemned, thundering
anathema. Our Lady cowers in her mantle at the sight of that destruction.
In a word, we have here the true Last Judgment, the real Condemnation,
the effectual Resurrection. Those who thought they knew art are overcome
by this work. They gaze upon the evidence of power in these contours and

* The Pope, to Messer Biagio: "If the painter had put thee in purgatory, I would
have done my utmost, but since he hath sent thee to hell, it is useless for thee to come
to me, since thence, as thou knowest, nulla est redemptio."

they tremble with fear as though some great spirit had possessed himself of the art of design. The more they examine this work, the more they are bewildered at the thought of a comparison of other paintings with this paragon.

Fortunate is he, and happy are his memories, who has seen this wonder. Thrice blessed art thou, O Paul, under whose protection was sheltered his renown! A great happiness has been his birth for all artists, since Michelangelo has solved all the difficulties that previously obscured painting, sculpture, and architecture.

Michelangelo worked at this painting for eight years and showed it to the public on Christmas day in the year 1541. Not Rome only, but the whole world, was filled with amazement and delight. For my part, I went from Venice to Rome to see it and I was utterly astounded by it.

Now Pope Paul resolved to have Michelangelo paint two large pictures in the Pauline Chapel. One was the *Conversion of Paul*, and the other the *Martyrdom of Peter*. We must not look for landscapes, trees, buildings, or any other attraction in this work. Perhaps it was because he would not debase his great genius to such matters. These were his last pictures, painted when he was in his seventy-fifth year, and, as he told me himself, at cost of great fatigue. Painting, and especially in fresco, is not for old men. He arranged that Perino del Vaga, an excellent painter, should decorate the ceiling after his designs, and to this Pope Paul consented, but the work was never completed.

Pope Paul had begun to fortify the Borgo, but, knowing that Michelangelo had directed the fortifications of San Miniato, he asked his opinion. That he disagreed with most of the other engineers, Michelangelo made perfectly plain. Sangallo told him that sculpture was his business, and not fortification. To this Michelangelo replied that he knew but little of sculpture and painting, but that he knew more about fortification than Sangallo and all his house put together. He then proceeded to point out their errors. One word leading to another, the Pope was compelled to impose silence. But soon afterward Michelangelo put the whole fortification in order, and the great gate of Santo Spirito, designed by Sangallo and then nearly completed, was left unfinished.

Michelangelo could not endure idleness. Since he was not able to paint any longer, he began to work on a piece of marble from which he proposed to extract a Pietà of four figures larger than life. He said he was doing it for his amusement and for his health. Our Saviour is being lifted down from the cross by the Virgin, who is powerfully aided by Nicodemus. One of the Marys comes to the aid of Our Lady, who is almost overcome by her grief. This is an absolutely new conception of the dead Christ. He sinks with the limbs in perfect abandonment. Such a work has rarely been extracted from a single stone. It is truly a beautiful and most laborious work, but it remained unfinished even though Michelangelo had intended it to be his own monument.

When Antonio da Sangallo died in 1546, a new director of the works of St. Peter's was required, and at length the Pope was inspired to send for Michelangelo. The master said that architecture was not his vocation, but the Pope commanded him, against his will, to accept the trust. One day when he had gone to the building to examine it and to see Sangallo's wooden model, he was met by a whole party of the Sangallicans who complimented him on his appointment and remarked that the model before them was a field on which he need never want pasture. "Well said," replied Michelangelo, thus implying, as he mentioned to a friend, that it was fit for sheep, who knew nothing of art. He often declared publicly that Sangallo had left the building without lights and that fifty years of work and three hundred thousand crowns might be saved by a simplification of the design, which he considered too elaborate with pinnacles, projections, and divisions of members. He made a model to prove this and it is the one that has since been used. This model cost twenty-five crowns and was finished in a fortnight, while Sangallo's cost four thousand and was several years in the making. It was easy to see that the church had become an endless source of income rather than a building to be finished. Such a state of affairs could not but displease so upright a man as Michelangelo, and he finally told the contractors that he knew they were doing their best to hinder him, but that, if he did undertake the charge, he would see to it that not one of them remained about the building. These words so publicly spoken aroused a great deal of ill feeling, and Michelangelo got no peace, since his adversaries constantly invented new ways of tormenting him.

At length the pontiff issued a decree that Michelangelo was to be in sole charge. Michelangelo inserted a clause that he was to receive no reward, but would perform his office for the love of God. Although Pope Paul more than once sent him money, Michelangelo would never accept any.

Michelangelo's model was approved by the Pope. Although it decreased the circumference of the building, it gave, in fact, greater space. It was now found that the four principal piers built by Bramante to support the weight of the tribune were too weak. I will not describe all the changes our artist made, but will be content to say that he caused all to be constructed with the utmost exactitude and added a degree of strength that should leave no pretext for anyone to disturb his plans.

Michelangelo was consulted on the plans to rebuild the Capitol. He made a rich and beautiful design with a fine front in travertine, a double flight of steps, and varied balustrades. He added statues of recumbent river gods, the *Nile* and the *Tiber*, eighteen feet high, and between them *Jupiter*, in a niche. On the south side a rich façade with a loggia of columns brings the building to a square plan. In the center of the piazza the equestrian figure of Marcus Aurelius was erected. The whole deserves to be considered one of Michelangelo's finest works, although it is not yet complete.

Antonio da Sangallo had worked on the Farnese Palace, but the upper cornice was still incomplete. His Holiness [Paul III was a Farnese] desired Michelangelo to design one. He made a model in wood, the actual size but only fourteen feet long, and had it fixed on one of the angles of the palace to try the effect. It was much admired and is the most beautiful ever erected. Michelangelo constructed the great window with the columns of varicolored marble that is over the principal entrance and added an escutcheon in marble bearing the arms of Paul III. He continued working on this palace until it became the finest in all Europe.

Pope Paul died in 1549, and Julius III was elected. There were disputes about the placing of Paul's tomb. Michelangelo made still another enemy, Fra Guglielmo della Porta, the designer of the tomb. That same year Pope Julius resolved to erect two tombs for his illustrious forebears, and Vasari made the designs and models. Pope Julius admired the genius of Michelangelo and loved Vasari, and he asked the former to set a price upon these labors. Vasari begged the Pope to put the whole work under Michelangelo's protection. Vasari also proposed that Simone Mosca should be engaged to prepare carvings for this chapel and that Raffaello di Montelupo should make statues, but Michelangelo advised against carvings of foliage or any of the usual decorations. Vasari was afraid the work would look poor, but when it was completed he saw that Michelangelo had displayed judgment, nay, great judgment. The master was unwilling that Raffaello di Montelupo should execute the statues because of the poor work he did under Michelangelo's guidance on the tomb of Julius II. He preferred Ammanati, who was also Vasari's choice. Michelangelo had a touch of personal dislike for this artist because he had taken some of the master's drawings from Antonio Mini. Michelangelo was once talking to Vasari about this matter. Vasari said, laughingly, that he himself would have taken all he could lay his hands on in pure zeal for the love of art.

The matter was thus turned into a jest and Ammanati went with Vasari to Carrara to prepare the marbles.

Vasari saw Michelangelo every day. One morning in the Jubilee year, the Pope kindly gave them a holiday to join the cavalcade that was visiting the Seven Churches and receive absolution together. They talked pleasantly, while going from one church to another, of the arts, and Vasari wrote down the whole dialogue, hoping to publish it some day. Pope Julius confirmed Michelangelo's authority over the work on Saint Peter's, in spite of the fault found by the followers of Sangallo. Vasari assured the pontiff that Michelangelo had given life to the edifice, which was the truth, and begged him not to alter the design for the building without Michelangelo's full consent. Nor did Pope Julius do anything without Michelangelo's advice at the Vigna Julia or the Belvedere.

It was in this same year that Vasari published his book, the *Lives of the Painters, Sculptors, and Architects.* He had written the life of no living artist, with the exception of Michelangelo. He now presented his work to that master, who received it gladly, for many of the facts were from his own wise and experienced observation. Soon afterward Michelangelo sent Vasari the following sonnet, which, in memory of his affection, I think it well to insert in this place:

TO GIORGIO VASARI

(On the *Lives of the Painters*.)

Se con lo stile

With pencil and with palette hitherto,
You made your art high Nature's paragon;
Nay more, from Nature her own prize you won,
Making what she made fair more fair to view.
Now that your learnèd hand with labor new
Of pen and ink a worthier work hath done,
What erst you lacked, what still remained her own,
The power of giving life, is gained for you.
If men in any age with Nature vied
In beauteous workmanship, they had to yield
When to the fated end years brought their name.
You re-illuming memories that died,
In spite of Time and Nature have revealed
For them and for yourself eternal fame.

—Translated by JOHN ADDINGTON SYMONDS

In 1551 a plot against Michelangelo was formed by the Sangallican faction, who protested to the Pope that Saint Peter's was going to lack light. A general meeting was called and the Pope told Michelangelo about the complaint. Michelangelo spoke directly to Cardinal Marcello, the chief of the deputies of the faction: "Monsignore, in the vaulting above, and which is to be of travertine, there are to be three other windows." "You have never told us so," said the cardinal. Then Michelangelo replied, "I neither am nor will be obliged to tell either your lordship or any other person what I intend or ought to do for this work. Your office is to procure money. The designs for the buildings are my concern." Then he turned to the Pope and said, "Holy Father, if these labors of mine do not benefit my soul, my time is ill spent." The Pope, who loved him, replied as he laid his hands on the shoulders of the master, "Your soul and body will both gain, never doubt it."

The day after these events the Pope invited Michelangelo and Vasari to come to the Vigna Julia. Here the pontiff talked long with them and discussed all the admirable improvements since carried out, all of which were done according to the judgment and opinion of Michelangelo. Once, on one of their frequent visits, they found the Pope with twelve cardinals, and His Holiness insisted that Michelangelo sit near him. The pontiff always did every possible honor to Michelangelo's genius. He also required that every other artist wait upon Michelangelo at his own house. His consideration for our artist was so great that he refrained from asking him to execute many a work that our master, notwithstanding his age, might very well have performed.

In the time of Pope Paul III, Michelangelo had been commissioned to repair the foundations of the bridge of Santa Maria. Much of the work had been done at great expense for timber and travertine. In the pontificate of Julius III there was agitation to bring the work to an end. It was suggested that Nanni di Baccio Bigio should finish it by contract, since Michelangelo took so little interest in it that at the present rate the work would never be done. The Pope was no lover of disputes and so gave his consent. Behind Michelangelo's back, Nanni set to work. He actually weakened the foundations by removing and selling foundation blocks of travertine. Nanni made bulwarks which looked strong, but five years later, when the flood of 1557 came down, the bridge fell in complete ruin. Michelangelo had frequently predicted this. I remember one day when we were crossing the bridge on horseback, he said to me, "Giorgio, this bridge shakes. Let us be gone before it falls with us on it."

When, in 1544, Vasari returned to Florence, Michelangelo was very grieved, as indeed was Giorgio, and they wrote each other daily. In April Vasari wrote Michelangelo that his nephew Leonardo had had a son at whose baptism Vasari had been present. The child was named Buonarroto. To this letter Michelangelo replied:

My dear friend Giorgio,

Your last gave me great pleasure for I see that you still remember the poor old man, and that you were present at the triumph of which you write, and have seen the birth of another Buonarroto. I thank you for telling me though I am displeased at so much pomp and merriment when the whole world is in tears. I think Leonardo should not rejoice so much over a birth but that such joy should be reserved for the death of one who has lived well. Do not be surprised that I have not replied immediately. As for the praises you shower upon me, if I deserved only one of them, I could repay you only by handing myself over to you soul and body, so much am I your debtor. I must acknowledge you my creditor for more than I can pay, and, being old, I have no hope of paying off the debt. In the next life, we may regulate our accounts. Pray be patient. I am wholly yours. Things here are much the same as usual.

Even in the time of Paul III, Duke Cosimo had tried to persuade Michelangelo to come back to Florence to finish the sacristy of San Lorenzo. The master excused himself, saying he was too old and could neither endure the labor nor leave Rome. Tribulo, the duke's messenger in this matter, tried to obtain Michelangelo's correct and final design for the steps of the library of San Lorenzo, for which there were a few sketches and a heap of stones all prepared. But all Michelangelo would say was that he could not remember.

The duke then commanded Vasari to write to the master, since it was hoped that for love of him Michelangelo would say something that would enable them to bring the work to some conclusion. Vasari wrote that he himself would be in charge of the work and take most minute care with it. Michelangelo replied by sending the plans in a letter written in his own hand on September 28, 1555.

Messer Giorgio, my dear friend,

About that staircase, believe me, if I could remember how I had arranged it, I should not need so many entreaties. There is a certain stair that comes into my thoughts like a dream, but I do not think it is exactly the one I had planned because it seems a clumsy thing. I will describe it for you nevertheless . . .

[a description of "oval boxes"]

What I am writing is laughable, but I know you will find something in it that you can use.

In those days Michelangelo wrote to Vasari that his enemies were tormenting him anew. The duke's private secretary sent to Rome to tell Michelangelo that, if only he would come back to Florence, the duke would ask nothing from him but occasional advice about his buildings. The messenger also carried a letter from Vasari to the same effect. But Pope Paul IV had been elected and he received Michelangelo most amiably and with generous offers. Michelangelo felt bound to continue his duties in the building of St. Peter's and so wrote to the duke and also wrote to Vasari as follows:

Messer Giorgio, my dear friend,
    I call God to witness how much against my will it was that I undertook the work on Saint Peter's, ten years ago. If the work had continued at the rate it was begun, I might now be able to leave it and return home. But lack of money has retarded it, and at the time when the most difficult part is still to be done. To abandon it now would be a great shame and sin and the labor of the last ten years would be lost. I am saying this in reply to your letter and because I have had a letter from the duke that is marvellously kind. I thank God and his excellency as much as I may and can. But I wander from my subject. I have lost my faculties. Writing is very hard for me since it is not my vocation. The conclusion is that you must understand that, if I were to abandon the building and depart, I would, first of all, rejoice many a scoundrel, and lastly, I should cause the ruin, or perhaps the full suspension of the edifice.

    He also wrote to Vasari that, since he had a house and establishment in Rome worth some thousands of crowns, and as he suffered from the infirmities of age, he was not fit for travel, as his physician, Messer Eraldo, to whom he owed his life, could testify. For all these causes, he was unable to leave Rome and had, indeed, courage for nothing more than to die and be at rest. Vasari has kept other letters in which Michelangelo begs to be excused to the duke. Had he been in a condition to travel, he would have gone at once to Florence. The kindness of Duke Cosimo moved him deeply, and I do not believe that, had he come, he would ever have departed again.

    Meanwhile Michelangelo pressed on the work at Saint Peter's in an effort to bring it to such a state that no further changes could be made. About this time he was told that Paul IV wished to change the paintings in the chapel because some of the figures in the *Last Judgment* were shamefully nude. Michelangelo said, "Tell His Holiness that this is a mere trifle, and can easily be done. Let him mend the world; paintings are easily mended."

Michelangelo's servant, who had become his trusted friend during the twenty-six years of his service, died that year. The master had nursed him in his sickness and slept in his clothes beside him at night the better to watch over him. When Urbino died, Vasari wrote to Michelangelo to console him and the master replied in these words:

My dear Messer Giorgio,

I am hardly able to write at this time, but I must try to reply to your letter. You know that Urbino is dead, which is both a great mercy from God and a great grief and infinite loss to me. The mercy is that, whereas in his life he kept me alive, in his dying he taught me to die, not only without regret, but actually with the desire to depart. I have had him twenty-six years, found him ever faithful, and now that I had made him rich and hoped to have in him the staff and support of my old age, he has disappeared from my sight. Nor have I any other hope than that of rejoining him in paradise. Of this God has given me a glimpse in the blessed death that he died. He did not grieve for himself, but for me, to leave me alone in this treacherous world with so many troubles. Truly the best part of my being has gone with him, nor is anything left me but an infinite sorrow. And herewith I bid you farewell.

Under Paul IV Michelangelo worked upon the fortifications of Rome. For Salustio Peruzzi, who was constructing the great gate of the Castello di Sant' Angelo, he undertook to distribute the statues required for that work and to superintend the work of the sculptors. But the French army was approaching Rome, and Michelangelo, fearing an evil end for himself and for the city, fled secretly to the mountains of Spoleto, where he visited several hermitages. At this time Vasari wrote to him and sent him a little book that was dedicated to Michelangelo [*Difesa della lingua e di Dante*]. Michelangelo replied:

Messer Giorgio, my dear friend,

I have received Messer Cosimo's little book, and in this shall be an acknowledgment, which I beg you to present to him with my service.

I have in these last days undertaken a visit to the mountains of Spoleto, to the hermits abiding there, at great cost of labor and money, but also to my great pleasure, so that I have returned to Rome with but half my heart, for there is no peace and quiet like that of those woods. I have no more to tell you. I rejoice that you are well and happy, and recommend myself to your friendly remembrance. This 18th day of Sept., 1556.

Almost every day Michelangelo worked for his amusement on the Pietà which we have mentioned. But at last he broke up the block, either because of defects in the marble, or because the stone was so hard that the chisel often struck sparks, or because he was too severe a judge of his own work and could never be content with anything he did. It is true that few of his mature works were ever completed and that those entirely finished were productions of his youth. Such were the *Bacchus*, the *Pietà* of the Madonna della Febbre [in Saint Peter's], *il Gigante* [the *David*], at Florence, and the *Christ Risen* of the Minerva [Santa Maria sopra Minerva], which are finished to such perfection that a single grain could not be taken from them without injury. Michelangelo often said that, if he were compelled to satisfy himself, he should show little or nothing. The reason is obvious: he had attained such knowledge in art that the slightest error could not exist without his immediate discovery of it. But once it had been seen in public, he would never attempt to correct it, but would begin a new work, for he believed that a similar failure would not happen again. He often declared that this was the reason that the number of his finished works was so small.

He gave the broken *Pietà* to Francesco Bandini. While it was still in Michelangelo's house, the Florentine sculptor, Tiberio Calcagni, inquired after a long discussion why he had destroyed so admirable a performance. Our artist replied that he had been driven to it by Urbino, his servant, who urged him every day to finish it. Besides, a piece had broken off the arm of the Madonna. This and a vein which appeared in the marble had caused him infinite trouble and had driven him out of patience. He would have dashed the group to fragments, if Antonio had not advised him to give it to someone, even as it was. Tiberio offered Antonio two hundred crowns in gold to persuade Michelangelo to allow Tiberio to finish the group for Bandini, that the labor already spent on it might not be lost. So Michelangelo gave them the pieces, which they instantly carried away. These were put together by Tiberio, and certain parts, I know not what, added. But the death of Bandini, of Michelangelo, and of Tiberio himself, left the work unfinished after all.

It now became necessary to find Michelangelo another block of marble in order that he might amuse himself daily with his chisel. He therefore took a much smaller block and began another Pietà, but in a different manner.

Paul IV engaged a new architect, Piero Ligorio, who went about saying that Michelangelo was in his second childhood. This offended our artist, who would have liked to return to Florence and was urged to do so by Vasari. But he was now eighty-one, and he excused himself in a letter to Vasari, to whom he sent several spirited sonnets. He said that the end of his days had nearly come and that no thought arose in his mind that did not bear the impress of approaching death. He added, in one of his letters:

"God has willed it that my life must be endured for some time longer. I know you will tell me that, being old, I am unwise to attempt sonnets, but, since they say I am in my dotage, I do but perform my proper office. I realize the love you bear me. You, on your part, must know that I would gladly rest my weak frame near the bones of my father, as you urge me to do. But if I left this place, I should cause great injury to the building of Saint Peter's. When all is so far completed that nothing can be changed, I hope still to do as you desire, if it is not a sin to disappoint a set of rogues who are daily expecting me to leave the world.

With this letter there came the following sonnet:

TO GIORGIO VASARI
(On the Brink of Death)

Now hath my life across a stormy sea,
    Like a frail bark reached that wide port where all
    Are bidden ere the final judgment fall
Of good and evil deeds to pay the fee.
Now know I well how that fond phantasy
    Which made my soul the worshiper and thrall
    Of earthly art, is vain; how criminal
Is that which all men seek unwillingly.
Those amorous thoughts which were so lightly dressed,
    What are they when the double death is nigh?
    The one I know for sure, the other dread.
Painting nor sculpture now can lull to rest
    My soul that turns to His great love on high,
    Whose arms to clasp us on the cross were spread.

Translated by JOHN ADDINGTON SYMONDS

From this we see that Michelangelo was drawing toward God and casting from him the cares of art. Vasari replied to Michelangelo's letter, by order of Duke Cosimo, in few words, but still encouraging him to return to his own country. To his verses, Giorgio replied with a sonnet of similar character. Michelangelo would have gladly left Rome, and even determined to do so, but the spirit was more willing than the flesh was able and his debility kept him in Rome.

In June, 1557, the builder made a mistake in the vaulting of the apse [of St. Peter's]. Michelangelo sent Vasari his designs for the vaulting with this note:

This mistake has been committed because I am too old to visit the building as often as I could wish, although I had prepared an exact model of the work as I do of everything. I had thought that part finished, and now it will not be done this winter. If a man could die of shame and grief, I would not be alive now. I beg you to account to the duke for my not being at this moment in Florence.

The duke at last realized that the continuation of St. Peter's was the most important thing in the world to Michelangelo and he no longer pressed him to return to Florence. Whereupon the latter wrote to Vasari that he thanked the duke with all his heart for that great kindness and added, "God give me grace to serve him with my poor person, for my memory and understanding have gone to await him elsewhere." The date of this letter was August, 1557.

Our artist was now pressed to make his final arrangements known, and because he saw that little was done on the building, he was encouraged by his best friends to make at least a model of the cupola. Several months elapsed, however, before he could resolve on anything, but at length he made a beginning. Slowly and by degrees he produced a small model in clay from which a much larger wooden one might be made later. Such a model was subsequently made by Maestro Giovanni Franzese, with all the parts executed with extreme nicety.

The completion of this model was a great satisfaction, not only to the friends of Michelangelo, but to all Rome. He continued to direct the work until the death of Pope Paul IV, when Pope Pius IV was chosen. That pontiff employed Piero Ligorio as his architect, yet he made many offers of service and showed much kindness to Michelangelo. His pension was continued, and some of the old allowances which our artist had lost in the pontificate of Paul IV were restored. The Pope employed him in many of his own buildings and during his reign the work of St.

Peter's proceeded busily. Among other things, Michelangelo was required to design a monument to the memory of the Pope's brother, and the Cavaliere Leone Leoni of Arezzo was commissioned to construct it in the cathedral of Milan.

About this time the Cavaliere Leoni made a portrait of Michelangelo, a very close resemblance, in a medal. This pleased Michelangelo greatly, and he presented Leoni with a model in wax of Hercules killing Antaeus. We have no other portrait of Michelangelo except two in painting, one by Bugiardino and the other by Jacopo del Conte, and a high relief in bronze by Daniello Ricciarelli.

In this same year, Giovanni de' Medici, son of Duke Cosimo, went to Rome to receive the hat [to be installed as cardinal] from Pope Pius IV. Vasari, his friend and servant, determined to go with him to spend a month in the society of Michelangelo, whom he held very dear. Vasari, by order of his excellency, took with him the model in wood of the ducal palace in Florence, together with the designs for the new apartments that he had himself built. Each of the new apartments was adorned with stories from the classics. The apartments beneath were decorated with the lives of the heroes of the house of Medici. A dialogue written by Vasari in which the paintings were explained was read by Annibale Caro to Michelangelo, who was much pleased with it.

A discussion arose about certain alterations Vasari proposed in the great hall. His excellency the duke had not yet agreed to lift the roof twenty-five feet, as Vasari wished, not that he feared the cost, but because of the danger to the building. A model of the hall as it was, and another of the proposed improvement, were now laid before Michelangelo, who was so much pleased that he became partisan rather than judge. When Vasari returned to Florence, Michelangelo wrote to the duke that his excellency ought to undertake the alterations, which, he affirmed, were worthy of his greatness.

Now Duke Cosimo went that same year to Rome with his consort, the Duchess Leonora. Michelangelo went to see his excellency, who received him with much favor and out of respect for his great genius caused him to be seated near himself. Michelangelo then encouraged Cosimo anew to undertake the alteration of the great hall and he expressed his regret that he himself was no longer young enough to do him service. Michelangelo visited the duke several times, to the great satisfaction of both. When the most illustrious Don Francesco, Cosimo's son, was in Rome a short time afterward, the master visited him likewise. This prince always spoke to Michelangelo with uncovered head, so great was his reverence for that extraordinary man. To Vasari, Michelangelo wrote that he grieved that he was too infirm to do anything for his excellency. He went about Rome looking for some fine piece of antiquity to send to Florence as a present to that Signore.

Pope Pius asked Michelangelo for a design for the Porta Pia, and the master made three, all singularly beautiful. The pontiff chose the least costly and this has been erected. Finding that His Holiness would willingly have the other gates of Rome restored, he made numerous designs for them. He also made a design for the new church of Santa Maria degli Angeli, constructed in the Baths of Diocletian when that building was brought into the service of the Christians. The design of Michelangelo surpassed those of many other excellent architects. His Holiness, and all who have seen it, have been indeed amazed at his judgment and in the use he made of the whole skeleton of those baths. He designed a ciborium for the Sacrament, later executed by the artist in bronze, Jacopo Ciciliano, for this church.

The Florentines in Rome had often considered beginning in good earnest to set about building the church of San Giovanni in the Strada Giulia. The richest families promised to contribute according to their means. A discussion then arose as to whether they should use the old plans or have something new and better. They determined that a new edifice should be raised on the old foundations. Three persons were appointed to be in charge, Francesco Bandini, Uberto Ubaldini, and Tommaso de' Bardi. These applied to Michelangelo for a design. They said it was a shame that the Florentines had spent so much money without results and that, if his genius failed them, they should be wholly without resource. The master assured them with the utmost kindness that the design would be the first thing he would turn his hand to and he said that he was glad to be occupied with sacred things and to be doing something for his own people.

With Michelangelo at this time was Iberio Calcagni, the young sculptor to whom he had given the Pietà which he had broken and also a head of Brutus copied from an antique carnelian. He could no longer execute the delicate details of his architectural designs, and therefore employed Tiberio to complete them under his direction. Tiberio made a floor plan of the original foundations of the church, and Michelangelo made five plans of different churches to show to the Florentines, who did not expect anything so soon. He bade them choose one, but they insisted that he decide. Yet the master would not, and with one accord they chose the richest. Michelangelo is reported to have said that, if ever they completed that design, they would do more than the Greeks and Romans. These words he certainly never said, he who was always so reserved and modest. It was determined that Michelangelo should direct the work and Tiberio should execute it. They made a model in clay which pleased all the Florentines, and afterward one in wood. As beautiful a church it is as ever man beheld. The building was begun, but, when five thousand crowns had been spent, the work stopped for lack of funds, to Michelangelo's infinite vexation.

Michelangelo had been working seventeen years on Saint Peter's, and the commissioners had more than once attempted to remove him. It chanced that Cesare da Castel Durante, overseer of the works, died, and Michelangelo put Luigi Gaeta, young but not inexperienced, in his place until he could find an overseer after his own heart. Some of the commissioners sent Luigi Gaeta away because they preferred Nanni di Baccio Bigio. Michelangelo, much displeased, would no longer go to St. Peter's. The commissioners announced that a substitute must be found since Michelangelo would and could do no more. When Michelangelo heard this, he sent to one of the commissioners, the bishop of Ferratino, who had spread the story that Michelangelo would have no more to do with the building, to say that he had no wish to give it up. Ferratino replied that he was sorry the master had not made his purpose known, but he added that a substitute was needed and that he would gladly accept Michelangelo's messenger as that substitute, a reply that appeared to satisfy Michelangelo. The bishop then told the other commissioners that a substitute was to be appointed and proposed Nanni Bigio, who was accepted and installed. Almost at once, Nanni Bigio had a great scaffolding built from the Pope's stable to the apse of Saint Peter's because, he declared, too many ropes were used in drawing up materials.

Michelangelo went to the Pope, whom he found on the piazza of the Capitol. His Holiness, speaking somewhat loudly, bade him go inside, when the master exclaimed, "Holy Father! A man of whom I know nothing has been made my substitute. If the commissioners and your Holiness are persuaded that I can no longer fill my office, I will return to Florence to rest, to be near the great prince who so often has desired my presence, and to finish my days in my own house. I beg leave of your Holiness to depart." The Pope sought to pacify the master with kind words and bade him come to Araceli on the following day to talk the matter over. His Holiness assembled the commissioners, who claimed the building was in danger of being ruined. The Pope sent one of them to examine the structure and to require Nanni Bigio to show where the errors might be found, for it was he who had made these accusations.

All the reports were found to be false and malignant, and Nanni was dismissed with few compliments. Michelangelo indeed has brought the building to such a state that the work has now a fair prospect of being completed. By all this we see that God, the protector of the good, has extended his hand over the fabric and the master, even to his death. Pope Pius IV, who survived Michelangelo, commanded that nothing should be altered, while Pius V, his successor, continued, with even greater authority, to command that the designs of Michelangelo should be followed exactly. When Piero Ligorio, who was directing the building, presumed to propose certain changes, he was dismissed with little honor. Pope Pius V was indeed as zealous for the honor of the edifice as for the glory of the Christian faith. When Vasari went to pay his respects, in 1565, the pontiff spoke of nothing but the regard that was to be paid to the designs of Michelangelo, and he commanded Vasari to go to Bishop Ferratino and to direct that prelate to guide himself by the records and memoranda which Vasari would give him, to the end that no presumptuous person should ever be able to alter a single point of those arrangements made by the admirable genius of Michelangelo. On this occasion, which was witnessed by Messer Giovambattista Altoviti, Ferratino solemnly promised to observe every order and arrangement left by Michelangelo.

To return to Michelangelo, I have to relate that about a year before his death, Vasari secretly prevailed upon Duke Cosimo to use his influence with the Pope to the end that, since Michelangelo was now much debilitated, His Holiness should keep a watch over him, have him visited daily and take measures that, in case of any sudden accident such as may easily happen to the very old, the plans for Saint Peter's, or for the sacristy, the library, or the façade of San Lorenzo might not be lost, as so frequently happens.

In Lent of this year, Leonardo, Michelangelo's nephew, resolved to go to Rome. Perhaps be sensed that his kinsman was near the end of his life. Michelangelo was already suffering from a slow fever and he had his doctor, Messer Federigo Donato, write Leonardo to hasten his coming. But the malady increased, in spite of the care of those around him. Still in perfect self-possession, the master at length made his will in three clauses. He left his soul to God, his body to the earth, and his goods to his nearest relatives. He recommended his attendants to think upon the sufferings of Christ, and departed to a better life on February 17, 1564.

Michelangelo found his greatest pleasure in the labor of art. He was a born genius and his studies were unremitting. He dissected the human frame and examined every part: the articulation of joints, the muscles, the nerves, and the veins. Of animals also, particularly of horses, he made exhaustive study. These labors enabled him to complete his works with inimitable perfection and to give them a grace, a beauty, and an animation that surpass even the antique. He has overcome the difficulties of art with so much facility that no trace of labor may be seen.

The genius of Michelangelo was acknowledged in his lifetime, and not, as happens in many cases, only after his death. He was favored by Julius II, Leo X, Clement VII, Paul III, Julius III, Paul IV, and Pius IV, Soliman, emperor of the Turks, Francis, king of France, the Emperor Charles V, the Signoria of Venice, and lastly, Duke Cosimo de' Medici would very gladly have favored him, too. They offered him the most honorable appointments. This does not happen to any except men of the highest distinction. To no other master has God granted such perfection in the three arts in all the years that the sun has been going round.

Michelangelo's powers were so great that his sublime ideas were often inexpressible. He spoiled many works because of this. Shortly before his death he burned a large number of designs, sketches, and cartoons so that none might see the labors he endured in his resolution to achieve perfection. I have, myself, some drawings by his hand which were found in Florence, and these, although they give evidence of his great genius, yet prove that the hammer of Vulcan was necessary to bring Minerva from the head of Jupiter. He used to make figures nine, ten, even twelve heads high, simply to increase their grace. He would say that the artist must have his measuring tools in the eye, rather than in the hand, as it is the eye that judges. He used the same idea in architectural designs.

None will marvel that Michelangelo was a lover of solitude, devoted as he was to art, and, therefore, never alone or without food for contemplation. Whoever thinks this solitude merely eccentricity is wrong. To produce works of merit, the artist must be free from cares and anxieties. Art does not permit wandering of the mind. Our artist did, nevertheless, prize the society of learned and distinguished men, more especially the illustrious Cardinal Ippolito de' Medici, who loved him greatly. He had a host of friends, but above all the rest, he loved Messer Tommaso de' Cavalieri, a Roman gentleman, still young and much inclined to the arts. For him, to help him in his drawing, he made superb cartoons, beautiful heads in red and black chalk and the Ganymede (carried to heaven by the bird of Jove), the Tityus, the Phaethon (falling from the chariot of the sun into the river Po), and also a Bacchanalia of Children, all most admirable. He also made a portrait of Messer Tommaso in a cartoon the size of life—he, who never painted the likeness of anyone before or after! The friendships of Michelangelo were all for deserving and noble persons. Messer Tommaso induced him to make drawings for his friends: an Annunciation for the Cardinal di Cesis, which was afterward painted by Marcello da Mantua, and another Annunciation, also painted by Marcello, the design for which is preserved like a jewel by Duke Cosimo. The duke has a statue ten feet high, representing Victory with a captive. He has, besides, a group of four captives, merely roughhewn, that show how Michelangelo extracted statues from the stone. The method is to take a figure of wax, lay it in a vessel of water and gradually emerge it, and then note the most salient parts. Just so, the highest parts were extracted first from the marble.

Michelangelo loved the society of artists, especially of Jacopo Sansovino, Il Rosso, Pontormo, Daniele da Volterra, and the Aretine, Giorgio Vasari, to whom he showed infinite kindness. Those who say he would not teach others are wrong. I have been present many times when he assisted his intimates or any who asked his counsels. It is true he was unfortunate in those whom he took into his house. His disciples were wholly unable to imitate their master. Even in his old age, had he found a disciple to his mind, he would have written a treatise on anatomy, in his desire to help artists, who are frequently misled by a lack of knowledge of anatomy. But he distrusted his ability to write, although in his letters he expressed himself well and tersely. He enjoyed reading our Italian poets, particularly Dante. Like Petrarch, he was fond of writing madrigals and of making sonnets. Michelangelo sent a large number of these verses to the most illustrious Marchesana di Pescara, and received replies both in verse and prose from that lady, of whose genius he was as much enamored as she of his. Michelangelo designed for her a Pietà with two angels of infinite beauty, a figure of Christ on the Cross, and one of Our Saviour at the Well with the Woman of Samaria. He delighted in the reading of the Scriptures, like the good Christian that he was, and honored the writings of Fra Girolamo Savonarola. He was an ardent admirer of beauty for art, and knew how to select the most beautiful, but he was not liable to the undue influence of beauty. This his whole life has proved. In all things he was most moderate. He ate frugally at the close of the day's work. Though rich, he lived like a poor man and rarely had a guest at his table. He would accept no presents for fear of being under an obligation.

Michelangelo slept little and often got up in the night to resume his labors with the chisel. For these occasions he had made a cap of pasteboard, in the center of which he placed his candle, which thus gave him light without encumbering his hands. Vasari had often seen this cap and had observed that Michelangelo preferred candles of goat's tallow. He sent the master four packets weighing forty pounds. Vasari's own servant presented them respectfully in the evening, but Michelangelo refused to accept them. The man said, "Messere, I have nearly broken my arms bringing them from the bridge, and I do not want to carry them back again. Here is a heap of mud before your door. I will just stick them up here and light them all." The master bade him lay down the candles, and declared that no such pranks should be played in front of his house.

He has told me that, in his youth, he often slept in his clothes, so tired that it did not seem worthwhile to undress only to dress again the next morning. Many have called him avaricious, but they are mistaken. He has given away his own work and other possessions. We have already mentioned many drawings and statues which he gave to Messer Tommaso de' Cavalieri, and also to others. These gifts might have been sold for many thousands of crowns. He made innumerable designs for buildings, and inspected many more, without receiving one scudo. But to come to the money he earned. It was not from holding official positions, nor yet by barter, but by the labor and thought of the master, I ask—can he be thought avaricious who assisted the poor as Michelangelo did, who secretly paid the dowry of many a poor girl, and who enriched all who served him? There was Urbino, whom he made very rich. One day, after the man had served him many years, Michelangelo said to him, "When I die, what wilt thou do?" "Serve someone else," replied Urbino. "Thou poor creature!" returned Michelangelo, "I must save thee from that." And thereupon, he gave him two thousand crowns, a gesture befitting the Caesars and high princes of the world. To his nephew he has more than once given three or four thousand crowns, besides the property in Rome.

Michelangelo had remarkable strength of memory. A work of art once seen he would remember perfectly and could make use of any portion of it, if he wanted to do so. In his youth he was once supping with his friends, when they amused themselves by trying to discover who could best produce one of those aimless, ugly drawings which are scratched on walls by those who know nothing. Here his memory served him well.

He produced one exactly as he had seen it, a most difficult feat for one accustomed to the most refined mastery.

He proved himself resentful against those who wronged him, but he never avenged himself by violence. He was orderly in all his proceedings, modest, reasonable in discourse, usually serious but sometimes amusing, ingenious and quick in reply. I will mention a few of his many well-remembered remarks. He was once looking at Donatello's statue of Saint Mark on Or San Michele, when a citizen asked him what he thought of it. He said that he never saw a face that looked more like that of a good man, and he added, "If Saint Mark looked thus, we may safely believe all he has written." A painter worked hard over a picture and earned a tidy sum when it was done. Asked what he thought of this painter, Michelangelo said, "While he works to become rich, he will always continue to be a poor painter." Of an artist who made excellent copies of the antique, Michelangelo said, "He who walks in the footsteps of another is not likely to walk before him, and an artist who cannot do good work by himself, cannot even make good use of the works of others." He said the gates of San Giovanni, in Florence, were so beautiful that they deserved to be used for the gates of paradise.

Vasari was sent one night by Pope Julius III to Michelangelo to get a design. The master was then working on the Pietà that he afterward broke. He knew by the knock who was at his door and came, lamp in hand, to let Vasari in. He sent Urbino after the drawing and fell into conversation on other matters. Vasari turned to look at the leg of the Christ, which Michelangelo was trying to alter. To prevent Vasari from seeing it, Michelangelo let the lamp fall, and they remained in darkness. He called to Urbino to bring a light, and, as he stepped away from the enclosure where the work was, he remarked, "I am so old that death often pulls me by the cape, and bids me go with him. Some day I shall fall like that lamp, and the light of life will be extinguished."

With all this he took pleasure in the society of men like Menighella, a rude person and a commonplace painter of Valdarno, but a pleasant fellow. Michelangelo, who would not work for kings without entreaty, often laid aside all other occupation to draw some simple matter for Menighella, "dressed after his own mind and fashion," as the latter would say. Among other things Menighella received the model of a beautiful Crucifix from which he made a mold and produced copies in various materials. He then went about the country selling them. This man would sometimes make Michelangelo laugh until he cried.

Another whom he favored was the stonecutter Topolino, who

imagined himself to be an excellent sculptor, though, in fact, he was a very poor creature. He spent much time at the quarries of Carrara, cutting marble for Michelangelo. He always sent some little figure of his own, along with the marble, at the sight of which Michelangelo would almost die of laughing.

While Michelangelo was finishing the tomb of Julius II he permitted a stonecutter to execute a terminal figure under his direction, saying, "Cut away here . . . level there . . . chisel this . . . polish that," until the stonecutter had made a figure almost before he was aware of it. He stood lost in admiration of his work. "What dost thou think of it?" inquired Michelangelo. "I think it very beautiful, and I am much obliged to you." "For what?" demanded our artist. "For revealing a talent I did not think I possessed."

But now, to conclude, I will only add, that Michelangelo had an excellent constitution, a spare form, and strong nerves. He was not robust as a child, and as a man he suffered two serious attacks of illness, but he could endure much fatigue. In his latter years he wore stockings of dogskin for months together, and when he took them off the skin of the leg sometimes came with them. His face was round, the brow square and ample, with seven direct lines upon it. The temples projected much beyond the ears, which were somewhat large and stood a little off from the cheeks. His nose had been flattened by the blow of Torrigiano. His eyes were rather small, dark, with blue and yellowish points. The eyebrows had few hairs. The lips were thin and the lower slightly projected. The chin was well formed, and the beard and hair were black mingled with gray.

This master, as I said at the beginning, was certainly sent by God as an example of what an artist could be. I, who can thank God for unusual happiness, count it among the greatest of my blessings that I was born while Michelangelo still lived, was found worthy to have him for my master, and was accepted as his trusted friend.

Michelangelo was followed to his tomb by all the artists and by his numerous friends. The Pope expressed his intention of commanding that a monument should be erected to his memory in Saint Peter's.

Michelangelo's nephew Leonardo did not arrive in Rome until it was all over, though he traveled post haste. When Duke Cosimo heard of his death, he resolved that, since he had not been able to do the master honor in his lifetime, Michelangelo's body should be brought to Florence and his obsequies solemnized with all possible splendor. But

Michelangelo's body had to be smuggled out of Rome in a sort of bale, such as merchants use, to prevent a tumult in the city.

A committee of four artists of the Academy of Painters and Sculptors of Florence was chosen to make all the arrangements. Agnolo Bronzino and Giorgio Vasari, painters, and the sculptors Benvenuto Cellini and Bartolommeo Ammanato formed the committee. First they decided to ask the duke if the funeral could be held in the church of San Lorenzo, where the greater part of Michelangelo's Florentine works were. Also, they requested that the distinguished Messer Benedetto Varchi pronounce the funeral oration. The duke most readily and graciously consented.

Leonardo Buonarroti directed the secret removal of his uncle's body from Rome and brought it to Florence, where it arrived on Saturday, March 11. The next day all the painters, sculptors, and architects assembled quietly, bearing only a pall of velvet rich with gold embroidery. This they placed over the coffin and the bier. At nightfall they gathered silently around the corpse. The oldest and most distinguished masters each took a torch, while the younger artists at the same moment raised the bier. Blessed was he who could get a shoulder under it! All desired the glory of having borne to earth the remains of the greatest man ever known to the arts.

A rumor had spread that the body of Michelangelo had come and was to be carried to Santa Croce. The news passed from mouth to mouth and the church was filled in the twinkling of an eye. It was with difficulty that the bearers made their way to the sacristy to place the body in the receptacle destined to receive it. Although the priests, the black-clad mourners, and the wax tapers are, without doubt, imposing and grand in funeral ceremonies, still the sight of so many artists gathered with so much affection around the corpse was also a very grand and imposing spectacle.

The number of artists in Florence, and they were all present, was very great, for, if I may say so without offence to other cities, Florence is the seat of art as Athens was of science. But there were also so many citizens that the place could hold no more. Nothing was heard but the praise of Michelangelo. True art has this power.

When the remains, with this magnificent attendance, had been carried to Santa Croce, the monks performed the customary ceremonies for the dead. The prorector [of the Academy] by virtue of his office, who wished to gratify the people, and, as he afterward confessed, to see him for himself, resolved to have the cerements taken off. This was done, and though the master had been dead nearly twenty-five days, we were tempted to think he lay in a sweet and quiet sleep. The features were exactly as in life except for their pallor, and the face and cheeks were firm to the touch, as though but a few days had passed since his death. So great a concourse hastened to look upon the corpse that the tomb was not closed without great difficulty, and, if it had been day instead of night, we must have left it open many hours to satisfy the general wish. Early next morning many verses, both in Latin and in dialect [Italian] were appended to the tomb, and this was continued for some time.

But to come to the obsequies. These were deferred until July 14. The three men of the committee (for Benvenuto Cellini, the fourth, had been indisposed from the first and had taken no part in the matter), chose the sculptor Zanobi Lastricati, as their chairman. His fellow artists agreed that such a man as Michelangelo should be honored by works of spirit and beauty rather than by costly ceremonies. Thus would they honor Art by art. Although this was their intention, the magnificence of the ceremonial was the equal of any ever held by those academicians in true splendor.

A catafalque was erected in the central nave of San Lorenzo. It was surmounted by a figure of Fame and decorated with symbolical sculpture and paintings from the life of Michelangelo. In the picture which faced the high altar was a Latin inscription, the meaning of which was as follows:

The Academy of Painters, Sculptors, and Architects, by favor of the Duke Cosimo de' Medici, their chief, the supreme protector of these arts, admiring the extraordinary genius of Michelangelo Buonarroti, and acknowledging the benefits received from his divine works, have dedicated this monument, erected by their own hands, and consecrated with all the affection of their hearts, to the eminence and genius of the greatest painter, sculptor, and architect that ever lived.

Not a surface in the church but was decorated, or draped in black, except only the pulpit from which Varchi pronounced the funeral oration. This was Donatello's pulpit, in bronze and marble. Whatever decoration the artists might have attempted must have proved less beautiful. The church, adorned by numerous lights, was thronged with an incalculable number of people, who abandoned every other care to behold that honorable solemnity.

The decorations were left for several weeks to allow the whole city time to examine the ornaments. The multitude of verses and epitaphs in

Latin and Italian are not repeated here, because they would fill a book by themselves and have, besides, been printed by others. After all the honors described above, the duke commanded that sepulture should be given the master in Santa Croce. His excellency gave to Leonardo, Michelangelo's nephew, all the marble for the tomb. The able sculptor Battista Lorenzi was commissioned to construct it after the designs of Giorgio Vasari. His excellency, that nothing may be wanting to the honor of so great a man, proposes to place Michelangelo's bust, with an inscription, in the cathedral, where there are the busts and names of many other distinguished Florentines.

Editorial Notes on Michelangelo

"Good painting is a music and a melody which intellect
only can appreciate, and that with great difficulty."
—MICHELANGELO

VASARI's life of Michelangelo, in the first edition of his Lives, was much enlarged for the second and complete edition. For the latter he used all the matter in Condivi's Life of Michelangelo. To read them both is to appreciate Vasari as an admirable art critic and understanding biographer.

When Michelangelo was a young sculptor in Rome, the antique was being born again; the very surface of the ground was alive with it. It must have been comparable to a gold rush, except that the treasure was simply unveiled to men able, for the first time in twelve hundred years, to see it where it lay, often just under the surface. The Apollo was already in the Belvedere. Francesco da Sangallo, the son of the architect, wrote, sixty years after it happened, an account of the unearthing of the Laocoön:

I was at that time a boy in Rome, when one day it was announced to the Pope that some excellent statues had been dug out of the ground in a vineyard near the church of Santa Maria Maggiore. The Pope immediately sent a groom to Giuliano da Sangallo to tell him to go right away and see what it was. Michelangelo Buonarroti was often at our house, and at the moment chanced to be there; accordingly, my father invited him to go with us. I rode behind my father on his horse. We had scarcely dismounted and glanced at the figures, when my father cried out, "It is the Laocoön of which Pliny speaks!" The laborers immediately began digging to get the statues out. After having looked at them very carefully, we went home to supper, talking all the way of antiquity.

Walter Pater, in his essay on the "Poetry of Michelangelo," speaks again and again of the sweetness of Michelangelo's work. Of the Bacchus, which was done for Jacopo Gallo, he says: "It was now, on returning to Florence, that he put forth that unique presentment of Bacchus, which expresses, not the mirthfulness of the god of wine, but his sleepy seriousness, his enthusiasm, his capacity for profound dreaming. No one ever expressed more truly than Michelangelo the notion of inspired sleep, of faces charged with dreams." This vivid criticism might apply to the figures on the Medici tombs, to the musing face of the Madonna in the sacristy of San Lorenzo, and most of all to the Adam of the Sistine Chapel.

It was Jacopo Gallo who wrote the contract for the Pietà, which was ordered by the cardinal of St. Denis. He added on his own account: "And I, Jacopo Gallo, promise his very reverend lordship that the said Michelangelo shall finish the said work in the space of one year and that it shall be the most beautiful work in marble in Rome, and that no living master shall be able to make one as beautiful." The contract is dated August 26, 1498. This Pietà, the Bacchus, and the Madonna of Bruges [which Vasari calls a bronze, and Dürer an alabaster, but which actually is a marble], have a quality of bewitching charm and grace.

But Michelangelo's growth paralleled the discoveries of his time. As a boy, Vasari has told us, he copied the Schongauer engraving. Though we do not possess this studious drawing, we may imagine it to have been as revealing as was Rembrandt's adaptation of the Mantegna. Even to look at the Schongauer with Michelangelo's copy in mind is to see what use the Italian might have made of the composition.

Then, as a young man, the antique presented itself to his imagination as colossal, impassioned, and nude. He was thirty-two when he began to paint the Sistine ceiling. He rejected the subject chosen by Julius II, "il pontifice terribile," as he wrote to Fattucci: "According to the first project, I was to paint the twelve Apostles in the lunettes and fill the rest of the space with the usual ornaments. In thinking of this work, it appeared to me, however, and I said this at once to the Pope, that it would never be more than a very poor thing." He painted an abridgment of sacred history from the Creation to the Deluge. Many years later he added, on the end wall of the same chapel, the Last Judgment. He used only the human form, colossal (if those garland-bearers stood up, they would be about eighteen feet tall), nude, and expressive of passion. There is no landscape, none of the ornamentation of flower forms so usual in Italian art. But what is the use of saying what is not there? The invisible grandeur of the human mind, the stature of the mind of Dante, the thought of Savonarola, above all, the mind of Michelangelo, is here made visible.

When the impetuous, furious, and magnanimous Pope threatened to have Michelangelo thrown from the scaffold (and meant it), unless the first half of the chapel was opened to the public, Julius II was the first one to enter, before the dust from the removal of the scaffolding had even settled. All Rome was at his heels. Raphael praised heaven that he had been born to live at the same time as Michelangelo.

The two great external sources of Michelangelo's inspiration were the formal might of the antique, and the Old Testament, illumined by the intellect of Savonarola. The moment of creation, to take but one example of the entirely new conception Michelangelo gave to his material, had been expressed in many ways. Once, God had breathed into the nostrils of Adam; then, in later pictures, the creative force was a ray of light; again, it was conveyed by the sign of benediction. Here, at last, life flows from the tip of the finger of God into man like a spark from space, an electric current.

"True art is made noble and religious by the mind producing it. For those who feel it, nothing makes the soul so religious and pure as the endeavor to create something perfect, for God is perfection, and whoever strives after perfection is striving for something divine."—MICHELANGELO

Glossary

Adoration of the Magi. The three wise men, led by a star, find the Christ Child in a manger and bring him gifts. The Three Kings of Orient are usually represented as an old man, a young man, and a Negro.

Adrian VI, Pope, 1522-23. Adrian of Utrecht had been the tutor of Charles V, emperor of the Holy Roman Empire. He was a dark horse in the election, a compromise nomination, and did not long survive in the atmosphere bequeathed by Leo X.

Alexander VI, the Borgia Pope, 1492-1503. This powerful political figure, the father of Lucretia and Caesar Borgia, lived the life of a Renaissance nobleman rather than that of a churchman.

Annunciation. The archangel Gabriel appears to tell the Virgin that she will bear the Saviour. The angel approaches the Virgin, and she receives the tidings in an ever-changing pattern, so that one might almost date the picture from the impetuosity of the angel's flight, at first so staid, and at last so swift.

Antimony. A chemical element of metallic appearance, hard and brittle, used in the making of glaze for terra cotta.

Apse. A projection, usually semicircular in plan, at the east end of a church.

Architrave. A beam resting on columns in the same way as a lintel rests above a doorway.

Armory. A cupboard for utensils or vestments.

Assumption. The Virgin soars to heaven while the disciples stand about her empty tomb.

Bargello. Ancient guardhouse of Florence, at once fortress and police headquarters.

Barrel vault. A series of arches roofed over to make a semicylindrical ceiling.

Bas-relief. Sculpture on a background. High relief may be figures in the round only attached to the background at the back. In half relief, figures half round are modeled against the ground. Low relief is bas-relief and may be no more than a very slightly raised drawing. Medals and coins are sculptured in bas-relief.

Belvedere. The building in the Vatican gardens was, in Vasari's day, a museum of newly discovered antiquities.

Boniface VIII, Pope, 1294-1303. His bull Unam Sanctam proclaimed the temporal as well as the spiritual supremacy of the popes.

Braccia. Twenty-three inches.

Byzantine. A style of art deriving from Byzantium or Constantinople. The art was rich in oriental pattern, stiff and unchanging. It survived in Russia until very recently. Vasari often calls it "modern Greek."

Campanile. A belfry, a separate tower, standing beside the church.

Campo Santo. A cemetery. The famous Campo Santo at Pisa is a long cloister-like building, housing the tombs.

Cartoon. A drawing the actual size of the picture. A cartoon for a painting in fresco is perforated along the lines of the drawing. Charcoal, or any powder, is dusted on the perforations while the cartoon is held against the new plaster. This outline is used as a guide in the painting of the fresco.

Casting. This is usually done in plaster of Paris. An impression is made in a mold. Then wet plaster is poured into the mold and allowed to set, after which the mold is removed. Casting in bronze is a complicated variation of the same process. The first cast is made in wax on a core. This is then incased in another mold which is pierced with vents at intervals. The molten bronze is poured in at the top. The liquid bronze melts the wax (this is called the cire-perdu, or lost-wax method). First the wax and then the bronze pours out the vents. The vents are stopped off when the bronze appears. When the lowest vent shows bronze, the cast is complete. The mold and core are removed (the core is of loose-textured material and may be shaken out), and all that is left is a thin layer of bronze the exact shape of the first wax.

Cella. The boxlike shrine or treasury of a Greek temple, surrounding which are the columns.

Chapterhouse of a monastery. The assembly hall.

Chiaroscuro. The use of light and shade in painting.

Ciborium. A goblet-shaped receptacle for the wafers of the communion service.

Classic. Pertaining to the Roman and Greek.

Clement IV, 1265-1268. This French pope held a high position at the court of Louis IX.

Clement VI, Pope, 1342-1352. Elected at Avignon, he established the custom of holding a jubilee for every fifty years.

Clement VII, Pope, 1523-1534. Giulio de' Medici forbade the divorce of Henry VIII of England from Catherine of Aragon.

Console. A scroll-like bracket to support a dais, chair, table, or shelf.

Cope. An ecclesiastical vestment, a sort of cape.

Corbel. A projection on the face of a wall supporting the ceiling.

Corinthian. The most ornate of the three orders of classic capitals. The column bears a bell-shaped capital enveloped with acanthus leaves. This was very popular with the Romans.

Cornice. A projecting molding at the top of a building. It may also be such an edging on a piece of furniture.

Coronation of the Virgin. The Virgin is crowned by Christ in heaven. This scene is imagined as taking place immediately after the Assumption.

Crown. A piece of money worth about half a ducat, which see for its value in terms of living costs.

Crucifixion. The infinite variations in this scene, the supreme symbol of the Christian religion, are a study in themselves. Before the fourth century, the cross appears without Christ sometimes marked with his symbol of the fish or his monogram. In the fourth century, Christ appears in a long tunic on the cross, though with no suggestion of pain

or death. In the eighth and ninth centuries, Christ is frequently shown, dressed only in a loincloth. Not until the eleventh century is He depicted suffering on the cross. Then His sufferings begin to play an important part in the redemption of mankind.

Deposition. The taking down of Christ's body from the cross.

Doge. Elected ruler of Venice or Genoa.

Saint Dominic, 1170-1221. Founder of the Dominican Order of Preaching Friars.

Doric. The simplest capital of a column of the three orders of architecture. The Capital has a plain, rounded, cushion shape.

Ducat. A piece of money. Muntz says, in La Renaissance en Italie et France, that in Florence in the fifteenth century, 50 ducats a year sufficed for the bare necessities of life; 100 or 150 was enough for ease; and 250 to 300 was moderate luxury.

Engraving. A means of reproducing a drawing. The lines are incised on a metal surface with a small v-shaped gouge, a burin. The lines are then inked and printed on paper.

Eugenius IV, Pope, 1431-1447. Besides signing a convention with the emperor John Palaeologus for the reunion of the Greek and Latin churches, he opposed the Council of Basel and ordered its dissolution.

Façade. An exterior face of a building.

Flemings. Flemish people.

Fresco. A painting in water color on wet plaster. The paint and the plaster dry together. Only enough of the finishing coat of smooth plaster is put on the wall to be painted in a day.

Gesso. A preparation, made of plaster of Paris and glue, used to make a suitable surface on wooden panels or canvas, for painting in tempera.

Ghibelline. A political party. See Guelph.

Glaze. A thin surface resembling glass applied to earthenware, such as terra cotta. Or a thin veil of transparent pigment in painting.

Gothic. A word applied by Raphael to everything that was not classic in style.

It has come to mean the culmination of the Byzantine style in Europe.

Guelph. A political faction in Italy, from the twelfth to the fifteenth century, which opposed the authority of the German emperors in Italy. The Guelphs were the church party and the city-state party against foreign domination. Their enemies were the Ghibellines.

High Altar. The altar at the end of the nave, at the point where the transept crosses the nave.

Illumination. A decoration or a picture in a manuscript which is then said to be illuminated. Gold leaf and beautifully durable colors were used so that these pictures may be as bright now as when they were painted.

Innocent IV, Pope, 1243-1254. He carried on the feud with Emperor Frederick II, who had been excommunicated by Gregory IX in 1239.

Innocent VIII, Pope, 1484-1492. Giovanni Battista Cibo received as ransom from the Sultan Bajazet 40,000 ducats a year and the sacred spear said to have pierced the side of the Saviour.

Ionic. An order of classic architecture which is distinguished by the scroll-like shape of the capital of the column.

John XXIII, Pope, 1410-1415. Baltassare Cossa succeeded Alexander V, whose death he was suspected of having encompassed. He was deposed by the Council of Constance.

Julius II, Pope, 1503-1513. The Della Rovere, il pontifice terribile, the awe-inspiring pope. He was the patron of Michelangelo, Raphel, and Bramante.

Julius III, Pope, 1550-1555.

Lady chapel. The eastern and main chapel of the apse, always dedicated to the Virgin.

Last Judgment. Christ in heaven judges mankind. It is the end of the world, when "a trumpet shall sound and the dead shall be raised incorruptible."

Leo X, Pope, 1513-1521. Giovanni de' Medici, the second son of Lorenzo de' Medici. He was not yet ordained a priest at the time of his election.

Litharge. A lead monoxide used as an ingredient of glaze for terra cotta.

Loggia. A roofed, open gallery, a porch.

Lunette. A circular or vaulted shape. It may be decorated with glass, painting or sculpture.

Lombard. A German tribe which invaded Italy in 568 and settled in the valley of the Po. Charlemagne overthrew them in 774, but the place is still called Lombardy, and the people Lombards.

Maul stick. A slender rod held in the left hand on which the painter steadies his right wrist, while painting details.

Mandorla. An almond-shaped halo which encloses the whole person. Christ in the Last Judgment is usually in a mandorla.

Martin V, Pope, 1417-1431. Oddone Colouna was elected by the Council of Constance after the deposition of John XXIII, Gregory XII, and Benedict XIII, thus ending a disastrous schism of the Church.

Medallion. A bas-relief sculpture on a disk. The size may vary from that of a coin to an ornament for the façade of a building.

Miniature. A hand-painted illustration for a manuscript. Byzantine miniatures were widespread in Europe and were the basis for the development of Gothic art.

Mosaic. Small, colored stones or bits of enamel set in cement to make a picture. Floors or walls, or ceilings may be decorated in mosaic.

Nativity. The birth of Christ in a manger.

Nave. The central aisle of a church. When the aisles are the same size, a church is said to have three, or more, naves. Usually, the nave is twice as wide as the side aisles.

Niche. A recess in a wall to be ornamented by a statue.

Nicholas V, Pope, 1447-1455. Tommaso Parentucelli fortified Rome to defend himself from enemies within and without.

Niello. A process for decorating metal with incised lines, which are then blackened.

Paul II, Pope, 1464-1471. Pietro Barbo, encouraged luxury and persecuted humanists.

Paul III, Pope, 1534-1549. Alessandro Farnese, excommunicated Henry VIII of England, 1538; approved the order of Jesuits in 1540.

Paul IV, Pope, 1545-1559. Giovanni Pietro Caraffa, restored the Inquisition.

Pedestal. The support or foot of a column or the base of a statue.

Pier. A structure, sometimes a cluster of columns, supporting a vaulted roof.

Pietà. The Virgin mourns over the dead Christ. Sometimes she is accompanied by Mary Magdalene, Saint John, and other saints.

Pilaster. A bas-relief column set against a wall.

Pius II, Pope, 1458-1464. Aeneas Sylvius Piccolomini, poet laureate at the court of Emperor Frederick III. He wrote a love story in his youth which he tried vainly to suppress when he became pope.

Pius III, Pope, 1503. Francesco Todeschini, nephew of Pius II, reigned for only two months.

Pius IV, Pope, 1559-1565. Giovanni Angelo Medici, reopened the Council of Trent in 1562.

Pius V, Pope, 1556-1572. Michele Ghis Cieri was the last sainted Pope.

Porphyry. A rock of felspar crystals embedded in a red or purple ground mass.

Predella. The small paintings in the wide frame of a larger picture, usually along the base. The subject matter of these small pictures is related to the subject of the large picture. For instance, an Adoration may have the Flight into Egypt in the predella.

Presentation. The occasion of the Purification of the Virgin Mary and the Presentation of Christ in the Temple.

Refectory. The dining hall of a religious house, monastery, or convent.

Reliquary. A container for a sacred relic. It was often of gold or silver, sculptured in relief and ornamented with precious stones.

Ressaut. A reinforcement of masonry against a wall.

Rusticated. Rough-hewn stone masonry, usually in the lower courses of a wall.

Sacristy. The vestry or a room attached to a church where the sacred utensils are kept.

San Giovanni. The church of John the Baptist, the Baptistery.

Sarcophagus. A coffin container which is not meant to be buried. It is often ornamented with sculpture in relief.

Signoria. A governing body. A sort of congress.

Silver point. A drawing with a silver point is possible on any coated paper. The line is light but definite.

Sixtus IV, Pope, 1471-1484. The founder of the fortunes of the Della Rovere family, uncle of Julius II. He built the Sistine Chapel in the Vatican.

Stigmata. The marks of the wounds of the Crucifixion. Saint Francis received these marks on his hands and feet.

Stories. The subject in a picture. Sometimes more than one episode appears in the same composition. In Perseus and Andromeda, by Piero di Cosimo, we see Perseus in the air, approaching, and also doing battle with the dragon.

Stucco. Plaster for walls or for statues.

Superimposed orders. The three orders of classical architecture used one above the other, usually on pilasters rather than on columns. The Colosseum has Doric on the ground floor, Ionic on the second, and Corinthian above.

Tabernacle. An ornamental niche or recess or an ornate receptacle for keeping a precious object, such as the consecrated elements of the Eucharist.

Tempera. A process of painting in which dry powdered colors are moistened in a medium of white of egg.

Terra Cotta. Sculpture in clay. The clay is modeled when moist, allowed to dry, and then fired in a kiln. It becomes the same substance as pottery.

Terra verde. A green earth color often used as an underpainting. The forms were often modeled on the green ground in black and white. The color of the picture was then painted on in a transparent glaze.

Travertine. A limestone building stone.

Tribune. The apse of a church contained a raised platform called the tribune.

Tuscany. West central Italy.

Tympanum. The space within the arch and above the lintel of a portal of a church.

Umbria. Central Italy—roughly, the land drained by the Tiber.

Urban IV, Pope 1261-1264. Jacques Pantaléon, opposed Manfred of Sicily.

Index

About the Author

Betty Burroughs was born on August 17, 1899, into a family of artists, and since that day her environment and interests have been consistently determined by art in its various forms. Her mother was the American sculptor, Edith Woodman Burroughs; her father was Bryson Burroughs, one of the best-known painters of his generation and for many years curator of painting at the Metropolitan Museum of Art; and from childhood Miss Burroughs planned to devote herself to the professions of her parents. Her formal schooling, after a confused start in French and American private schools, was crammed into the six years which ended with her graduation from high school.

After a period of apprenticeship in painting and sculpture at the Art Students League, Miss Burroughs continued her studies abroad, where her father's reputation gave her entrée into artistic circles in Paris, London, Madrid, and Florence. She made her headquarters in Paris, but her studies carried her over most of Europe and widely extended both her personal contacts with various artists and critics and her understanding of the techniques and theories of art.

The continuity of Miss Burroughs' life as a studious artist has remained unbroken in more recent years. She has continued her own work in sculpture and has also devoted much of her time to teaching. For the past ten years she has taught painting and sculpture in the Birch Wathen School and during the last four years she has also taught history of art. It was this latter course, for which she wrote her own outline, that suggested a new edition of Vasari, the indispensable source of information on Renaissance art.

Simon and Schuster books that might be of interest
to readers of *Vasari's Lives of the Artists*

FINE ARTS

MEN OF ART *by* THOMAS CRAVEN $3.75

THE STORY OF PAINTING *by* THOMAS CRAVEN $5.00

A TREASURY OF ART MASTERPIECES, *edited by* THOMAS CRAVEN $10.00

PICASSO: FIFTY YEARS OF HIS ART, *by* ALFRED H. BARR, JR., A MUSEUM OF
MODERN ART PUBLICATION $5.00

HISTORY OF IMPRESSIONISM *by* JOHN REWALD, A MUSEUM OF MODERN ART
PUBLICATION $7.50

ARTS OF THE SOUTH SEAS *by* RALPH LINTON, PAUL S. WINGERT, *and* RENE
D'HARNONCOURT, A MUSEUM OF MODERN ART PUBLICATION $5.00

THE ARTS *by* HENDRIK WILLEM VAN LOON $3.95

MUSIC

BEETHOVEN'S 32 SONATAS, *edited by* ARTUR SCHNABEL, *paper edition* $6.00,
cloth-bound edition $8.75

SYMPHONY THEMES *by* RAYMOND BURROWS *and* BESSIE C. REDMOND $2.50

MUSIC FOR ALL OF US *by* LEOPOLD STOKOWSKI $2.50

THE VICTOR BOOK OF THE SYMPHONY *by* CHARLES O'CONNELL $3.50

THE VICTOR BOOK OF THE OPERA *by* CHARLES O'CONNELL $2.00

THE WELL-TEMPERED LISTENER *by* DEEMS TAYLOR $2.50

THE OPERA *by* WALLACE BROCKWAY *and*
HERBERT WEINSTOCK $3.75

A L P E S

4s

44

Iouxta
sid   Comu   Teramira
Milan   bergamo   Coneglian forum uliu   Aquaria Tarostini
1   Crema   oriesta   2   belpacto   HIS
nouaria   lodi   pisac   Teruis   TR huma
auretti   pauia   4   Verona   esti padua   TA pareti pola
Cremo   Mantua   5   6
na   3   Vinena   Venenae
Salugia   Tortona   Placentia   munni   ferraria
Turino   Alisandria   7 parma   dula   piss   Argenta
brasi   isola   8 9 10   11   imola   12°
Amirü   sauota   Genua   3   Bononia
          d.oriole   Capal Spena   Luna   fiuefu   MARE
          fragari   la   15   luca floretia   14   sauena   18
43   Gorgona   16   17   Arimini
                    19   22 .23   lauerma   25   Cusibeni
          Caprasi   21 pisa   24   urbino   fino
42   liuerno   Sena   28   fosso sanua
                    Vda   27   peruha   29   Fananm
                    elba   Campighia   30   norba
41   planofa   prombino   Spoliti   31   ferma   S.fabiao
          CORSICA   Calighia   Aqua pedis   32   33   Aquila
          INSVLA   Iamin   giglio   Vitirba   34
                    'M.opi   bestin   Roma   Tagle
40   35   Sosa S.benebuto
                                        Capua
                    ponja   ristua   36   Neapol
                                        forini   Salg

39

SARDINIA   MARE   TYRENVM
INSVLA

38

37

SICILIE PA

Scala   Miliar   Italie
50   100   150   200   250   300

Based on the maj